Also by James Michael Fleming

Townsville or Hell!

Kessey photograph catalogue

Fleming photograph catalogue

The book's title *All our tracks and ways* is inspired by the first line of Henry Lawson's 1902 poem, *Bourke*.

> *I've followed all my tracks and ways,*
> > *from old bark school to Leicester Square,*
> *I've been right back to boyhood's days,*
> > *and found no light or pleasure there.*
> *But every dream and every track*
> > *- and there were many that I knew -*
> *They all lead on, or they lead back,*
> > *to Bourke in Ninety-one, and two.*

As we see in chapter 19, he was in the Bourke district in 92 and 93, not 91 and 92; but that didn't rhyme as well!

*

The title of chapter 20 *Brassy skies and bare plains* is inspired by the first line of Lawson's 1899 poem, *The Song of the Darling River*.

> *The skies are brass and the plains are bare,*
> > *Death and ruin are everywhere —*
> *And all that is left of the last year's flood*
> > *Is a sickly stream on the grey-black mud;*
> *The salt-springs bubble and the quagmires quiver,*
> > *And — this is the dirge of the Darling River:*

All Our Tracks and Ways

about
Bourke's Pioneering Reed Dynasty

James Michael Fleming

Flamingo Publishing

Flamingo Publishers
4 Currawang Street
Cammeray   NSW   2062

This hardback edition 2024

James Michael Fleming asserts the moral right
to be identified as the author of this work.

ISBN: 978-0-9923438-3-5

Printed and bound in Australia by
Ingram Spark

www.jmfwriter.net

Contents

If you would not be forgotten,
as soon as you are dead and rotten;
Either write things worthy of reading,
or do things worthy of writing.

— Benjamin Franklin, May 1738

In memory of Ena Ruby Murphy
a great granddaughter of James and Frances

William Reed
b ca 1745
d 7.1.1786, Chapel Chorlton

m 26.12.1764
Stoke-on-Trent

Sarah Martin
b ca 1745
d Whitmore

Thomas Reed
b x.8.1765, Chorlton
d 17.2.1853, Trentham
m 13.7.1789, Stoke

Ann Reed
b x.7.1767, Whitmore

William Reed
b x.4.1771, Whitmore
d 6.4.1772, Whitmore

William Reed
b x.6.1773, Whitmore

Elizabeth Sutton
b ca 1767
d 1.4.1809, Chapel Chorlton

Mary Reed
b 2.5.1790, Trentham
d after 1853
m John Grindley

Ann Reed
b 17.12.1791,
Trentham
d 6.3.1810, Trentham

Elizabeth Reed
b 1.2.1794, Trentham

William Reed
b x.12.1796, Trentham

Thomas Reed
b x.1.1799, Trentham

John Reed
b x.6.1801, Trentham

Prudence Reed
b 5.8.1803, Trentham

Edward Reed
b 27.1.1806,
Trentham

James Reed
b 14.12.1808, Trentham
d 30.1.1898, Bourke
m 28.6.1830, Monkwearmouth

Frances Heazle
b ca 1812, Canterbury
d 5.4.1895, Bourke

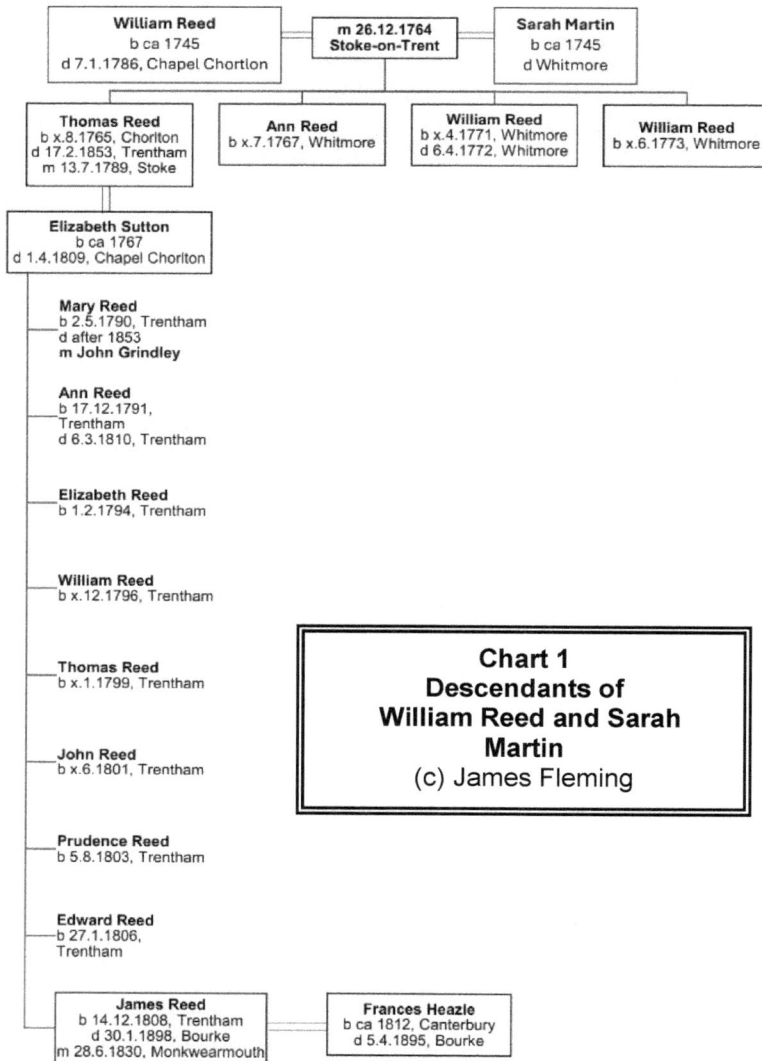

Chart 1
Descendants of
William Reed and Sarah
Martin
(c) James Fleming

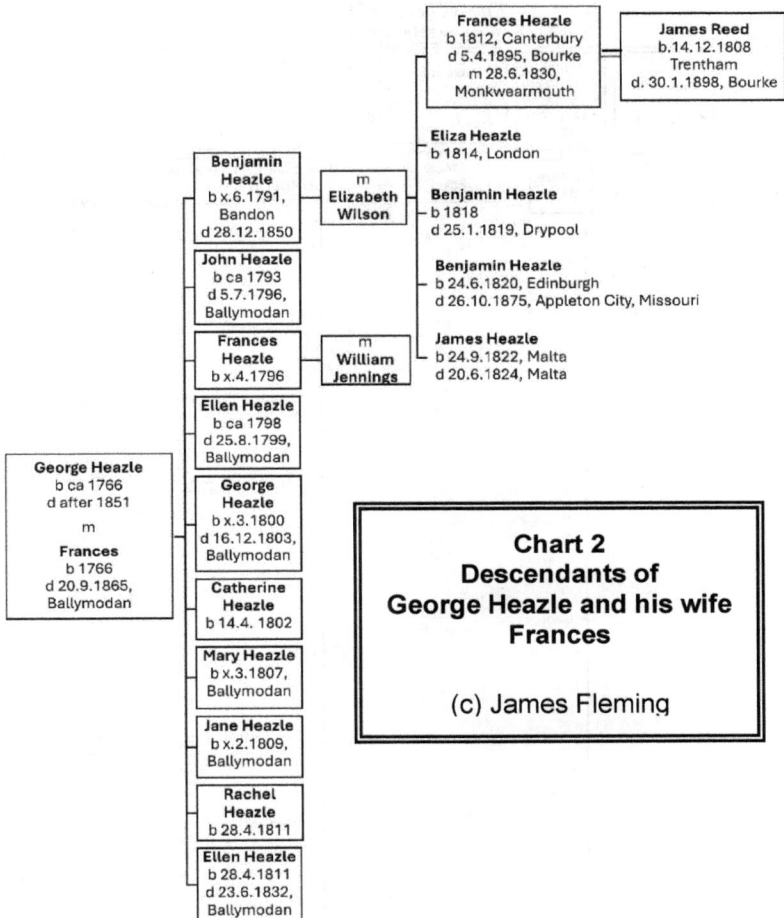

Chart 2
Descendants of George Heazle and his wife Frances

(c) James Fleming

George Heazle
b ca 1766
d after 1851

m

Frances
b 1766
d 20.9.1865, Ballymodan

Children:

Benjamin Heazle
b x.6.1791, Bandon
d 28.12.1850

m **Elizabeth Wilson**

- **Frances Heazle**
  b 1812, Canterbury
  d 5.4.1895, Bourke
  m 28.6.1830, Monkwearmouth
  — **James Reed**
    b.14.12.1808 Trentham
    d. 30.1.1898, Bourke

- **Eliza Heazle**
  b 1814, London

- **Benjamin Heazle**
  b 1818
  d 25.1.1819, Drypool

- **Benjamin Heazle**
  b 24.6.1820, Edinburgh
  d 26.10.1875, Appleton City, Missouri

- **James Heazle**
  b 24.9.1822, Malta
  d 20.6.1824, Malta

John Heazle
b ca 1793
d 5.7.1796, Ballymodan

Frances Heazle
b x.4.1796

m **William Jennings**

Ellen Heazle
b ca 1798
d 25.8.1799, Ballymodan

George Heazle
b x.3.1800
d 16.12.1803, Ballymodan

Catherine Heazle
b 14.4. 1802

Mary Heazle
b x.3.1807, Ballymodan

Jane Heazle
b x.2.1809, Ballymodan

Rachel Heazle
b 28.4.1811

Ellen Heazle
b 28.4.1811
d 23.6.1832, Ballymodan

James Reed m Frances Heazle

William	John Benjamin	James	Alexander	Sarah	Eliza Emily		Sarah Ann
b 1831 Southampton d ca 1836	b 1832 Belfast d 15.9.1881 Bourke	b 1835 Manchester d 19.4.1916 Qld	b 1837 Linden d 21.11.1917 Qld	b 1839 Sydney d 11.5.1843 Sydney	b 1841 Wollongong d 22.8.1925 Bourke		b 1844 Sydney d May 1932 Bourke

John Benjamin — m Eliza Jane Green
- William John
- Frances Eliza

James — m Eliza Bend
- John
- Eliza
- James
- Charles Alexander
- George
- Henry
- Frank Edward
- Frances
- Thomas
- Mary Jane

Alexander — m Mary Eckel
- Margaret "Maggie"
- Eliza Jane
- Christina Wingfield
- Henry James
- George Charles Alexander
- William Edward
- Ernest John

Sarah — m2 Henry JOHNSON / m1 Anders BUFE
- Frances Eliza
- James Henry
- Alexander George Oxley
- Sarah Jane Heazle
- John Benjamin Linley
- George
- Henry Sampson
- Emily Jane
- Albert William
- Mary Ann "Maud"

Sarah Ann — m Michael BRENNAN
- Sarah Ellen
- Frances Eliza
- Emeline
- Isabelle "Maude" Mary
- Victoria Prudence
- William J
- Mary Jane Heazle
- Josephine Whelan
- Annie
- Michael James
- Alfred John

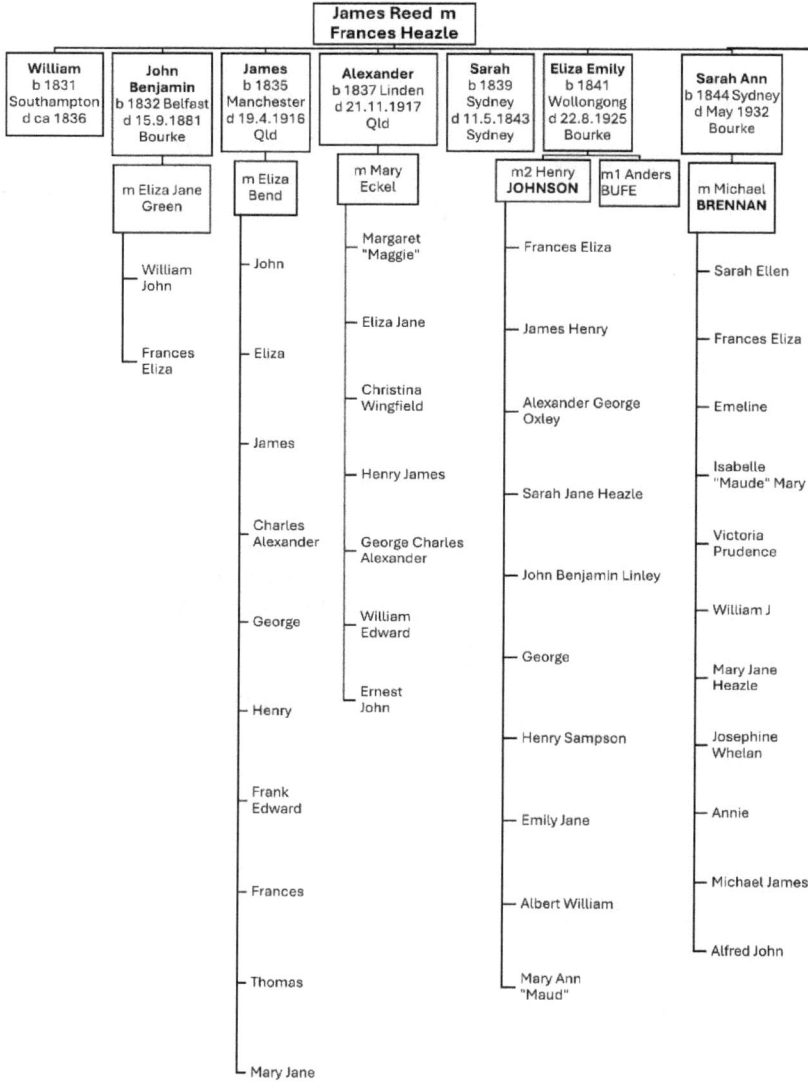

Chart 3 – across both pages
Descendants of James Reed and Frances Heazle
including all 12 children and 89 grandchildren
(c) James Fleming

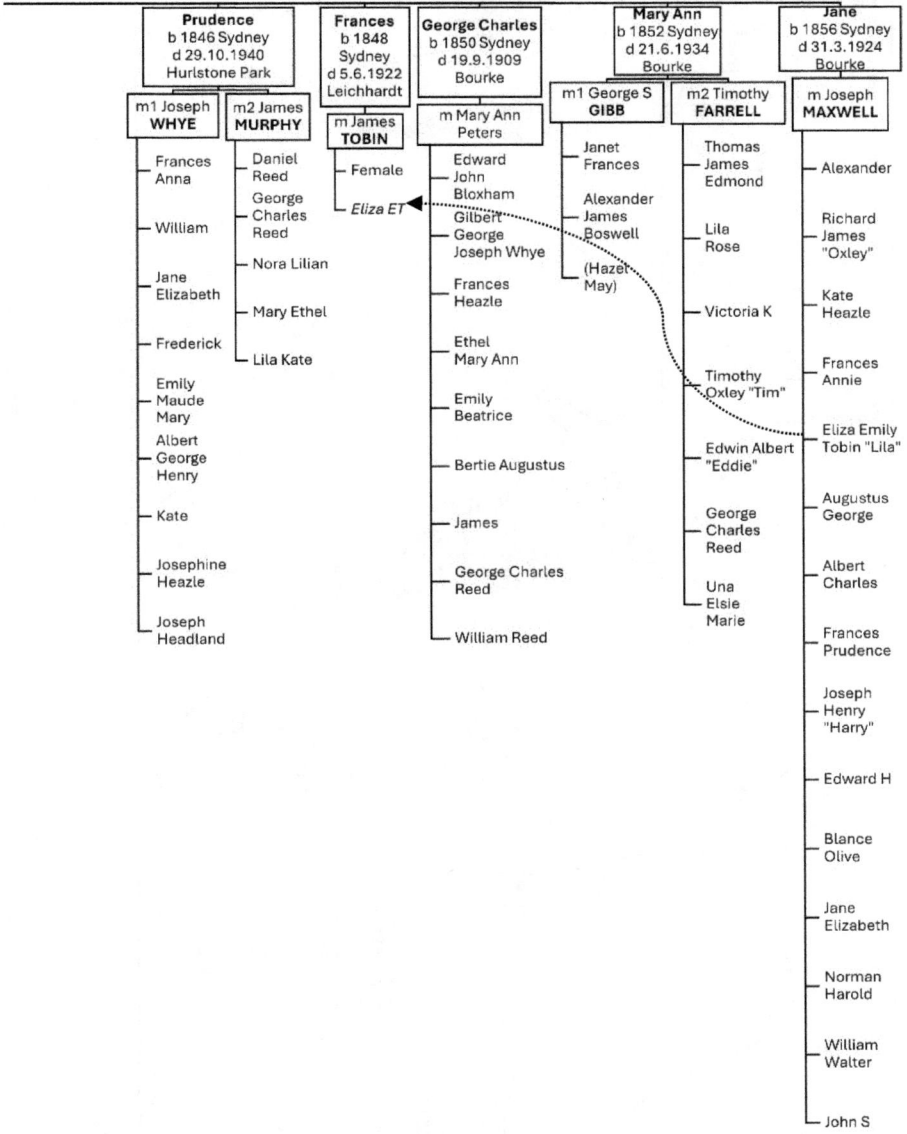

Prudence
b 1846 Sydney
d 29.10.1940
Hurlstone Park

m1 Joseph WHYE | **m2 James MURPHY**

- Frances Anna
- William
- Jane Elizabeth
- Frederick
- Emily Maude Mary
- Albert George Henry
- Kate
- Josephine Heazle
- Joseph Headland

- Daniel Reed
- George Charles Reed
- Nora Lilian
- Mary Ethel
- Lila Kate

Frances
b 1848 Sydney
d 5.6.1922
Leichhardt

m James TOBIN

- Female
- *Eliza ET*

George Charles
b 1850 Sydney
d 19.9.1909
Bourke

m Mary Ann Peters

- Edward John Bloxham
- Gilbert
- George Joseph Whye
- Frances Heazle
- Ethel Mary Ann
- Emily Beatrice
- Bertie Augustus
- James
- George Charles Reed
- William Reed

Mary Ann
b 1852 Sydney
d 21.6.1934
Bourke

m1 George S GIBB | **m2 Timothy FARRELL**

- Janet Frances
- Alexander James Boswell
- (Hazel May)

- Thomas James Edmond
- Lila Rose
- Victoria K
- Timothy Oxley "Tim"
- Edwin Albert "Eddie"
- George Charles Reed
- Una Elsie Marie

Jane
b 1856 Sydney
d 31.3.1924
Bourke

m Joseph MAXWELL

- Alexander
- Richard James "Oxley"
- Kate Heazle
- Frances Annie
- Eliza Emily Tobin "Lila"
- Augustus George
- Albert Charles
- Frances Prudence
- Joseph Henry "Harry"
- Edward H
- Blance Olive
- Jane Elizabeth
- Norman Harold
- William Walter
- John S

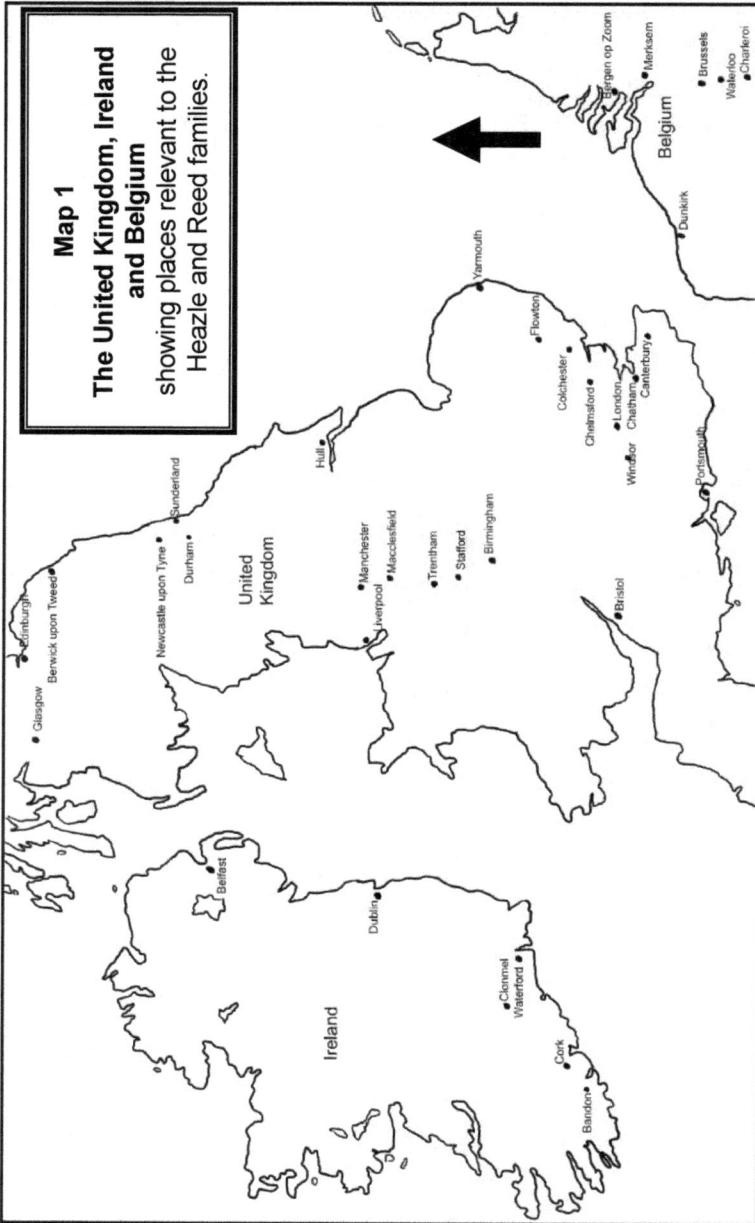

Map 1
The United Kingdom, Ireland and Belgium
showing places relevant to the Heazle and Reed families.

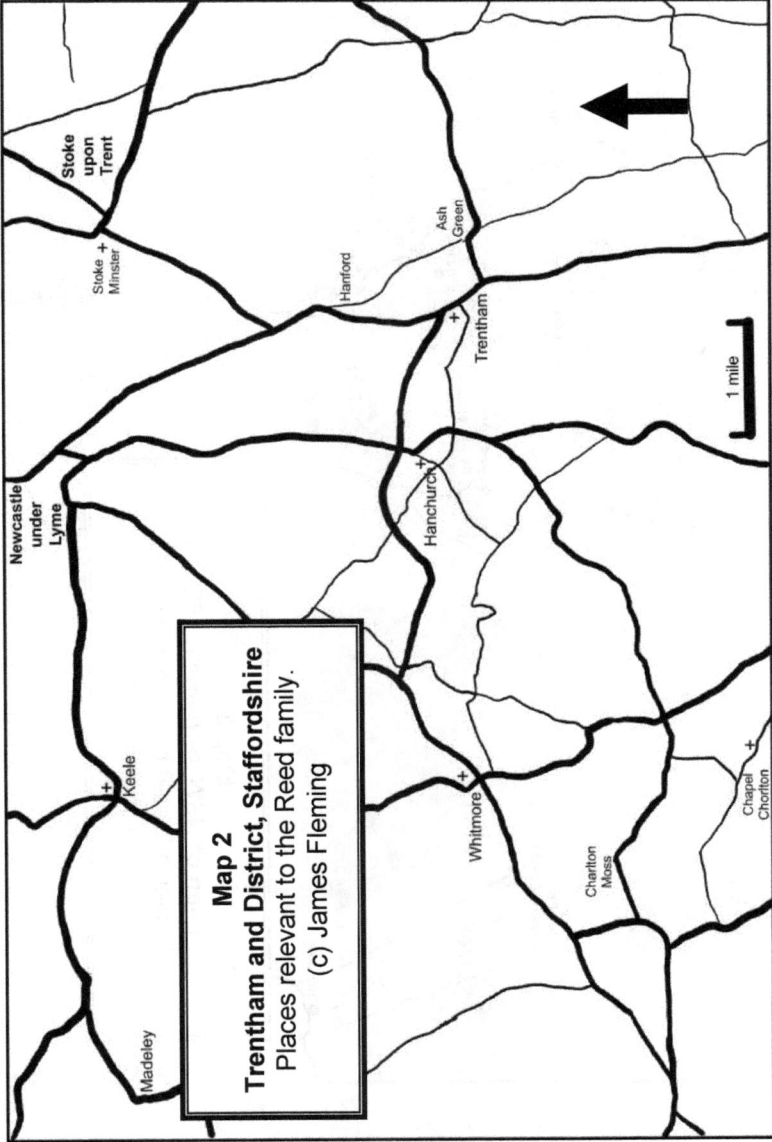

Map 2
Trentham and District, Staffordshire
Places relevant to the Reed family.
(c) James Fleming

Stoke upon Trent

Stoke + Minster

Hanford

Ash Green

Trentham +

Newcastle under Lyme

Hanchurch +

1 mile

Keele +

Whitmore +

Madeley

Charlton Moss

Chapel Chorlton +

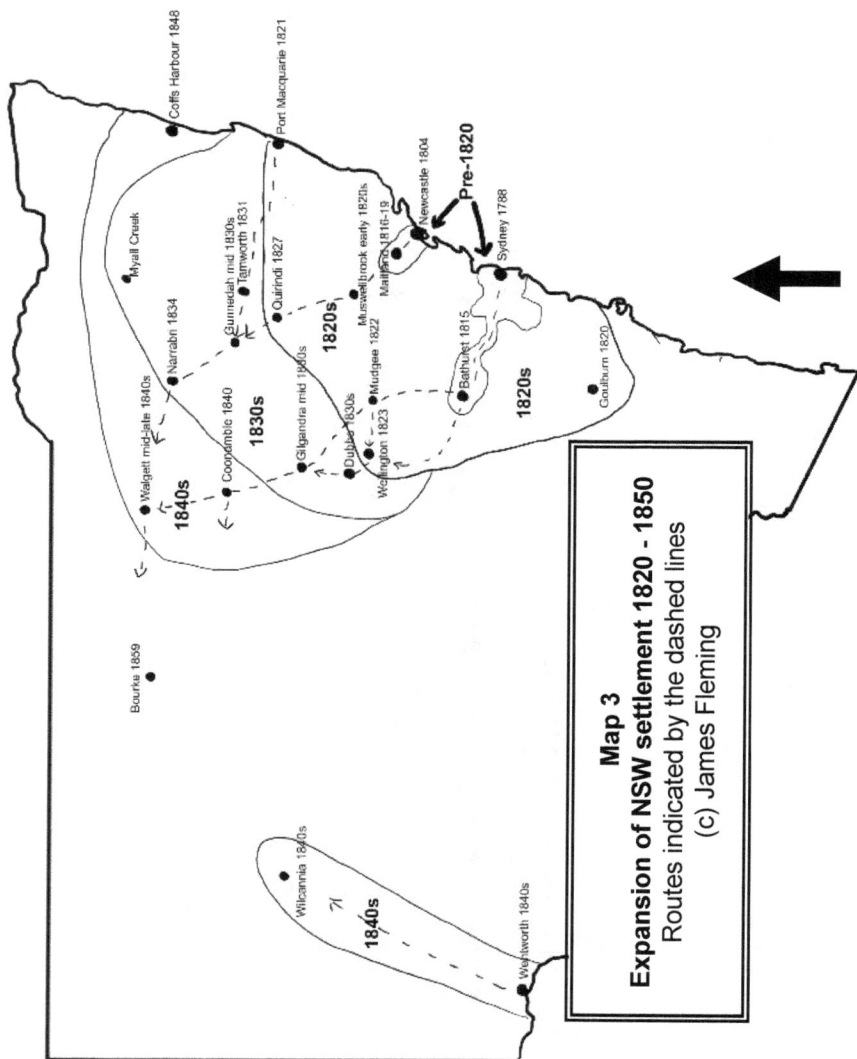

Map 3
Expansion of NSW settlement 1820 - 1850
Routes indicated by the dashed lines
(c) James Fleming

Coffs Harbour 1848
Port Macquarie 1821
Myall Creek
Gunnedah mid 1830s
Tamworth 1831
Quirindi 1827
Narrabri 1834
Muswellbrook early 1820s
Maitland 1816-19
Newcastle 1804
Pre-1820
Sydney 1788
1820s
Walgett mid-late 1840s
Coonamble 1840
Gilgandra mid 1840s
Dubbo 1830s
Mudgee 1822
Wellington 1823
Bathurst 1815
1830s
1840s
Goulburn 1820
1820s
Bourke 1859
Wilcannia 1840s
1840s
Wentworth 1840s

xiv

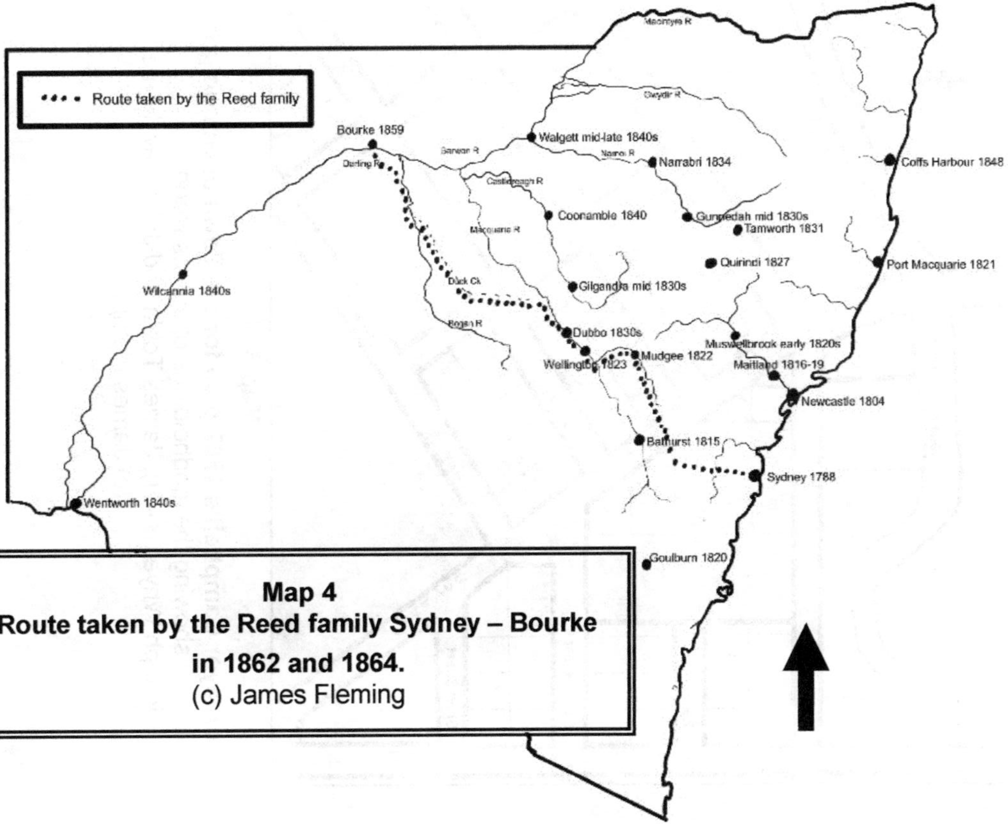

Map 4
Route taken by the Reed family Sydney – Bourke
in 1862 and 1864.
(C) James Fleming

•••• Route taken by the Reed family

Coffs Harbour 1848
Port Macquarie 1821
Gunnedah mid 1830s
Tamworth 1831
Quirindi 1827
Narrabri 1834
Murrurundi early 1820s
Maitland 1816-19
Newcastle 1804
Sydney 1788
Walgett mid-late 1840s
Cooramble 1840
Gilgandra mid 1830s
Dubbo 1830s
Mudgee 1822
Wellington 1823
Bathurst 1815
Goulburn 1820
Bourke 1859
Wilcannia 1840s
Wentworth 1840s

Macintyre R
Gwydir R
Namoi R
Castlereagh R
Macquarie R
Duck Ck
Bogan R
Darling R

xv

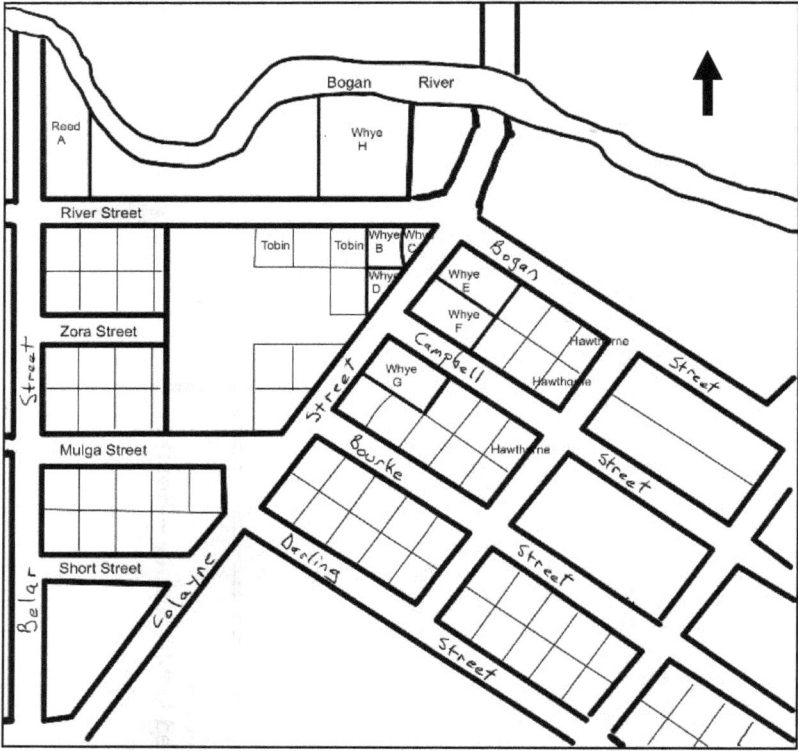

Bogan   River

Reed
A

Whye
H

River Street

Tobin   Tobin   Whye | Whye
                        B | C

Whye
D

Whye
E

Whye
F

Bogan

Zora Street

Hawthorne

Street

Whye
G

Hawthorne

Street

Campbell

Mulga Street

Hawthorne

Street

Bourke

Short Street

Street

Belar

Colayne

Darling

Street

Street

Map 5

Surveyor Campbell's 1867 plan for the Town of Gongolgon
showing the landholdings of James Reed (A),
Joseph Whye (B - H), James Tobin and John Hawthorne.
(c) James Fleming

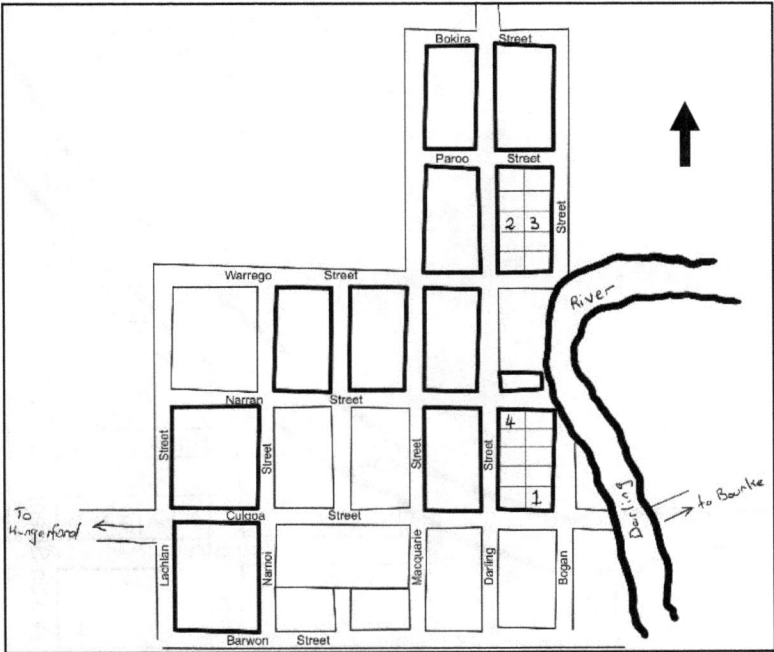

Map 6
North Bourke 1860s
(c) James Fleming

Michael Brennan's land is marked 1. The blocks marked 2 and 3 were owned by Joseph Lunn. The block marked 4 would be acquired from Joseph Becker by George Charles Reed in 1881.

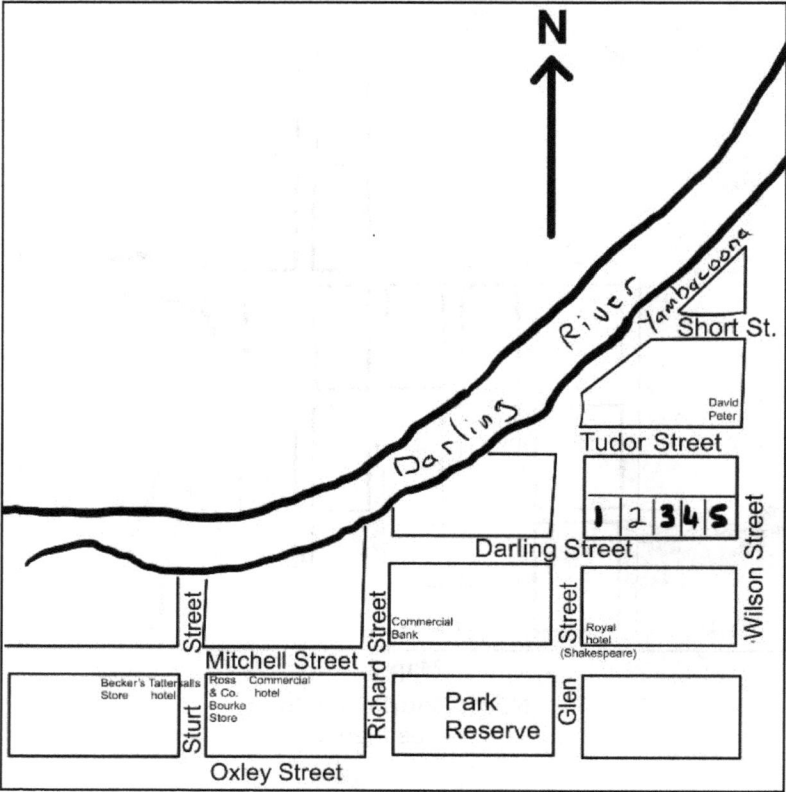

Map 7
Bourke in 1872
(c) James Fleming

The Reed family owned the blocks marked 1, 2, 3, 4 & 5 in
Darling Street.

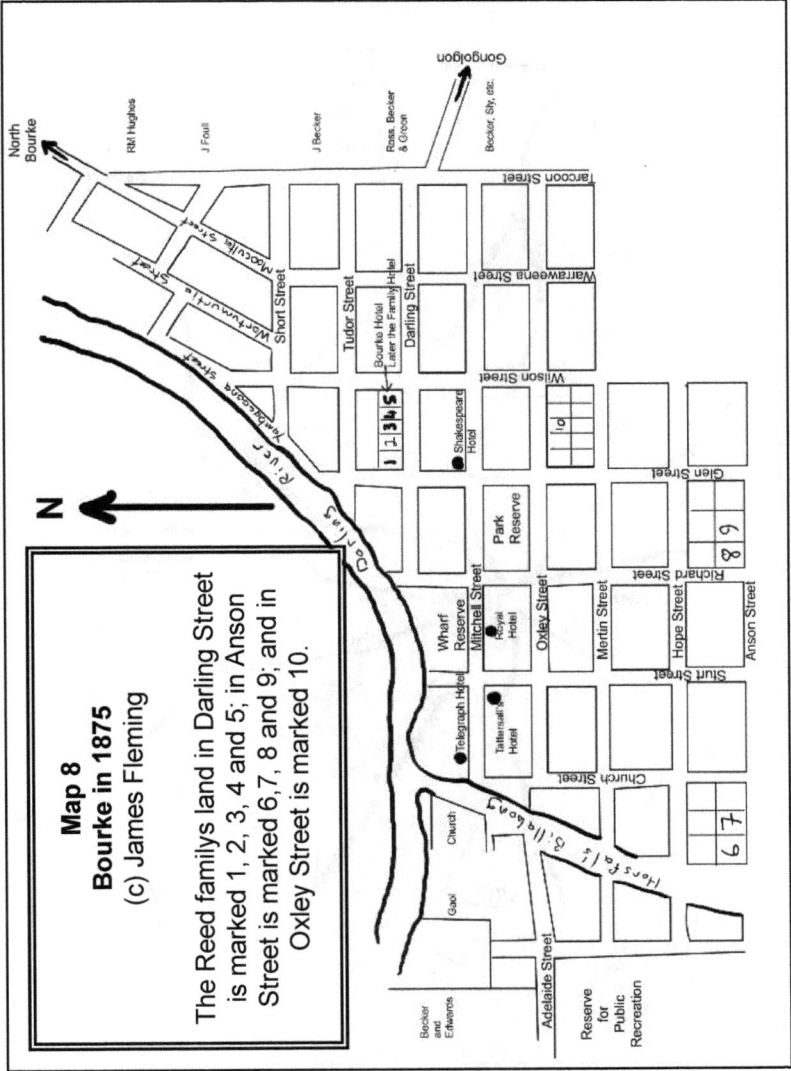

Map 8
Bourke in 1875
(c) James Fleming

The Reed familys land in Darling Street
is marked 1, 2, 3, 4 and 5; in Anson
Street is marked 6,7, 8 and 9; and in
Oxley Street is marked 10.

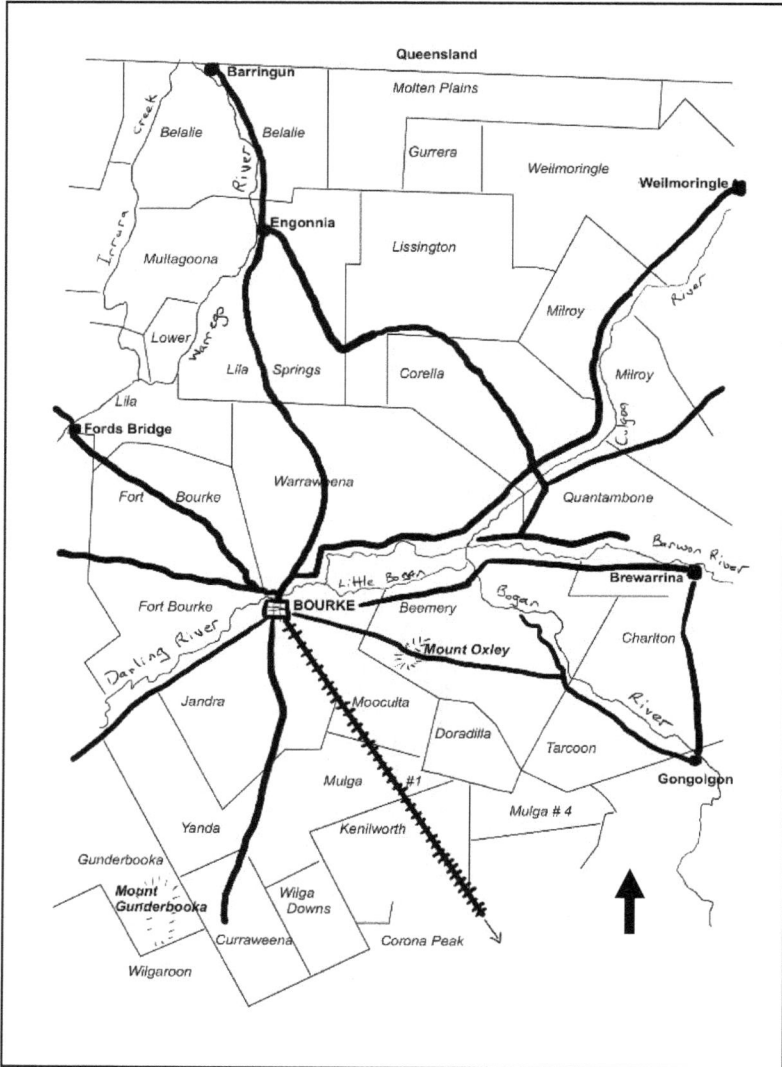

Map 9
Bourke district circa 1885
(c) James Fleming

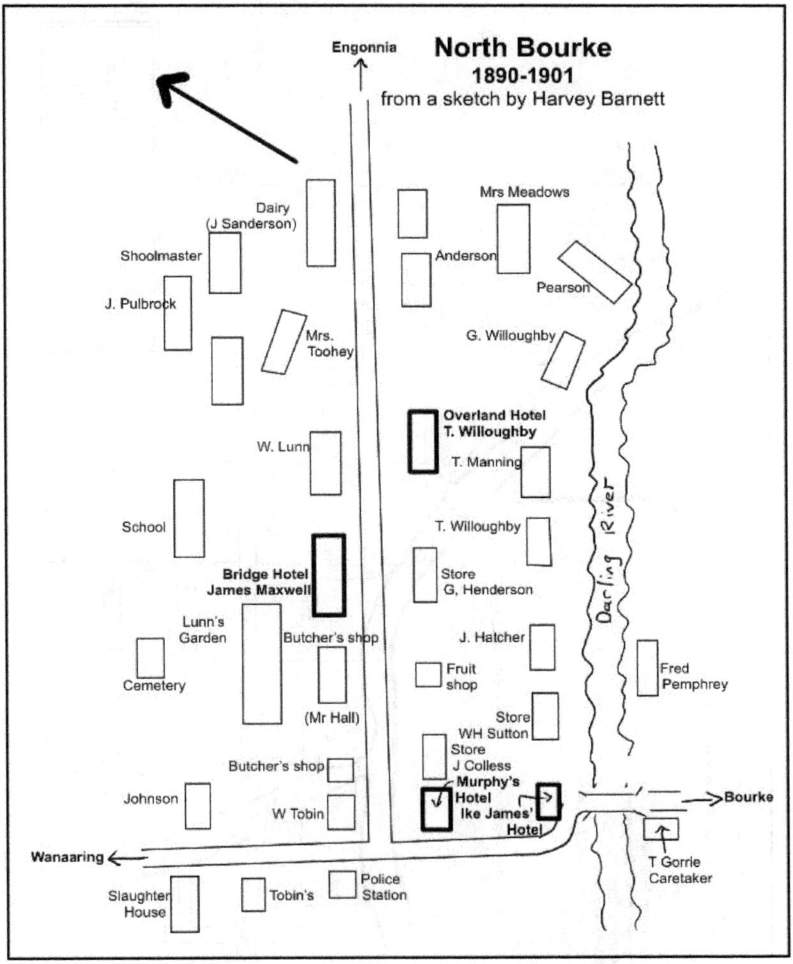

Map 10
North Bourke 1890
(c) James Fleming

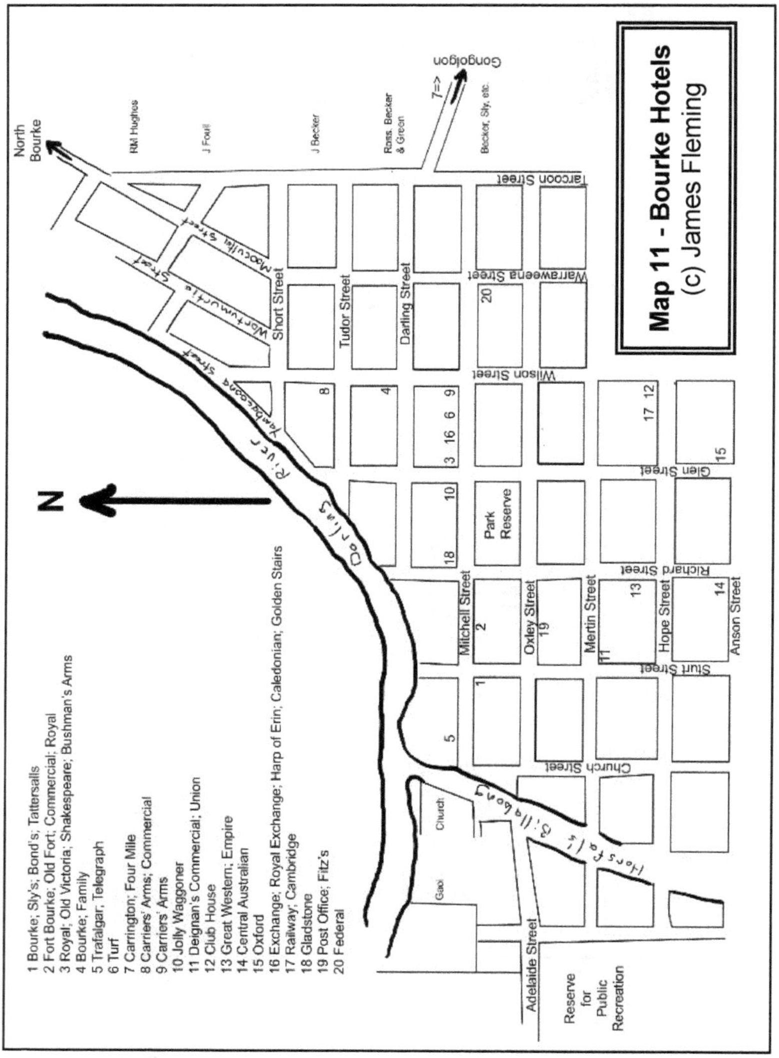

Map 11 - Bourke Hotels
(c) James Fleming

1 Bourke; Slys; Bond's; Tattersalls
2 Fort Bourke; Old Fort; Commercial; Royal
3 Royal; Old Victoria; Shakespeare; Bushman's Arms
4 Bourke; Family
5 Trafalgar; Telegraph
6 Turf
7 Carrington; Four Mile
8 Carriers' Arms; Commercial
9 Carriers' Arms
10 Jolly Waggoner
11 Deignan's Commercial; Union
12 Club House
13 Great Western; Empire
14 Central Australian
15 Oxford
16 Exchange; Royal Exchange; Harp of Erin; Caledonian; Golden Stairs
17 Railway; Cambridge
18 Gladstone
19 Post Office; Fitz's
20 Federal

North Bourke

Gongolgon

RM Hughes
J Foat
J Becker
Ross, Becker & Green
Becker, Sly, etc.

Tarcoon Street
Warraweena Street
Wilson Street
Glen Street
Richard Street
Sturt Street
Church Street
Adelaide Street

Short Street
Tudor Street
Darling Street
Mitchell Street
Oxley Street
Mertin Street
Hope Street
Anson Street

Wortumurtle Street
Moculta Street
Anabranch Street

River Darling

Horsfall's Billabong

Gaol
Church

Reserve for Public Recreation

Park Reserve

N

Illustrations

Photographs

Preface

Forty six year ago, on a whim, I undertook an adult education course on tracing family history. Within months I had discovered more of our family's history than my parents and grandparents knew. Their interest in these revelations inspired me to delve deeper and earlier, continuing until the present day.

Two years ago, I was preparing to write my annual entry in the Society of Australian Genealogists' Croker Prize biography competition. The topic was "Where did I come from". Well, I had come from Bourke, as had my mother, grandmother and G-grandfather; all because my GGG-grandparents James and Frances Reed and all their children went to Bourke at its inception. So, my essay was about Frances Reed, who lived the last 33 of her 83 years there and is buried in Bourke cemetery with her husband.

I was aware of her parents' and children's names and that she had emigrated on the *Earl Grey* in 1836 as the wife of a soldier, but I needed more than these scant details. Further research soon identified two more children and three more siblings than previously known; and established that the family was very securely settled in Sydney before venturing to Bourke.

But why would a middle-aged couple suddenly move their family 800 kilometres from a booming modern city to a barely existent place on the settlement frontier? And how did they then make a living? Having answered these questions and more, I wrote Frances' biography. It then occurred to me that the Reed family story, including their part in the creation and success of Bourke, was deserving of a book. It then took two years to complete more research and to write the manuscript.

All our tracks and ways provides a comprehensive history of three generations of the Reed and Heazle families and a detailed overview of the first fifty years of Bourke history. It reveals details of the family not previously known and explains their motivations in moving to Bourke. The Epilogue identifies a Bourke soldier who lost his life in World War 1 whose sacrifice is not memorialised on the town's War Memorial.

Because many family members were publicans, Bourke hotels are a particular focus. Appendix 1 provides a detailed summary of all Bourke hotels and publicans throughout the nineteenth century. The book refutes the very existence of the Bourke Club hotel; disproves claims that the town had 21 hotels in 1882; clears up confusion over the early years of the Royal hotel; and corrects the identity of the building in the National Library's photograph captioned "Bourke's first hotel 1866".

Family and local history relies on cooperation and information sharing between historians. This book builds on the work of others and is designed to inform future researchers (hence the detailed end notes). I acknowledge all contributors to the *History of Bourke* journals, particularly memoirist Harvey Barnett, medical historian Dr RE Coolican and hotel historian Bill Cameron. Fellow Reed genealogists Kayleen Vallance, Sarah McKibbin and Noreen Watts have assisted me with information, guidance, documents and photographs.

Jim Fleming
Cammeray
September 2024

CHAPTER ONE

James Reed's origins

James Reed was the youngest in a brood of nine children born to shoemaker Thomas Reed and his wife Elizabeth (nee Sutton) who lived out their lives in the English hamlet of Ash Green (near Trentham in Staffordshire). As a young adult James would work briefly as a brick maker before joining the army, a life-defining decision that would introduce him to his future wife Frances Heazle and eventually take them to Australia, where they and their large family would help to found the town of Bourke in far-western New South Wales (NSW).

On 22 January 1809, just like every other Sunday, Thomas and Elizabeth Reed observed the sabbath by mustering their many children and walking the mile from their house at Ash Green to the local church of St Mary and All Saints at Trentham. It was a handsome edifice set in picturesque grounds near the junction of Park Brook and the River Trent. The Reeds and other churchgoers could see, on the farther bank of the river, the Mausoleum that had very recently been built by the

Duke of Sutherland as a final resting place for himself and his successors.

After the normal Sunday service, the Reeds remained behind to witness Reverend Thomas Butt baptise two infants, including their youngest member, three-week-old James.[1] His siblings, from nineteen-year-old Mary down to two-year-old Edward, had all been welcomed into the Anglican community in this same church (see Chart 1). Young James would attend many more Sunday services here over the next eighteen years before entering an adult life that would take him to numerous places in England, Scotland and Ireland, before emigrating to Australia.

Staffordshire historian William White described Trentham as

a small but handsome village, on the east bank of the River Trent, from which it has its name, and on the turnpike road, five kilometres SSE of Newcastle-under-Lyme, and ten kilometres NNW of Stone. It ... derives most of its beauties from its close proximity to the elegant and picturesque seat of the Duke of Sutherland, the lord of the manor and owner of nearly all of the parish.[2]

The village had been anciently called Trichingham, where St Werberga (sister of Ethelred, King of Mercia) had been abbess of a small nunnery before her death in 683. By the twelfth century it had been re-founded by the second Earl of Chester as a priory for an order of canons who remained until the dissolution of the monasteries in 1537.[3]

Three years later the village was owned by the Leveson family, who were to build Trentham Hall in 1730 based on the architecture of Buckingham Palace (which is 27 years older). This grand house was set within an impressive park designed by Lancelot ("Capability") Brown, much of which has survived into the 21st century.

The church where the Reed children were baptised was largely rebuilt in 1844, although the South wall of the new building is of old stone from the former church and the Norman pillars were also reused.

***

The origins of James Reed's mother are obscure. Given that she was to marry in 1789 and bear her first child in 1790, it is likely that she was born between 1765 and 1772. There were nine babies named Elizabeth Sutton baptised in Staffordshire during those years but, without knowing her parents' names, it is impossible to know which of these she was.

Her surname Sutton derives from a place with that name that was associated with the family. The place name was created by combining the Anglo-Saxon words *sudh* (south) and *tun* (a homestead, village or town). This was a very common place name throughout Britain, being recorded as early as the Domesday Book in 1086. The nearest of these places to Trentham is the village of Sutton, just 27 kilometres to the south.

During the 14th century, John de Sutton had inherited Dudley Castle (41 kilometres further south) through marriage to Margaret, daughter of Roger de Somery. Their son, Sir John de Sutton II (1310-1359) was the first Baron Sutton of Dudley[4]. Four centuries later, Elizabeth Sutton lived nearby, so it is possible that she had descended from this family.

Elizabeth married Thomas Reed at the church of St

Peter ad Vincula at Stoke upon Trent (see Map 2), just 5 kilometres north of the church at Trentham where her children would later be baptised. The dedication to St Peter ad Vincula means "Saint Peter in Chains" but the name was formally changed to Stoke Minster in 2005. The banns of marriage had been read three times before the marriage ceremony was performed on 13 July 1789 by William Fernyhough, who also married John Booth and Martha Simpson on the same day. Both marriages were witnessed by Samuel Poulson and Daniel Rhodes. Elizabeth Sutton signed the marriage register with a cross, but her husband signed his name.

William Fernyhough was a Minister of Stoke-upon-Trent for many years and had recently published a slim volume of poems that all related to the famous pottery industrialist, Josiah Wedgewood and his family.[5] Fernyhough would later officiate at Wedgewood's burial in 1795.[6]

Elizabeth's husband Thomas Reed had been born at Chorlton in about 1765[7]. This would have been near Chorlton Moss and Chapel Chorlton, both of which are about 11 kilometres west of Ash Green, where they were to live for the remainder of their lives.

It is possible that he was the son of Thomas and Elizabeth Reade of Hanchurch who had been baptised in the church of St Mary and All Saints at Trentham on 27 September 1767.[8] The parents of this child were very probably Thomas Reed (a husbandman) and Elizabeth Hemmings who had married by banns on 21 March 1766 in the church of St Peter ad Vincula in Stoke on Trent. The husband, Thomas Read of Hanchurch, was later buried at St Mary and All Saints Church at Whitmore on 2 April 1776.

This family lived at Hanchurch, which is about 7 kilometres from Chorlton and 3 kilometres from Ash Green. Their son Thomas Reade was born close to Chorlton and at about the right time, so it is <u>possible</u> that he was to later become a shoemaker at Ash Green. But he was two years younger than shoemaker Thomas Reed was later said to be on both the 1851 census and his death certificate; and there is a better candidate.

It is more likely that the shoemaker-to-be was baptised in the church of St Mary and All Saints at Whitmore on 30 August 1765, a son of William Reed and Sarah Martin.[9] Whitmore is (at 2.5 kilometres) much closer to his recorded birthplace of Chorlton than Hanchurch. It may also be significant that shoemaker Thomas later named his eldest son William (although he did not name any of his daughters Sarah).

His parents, William Read (a farmer) and Sarah Martin of Whitmore had been married in Stoke upon Trent on Boxing Day in 1764.[10] They had at least three children in addition to Thomas, all baptised in the same church. These included Ann, who was baptised on 19 July 1767;[11] William, baptised on 5 May 1771[12] and buried there on 7 April 1772;[13] and another William, baptised on 29 June 1773.[14]

Their father (William Read) may be the person of that name who was buried in the church of St Lawrence at Chapel Chorlton on 8 January 1786.[15] That burial place would also provide his son with a reason to later state that Chorlton was his birthplace. In contrast, the son of Thomas Reed and Elizabeth Hemmings had probably been born at Hanchurch.

William Read's wife Sarah Martin may be the Sarah Rhead who was buried in the church of St Mary and All

Saints at Whitmore on 17 August 1802.[16]

The Reed surname was common throughout England, including in Staffordshire. One theory is that the surname derives from a nickname that was applied to people with red hair or a ruddy complexion (based on the Old English word *read* meaning red). Another theory is that it may have been a topographical name for someone who lived in a woodland clearing (based on the Old English word *ried* or *ryd*). Other theories are that it could be a locational name contracted from the Old English word *hreod* meaning reeds; or from *rhyt* meaning brushwood; or from combining *roege* (female roe deer) and *heafod* (headland). It is quite possible that the surname was adopted by many different families scattered across England and that several or all these derivations may be correct.

The multiple origins of the name could have also contributed to the many spelling variants that have been used over time, including Rade, Read, Reade, Rede, Reede, Reid, Ried and Rood. In Staffordshire, it was common to spell the name Rhead for many years. In fact, James Reed's baptism record on 22 January 1809 reads:

James son of Thos Rhead shoemaker of Ash Green & Elizh h. wife...

Nevertheless, his descendants eventually settled on the "Reed" spelling, used throughout this book.

Thomas and Elizabeth Reed lived during a tumultuous time. England's power had grown over the previous two centuries into a worldwide empire, but the tide was starting to turn. Her American colonies rebelled and revolution in France disrupted the peace in Europe and threatened England with invasion. The lives of all people living in England were affected.

One of the first missteps taken by the English government had occurred around the time of Thomas Reed's birth in 1765. The recent signing of the Treaty of Paris had formally ended the Seven Years' War between France and Great Britain over control of North America, with Great Britain gaining most of France's possessions there. But the war had been costly and British taxpayers were demanding cuts to government spending. To achieve that, Parliament decided that the colonies would need to fund their own defence. The government instructed the Royal Navy to enforce the payment of customs duties levied in American ports and to stop the trade of smuggled goods.

This led to great discontent, as Americans noted that they were being taxed by a distant government in which they were not represented. Tensions escalated after the Boston Massacre in 1770, when British troops fired on rock-throwing civilians, killing five. Nevertheless, the British government raised taxes and further angered Americans by passing the Tea Act that gave a trade monopoly in tea to the failing East India Company at the expense of American merchants.

Three years later a group called the Sons of Liberty disguised as Mohawk natives dumped 342 crates of tea into Boston Harbour, an event later known as the Boston Tea Party. The British Parliament responded by passing the so-called Intolerable Acts to punish Massachusetts colonists for expressing their defiance. The Acts rescinded self-government and removed rights that the colony had enjoyed since its foundation, triggering outrage and indignation in all thirteen American colonies. This surge in popular sympathy for the

American Patriot cause led to an increase in unrest throughout the colonies.

Twelve American colonies sent delegates to Philadelphia in early September 1774 to organise a protest as the First Continental Congress. Despite attempts to achieve a peaceful solution with Britain, fighting between American Patriot forces and the British army began with the Battle of Lexington on April 19, 1775. In June, the American Congress authorised the creation of a Continental Army with George Washington as commander-in-chief. The British government's attempts to impose its will in America had led to war. On July 4 1776 the Second Continental Congress formally adopted the United States Declaration of Independence.

None of this had any direct impact on Thomas Reed, who was about to enter his teenage years. He would then commence the apprenticeship that would eventually see him recognised as a qualified shoemaker. Soon after his 18th birthday, the British government signed another Treaty of Paris, officially accepting American independence and ending the war.

Thomas was 23 years old and well-established in his new profession when he married Elizabeth Sutton on 13 July 1789. They soon made their home at Ash Green near or above a small shopfront where customers could be fitted for new shoes and could bring their existing shoes for repair. It is likely that he also made and repaired other leather goods, such as belts and aprons for humans and harness for horses and other animals.

Their marriage came just two months after the first meeting in Paris of the Estates General, a parliamentary assembly that is recognised as the start of the French Revolution. This political movement would disrupt the whole of Europe and affect the lives of all members of the Reed family over the next few decades.

The general assembly comprised three estates: the clergy, the nobility and the commoners. The third estate proposed reform of the powers of the three estates but negotiations failed, so they acted unilaterally to redefine themselves as the National Assembly; an assembly of the people, not the estates. On 20 June, King Louis XVI attempted to frustrate the upstart Assembly by ordering the closure of the hall where it met. Members of the Assembly then went in search of a building large enough to hold them, taking their deliberations to a nearby tennis court, where they proceeded to swear the 'Tennis Court Oath', agreeing not to disband until they had settled on a new constitution for France. Messages of support poured in from Paris and other cities and by 27 June they had been joined by most of the clergy and forty-seven members of the nobility. The King backed down.

These limited reforms were nevertheless too much for Louis' wife, Marie Antoinette and his younger brother the Comte d'Artois. On their advice, Louis dismissed the chief minister on 11 July. A day later the Assembly went into a non-stop session after rumours circulated that the King was planning to use his Swiss Guards to force it to close. The news brought crowds of protesters into the streets and soldiers of the elite Gardes Françaises regiment refused to disperse them.

On the 14th, many of these soldiers joined a mob that attacked the Bastille, a royal fortress with large stores of arms and ammunition. Its governor surrendered after several hours of fighting that cost the lives of 83 attackers. He was taken to the Hôtel de Ville (the Town Hall); executed; and his head was paraded around the city on a pike. The Bastille was then torn down in a remarkably short time. Its destruction was viewed as a triumph for the ordinary people and Bastille Day is now France's National Day, celebrated on 14 July every year. The French Revolution had started.

King Louis appointed the Marquis de Lafayette as commander of the National Guard that was charged with defending the capital. Nevertheless, a week later the former Finance Minister Joseph Foullon and his son were lynched by a Parisan mob. In rural areas rumours and paranoia led to the creation of militias and an agrarian insurrection. Law and order broke down and there were frequent attacks on aristocrats and their property across the country. Many of them fled abroad to implore foreign monarchs for help to restore order.

The Assembly abolished feudalism and decreed equality before the law, freedom of worship and the abolition of feudal dues and church tithes. Assisted by the future American President, Thomas Jefferson, Lafayette prepared a draft constitution known as the Declaration of the Rights of Man and of the Citizen, which echoed some of the provisions of the American Declaration of Independence, now thirteen years old. The document was later heavily edited to highlight equality in a way that the American Declaration of Independence does not.

The newly married Reeds had now settled into life at Ash Green and Elizabeth was pregnant. Their first child was a daughter born on 2 May 1790 but she was not baptised until three months later,[17] when she was christened Mary Reed at Trentham on 15 August in the church of St Mary and All Saints. In later years, Mary was to play an important role in the lives of both her father and her youngest brother, James Reed.

A second daughter, born at the end of the following year, was baptised Ann, at eight days old, on Christmas Day 1791.[18]

By 1792, the pleas of French refugee aristocrats had successfully mustered support abroad and they threatened 'unforgettable vengeance' should anyone oppose them or their allies in seeking to restore the power of the monarchy. This only served to increase anger among the ordinary people of France. On the morning of 10 August, a combined force of the Paris National Guard and provincial forces attacked the Tuileries Palace, killing many of the Swiss Guards protecting it. Louis and his family took refuge with the Assembly and shortly after 11:00 am, the deputies present voted to 'temporarily relieve the king', effectively suspending the monarchy.

Five months later the Assembly condemned King Louis to death for conspiring with others to restore the monarchy to its former status. The sentence was carried out four days later at the Place de la Révolution, now the Place de la Concorde (Harmony Plaza). Horrified conservatives across Europe called for the destruction of revolutionary France. In February the Convention anticipated this by declaring war on Britain and the Dutch Republic. These countries were later joined by Spain, Portugal, Naples and Tuscany in the War of the First Coalition.

During the next three years the political situation in France was marred by social disorder and shifting loyalties. Prussian forces invaded and had early success but were defeated at Valmy in September. The emboldened National Convention abolished the monarchy and established the First Republic.

Britain's state of war with France would remain in place for more than twenty years, resulting in many battles on both land and sea. Britain also went to war against Spain from 1797 after the Spanish allied with France. The warfare would have created significant demand for boots and shoes which had hitherto been made by hand by skilled tradesmen like Thomas Reed. But the long war provided an incentive for inventors to look for ways to mechanise the processes to produce boots more quickly and cheaply. While widespread mechanisation of the industry was still decades away, in 1812 engineer Marc Brunel developed a machine that automatically fastened soles to uppers using metal pins and nails. While it fell into disuse at the end of the war, the process of mechanisation of the industry had begun.

The Reed's third daughter was born on 1 February and was baptised Elizabeth (after her mother) on 13 April 1794.[19] The three daughters were then followed by three sons: William was baptised on 11 December 1796;[20] Thomas was named after his father on 3 February 1799;[21] and John was baptised on 14 June 1801.[22]

During the 1790s the new French republic was involved in war across much of Europe. In 1796, a hitherto unknown general named Napoleon Bonaparte began his first campaign in Italy. Within a year, his armies had decimated the Habsburg forces and evicted them from the Italian peninsula, winning almost every battle and capturing 150,000 prisoners.

Despite the new French Constitution abhorring wars of conquest, its armies under Napoleon invaded Egypt in 1798. European countries responded to the French troops' absence by attempting to re-take territories recently lost. They gradually pushed the

French out of Italy and Switzerland before France won a significant victory at Zurich in 1799. Meanwhile, Napoleon's armies had carried all before them in Egypt and he returned in triumph in late 1799, enhancing his popularity at home. Nevertheless, the British Navy had won a famous victory over the French navy in the Battle of the Nile in 1798, strengthening British control of the Mediterranean and weakening the French Navy.

Napoleon installed himself as Consul and reorganised the French army before launching new assaults against Austria in early 1800. He won conclusively, leaving isolated Britain to agree peace terms in 1802. However, lingering tensions proved too difficult to contain, and the Napoleonic Wars recommenced just over a year later.

In England, William Pitt (with strong support from King George III) had become Prime Minister of Great Britain in December 1783 at just 24 years of age. He was widely expected to fail, like the three who had preceded him over the previous two years, but he proved to be an outstanding administrator who worked for efficiency and reform, bringing in a new generation of competent administrators. His government increased taxes to pay for the great war against France and cracked down on radicalism to ensure that the seeds of revolution did not find root in Britain. In response to the threat of Irish support for France, he engineered the Acts of Union 1800 which united the Kingdom of Great Britain and the Kingdom of Ireland (previously in personal union) to create the United Kingdom of Great Britain and Ireland. So, in January 1801 he served as the last Prime Minister of Great Britain before becoming the first Prime Minister of the United Kingdom (of Great Britain and Ireland). His combined service as Prime Minister eventually totalled almost twenty years.

In Trentham, the Reed family's seventh child was a daughter who was born on 5 August 1803 and baptised Prudence on 4 September.[23] She must have become a favourite of her younger brother in future years, because her Christian name was to feature prominently amongst his descendants in years to come.

On 27 January 1806 a fourth son was added to the family, who was baptised Edward on 7 February.[24] Nearly three years later the last member of the family was born on 14 December 1808 and baptised James Reed on 22 January 1809.[25] He is one of the two main subjects of this book.

His mother, Elizabeth Reed (nee Sutton), had now given birth to nine children over a period of nineteen years and was only about 42 years old, but died with her new baby less than four months old. She was buried at Chapel Chorlton on 2 April 1809,[26] where her father-in-law William Reed had been buried 23 years earlier.

Thomas Reed was now a 43-year-old widower who had a baby, a toddler and two other children under ten years old to raise while also running his shoemaker business. Despite the extensive demands that this would have placed on him, he did not re-marry. It is likely that he received strong support from his older children, especially Mary (now nineteen), Ann (eighteen) and Elizabeth (fifteen).

Unfortunately, his daughter Ann died less than a year after her mother and was buried on 7 March 1810 in the church where she had been baptised eighteen years earlier.[27]

Her older sister Mary would now have had to

assume a much greater share of the work associated with raising her younger siblings and running the household. Her father would have relied heavily on her during this time and she seems to have run his household for the rest of his life, which may explain why she did not marry until she had reached 32 years old, by which time her youngest brother James was fourteen and able to look after himself.[28]

James Reed had probably picked up many shoe-making skills by watching his father work over the years but he did not follow him into that profession. Instead, he found work in one of Staffordshire's oldest industries, brick making. In making this decision he may have been influenced by the prospect of increasing competition in the shoe making industry due to the invention of automated machinery and the introduction of specialised factories into the market.

There were two brick works within two kilometres of the family home at Ash Green. The nearer was about one kilometre northwards, on the road towards Hanford (see Map 2). Another kilometre further on was a major brick works at Trent Vale where there had been a kiln in Roman times.[29] Other brickworks were at nearby Spring Fields, Hartshill and Brick Kiln Lane.

As early as the 15th century there had been small-scale pottery making in Stoke-upon-Trent, the nearest large town. By 1600 Stoke had three factories producing coarse brown pottery and thereafter the industry gradually grew in importance by developing new products including butter pots, smoking pipes and buttons. It also expanded into more refined products such as earthenware, fine crockery, bone china and porcelain. "Staffordshire" eventually became a byword for quality products of the potting industries and names such as Spode, Minton and Wedgewood became valuable brands.

The only real issue holding the industry back in the early times was the distance to large markets. Road transport was not ideal because it was slow and the rough roads meant that breakage was a significant problem. This was overcome when the Trent and Mersey canal was built between 1766 and 1777, partly because of vigorous lobbying for it by Josiah Wedgewood who wanted faster and smoother transport for the output from his factory.

With that problem solved, the pottery industries boomed and the construction of several new factories caused a significant increase in the population of the area. There had been only about 7,500 people in Stoke-upon-Trent when Thomas Reed was born in 1765, but this had more than doubled by the time of his marriage in 1789. Thirty years later, as his 13-year-old son James prepared to enter the workforce, the town's population exceeded 40,000.[30] Male adults were the best paid manufacturing workers in England, with many of them earning 30 to 40 shillings a week, which may explain why James Reed chose this career rather than following his father into the shoe making trade.

The pottery factory owners expanded into brick and tile making in the early nineteenth century, just as James Reed was entering the workforce. The district was very well suited to these industries because of its geology. Stoke-upon-Trent is well supplied with beds of heavy clay suitable for making bricks, including Etruria marl and Old Mill marl, together with the associated coal seams to power the kilns. All these basic raw materials were quite near the surface and easily available.

The Staffordshire historian Robert Plot recorded in the late 17th century that '*on a bank by the way betwixt Newcastle and Keele*' he met with a peculiar sort of brick-earth which became blue when heated.[31] This was the basis for the "Staffordshire blue" brick which, when fired at a high temperature in a low-oxygen environment, takes on a deep blue colour and attains a very hard, impervious surface with high crushing strength and low water absorption. It is ideal for building work and was subsequently used in the construction of almost every railway, road and canal bridge in England. This "Staffordshire" brick is still in high demand throughout the world four centuries later.

The brick workers may have been relatively well paid, but they toiled long and hard; 72 hours a week. The clay was always mined in Autumn, extracted by hand shovels. It was then exposed to the weather, so winter's freeze-thaw cycle would break it down, making it easier to work. The elements softened the clay and removed unwanted oxides.

In Spring, the clay was thinned with water and sieved to remove stones. It then had to be tempered or pugged, so that all the elements were thoroughly mixed. This was very hard work, kneading the clay by hand and foot (later replaced with horse-powered pug mills).

The clot moulder would then extract a lump of clay and pass it to the brick moulder, who was the key to the whole process and head of his team. He would stand at the moulding table for twelve to fourteen hours a day during which, with the help of his assistants, he could make 3500 to 5000 bricks.

To make each one he would take the clot of clay, roll

it in sand, and "dash" it into a sanded mould. The sand ensured that the brick would then slide easily out of the mould. Next an off bearer would remove the filled mould from the table and place the brick out to dry on a barrow covered with a bed of sand, before sanding the empty mould and returning it to the moulding table.

The moulded bricks were stacked in a herringbone pattern and left in the open air to dry for a couple of days, when they were turned over to ensure uniform drying and to prevent warping. Edgers straightened and trimmed the bricks to obtain a smooth surface. The bricks were then re-stacked under cover for another two weeks of drying before being placed in a kiln.

The kiln was kept at a low heat for two days to complete the drying process. Then, once the bricks stopped producing steam, they were fired for a week at about 1800 degrees. Once the kiln had cooled, experienced workers would sort the finished bricks into different qualities, based on their appearance.

Because of this process, brick making was highly seasonal work. Typically, the owner would subcontract the whole process to the moulder at a given rate per thousand bricks. The moulder would then hire the rest of the team based on the quantity of bricks required. It is not clear whether it was the very hard labour, the long hours or the seasonal nature of the work that prompted James Reed to turn his back on the brick making industry and to instead seek a career in the army.

He was eighteen years old when he attested to the 35th Regiment at its depot in Newcastle upon Tyne (300 kilometres from his home in Trentham) on 13 June 1827.[32] His recruiter, Private Thomas Gillen, noted that James stood 5 feet 6 inches tall and had dark brown hair above an oval face with light brown eyes and a fresh complexion. The new soldier would have been immediately housed with a detachment of the regiment in the Sunderland Barracks, 20 kilometres south-east of Newcastle.

It is also unclear why he transferred to the 80th Regiment six months later. It could have been simply because it was a Staffordshire Regiment and he may have had a friend there. Or it could have been because he had noticed a young woman who was attached to the 80th. While the main body of the 80th had by this time been serving for six years on the Mediterranean island of Malta,[33] its depot was stationed in the Sunderland Barracks along with the 35th regiment. There is no doubt that one of his new instructors was the battle-hardened Sergeant Benjamin Heazle who was soon to become his father-in-law. Two years later, Sergeant Heazle's 18-year-old daughter Frances married James Reed on 28 June 1830 in St Peter's church, just across the river from Sunderland Barracks.[34]

James Reed could have followed his father into the shoe making industry, but sole trader shoemakers were facing increased competition from factories that could reduce production costs through specialisation, mechanisation and the economies of scale. Instead, he initially chose to work as a brick maker, probably because it paid well. But he had eventually rejected those conservative options to instead join the army and see the world.

James Reed's origins

CHAPTER TWO

Frances Heazle's origins

Frances Heazle was the oldest of five known children born to Sergeant Benjamin Heazle and his wife Elizabeth Wilson. Little is known with certainty about her mother, apart from a name, but her father was an Anglo-Irish weaver who had joined the British army three years before Frances' birth. He was promoted quickly and fought in Europe against Napoleon's forces while his daughter was a toddler. During Frances' formative years the family accompanied him to many postings across the United Kingdom and the Mediterranean. After she married James Reed (a Private in her father's Regiment) she continued to accompany the regiment until it eventually took her to a new life in Australia.

Benjamin Heazel was baptised on 30 June 1791 in St Peter's Church of Ireland within the Ballymodan Parish for the town of Bandon in County Cork, Ireland.[35] He was the oldest of ten known children of George and Frances Heazle (see Chart 2). His siblings included John (1793 - 1796[36]), Frances 1796,[37] Ellen[38] (1798 - 1799), George (1800

- 1803[39]), Catherine[40] 1802, Mary[41] 1807, Jane[42] 1809 and twins Rachel and a second Ellen[43] 1811. Theirs was a female-dominated household, with Benjamin's two brothers dying when he was five and twelve years old, respectively. Some of the children were baptised in the nearby rural parish of Kilbrogan.

The fact that Benjamin Heazle was a weaver prior to joining the army indicates that he came from a poor background. His father may have been employed on the Irish estate of the Duke of Devonshire, as Benjamin was to be in his later years.

The main street of Bandon is named for the Boyle family who had been Earls of Cork since the 1620s. In 1753 that family's Lismore estates (including those in the parish of Ballymodan) had been passed to the Cavendish family following the marriage of Charlotte Boyle to William Cavendish. He later succeeded as 4th Duke of Devonshire and was briefly Prime Minister of Great Britain in 1756-7.

Despite his Irish origins, Benjamin's surname is English. The name may be of Anglo-Saxon origin, a topographical name for someone who lived near a hazel tree or grove, deriving from the Olde English word *haesel*. Alternatively, it may be a locational name of Viking origin, deriving from the Old Norse *hesli* meaning hazel grove. There are several such places that were formerly under Viking control such as Hessle (in both the East and West Ridings of Yorkshire), Heazille Barton and Heazle Farm (both in Devonshire). The various spellings include Hazel, Hazael, Hasel, Hasell, Haisell, Heazell and Hessel. There are some very early examples of people with this name, including Alured del Hesel (Worcester c. 1182), Gamel Hesel (Pipe Rolls of Lincolnshire in 1203) and

Hugh de Hesill (Assize Rolls of Yorkshire in 1204). The surname is rare in Ireland generally but was well-established at Bandon long before Benjamin's birth, indicating that it had probably been brought there from England a few generations before.

Two days after Christmas in 1809 Benjamin signed on for military service at Bandon. This decision may have been influenced by the Duke of Devonshire given that he would, years later, provide Benjamin with a sinecure after his retirement from the army.

The recruiting officer (Captain Evatt of the 55th Regiment) recorded that Benjamin was about 17 years old and "well made", standing 5 feet 9 inches tall, with dark brown hair above a full face, grey eyes and a fresh complexion.[44] The British army had a keen need for recruits at this time because it was engaged in war with France and its allies on several fronts. The Regiment had been stationed in the West Indies for several years and had gone to the aid of Britain's new-found Spanish allies during the Spanish re-conquest of Santo Domingo just six months before Benjamin joined.

Even though he originally signed on for a limited time, Benjamin must have found that he was suited to military life as he would remain in the army for more than 22 years. His leadership qualities were quickly recognised with promotion to Sergeant after just 13 months in the regiment,[45] thus skipping the ranks of Lance-Corporal and Corporal altogether!

Around this time, he married Elizabeth Wilson[46]. Their daughter Frances Heazle was, according to her death certificate, born at Canterbury in 1812, but records of both the marriage and Frances' baptism remain elusive. It is possible that both ceremonies were performed by an army chaplain whose records have not yet made it into publicly available indexes.

The British army did not encourage marriage, especially for those in the lower ranks where a mere six percent were allowed to marry "on the strength" (meaning that the regimental colonel had given permission for the nuptials).

> There is no doubt that the ordinary rank and file did marry, [but] these wives were considered "off the strength". Wives who were "on the strength" lived inside the barracks, fed free on army rations, and could enrol their children in the regimental schools. Separate married quarters were only provided in 20 of the 251 stations, which sent returns to the Sanitary Commission in 1857. Marriages were consummated and babies were born in communal barrack-rooms, in the presence of other soldiers, screened by a flimsy curtain usually no more than a blanket strung up around their bunk. These conditions, though difficult, involved less heartbreak and suffering than those endured by the couples who married "off the strength." The wives of these marriages were neither allowed in barracks, nor granted separation allowances, nor entitled to accompany their husbands abroad (though this rule was sometimes evaded.) Undoubtedly these women suffered considerably from the regulations imposed by the army. Unofficial accommodation, often known as 'married patches' comprising whatever small huts that could be cobbled together, sprung up around encampments.[47]

This prompts the question of how Benjamin Heazle had met Elizabeth Wilson. It is possible that they met because she was herself attached to the 55th regiment as a camp follower - her father may have been in that regiment.

> *Reviews of the lists of dependants for a regiment of the British line show that many women carried the maiden names of other soldiers in the same regiment. It would appear from this that marrying the daughter of a colleague in the same regiment might have been a common occurrence. (Unknown, 'Camp Followers'.)*

After their marriage, Elizabeth Heazle accompanied Benjamin on all or most of his subsequent postings, so their marriage was clearly "on the strength". This is another indicator that Elizabeth's family may have already been attached to the regiment and that Benjamin was held in high esteem by his officers.

> *The wives of the Regulars served a very necessary function. They washed, cooked, mended uniforms and served as nurses in the time of battle or sickness. They also helped keep the morale of the men up. The women were expected to cook the meals for the company, clean the mess and wash the company laundry. At times the accepted women of the regiment were permitted to work for the Officers as well. (Unknown, 'Camp Followers'.)*

The main body of the regiment had been stationed in the West Indies during the previous decade but had seen little in the way of active service beyond the quelling of a mutiny in 1808 and a rebellion in 1811. This lack of action may explain the fractious relationships between its officers when the regiment returned to Britain in 1812. In a hot climate with little to do but drills, quarrels and slights can grow into lasting enmity. Now that he was a Sergeant, Benjamin Heazle would have become acutely aware of the volatile relationships among the officers that had lately returned from the Caribbean, particularly that between the aristocratic Lieutenant Richard Blake and his superior, Captain Hamilton Clune.[48]

Blake was clearly an abrasive character with fixed views on class, status and how a gentleman should behave. This led to the souring of his relationships with fellow officers to such an extent that his commanding officer, Colonel Robert Douglas, obliged him to sign a written declaration expressing his *"contrition for having disturbed the harmony of the corps"* and promising his future good conduct. But Blake was about to make things much worse and deprive everyone in the regiment of the honour of fighting at the Battle of Waterloo.

In that same year, Napoleon made the fateful decision to send his forces into Russia. On September 14, 1812 he arrived in Moscow at the head of an army of 600,000 men to find that the inhabitants had abandoned the city and set it alight. In addition to these scorched-earth tactics, the Russians harried the French with cavalry, resulting in huge French losses. Napoleon's proposals for peace failed because the Czar refused to capitulate. In October, with no sign of a clear victory in sight, he began the disastrous Great Retreat from Moscow. During the following weeks, the French Army was dealt a catastrophic blow by the onset of the savage Russian winter, worsened by a lack of supplies and constant guerilla warfare by Russian peasants and irregular troops. By November, only 27,000 fit soldiers had survived, with 380,000 men dead or missing and 100,000 captured.

Despite this humiliating defeat, Napoleon retained power in France and was still a force in the rest of Europe. But the coalition that opposed him recognised an opportunity and was strengthened when Prussia, Sweden, Austria and several German states switched sides to oppose France.

Napoleon vowed that he would create a new army as large as the one he had sent into Russia. He quickly built up his forces in the east from 30,000 to 130,000 and eventually to 400,000. He inflicted 40,000 casualties on the Allies in Germany at Lützen on 2 May and Bautzen on 20–21 May. Both battles involved forces of over 250,000, making them some of the largest conflicts of the wars so far.

Nevertheless, the anti-France coalition now had a clear numerical superiority, which they eventually brought to bear on Napoleon's main forces. In October 1813 he suffered a pivotal defeat in the Battle of Leipzig, thus breaking his hold over Germany.

In this atmosphere, Benjamin Heazle and the 55th regiment were sent to Europe in 1813, but not before the feud between officers Blake and Clune had mushroomed into full-scale conflict.

> Blake, having taken exception to some unspecified act on Clune's part, sought to obtain satisfaction by attempting to force him into a duel. Blake offered 'many insults of a gross nature', but Clune refused to be drawn. In this, of course, Clune was only following regulations, but it is clear from Blake's subsequent conduct that he felt that Clune had shown himself up as falling short of his concept of the behaviour expected of a gentleman. (Bamford, 'Dastardly 2014', p.212).

Blake brought matters to a head in the most public place possible: on the parade ground in front of the whole Regiment, including Benjamin Heazle. After a series of provocations, Blake said to Clune (who had just overseen the parade), "Let me tell you, you are no gentleman". Clune could not ignore this public challenge to his authority but didn't wish to give Blake what he wanted, a challenge to a duel. Instead, he had him arrested and charged with actions "subversive of good order and discipline". Blake then let fly with a tirade of gross and vulgar language which led to a second charge of "conduct disgraceful to the character of an Officer and a Gentleman". Clearly, Clune knew how to twist the knife!

Blake was confined to quarters but did not suffer the indignity of being placed under guard. He abused this privilege by attending a dance in Windsor Town Hall, leading to a third charge. Worse was to come. Three days later he ambushed Captain Clune in a Windsor Street, inflicting several violent blows with a stick and knocking him down. He stopped only when Clune managed to regain his feet and draw his sword. Blake fled to London but gave himself up a week later. He was then placed in close confinement pending court martial.

Despite these headstrong actions, it seems that Blake had some support from fellow officers! General Disney commented on this when he inspected the Regiment in early October.

Despite the need to clear the air by completing the court martial, fate intervened when the 55th was ordered to Europe as part of a force to be led by General Sir Thomas Graham, who had previously served as Wellington's second-in-command in Spain in 1811-1813. The aim of Graham's force was to drive the French out of Belgium and Holland with support from Prussian forces. The initial objective of the combined forces was Antwerp and, more specifically, the French naval squadron that was based there.

For the initial attack, the inexperienced soldiers of Benjamin Heazle's Regiment were combined with experienced men under the leadership of Major General Sir Herbert Taylor. He was a soldier-diplomat who had served as Private Secretary to King George III and later to Queen Charlotte. His force (including 340 from the 55th) attacked the village of Merksem near Antwerp on 13 January 1814. The village was taken but the attackers were obliged to fall back to conform with a Prussian withdrawal.[49]

A second attack on Merksem was launched on 2 February. This time the brigade (now led by Major General Skerrett) included 295 troops from the 55th. The operation was, again, successful and the following day the British and Prussian forces started a bombardment of the French fleet that lasted for three days. This, however, was ineffectual due to the inadequate artillery available. Withdrawal of the Prussian troops necessitated the falling back of the British troops also, to await the arrival of a better siege train.

Without allied help, the British were unable to operate against Antwerp, so Graham ordered an alternative attack against the fortress of Bergen-op-Zoom (40 kilometres to the north) on the night of 8-9 March. It was to be a disaster.

Graham decided to storm the fortress with three genuine attacking forces and a feint (or false attack to draw defenders away). Benjamin Heazel and 250 of his comrades from the 55th participated in the Centre Attack that consisted of 600 troops and 600 supports under Lt Colonel Charles Morrice. The Left Attack had 600 troops and 400 supports while the Right Attack had 300 troops and 600 supports. The Feint Attack had 650 troops.

On the day of the attack, the 55th marched from Santvliet (9 miles south) before assembling in their columns to await the attack signal. Ensign George Goodall later described the events that followed.[50]

> *Our column did not move till we heard a solitary shot a considerable distance to our right followed soon after by a volley as if from a sentry or guard. We then proceeded and had got well up to the works when suddenly a most tremendous fire was opened on us from the walls, as if the whole garrison had been assembled at that one point.*

Ensign Goodall found himself isolated with a small party led by Colonel Morrice. Twice Morrice sent a messenger to the rear for orders, but the messenger was unable to find the Commander in Chief. Morrice then ordered the retreat on his own authority.

> *Just after the retreat was ordered, however, the enemy opened from the guns which scoured that part and did some harm, but the firing on the whole must have been very wild or a man of our column should not have remained alive. ... Afterwards we were ordered to surrender, before doing which however I had secured the King's Colour about my person, as had also the other Ensign ... the Regimental [Colour]. (McCance, 'Colours 1928' p. 202-203.)*

So, while the initial British assault had seized part of the defences, a well-managed French counterattack had compelled a great many of their forces to surrender. The two Ensigns of the 55th Regiment had, nevertheless, managed to wrap the Regimental Colours (flags) around their bodies and under their jackets, to ensure that those sacred emblems would not suffer the indignity of being captured by the French.

The operation had failed despite heavy losses, with Major General Skerrett, Brigadier General Gore and Lt Colonel Carleton being amongst those killed. Benjamin Heazle's commander Morrice was wounded.

The 2,700-man French garrison had sustained 500 killed and wounded and 100 captured during the action. Of the 4,000 troops in the British assault force, casualties totalled 3,183 all ranks, the bulk of those being prisoners. 98 of the 250 troops from Benjamin Heazle's 55th Regiment were casualties, with 5 killed, 31 wounded and 62 captured.

For political reasons, various obstacles delayed the exchange of the men taken prisoner at Bergen-op-Zoom for a month. Nearly thirty years later, a colleague who was also present at that surrender, recalled that *"on the prisoners subsequently being given up* [i.e. exchanged], *the old well-riddled Colours were remounted on temporary poles"*. (McCance, 'Colours 1928' p. 201.)

After this loss, Graham's force was unable to mount any further attacks and some battalions were withdrawn. Nevertheless, his force was ultimately reinforced to maintain a military presence in Holland. Despite having acquitted itself admirably in battles at Merksem and Bergen-op-Zoom, the 55th Regiment returned to England in June 1814.[51]

This was very probably because of the need for regimental witnesses to provide evidence at the impending court martial of Lieutenant Blake. In the meantime, Colonel Clune had died (of natural causes) in England. Blake was tried by a General Court Martial at Harwich, found guilty on all charges and was cashiered.

Most of the regiments that had remained in Europe

would eventually form the nucleus of Wellington's force that won the final victory over Napoleon at Waterloo a year later, but Benjamin Heazle did not fight at Waterloo because of the indiscipline amongst the Regiment's officers and the Court Martial.

Judging by the Regiment's performance in action under Graham, where it was one of the few units to come out of the Bergen-op-Zoom debacle with much credit, the 55th got over this, but the urgency with which it was pulled back to England for Blake's court martial and the consequent re-opening of old wounds when the case was brought to trial, seems to have set matters back anew. Certainly, when the call came for units to go back to the Netherlands in 1815 for the Hundred Days campaign, the 55th, though available, was not chosen to form part of the army that fought at Waterloo. ... it does seem likely that it was owing to Blake's twisted conception of his own personal honour that the 55th missed out on the greatest battle honour of all. (Bamford, 'Dastardly 2014', p. 222).

Following the ending of hostilities after the second abdication of Napoleon Bonaparte, the Treaty of Paris was signed on 20 November 1815. Graham was ultimately able to negotiate the evacuation of both Bergen-op-Zoom and Antwerp by their French garrisons.

With Napoleon's ultimate defeat, Europe was finally at peace, sixteen years after he had risen to prominence. Fighting in the War of 1812 between the United Kingdom and the United States also ceased, peace terms having been agreed at the end of 1814.

While her husband was fighting in the European war, Elizabeth Heazle was heavily pregnant. During the war's dying days she gave birth to a daughter who was baptised Eliza.[52] Further records of this child are elusive.

The 55th Regiment disembarked at Yarmouth in Norfolk in June 1814 on return from Europe.[53] During the next three years, the people of the regiment moved around a lot, spending a few months at one or more of several places in Southern England. Some of these moves may have been tactical troop movements to allow for the possible need for reinforcements during the dying days of the war in Europe, but that potential requirement was never realised.

Benjamin Heazle was based firstly at Chelmsford, 50 kilometres northeast of central London, from where he took two months furlough in January and February 1815. This seems like a long break, considering that his army career was just six years old at this stage. It hints that there may have been a family issue that required his undivided attention. It is possible that his wife Elizabeth was suffering ill health or complications resulting from another pregnancy. Nevertheless, he returned to duty at Chelmsford in early March.[54]

Some members of the regiment were stationed at the Tower of London in April 1815, but they may not have included Benjamin Heazle. He was stationed at Brighton (87 kilometres South of London) during the June and September Quarters. For Muster 2 of the September Quarter (presumably August 1815) he was "on Command in London". This London posting continued until 25 October, after which he was posted to Bristol (190 kilometres west of London).

His head station remained Bristol throughout most of 1816, but he was seconded for three months to recruiting duty from February to May. For the third muster of the September Quarter he was again seconded, this time to Command at Chelsea (back in London). This secondment continued for about three months during which the main part of the regiment was posted to the island of Guernsey in the English Channel.

A year later, on 24 October 1817, Benjamin obtained a limited discharge from the 55th Regiment at Chatham in Kent (56 kilometres east of Chelsea) to re-enlist as a Sergeant in the 80th Regiment.[55] The reasons for this change are lost in the mists of time but may be related to continuing bad blood amongst the officers of the 55th.

The 80th Regiment had recently returned from India where it had seen action in the Second Anglo-Maratha War (1803-1805) and the Travancore War (1808-1809). Benjamin Heazle joined it as part of a recruiting drive to bring it back up to strength on its return to England. It is possible that he had met soldiers of the 80th regiment during his secondment to recruiting duties, or on one of his postings to London.

With recruitment completed, the 80th was ordered to Scotland for police duties. On 8 January 1818 they marched out of Chatham bound for Canterbury; left there on 2 February to march to Sheerness; and left there on 19 April for Colchester. Five months later, on 11 September they marched to Hull, where the regiment had its headquarters for the North of England. Detachments also went to Manchester, Rochdale and Stockport.[56]

On 26 January 1819 a one-year-old Benjamin Heazle was buried by the minister of St Andrews parish church at Drypool in Hull.[57] His abode was recorded as the Citadel, a triangular artillery fort that had been built in the 1680s at the confluence of the Hull and Humber rivers and which continued in military use until 1848. Given that Benjamin and Elizabeth Heazle were stationed in Hull on this date, presumably in barracks at the Citadel, it seems clear that the young boy who died was their son. He may be the Benjamin Heazle who had been baptised exactly a year earlier at Flowton in Suffolk on 25 January 1818.[58]

On 14 July 1819 the regiment marched north again, for Glasgow. On arrival a month later, detachments were sent to Fort George and Dunbarton. On 29 September they marched for Aberdeen by way of Sterling, arriving there on 14 October (with a detachment at Dundee). On 11 March 1820 a detachment went to Brechin. Two months later, on 25 May, the regiment was stationed at Edinburgh Castle where it remained for three months.

A gravestone in the Appleton City Cemetery (Missouri, USA) records the burial of a Benjamin Heazle[59] who died on 26 December 1875. The inscription states that he had been born on 24 June 1820 and had later married Margaret Hill. His descendants indicate that he had been born in Edinburgh, although the source of this information is not stated. Nevertheless, since the Heazle family was in Edinburgh on that date, it is likely that Benjamin Junior was a younger brother to Frances and Eliza Heazle and their late brother (also called Benjamin).

On 4 September the regiment commenced a three-day march for Berwick on Tweed. They later marched for Macclesfield, arriving on 22 September, from where (on 14 October) they left for Liverpool to embark aboard a ship bound for Dublin in Ireland, arriving on 31 October. Four days later, they marched for Fermoy where they arrived after ten more days. They left for Cork in December 1820.

During the three years from January 1818 to

January 1821, Benjamin Heazle and his regiment had
walked from southern England to northern Scotland,
returned to the midlands and then walked half the length
of Ireland. This would have amounted to at least 2000
kilometres as the crow flies. But it was not just the
soldiers who put in so much effort; Benjamin's wife
Elizabeth and six-year-old daughter Frances would have
accompanied him every inch of the way, although they
may not have been made to walk for the whole distance.
During that time Elizabeth had also given birth to their
daughter Eliza and two sons, both named Benjamin.

After traipsing all over England, Scotland and part
of Ireland, Benjamin Heazle suddenly found himself near
his birthplace in County Cork. But it is unlikely that he
was granted leave for a sentimental visit to introduce his
wife and children to his parents George and Frances at
Bandon. The regiment had orders to immediately embark
aboard a ship bound for Gibraltar, where it arrived on 15
January 1821.

The regiment spent five months at Gibraltar
acclimatising to the Mediterranean before continuing to
Malta where it would undertake garrison duties for
seven years. The island of Malta is strategically located
near the centre of the Mediterranean Sea. It had been
captured by France in 1798 but the locals revolted against
Napoleon a year later and were supported by Britain. It
then became a British Protectorate and, in 1813, a
recognised British colony. The British turned it into the
main base for their Mediterranean Fleet and it became
one of the most prestigious commands in the navy.

The 80th Regiment arrived at Malta in mid-
September 1821 aboard the transport ships *Clansman* and
Star. On arrival, the men marched to their quarters in the

outworks of Floriana, north of the harbour at Valetta. Later, detachments were deployed across the island and the neighbouring island of Gozo.[60]

Inspector of Hospitals John Hennen reported that the 80th Regiment was of the ordinary class of materials and [the] least effective corps in the garrison from the prevalence of fever amongst them. This statement was disputed by the adjutant Captain William Henry Penny [of the] 80th Regiment who had served in Malta from 1821 to 1 January 1828. Captain Penny stated that [his] Regiment was sickly during the first excessively hot summer, when the men were in hospital on average three times more than usual. However, once the men became accustomed to the heat, it was the 95th Regiment that was sickly on its arrival in 1824, and unable to perform guard duty, which consequently had to be carried out by soldiers of his regiment.[61]

There is no doubt that the 80th Regiment brought sickness with them to Malta because Lieutenant Hugh MacDougal, the 36-year-old Quarter Master of the regiment, died at the Quarantine Bastion on 19 November 1821, just two months after their arrival in Malta. Another three men died during that same winter and four soldiers were admitted to hospital with fever, at least one of whom had previously suffered with the same illness at Gibraltar. There were more than forty cases of fever during the Spring and nearly 200 cases with three deaths in the summer. In Autumn 1822 there were another 44 cases and five deaths. The medical officers thought it was typhoid fever, which is caused by salmonella bacteria and is transmitted via human faeces. (Various, 'Malta Garrison'.)

A year after their arrival in Malta, Elizabeth Heazle gave birth to a son on 24 September 1822[62] and he was baptised James Heazle on 20 October. Fortunately, his birth coincided with a reduction in the typhoid fever epidemic, although there were 159 admissions and one death during 1822. There were also cases of pneumonia, catarrh and tuberculosis, including two deaths. (Various, 'Malta Garrison').

During 1823 there was an average of two burials per month from all causes, but this increased dramatically in 1824 because of the great sickness that decimated the garrison. This time it was most likely phlebotomus fever (sandfly fever) which was known to affect all regiments arriving in Malta during the summer months. The 95th Regiment contracted nearly 300 cases soon after its arrival and was unable to provide men for guard duty for the first ten months after its arrival in Malta. (Various, 'Malta Garrison').

It was almost certainly this illness that accounted for a sudden spike in regimental deaths in June and July 1824, when 22 of the regiment's children died. Unfortunately, one of these victims was the Heazle's son James, who was buried on 21 June 1824, three months short of his second birthday.[63] This would have been a sober and formative experience for James' older siblings Frances, Eliza and Benjamin, then aged about twelve, ten and four years respectively. It is also possible that their mother died around this time, because she did not produce any more children and there is no further record of her.

According to his discharge papers, Benjamin Heazle served in the Mediterranean for five years, so he must have returned to England in 1825. While the bulk of the regiment went to Corfu from Malta, Benjamin went with the contingent that was stationed at the regimental depot in Sunderland from March of that year. He had now served in the army for sixteen years and would serve a further six years at home. Given his experience of active service and garrison duties, his work during the next six years would have probably involved him in both recruitment and training.

At the end of the following year, on 27 December 1827, James Reed transferred into the 80th Regiment from the 35th (as we saw in the previous chapter). It is almost certain that part of his training was then supervised by Benjamin Heazle, his future father-in-law. In any case, Benjamin's 15-year-old daughter Frances Heazle was among the camp followers and this is surely how she came to meet her future husband.

Nine months after his daughter's marriage, the regiment's depot contingent, including Sergeant Heazle, marched south to Portsmouth and was reunited with the main body of the regiment that had just returned from Kephalonia.[64] After resting there for two months, the whole regiment marched north to its main base at Stafford, arriving on 15 June 1831.[65] Detachments were stationed at Macclesfield, Manchester, Bolton, Blackburn, Oldham, Rochdale, Hyde and Wrexham.

Benjamin Heazle was stationed at Salford Barracks in Manchester for the next few months before he was discharged on 23 January 1832.[66] His discharge papers record that he had served "*In the 55th Foot on the Continent in the Years 1813 and 14; was present at the affair of Merxham and the subsequent bombardment of Antwerp & storming of Bergem op Zoom; In the 80th Regiment in the Mediterranean Five Years the remainder at Home*". The document also records that he had been discharged *"at his own request"*. The Regimental Board was of the opinion *"that his general character has been good"*.

He was now 41 years old and had served 1 year and 29 days as a Private plus 20 years and 361 days as a Sergeant; a total of 22 years and 25 days. He was admitted to a daily pension of 1 shilling and 8 pence from 8 January 1832 and indicated that he intended to reside at Clonmel, more than 200 kilometres north of his home parish of Ballymodan in Cork.

His son Benjamin (born in Edinburgh in 1820) may be the 20-year-old person of that name who was recorded on the 1841 census as a Smith Journeyman living in Liverpool, although that document states that he had been born in Ireland.[67] Descendants claim that young Benjamin was to marry Margaret Hill in St Louis, Missouri on 21 October 1854 and that they produced a family of six daughters named Elizabeth, Mary Ann, Eliza, Margaret, Frances and Adelaide.[68] He eventually died at Appleton City, Missouri, on Boxing Day 1875 and is buried in the local cemetery.

On 20 January 1853, a 23-year-old Benjamin Heazle married Maria Burchill at Ballymodan where Sergeant Benjamin Heazle had been born about 60 years earlier. This Benjamin was a son of Henry Heazle who may have been a brother or cousin of Sergeant Benjamin Heazle.

Benjamin's father George Heazle was recorded as living in a house in Bandon's Boyle Street on both 22 November 1848[69] and 24 July 1851[70] (when he paid an annual rent of 2 pounds and 15 shillings). While the details of George's death are obscure, his wife Frances was buried at Ballymodan on 21 September 1865 aged 99 years.[71]

In the years before his death, Benjamin lived rent-free in a house and garden owned by William Cavendish, the 6th Duke of Devonshire, in return for his services as canal lockkeeper at Ballynadeige (41 kilometres south of Clonmel) in Waterford, Ireland.[72] Cavendish, the Lord Lieutenant of Derbyshire, had a keen interest in gardening and horticulture and, as President of the Royal Horticultural Society, was chiefly responsible for the establishment of the Royal Botanic Gardens at Kew. The world's most commercially exploited banana, the Cavendish, was named in his honour.[73] Since the Duke's Irish estate included holdings at Kilbrogan (Benjamin's birthplace near Bandon in County Cork), it is likely that the lock-keeper position was a sinecure provided by the Duke in recognition of his military career. He or his representative may have been instrumental in Benjamin's decision to join the army all those years earlier.

Sergeant Benjamin Heazle died on 28 December 1850, aged 58, survived by his son Benjamin, daughter Frances and both his parents. He had lived a life of service to the aristocratic family that owned much of the land around his birthplace and elsewhere, including through his military career of 22 years where he had seen action against Napoleon's forces in Europe. He had then been rewarded with a welcome sinecure that enabled him to spend his declining years in security, dignity and comfort.

Frances Heazle's origins

CHAPTER THREE

Married life

Frances Heazle and James Reed had been brought together by the 80th Regiment of Foot which would also dictate the course of the early years of their married life during which they would start a family while traversing the length and breadth of the United Kingdom.

Thirty months after James transferred into the Regiment, he and Frances married at Monkwearmouth in Sunderland, Durham on 28 June 1830. This was just a few hundred metres from their home at Sunderland Barracks where the regiment's depot had been stationed for several years. The curate who performed the marriage, Reverend Benjamin Kennicott, noted that James (who signed the register with a mark) was a 21-year-old bachelor while Frances (a spinster who signed her own name) was three years younger.[74]

The Reverend Kennicott was a Hebrew scholar who had followed in the footsteps of his eponymous father,[75] who had endowed Oxford University with two scholarships for the study of Hebrew, now the Kennicott Fellowship.[76]

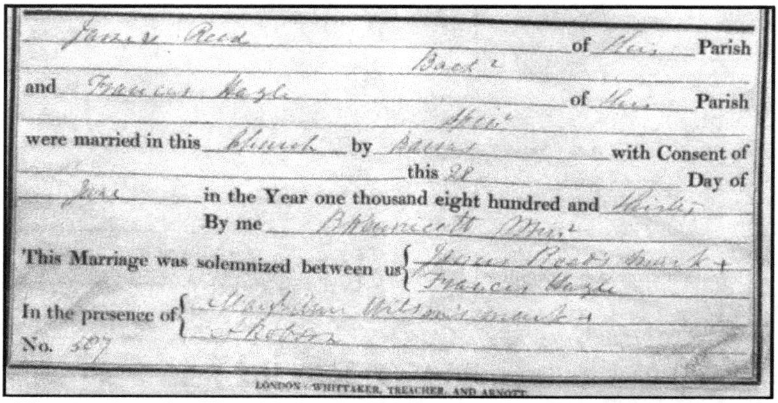
James Reed of this Parish
Bach.r
and Frances Hazle of this Parish
Spin.r
were married in this Church by Banns with Consent of
this 28 Day of
June in the Year one thousand eight hundred and Thirty
By me B Kennicott Min.r
This Marriage was solemnized between us { James Reed's mark +
Frances Hazle
In the presence of { Margaret Ann Wilson's mark +
J Robson
No. 507
LONDON : WHITTAKER, TREACHER, AND ARNOTT.

Illustration 1 - The 28 June 1830 entry for James Reed and Frances Heazle in the Marriage Register of St Peter's church at Monkwearmouth, Sunderland.

It may be significant that one of the marriage witnesses was Margaret Ann Wilson. This gives credence to the information on Frances' 1895 death certificate that her mother's maiden name was Elizabeth Wilson.[77] While church records reveal that there was a large extended Wilson family established at Monkwearmouth, it is equally possible that Margaret was attached in some way to the 80th Regiment, perhaps the daughter or wife of another soldier. She may indeed have been Frances' aunt, although there is no direct evidence for this proposition.

Two days before their wedding King George IV had died, after ten years on the throne. He had also served several periods as Regent before he became king, during the irregular bouts of illness suffered by his father, George III. He had been an active king known for his personal charm and culture, despite being unpopular with the general population due to an extravagant lifestyle and the poor treatment of his wife, Queen Charlotte (whom he had tried to divorce). He had built the Brighton Pavilion, remodelled Buckingham Palace and rebuilt Windsor Castle. During his short reign,

Britain had defeated Napoleon and emerged as a superpower, but his ministers found him to be biased, selfish, irresponsible and unreliable. His only legitimate child, Princess Charlotte, predeceased him, so he was succeeded by his younger brother.

The new monarch, William IV, was known as the "sailor king" because he had served in the Royal Navy as a young man, being stationed in both North America and the Caribbean. Despite this experience, the Admiralty had declined to give him a command during the Napoleonic wars so the nearest he came to combat was when he reviewed British troops in the Netherlands in 1813. He may well have swept past Sergeant Benjamin Heazle while on parade during his inspection before the affair at Merksem. He had then observed the bombardment of the French fleet at Antwerp from the steeple of a nearby church where he came under fire and a bullet had pierced his coat.

The reign of William IV ushered in several reforms, including an update of the poor law, restrictions on child labour, the abolition of slavery in nearly all the Empire and reform of the British electoral system.

Frances conceived a child within the first weeks of marriage as James continued his duties in the regiment's depot at Sunderland Barracks. The main body of the regiment was then stationed on the island of Kephalonia in the Aegean Sea but their Mediterranean service was ending after ten years.

About seven months after the Reed marriage, the 80th Regiment's posting to Kephalonia ended and it embarked aboard the transport ship *Pamelia* bound for home[78] eventually dropping anchor at the Mother Bank off the Isle of Wight on 8 March 1831. The soldiers landed at nearby Portsmouth two days later and then marched the short distance to their barracks at Southsea Castle for a brief period of garrison duty.

Meanwhile, their counterparts from the regimental depot at Sunderland, including Sergeant Heazle and Private Reed had marched south to Portsmouth so that the whole regiment was reunited.

Southsea Castle had originally been built by King Henry VIII in 1544 to protect against invasion by France and the Holy Roman Empire; and had been expanded in the 1680s. After many years of neglect, it had been redesigned in 1814 to protect against an invasion by Napoleon's France and was to later see service in both world wars.[79]

Frances' pregnancy was now well advanced and she gave birth to a son a few days after their arrival. He was baptised William Reed by Reverend Samuel Slocock on 24 April 1831 at St Paul's church in nearby Portsea.[80] On the previous day, Reverend Slocock had signed a petition desiring the proprietors of the Portsmouth and London coaches of discontinuing their Sunday coach services to *promote better observance of the Sabbath*[81]. The church at Portsea had been consecrated in 1822 but was to be destroyed by German bombs on the night of 10/11 January 1941.[82]

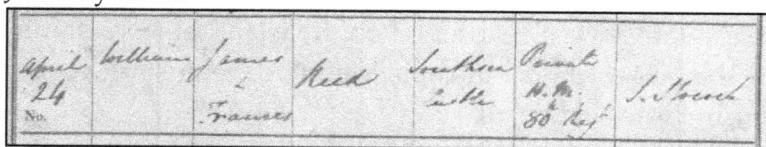

Illustration 2 - The 24 April 1831 entry for William Reed in the Baptism Register of St John's church at Portsea.

The choice of William for the baby's name is interesting, because none of his near ancestors had borne this name. In some families it was traditional to name the eldest son after his father's father but James and Frances Reed did not name any of their sons Thomas. Either they did not adhere to the naming tradition or James Reed did not wish to honour his father, although it is possible that the baby was named after his grandfather, William Reed. James and Frances would later name a daughter Sarah, possibly in honour of James' grandmother, Sarah Martin, wife of William Reed. Nevertheless, it must be acknowledged that both grandparents had died long before James' birth in 1808.

At the end of May, after about ten weeks at Southsea Castle, the regiment started a 300 kilometre march to its home base at Stafford, arriving two weeks later.[83] Presumably, Frances would have been provided with wheeled transport for herself and baby William. Soon afterwards, detachments were sent north into Lancashire where they were stationed at Macclesfield, Ashton, Manchester, Bolton, Blackburn, Oldham, Rochdale and Hyde. It is to be hoped that James and Frances were allowed to stay at the main barracks in Stafford, because that would have allowed them to show off their first child to James' father and siblings at Ash Green, just 22 kilometres away.

Six months later the regiment was on the move again. This time those that had remained at Stafford marched 90 kilometres north to Manchester (AJCP, 'Record of Stations'). The route would have taken them through Trentham, affording another opportunity for a reunion with grandpa Thomas Reed and baby William's aunt Mary and her husband John Grindley who had been married at nearby Keele nine years earlier.[84]

Soon after arriving in Manchester, Sergeant Heazle was discharged from the regiment and went to live in retirement in Ireland. It is unlikely that his daughter and son-in-law ever saw him again.

Two months later the regiment was split into detachments that were sent to various towns nearby, including Warrington and St Helens. Then on 2 June they left for Ireland via Liverpool, landing at Dublin on 3 June (AJCP, 'Record of Stations').

After a week there, they embarked aboard the steamship *Messenger* that carried them north to Belfast, from where detachments were stationed at Carrickfergus, Downpatrick, Castle Wellan, Port Glenone and Magherafelt (AJCP, 'Record of Stations').

The young couple's second son, John Benjamin Reed, was born soon after while they were stationed in the Belfast district.[85] His age was estimated to be six in 1836, but he was clearly younger than that because even his older brother would have been only 5 years old by then. If James and Frances had been following the naming convention, their second son would have been named Benjamin in honour of Frances' father. Clearly they decided to follow the tradition in their own way by using Benjamin as his second name. None of his known ancestors had been named John, unless this was the name of Frances' maternal grandfather.

One of the reasons for posting the regiment to Ireland was the Tithe War of 1831-36, a campaign of mainly non-violent civil disobedience in response to the continued imposition of tithes on the Catholic majority. Every landholder was obliged by law to contribute ten percent of their income as a tithe to the established Church of England, although most people belonged to the Catholic church and were therefore, at the same time, making voluntary contributions to support Catholic clergy. In 1829 a government led by the Duke of Wellington had enacted a Catholic Emancipation Act, despite a defiant King George IV, but this had not removed the tithe burden, thus leaving Catholics to continue bearing an intolerable burden of double taxation.

A year earlier the Irish Constabulary had opened fire on protesters in County Wexford, killing twelve and wounding twenty. Six months later resisters retaliated by ambushing 40 constables in County Kilkenny and killing twelve, including the Chief Constable. A few months after that a crowd of 200,000 had gathered at Ballyhale, in Kilkenny, as feelings ran even higher. During the next two years there were regular clashes that resulted in casualties, prompting the authorities to reinforce selected army barracks in fear of an escalation. Soldiers were also regularly used to provide additional security for Irish constables engaged in tithe law enforcement.

In this environment, James and Frances Reed remained in Ireland with the 80th Regiment throughout 1833. The regimental diarist recorded that:

> *While at Belfast many parties were sent out at different periods for the purpose of assisting the Civil Power in collecting tithes as also in aiding the Revenue Officers which duty was often harassing from long marches and inclement weather. (AJCP, 'Digest')*

Nevertheless, the most serious protests were in the south, not in the area around Belfast. So, in 1834 it was decided that the regiment could therefore return to the Royal Barracks in Dublin. In mid-April, after a long parade drill, they were given a sudden and unexpected order at one o'clock to depart for England forthwith.

There were at the time 70 men on Guard. At a quarter to 5 o'clock the Regiment marched out of the Royal Barracks and at 6 o'clock (being five hours from the receipt of the order) was clear of Dublin Harbour. (AJCP, 'Digest')

Such was the state of readiness and the level of efficiency required of soldiers in the regiment. The diary notes (in relation to their sudden departure) that *"this sudden movement was in consequence of the Political Union having assumed a formidable aspect and one menacing to the Government and likewise owing to serious riots in Oldham"*. There was a general expectation that the political unrest would be quickly suppressed, which would allow the regiment to return to Ireland after this short and unplanned deployment to England, but those expectations and plans were shortly abandoned. Soon afterwards, Major General Sir Edward Blackency of the Dublin Barracks expressed his appreciation of the regiment to its commanding officer Lieutenant Colonel Pitt in the following terms.

I cannot tell you the disappointment I felt in learning that your excellent corps was to be detained in England, be assured however that you will all of you ever retain my admiration .. As a high and well disciplined Corps, and one that I should only be too proud to have near in any day of need. Your admirable style of embarkation has been the theme of every one's commendation here since you left us, and I can assure you that you have left a stamp here not easily to be forgotten. (AJCP, 'Digest')

Despite the 80th Regiment's withdrawal from Ireland, the Tithe War continued. On 18 December the conflict came to a head near Rathcormac in County Cork, when armed constables reinforced by the regular British

Army killed twelve and wounded forty-two. This event, known as the Rathcormac-Gortroe massacre, took place during several hours of fighting while officials were trying to enforce a tithe order of just 40 shillings. One official observed that "it cost a shilling to collect tuppence"; and he was discounting the cost in blood. The government was forced to concede by suspending the collection of tithes.

After King William IV died in 1837, the government passed a law that reduced the direct tithe by a quarter and made the remainder payable in rent to landlords (who were required to remit it as part of their tithe). This effectively incorporated part of the tithe within a tenant's rent payment, providing partial relief. At the same time, elimination of the confrontational collections system ended the violent aspect of the Tithe War. However, full relief from the tax was not achieved until the Gladstone government passed the Irish Church Act of 1869, which disestablished the Church of Ireland.

On arrival at Liverpool the regiment was divided into two detachments of three companies each, stationed at Wigan and Chester. By 1 May they had moved to Blackburn in Lancashire, with detachments at Rochdale, Bolton, Bromley and Nottingham; all near Oldham where the political unrest had been manifested earlier.

Lancashire was the seat of the Industrial Revolution and the centre of the political unrest mentioned in the Regimental diary, particularly since the events in Manchester fifteen years earlier. Tension had been building in the area since the end of the Napoleonic Wars in 1815 because the resultant reduction in Government spending had caused an acute economic slump with chronic unemployment. The following year was the coldest in 250 years of records and was known as "the year without a summer", probably caused by the largest volcanic eruption for 1300 years that had occurred in 1815 at Mount Tambora in Indonesia. Huge quantities of ash and dust from the eruption remained in the atmosphere for many months, circling the earth and partially blocking the sun. This caused a "nuclear winter" that resulted in crop failures and major food shortages throughout the world, including Europe. To assist farmers, the British government passed the Corn Laws that kept the price of bread high, adding to the mounting unrest that stemmed from widespread unemployment. These disruptions added fuel to the existing popular discontent that had resulted from increasing mechanisation in many industries. Only 11 percent of males were then eligible to vote so reformers started to push for widespread suffrage, but this was rejected by Parliament.

In 1819 a second slump had prompted reformers to resume agitation for their cause, particularly in the areas of England that were the centre of the Industrial Revolution, such as Lancashire. The Manchester Patriotic Union had organised a mass rally in August 1819 at St Peter's Field. The local magistrates tried to stop the meeting by sending a cavalry regiment through the crowd to arrest the speakers. A woman was knocked down and a child killed. The magistrate's chairman then summoned the 15th Hussars to disperse the crowd. They charged with sabres drawn, killing at least nine people. The local newspaper dubbed it the Peterloo Massacre in an ironic reference to the recent victory at Waterloo. The Peterloo Massacre was described by historian Robert Poole as *the bloodiest political event of the 19th century on*

English soil.[86]

One immediate outcome from this incident was that the government passed the Six Acts, aimed at suppressing any meetings for the purpose of radical reform. Another outcome, it seems reasonable to conclude, was the erection of the Salford Infantry Barracks in Manchester, designed to garrison the troops required to quell any future insurrection in the district.

The Reed family was posted to that barracks on 17 October 1834 after having initially spent five months in the Blackburn district. They were to spend the next six months there but fortunately, nothing like the Peterloo Massacre occurred during that time.

On the contrary, their third son was born during this posting. He was baptised by the Reverend Isaac Robley in St Philip's church at Salford on 5 April 1835 and named James Reed after his father.[87]

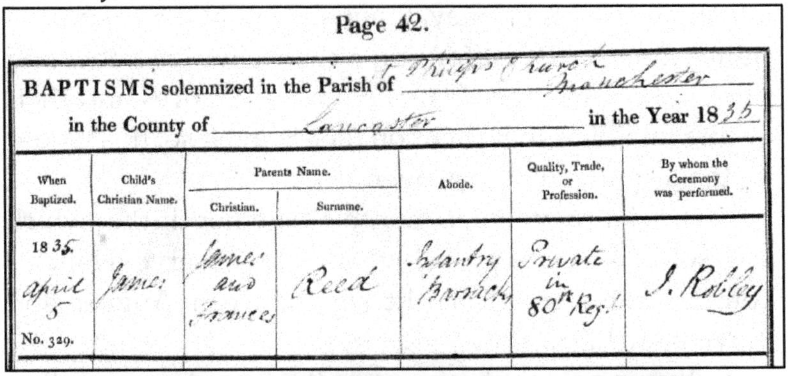

Page 42.

BAPTISMS solemnized in the Parish of St Philip's Church Manchester in the County of Lancaster in the Year 1835

When Baptized.	Child's Christian Name.	Parents Name. Christian.	Parents Name. Surname.	Abode.	Quality, Trade, or Profession.	By whom the Ceremony was performed.
1835. April 5 No. 329.	James	James and Frances	Reed	Infantry Barracks	Private in 80th Regt.	I. Robley

Illustration 3 - The 5 April 1835 entry for James Reed in the Baptism Register of St Philip's church at Manchester.

The church was even newer than the barracks, having been completed in 1824. It had been designed in the Greek style by architect Sir Robert Smirke with a semicircular porch featuring unfluted Ionic columns, a balustraded parapet, a round pilastered tower in diminishing stages, with a domed cap.

A month after young James was baptised, the regiment's Manchester posting ended and they were marched 50 kilometres east to Liverpool, with detachments sent to Haydock Lodge, Wigan and Chester. At some time during the next few months, it was decided to include the regiment in the garrison at New South Wales.

In the beginning of September of the same year the Regiment received orders to proceed to Chatham for embarkation in Convict Guards for New South Wales. (AJCP, 'Digest')

The regiment marched 400 kilometres southeast to Chatham (south of London) via Weedon (where they rested for twelve days). It is possible that the regiment would have marched through James' hometown of Trentham on this journey. If not, they would have passed quite close by, thus affording a chance for his father and other family members to meet James, Frances and their young family as they went on their way. If so, this would be the last time that they ever met.

The journey took a month altogether during which the soldiers were probably able to observe Halley's comet, visible in the night sky between August and November 1835.

It was not until seven months later, however, that the first detachment embarked for NSW at Gravesend, 15 kilometres north of Chatham (AJCP, 'Digest'). The Reed family had to wait a further two months before they embarked aboard the *Earl Grey* on 25 July 1836, the sixth of twenty-four ships that transported the Regiment to NSW between May 1836 and October 1837. (AJCP,

'Digest')

If the Reeds harboured concerns about the prospect of a lengthy ocean voyage, they were immediately validated when their son John became gravely ill while the ship was en route to Ireland.

The *Earl Grey* was a new ship, having been built at Newcastle a year earlier.[88] She was named for Charles, the second Earl Grey, a prominent Whig politician who had served as Prime Minister of the United Kingdom from 1830 to 1834. His government had introduced the Great Reform Act of 1832 that improved the electoral system and gave the vote to a much broader range of men, including small landowners, tenant farmers, shopkeepers, some householders and even some lodgers; but specifically excluded women. A year later, his government had abolished slavery throughout the British Empire.

Whether Earl Grey tea (a blend of tea flavoured with bergamot oil) was named after him is disputed. During his lifetime, bergamot was used to enhance the taste of low-quality tea, but this practice was frowned upon, so it is unlikely that he would have chosen to promote it. Later members of his family claimed that the blend was specially made to suit the water at Howick Hall, the family seat in Northumberland, which has a preponderance of lime. There were advertisements for "Grey's Tea" in the 1850s and 1860s, firstly associated with the tea merchant William Grey, but the first mention of "Earl Grey tea" did not come until the 1880s.[89]

The *Earl Grey* had a seasoned captain in James Talbert (or Talbot) and her Surgeon Superintendent (William Evans) was very experienced. A knowledgeable surgeon was a decided advantage on a convict voyage, because outbreaks of all kinds of diseases were common. Evans had enjoyed a long naval career and had also been employed by the army. The 1836 voyage of the *Earl Grey* was to be the last of his ten voyages on convict ships![90] His Surgeon's Journal provides a great deal of detail about the journey to Australia.

Joined the Earl Grey convict ship on the 15th of July 1836 at Deptford. On the 25th of the same month the Guard embarked comprising the following personnel viz. Lieutenants McDonald 80th, Hill 41st, Quarter Master Potter 4th, Assistant Surgeon Graydon 50th, Assistant Surgeon Allman 4th, One Sergeant and 29 rank and file of the 28th, 50th and 80th regts. Officers' wives Mrs MacDonald, Mrs Allman and Mrs Potter, 5 women and 7 children.[91]

One of those women was Frances Reed and two of the children were her sons John Benjamin Reed (who was about 4 years old) and James Reed (about 15 months old). Her eldest son William Reed (who would have been 5 years and three months old) was not aboard, so he must have died at some time during the previous five years, but his burial record is elusive. In fact, the only record of his existence is his baptism in April 1831.

Surgeon Evans recorded that the ship was new and very damp, so several of the guard suffered *catarrhal affliction*. To dry out the ship, fires were burnt in swing stoves fore and aft between decks and the barracks and prison were *dry holy stoned with hot sand and lime*. Holy stone was soft sandstone that was used on all wooden ships to scrub the decks to a fine smoothness; the forerunner to our modern sandpaper. The addition of lime to the sanding process was designed to kill bacteria and reduce the likelihood of further infection. This was good preparation, during the voyage from Gravesend to Kingstown, Ireland, prior to the embarkation of the Irish convicts.[92]

During the passage to Ireland, on 29 July, four-year-old John Reed took sick with croup and became dangerously ill. The little boy was bled and given aperient powders to make him vomit, to the extent that his *countenance became pale and sunk* and *symptoms of sinking of the powers of life were manifest - the powders were discontinued.* He was then treated with poultices and began to improve, but it took him two weeks to recover from this treatment, being finally discharged from the ship's hospital on 12 August.

Four days later, having arrived at Kingstown, ninety one convicts were brought on board from the *Essex* Hulk. A hulk was an old ship, now too weak and leaky to withstand the rigours of an ocean voyage, that had been stripped of all its masts and rigging and was now moored close to shore for use as a prison. This hulk had originally been the USS *Essex*, a frigate in the United States Navy that had participated in the Quasi-War with France, the First Barbary War, and in the War of 1812. The British had captured her in 1814 and she had been put into service as HMS *Essex* (a troopship) in 1819 before being converted to a prison hulk at Cork in 1823. She had housed Irish prisoners at Kingstown since 1824 but was about to be sold at public auction in 1837. Having now housed hundreds of emaciated and ill prisoners for a dozen years, the *Essex* would have been a real crucible for infection, all of which was now coming aboard the *Earl Grey*.

On the following day they sailed for Cork, reaching

there on 21 August. Frances Reed was now just 33 kilometres from her father's hometown of Kilbrogan, but she would have been unable to leave the ship. In any case, since retiring from the army four years earlier he had probably been living at Ballynadeige in County Wexford, 60 kilometres away. She would not have had an opportunity to say goodbye.

> *On Thursday the 23rd we received One Hundred and Ninety two Convicts and Five free boys (the sons of convicts in the colony) making the Grand Total of persons on board to be Three Hundred and Eighty Four. (Evans, Surgeon's Journal).*

James and Frances had now enjoyed six very busy and varied years of marriage during which they had celebrated the birth of three sons, albeit the eldest of these had since died. They would now have been feeling quite apprehensive, not only about what to expect in far-off and little-known Australia, but also about the more immediate prospect of a long and dangerous ocean voyage.

CHAPTER FOUR

Emigration

The Reed's knowledge about Australia would have been extremely limited. Like most of the other military families, what little understanding they had was likely based on misinformed prejudice and hyperbole. Consequently, they would have approached this new phase of their life with a significant amount of dread.

Four days after the last of the convicts embarked, the *Earl Grey* sailed and, over the next week or two, the ship gradually fell into its daily routine at sea. James would have mainly performed sentry duty on shifts that were scheduled out around the clock. Sentries were routinely posted outside the convicts' gaol, the captain's cabin, the armoury and the food store. Soldiers on guard duty were regularly inspected by an officer and could be punished for derelictions like sitting down or sleeping, talking to prisoners, having a dirty weapon, quarrelling or insolence.

Frances would have been mainly occupied in washing, drying and mending the family's clothes while supervising her sons John and James. Nevertheless, there would have been plenty of time to relax on deck and watch the sailors working the ship, the waves, passing birds and the occasional fish. No doubt she would have been super-vigilant whenever the children were on deck, for fear of them going overboard to a certain death.

As the ship proceeded southward towards the tropics, the weather gradually warmed until the thermometer reached 83 degrees Fahrenheit (28 degrees Celsius) as they rounded the Cape Verde Islands. In the convicts' prison, so far below decks, conditions for both the prisoners and their guards would have been uncomfortably hot and humid with very stale air. Surgeon Evans observed that embarking Irish convicts were generally in much worse shape than English ones, as was the case here. He considered that English prisons provided far superior food than Irish prisons and noted that Irish prisoners usually had no clothing of their own at all, other than that supplied as they came aboard. It is likely that their prison hulk clothes had been infested with vermin and therefore taken away and burnt.

He soon had thirteen cases of scurvy to deal with. This was always a risk on long sea voyages because it is caused by a lack of vitamin C, which is normally absorbed from fruit and vegetables. Since these don't grow well aboard ship and don't last very long while stored, the diet of everyone aboard was deficient in this vital nutrient.

As an experienced naval surgeon, Evans was well-acquainted with scurvy. Early stage sufferers bruise easily and their faces take on a pinched look. They gradually grow weaker and develop aching limbs, swollen and bleeding gums, foul breath, loss of appetite and anaemia. Left untreated, they are soon bedridden and eventually waste away to death.

Evans blamed the poor quality of water provided at Deptford; the hot, humid, foul and stagnant air experienced in the tropics; the "depression of spirits" experienced by each convict; and the inferior diet at sea. He noted that Irish convicts were much more likely to dislike food that they didn't normally experience, even simple things such as soup (which generally had reasonable nourishment).

The ship crossed the Equator on 1 October and benefited from a fine breeze. This should have helped the scurvy patients, some of whom did improve, but others were soon afflicted and the number of patients grew to nearly thirty.

> On the 19 October, after Mature Consideration, I recommended the Master to proceed to the Cape for refreshments; experience, to which all Theory is subordinate, convinced me in several former voyages that Lime Juice and Nitrate of Potash are mere Prophylactics and inadequate though very useful in their way, and that a liberal mixed diet of Animal and Vegetable Food are the only sure and permanent means of ensuring convalescancy and health for the remainder of the voyage. (Evans, Surgeon's Journal).

The use of citrus juice to ward off scurvy had been well known since before the voyages of Captain Cook, seventy years earlier. But Evans was wisely observing that lemon and lime juice, while very useful, were no substitute for a decent diet. The ship's captain knew that he could not ignore the advice of an experienced surgeon in a case like this. To do so would risk many deaths, which would probably result in his own court martial. So, he followed Evans' advice and made for Cape Town.

In the meantime, the weather worsened and two of the convicts died. By October 26 Evans had thirty five scurvy patients but his experience revealed that most of the other convicts were displaying the tell-tale early signs. They were coming down with disease before anyone else because they had started the voyage in poor health due to an inadequate diet while they were confined in the prison hulk.

So, it was with relief that the ship dropped anchor in Simon's Bay at the Cape of Good Hope on 4 November. During a stay of eight days, they took on fresh beef, mutton and vegetables for the soldiers and convicts and replenished their fresh water. In addition, they received five live bullocks and sixty sheep for later slaughter and consumption, with vegetables in proportion.

It was surprising to witness the beneficial effects resulting from this timely change of diet on the health and spirits of the Scorbutic Patients as well as the rest of the convicts. Indeed, in less than a fortnight, upwards of thirty who were before bedridden, were in a forward state of convalescency and continued to improve. (Evans, Surgeon's Journal).

Eight more convicts joined the ship before it departed Cape Town. Thereafter, as they sailed west across the Indian Ocean, the weather proved to be cold and wet and the seas boisterous. Finally, on 20 December 1836, Cape Otway was sighted and soon after the north end of King Island. These landmarks are the westerly gateway to Bass Strait, which they passed through with a fine following breeze over the course of the next day, before turning north towards Sydney. (Willets, *Earl Grey*).

As they sailed up the coast during the next ten days, the Reed family would have had a distant view of the coast, which comprised a series of long beaches interspersed between massive high cliffs. The temperature would have risen significantly as they sailed into their first Australian summer. They probably got an occasional whiff of smoke from the fires lit by the aboriginal population to control the dry undergrowth. No doubt their minds drifted and they probably started to wonder what their life would be like in Sydney and beyond.

The parochial English view of New South Wales would have told them that they were about to enter a wilderness where a few reluctant Europeans eked out a sad existence far from the civilisations of the northern hemisphere. Accordingly, they may have started to feel a bit sorry for themselves while clinging to hope that the posting would be at least bearable before returning home in a few years' time.

The *Earl Grey* entered Sydney harbour on the last day of 1836, the middle of Sydney's hot summer. The ship's occupants were, no doubt, breathing sighs of relief after having survived the journey. Only the previous year, the convict ship *George III* had sunk near Bruny Island in Tasmania with a loss of 134 of its 294 people; and the convict ship *Neva* had been wrecked in Bass Strait with the loss of 224 people and only 15 survivors.

The soldiers and their families had to remain on board for another day, while arrangements were made for their accommodation ashore. This would have given them plenty of opportunity to go up on deck and gaze at the shoreline of Sydney Cove. Their spirits may have lifted a little as they admired the beauty of the harbour and gazed at the buildings around the cove. The western shore was the busy area, featuring Cadman's Cottage, the Commissariat stores and a naval dock, with a maze of buildings lining the higher ground behind them in an area called The Rocks. There was plenty of commercial activity on the eastern shore as well, with wharves, storehouses and other buildings. On this side there was also a quarry and construction site for the land reclamation project that the government had authorised on the southern side of the cove to construct a Semi-circular Quay.

On their second day at Sydney, they would have woken in the dark as the first hint of the new day caused the kookaburras to launch into a raucous and soon-to-be-familiar dawn chorus. This may have prompted James and Frances to fully realise that they were entering a place that was very foreign to their previous experience. Between them the Reeds had, of course, lived in the Mediterranean island of Malta; the English towns of Sunderland, Stafford, Manchester and Blackburn; and Belfast in Ireland. They had been to Portsmouth, Liverpool, and Chatham in England; Dublin in Ireland; and Cape Town in South Africa. But this new land was already showing itself to be very different from everywhere they had been before.

The Reed family may have expected to find a backwater, a near-forgotten outpost of Britain's empire. They may or may not have heard stories of the bleak first few years of the settlement, when crops failed, stock wandered off and much-needed store ships were delayed by many months. The population had been on the brink of starvation, despite their situation in a land that had produced an easy living for its native inhabitants for millennia. But those desperate days were now a very distant memory.

In fact, Sydney's civic leaders were now preparing for the fiftieth anniversary of the colony, to be celebrated in thirteen months' time. Far from a struggling outpost, Sydney had developed into a thriving hub of industrious activity; the centre of a prosperous and energetic colony that now reached for hundreds of kilometres up and down the coast and well into the inland of the country. James and Frances would soon discover that the standard of living of most people in the colony was equal to or higher than that of the ordinary person back home.

The land where they were about to disembark had been occupied by aboriginal people for at least 30,000 years. Prior to the arrival of the First Fleet at this same location 49 years earlier, there had been up to 4,000 native people living in the Sydney region as part of nearly thirty clans, collectively forming the Eora nation. On 26 January 1788 the new colonists had raised the British flag at Sydney Cove on Cadigal land, which comprised the Southern side of the harbour between the Heads and Cockle Bay (now Darling Harbour), including the area around Sydney Cove (which they called *Warrung* meaning little child). The Cadigal camped on harbour islands and near the harbour shore where they fished from bark canoes. Large middens revealed that shellfish formed an important part of their diet. Unfortunately, the Reed family would not have seen any of this, because more than half of the people of the Eora nation had died of smallpox by 1789, a disease previously unknown in Australia and for which they had no natural immunity.

The Cadigal clan was hit hardest, as the new arrivals had immediately taken possession of most of their land. Those that survived the introduced illnesses had therefore been unable to make a living on their own country and were consequently forced to move south, where they had settled in the Concord area. Any that stayed on their traditional land had become dependent on the colonisers for food and clothing. Their former lifestyle had disappeared from the central Sydney area within a couple of years and was almost completely absent when the Reed family arrived 47 years later. This process of dispossession was to be echoed throughout the continent for decades to come.

After a quick breakfast and the completion of last-minute packing, they landed on 2 January and the soldiers marched the short distance to the Military Barracks on George Street.[93] It was confined inside a sandstone wall three meters high and occupied a large plot of prime real estate in central Sydney, bounded by George, Barrack, Clarence and Margaret Streets. The wall had been ordered by Governor Macquarie three decades earlier *"to restrain as much as possible intercourse between the military and the inhabitants of the town"*. He wanted his military forces to stand aloof from the general population to reduce the likelihood that they would be corrupted and sink into dissolute behaviour.

Inside the wall were barracks for officers and men, storehouses, parade grounds and exercise grounds. From the main entrance in George street a broad gravel path led straight up to the barracks, with the large parade ground on either side (see Illustration 4). The main row of barracks stood along the western side of what is now York street, with the men's accommodation in the centre and the officers on either end.

James and Frances Reed would have relished the opportunity to move into the sturdy barrack room after so many months at sea. Frances would have been preoccupied with settling nine-month-old James into his new home while trying to keep tabs on young John Benjamin who was now four years old and could disappear at a moment's notice. But she knew not to ever get too settled in barracks, because it was a soldier's lot to be redeployed to another station with very little notice.

The *Earl Grey's* convicts had to remain on board while a muster took place. All their particulars were meticulously recorded by the Governor's clerks in Indents that would form the basis of the administration of these men for years to come. When they landed on Bennelong Point on 18 January 1837, Surgeon Evans was justifiably pleased that they were all in good condition.

> *By the time they were disembarked we had not an individual but what could walk up to the Convict Barracks to be Inspected by His Excellency the Governor. The number landed were Two Hundred and Eighty Eight. (Evans, Surgeon's Journal).*

James Reed would probably have been a member of the Guard that escorted the convicts up the hill and along Macquarie Street to the Convict Barracks. Much of what they saw on the eastern side of the street remains in place nearly two hundred years later. On the harbour end were the public Domain and Botanic Gardens. He may have noticed lots of activity in the Domain as construction work was about to commence on a new Government House. Further along were several fine buildings that comprised Sydney Hospital, although some were to be re-purposed in later times. Next came their destination, the Convict Barracks, a three storey red brick structure surrounded by a high brick wall. It provided convict accommodation and was the hub of convict administration for the whole colony. Inside the wall was a large treadmill that was used as extra punishment for prisoners who had been convicted of minor crimes in the colony.

On arrival at the Convict Barracks, the convicts would have been assembled for inspection by the Governor, Major-General Sir Richard Bourke. Little did the Reeds know at that time that they were destined to spend more than a third of their lives in a town that would be named after this Governor.

Bourke was a 59-year-old member of the Irish aristocracy who, as a child, had spent his vacations with a distant relative, Edmund Burke (the Irish-born British statesman, economist and philosopher), who was a proponent of underpinning personal virtues with good manners; and of the importance of religious institutions for the moral stability and good of the state.[94] Governor Bourke had been educated at Westminster school and Oxford University before joining the army and seeing active service in the Netherlands in 1799, where he had been badly wounded. Eight years later he again saw active service in South America followed by administrative roles where his Spanish language skills proved useful. Before his appointment as Governor of NSW he had acted in a similar capacity in the Cape Colony during the 1820s where he did much to improve government administration and attempted to repair relations between the various races. He was now entering his sixth year as NSW Governor, where he was popular with ordinary people and those with liberal views but opposed by the "exclusive" faction that controlled the Legislative and Executive Councils.[95]

The Governor inspected the prisoners and gave them an address that laid out what was expected of them in their new lives in NSW. With the official ceremonies completed, the Governor left and there was a chance for everybody to relax and look around at their new surroundings.

Across the road was the impressive St James Anglican church, that had, like the Convict Barracks itself, been built in 1819. Behind the Convict Barracks was the 15 year old St Mary's Catholic church, now administered by Bishop John Bede Polding who had arrived in Sydney a year earlier. His cousin, Bishop Edward Bede Slater, had been, for many years, vicar apostolic with jurisdiction over Australia, Mauritius, Madagascar and the Cape. Polding had already impressed Governor Bourke so much for his positive influence on Catholic convicts that he had been given access to them during the first several days after arrival. He and his assistants would have personally visited each of the *Earl Grey's* convicts and done whatever they could for them before they were drafted to their first assignment in NSW.

The Reeds did not have long to enjoy the dry and relatively comfortable accommodation of the Sydney Barracks before orders came to move west. A detachment of the regiment was dispatched to Bathurst in mid-February, to relieve the 28th Regiment[96]. The Reed family was almost certainly in the party that headed west, but fortunately they would not be required to go the whole way to Bathurst, because they were to remain with a smaller detachment that manned the station at Seventeen Mile Hollow (now known as the town of Linden) in the Blue Mountains. It was so named because of its location, 17 miles (27 kilometres) west from the Nepean River.

From Sydney the party would have first marched the 25 kilometres to Parramatta (although they may have been allowed to travel this first leg by boat up the Parramatta River). They probably rested there for a day or two, giving them an opportunity to admire the thriving settlement. The town's name was a Darug word meaning place of many eels, which remain very numerous in the river into modern times. It had been selected by Governor Phillip in 1788 as an ideal farming locality (an early imperative due to Sydney's poor soils) that was easily accessible by boat from Sydney. It grew rapidly and was for many years larger and more important to the colony than Sydney itself. Parramatta was the first place in the colony to be given a name sourced from an aboriginal language.

The town now had a very pleasant Government House, a military barracks, convict huts, a hospital, a gaol, St John's church and graveyard, a granary, warehouses, brick kilns and other industries such as brewing and weaving. The Reed family would have also seen the Female Factory and Orphan School, the central hub for the administration of female convicts throughout the colony. The town also had a courthouse and a busy shopping centre that provided not only ordinary goods but also specialist wares and professional services in law and medicine. There was a newly opened school (the King's School).

After taking in the sights of the town, the Reed family would have moved further west along with the detachment bound for Bathurst. It was 35 kilometres to Penrith, on the banks of the Nepean River. The town was built above the flood level and had a depot, a guard house, a gaol, gardens and farms. It had originally been named *Penrhyn* by William Cox, a reference to the *Lady Penrhyn*, one of the ships of the First Fleet. That name had since been corrupted to Penrith.

Nearby was Emu Ford, where the riverbed was covered in thousands of rounded rocks that provided a firm base for people and wagons to ford the river. Whenever the river was too high, travellers had to rely on a punt as there would be no bridge for another 20 years. On the western bank was the small village of Emu Plains, sitting at the foot of the Blue Mountains and catering for people travelling from the west while they prepared to cross the Nepean.

The road from Emu Plains to Bathurst, a distance of 163 kilometres, had been completed 22 years earlier in only six months by a working party composed mostly of convicts. Heading west from Emu Plains there was a very steep and extremely arduous climb up Lapstone Hill to the top of the ridge, 140 metres above the river flats. From there the road wended its way along the ridge, gradually climbing for 27 kilometres to 17 Mile Hollow. The ridge is only a kilometre or two wide for the most part, so there would not have been much scenery for the Reed family to admire along the road.

They would not have reached 17 Mile Hollow on that same day. It is much more likely that they stayed for a night or two at Springwood, 15 kilometres from Emu Plains, where the government had built a military stockade.

By early March 1837, the Reeds would have reached

their new home at 17 Mile Hollow where they were destined to remain for about fifteen months. It was situated in a slight dip on top of the ridge 526 metres above sea level. The mountain road was still quite primitive requiring constant maintenance by convict gangs, the main function of the place. Part of James Reed's duties would have been to provide security for the road gang overseers and for passing travellers.

The Reed family had now been in Australia for several months during which they would have had very little contact with the vanquished original inhabitants of the settled areas. The frontier between the colonists and the traditional owners of the land had advanced inexorably north, south and west every year, creating new tensions with natives whose land had been previously out of reach of the colonists.

17 Mile Hollow lay between the land of the Gandangarra aboriginal tribe to the west and south-west (the great valleys and Upper Blue Mountains) and the Dharug tribe's territory to the east (Cumberland Plains and Lower Blue Mountains). It is likely that the ridge lines (where the Europeans gathered along the road from Penrith to Bathurst) had been a boundary between the tribes, a neutral area where inter-tribal ceremonial activities were focussed. Both tribes had participated in the Hawkesbury and Nepean Wars of 1814-1816, armed resistance to the colonists' settlement on their land.

For two violent years between 1814 and 1816 the so-called 'Wild Mountains Natives', mostly Gandangarra people, were seen by the Sydney colonists as a major threat. Their raids on the fringes of the Cumberland Plain were regular and at times deadly. There were reports they would ally with the Dharawal warriors and

attack the settlements, and 'murder all the white people
before them'. Gandangarra warriors had been seen in
warbands of several hundred and settlers had been forced
to flee outlying farms for the safety of townships.[97]

In March 1816 warriors had attacked the
MacArthur family's farm at Camden and killed three
servants. Nearby settlers quickly raised a force of about
forty able-bodied volunteers led by local magistrate
Robert Lowe and including a detachment of soldiers.
While pursuing the warriors they were attacked
somewhere on the nearby Razorback Range. Samuel
Hassall, a settler at Macquarie Grove who was in Lowe's
force, later wrote that the warriors "began to dance in a
manner daring our approach" and, when the militia did
advance, it met a shower of spears and stones and was
forced to retreat.

Soon afterwards, Governor Macquarie mobilised
the largest military expedition in the history of the colony
"so as to Strike them with Terror against Committing
Similar Acts of Violence in future".

Macquarie's infamous campaign of April 1816, which
resulted in the massacre of at least 14 Dharawal people
at Appin, involved well-coordinated infantry
detachments sweeping through the west and southwest
of the Cumberland Plain. The campaign effectively ended
resistance to the Europeans in the Sydney region and on
its fringes (although there were smaller conflicts into
1817). Gapps, The Sydney Wars.

The native warriors had eventually been forced to
retreat into the safety of the "impenetrable barrier" of the
Blue Mountains from where they carried on a campaign
of ambushes and sudden attacks in a long-running

guerrilla war with the settlers. But the Hawkesbury and Nepean War of 1814-16 was neither the beginning nor the end of the conflicts between the original inhabitants and the newcomers. As the colonists advanced further and further along the coast and into the interior of the continent, conflict erupted whenever they encountered previously undisturbed clans, a process that was to continue for several decades until the frontier finally reached the Kimberley region in Western Australia.

James and Frances would have been largely unaware of the details of aboriginal dispossession in the districts around Sydney because twenty years had since passed. But they would be made aware of the continuing process of displacement two years later when news broke about the Myall Creek massacre.

The dread that James and Frances had probably felt about this new posting may have ebbed away somewhat during their first seven months in Australia. Sydney and Parramatta had proved to be far more hospitable than feared, but some trepidation would have lingered as they faced the prospect of living in a lonely Blue Mountains outpost as winter approached.

Illustration 4 - Barracks, George Street, viewed through the George Street Gate, 1845
by George Roberts.
State Library of NSW[98]

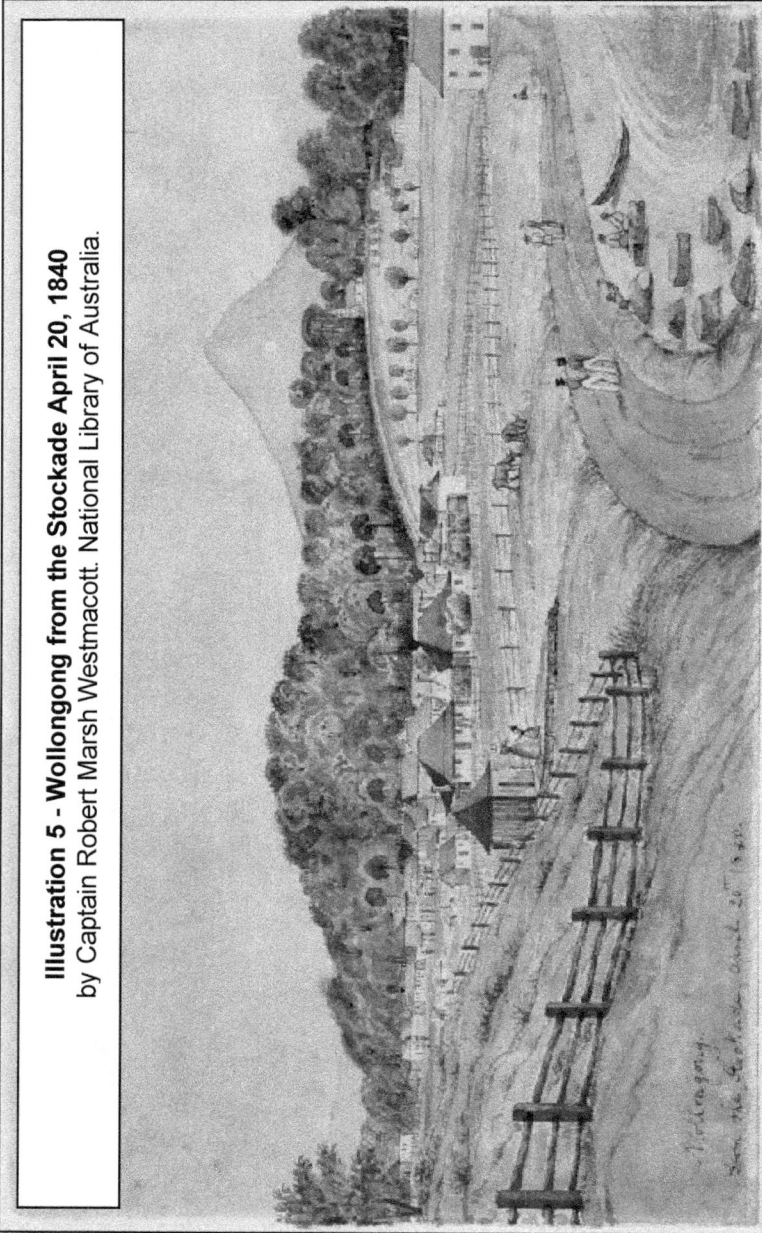

Illustration 5 - Wollongong from the Stockade April 20, 1840 by Captain Robert Marsh Westmacott. National Library of Australia.

Illustration 6 - The sailing steamer *Sophia Jane* that transported the Reeds to and from Wollongong.
Source: JHM Abbott. The Newcastle Packets and the Hunter Valley, Currawong Publishing Co, Sydney 1942.

Illustrations 7 (top), 8 & 9 (bottom)

7. Alexander Reed was baptised by the Reverend Henry Fulton at 17 Mile Hollow on 10 July 1837.

8. Sarah Reed was baptised by the Reverend George Napoleon Woodd in St James church at Sydney on 1 December 1839.

9. Eliza Emily Reed was baptised by the Reverend Matthew Devenish Meares in St Michaels parish at Wollongong on 7 November 1841

CHAPTER FIVE

Duty and discharge

During their first few years in Australia James and Frances welcomed three more children into their family as they moved between postings that gave them an overview of the Sydney environs, from the Blue Mountains and Windsor in the west to Wollongong in the south. They witnessed the rapid development of colonial society, the establishment of representative government and the end of convict transportation to NSW. These developments may have prompted them to start imagining life outside the army.

The Reed family did not arrive in the Blue Mountains until twenty years after the Hawkesbury and Nepean War, by which time the colonists were established as the victors and settlement was proceeding apace.

On arrival at 17 Mile Hollow, they would probably have welcomed the change in climate, with the mountain elevation providing some relief from the heat. But as the weeks wore into months, the temperature would have dropped significantly as they transitioned from autumn into winter. During the night it would regularly have fallen below freezing and they would have seen many a frosty morning.

Frances was pregnant, so she must have had a very strong constitution to have walked all the way from Sydney while supervising her young sons. When their brother **Alexander Reed** was born at 17 Mile Hollow on 10 July 1837, John was about 5 years old and James about two. He was baptised by the Reverend Henry Fulton on 26 July (see Illustration 7).

Reverend Fulton was a curate of the Church of Ireland who had been caught up in the cause of the United Irishmen in 1798. He had then been convicted of sedition and sent to Australia as a convict but Governor Hunter recognised him as a genteel scholar and soon allowed him to resume his clerical profession, firstly at the Hawkesbury and then at Norfolk Island. Governor King had subsequently given him a full pardon and brought him back to the mainland where he had worked for the Reverend Samuel Marsden at both Sydney and Parramatta. In 1808 Fulton had strongly supported Governor Bligh following his arrest by the Rum Corps, eventually travelling with Bligh to England to give evidence at the court-martial of the rebellion's leader, Lieutenant-Colonel George Johnstone. On his return to NSW, he was promoted to chaplain in charge of Castlereagh and Richmond. By the time he baptised Alexander Reed, Fulton was 76 years old and still very active as both a churchman and an educator of young men in the classics, particularly mathematics. He was to die at Castlereagh four years later.[99]

On the same day that Alexander was baptised, the Regimental Headquarters were moved from the Military Barracks in Sydney to Windsor, downstream from Penrith. By that time the regiment had small detachments deployed at a dozen places throughout the colony. Along the western road were detachments at Emu Plains, 17 Mile Hollow, Hassans Walls (near Lithgow), Cox's River and Bathurst. South of Sydney they were at Liverpool, Berrima, Wingello and Illawarra while others were in the more distant settlements at Newcastle, Moreton Bay (now Brisbane) and Port Phillip (now Melbourne). In early 1838 detachments were sent to the penal settlements at Port Macquarie and Norfolk Island. (AJCP, 'Digest')

A month before Alexander's birth, King William IV had died. He was the third son of King George III and had succeeded his brother George IV seven years earlier. At the time of his death, William had no surviving legitimate children (although he was survived by eight of the ten children he had fathered with actress Dorothea Jordan, with whom he lived for twenty years). William was succeeded by his niece Victoria, who was to reign for nearly sixty four years, surviving both James and Frances Reed.

The reason for the choice of Alexander for the new baby's name in unclear. It is possible that his name was inspired by the new queen, whose full name was Alexandrina Victoria, although it is unlikely that James and Frances Reed knew about her ascension to the throne when their son was born.

Soon after Alexander celebrated his first birthday, the detachments at both 17 Mile Hollow and Cox's River were withdrawn to Headquarters at Windsor. They would have had to re-trace their steps back to Penrith before turning north and proceeding along the Northern Road for another 22 kilometres.

The area around Windsor had been first populated by Europeans in 1791, just three years after the arrival of the First Fleet, making it the third settlement in NSW after Sydney and Parramatta. After another three years, a settlement had also been made at Richmond, just 7 kilometres west of Windsor. The fertile river flats in this district were ideal for cultivation but the area was vulnerable to floods. The town is below the junction of the Grose and Nepean rivers (prompting a name change to the Hawkesbury) and just above the junction with South Creek, so floods could come up suddenly. Fortunately, the Reed family was stationed at Windsor during an unusually long period without a really major flood.

After an uneventful year at Windsor, they were posted back to Sydney.

> *On the 10th September [1839] a party consisting of 1 Sub 2 Serjts and 32 rank and file proceeded from Head Quarters at Windsor to Sydney for the purpose of taking a share in the duties of the latter station. (AJCP, 'Digest')*

It is possible that this journey was made by boat, over two or three days. There were small vessels regularly plying this route to bring provisions into Windsor and to take farm produce back to market in Sydney. They would firstly follow the river north to Wiseman's Ferry where it turns eastwards into Broken Bay and so through to the ocean; then south to the opening of Sydney Harbour; and westward up the harbour to Sydney Cove. This is much further than the land route of 55 kilometres via Parramatta but would have been a much less arduous journey. It is also possible that the soldiers marched and the families travelled by boat.

About a month after arriving back into the Military Barracks at Sydney, Frances gave birth to their fifth child. After four consecutive sons they were overdue for a girl and would have no doubt been delighted with the arrival of their first daughter on 20 November. **Sarah Reed** was baptised in St James church ten days later (see Illustration 8) by Reverend George Napoleon Woodd.[100]

Reverend Woodd had arrived in Australia in 1837 after being ordained by the Bishop of London three years earlier. He was to serve at St James for only two years before moving inland for his health. He is reputed to have worked every day for the first 50 years of his life in Australia, without a single holiday.[101]

Photograph 1
A button from the uniform of an 80th Regiment soldier who served in Australia.

Two days before little Sarah celebrated her first birthday, the last convict ship to NSW, the *Eden*, arrived in Sydney. Opposition to convict transportation had been growing in England for nearly two decades and during the 1830s, many citizens of NSW also started to voice their opposition to it. Humanitarian and liberal views had gradually gained traction in Britain after the abolition of slavery in most British colonies from 1834.

Prior to 1825, NSW had been an autocracy, ruled by a Governor appointed by the British Government who generally exercised his powers within the constraints of British law. In practice the Governors ruled by consent, based on advice from the military, officials and free settlers. This system had been formalised in 1825 through the establishment of the NSW Legislative Council to provide advice to the Governor. It was not proper democracy, because all members of the Council were appointed, but it was a step towards it. Trial by jury was introduced at the same time, thus reducing the judicial power of the military.

Over time, the harshness of the British penal code had been reduced, so that fewer minor offenders were transported. This meant that hardened criminals now made up a much higher proportion of transportees and consequently, Sydney's population had less and less sympathy for newly arrived convicts. Newspapers editorialised that the fabric of society was fraying because of crimes committed by disgruntled and desperate convicts. Opposition to transportation was strongest amongst urban dwellers, free immigrants and the working classes (who felt that their wages were depressed by the availability of convicts whose labour was free).

So, in August 1840 the British government decided to end convict transportation to NSW (including Victoria and Queensland) immediately, although ships continued to bring convicts to Van Diemen's Land and Western Australia.[102]

Despite this, there were powerful conservative forces in NSW that wanted to reverse the decision. Squatters and landowners had become wealthy using cheap convict labour and didn't want to have to pay proper wages to free citizens for the same labour services. These views were over-represented in the NSW Legislative Council which had become partly elective in 1842 (with the vote restricted to landowners). The British government agreed to resume transportation if the Legislative Council officially endorsed the proposal. A committee chaired by William Charles Wentworth recommended endorsement but, after a popular backlash, the full Legislative Council voted against it.

Undeterred, the conservatives managed to convince the Legislative Council to change its position two years later, by restricting transportation to "high class" convicts. The anti-transportation movement, led by Henry (later Sir Henry) Parkes, redoubled its efforts. They attracted a crowd of seven or eight thousand people to a rally at Circular Quay in 1849 and held another huge rally at Barrack Square two years later, where a petition was signed by 16,000 people. The plans to reintroduce transportation were abandoned (although convicts continued to be sent to Western Australia until 1869).

So, from 1840 very few convicts arrived in Sydney. The general population of NSW now saw themselves as a free people and began to demand the same rights that were enjoyed by their peers in Britain. Nevertheless, there were still plenty of existing convicts with many years of their sentences left to serve, so the work of James Reed and his fellow soldiers of the guard continued unchanged for many years.

A census was conducted in England in June 1841. James Reed's father Thomas was recorded as a 75-year-old shoemaker living at Trentham with labourer Joseph Perrins, aged 35 years, residing at the same premises.[103]

Thomas Reed's daughter Mary was living with her husband John Grindley (a sawyer), his brother William (an agricultural labourer) and their 80-year-old mother Sarah Grindley at Keele, Staffordshire.[104] Thomas Reed's son Edward was an agricultural labourer living at Trentham with his wife Elizabeth and six children.[105]

A similar census had been conducted throughout NSW three months earlier, but no record of the Reed family seems to have survived. There is a record of the family of another James Reed who lived with his wife and family in Nichol Street, Surry Hills.[106] This James Reed was also recorded at the same Surry Hills address on the Electoral Roll for 1842, but James and Frances Reed had moved to Wollongong before then[107] because their next daughter **Eliza Emily Reed** was born at the Wollongong Stockade on 22 October 1841.[108] She was baptised by the Anglican Reverend Matthew Devenish Meares in St Michael's parish at Wollongong on 7 November (see Illustration 9). The ceremony would have been celebrated in the Anglican school building (which doubled as a church until 1847 when the new St Michael's church commenced service).

Reverend Meares had been born in Cork (Ireland) in 1800 and had graduated 22 years later with a BA from Trinity College in Dublin. After joining the church, he arrived in NSW in 1825. The people of his parish found much to admire in his role as a churchman over a long period of time, but they were unaware of his double life. Like many of the Anglican clergy in NSW at that time, he devoted an inordinate amount of time and energy to the acquisition of wealth, particularly land. But all of that came undone in 1860 when he was defrocked after being discovered staying at a hotel for two days with a young woman who he had passed off as his wife. After the story broke, a journalist with the *Goulburn Herald* accused him of Pecksniffdom, an allusion to the character Seth Peckniff in Charles Dickens' 1844 novel, *Martin Chuzzlewit*. Pecksniff liked to preach morality and brag about his own virtue, but in reality he was a rascal who used any means to advance his own selfish interests.

Soon, Meares found that, without his church stipend, he was unable to keep up the payments on his highly geared property portfolio and he therefore faced bankruptcy. Fortunately for him, his adult sons came to the rescue and Meares was able to make a living from teaching in his final years.[109]

The Reed family would have travelled to Wollongong aboard the steamship *Sophia Jane*, which ran a regular service from Sydney to Broulee via Wollongong, Jervis Bay and Bateman's Bay.[110] She was a small wooden paddle steamship with two masts that had been built at Rotherhithe (England) in 1826 (see Illustration 6). An auxiliary steamer, she used her paddle wheels only when winds were inadequate or contrary. She had sailed (not steamed) to Australia in 1831[111] (but is recognised, nevertheless, as the first steamship to arrive in the colony). In 1845 she was to run aground on a reef near Wollongong. While her owners managed to refloat her, they found that extensive repairs were required, so they decided to lay her up.[112]

The Wollongong Stockade, where the Reed family lived in 1841, was built on a tongue of land immediately south of Brighton Beach. An evocative impression of the place had been recorded two years earlier in the diary of Lady Jane Franklin, wife of the Governor of Van Diemen's Land.

*We walked on the rock under the tongue of land, round
to a break in the rock ... through a natural hole ... in the
face of the rock ... and [found] a ladder into a bathing
cove where the military officers of the stockade ... [had]
erected a hut for ladies. Another for gents is over the cliff
... We got out of the cove and ascended to the top of the
tongue of land whence there is a pretty view ... with
sandy beach, woods, harbour and mountains ... The
barracks and huts of the prisoners and military are
here.*[113]

Lady Franklin then inspected the huts that housed
the 115 convicts and those for the 30 soldiers of the 80th
Regiment. The convicts' five or six wooden huts were
arranged in a square. There were no windows, with air
admitted only through iron bars above the door. Convicts
slept on the bare wooden floor with no mattresses and
were locked in before her visit, even though they were
only supposed to be locked in at night.

The convicts were employed on excavating the new
harbour basin nearby. They drilled holes in the rock
which were then filled with gunpowder and blasted. The
resulting rocky debris was then hauled away for use in
building a nearby breakwater. Any misbehaviour would
result in transfer to a road gang where they would
undertake similar work while encumbered with leg
irons.

The convicts' diet was inadequate for people who
were undertaking extremely hard physical work. In
reminiscences published in the *Illawarra Mercury* in 1924,
Albert Organ recalled his soldier father guarding road-
gang convicts near the stockade at Flagstaff Hill

... when Mrs Fuller's bread cart was coming up with a

supply of bread for the prisoners the men were that hungry that they mobbed the cart and cleaned out all the bread.[114]

Housing in the Wollongong Stockade was originally tents, but these had gradually been replaced as the settlement became better established during the 1830s. Tradesmen had been brought in and had built a courthouse with a watch house (or lockup) behind it. Further back were cells, then residences of the commandant and the magistrate and, finally, the soldiers' barracks.

A picture (see Illustration 5) of the Wollongong Stockade that was probably painted by Captain Robert Marsh Westmacott on 20 April 1840 shows just how close it was to the beach.[115] The church on the hill in the middle distance must be the 250-seat Catholic chapel that had been built in 1836, because the first Anglican church was not even started until October 1840.[116]

Accommodation for soldiers and their families was more comfortable than that endured by the hard-working convicts, including both mattresses and windows! But their role was akin to a prison warder, providing a deterrent against escape and conducting search and re-capture missions when necessary. They guarded the convicts during working hours and performed sentry duty outside the stockade, constantly marching backwards and forwards to ensure that no convicts escaped.

The stockade buildings were very basic, having been constructed quickly by tradesmen who were always in high demand elsewhere. The general conditions were primitive, without even a secure water supply. The soldiers eventually dug a well, but it was not adequate to meet the demands of the growing settlement, so residents had to continue carting water from local creeks or from Tom Thumb Lagoon.

The whole of the Illawarra was isolated because it relied heavily on the regular steamship run. There was no road access to Sydney; just a very rough bush track. Due to the need to be very self-reliant, the district had grown slowly. Nevertheless, Wollongong was starting to find its feet by the time the Reed family lived there, with the population numbering 825 on the 1841 census. But there was an economic depression throughout the whole colony in 1842 and the population fell to 546 in 1846. The Reed family was part of this exodus, returning to Sydney in late 1842 or early 1843, where they were, once again, accommodated at the George Street Barracks.

The Australian Patriotic Association, considered the first political party in Australia, had been formed in 1835 by William Charles Wentworth, Sir John Jamison and Dr William Bland. The Association lobbied the British government for political changes in the administration of NSW. Some of these were introduced when the British parliament passed the NSW Constitution Act in 1842. The constitution gave freed convicts the same rights as free settlers, subject to a property test. The right to vote was limited to men who owned land worth two hundred pounds or to householders who occupied houses that attracted a rental of at least twenty pounds per year. James Reed's annual income as a soldier was 365 shillings or about 18 pounds.

The Sydney Municipality was also first created in 1842, with Charles Windeyer serving as interim mayor from August of that year until John Hosking became the first person elected to that position in November. Voting was open to all adult males who occupied a house, warehouse, counting house or shop in the city with an annual rental value of 25 pounds. Since James Reed was a soldier, he would not have been able to vote.

On 11 May 1843 three-year-old Sarah Reed died. She was buried three days later at St Phillip's church where her age was incorrectly estimated at 2 and a half years by the Minister, Thomas Wall Bodenham.[117] Her death would have plunged James and Frances into a deep melancholy, especially as they had experienced such tragedy before, when their eldest son William had died prior to their voyage to Australia. This time the grief would have also been shared by their surviving children, John Benjamin (now aged 11 years), James (8), Alexander (nearly 6) and Eliza Emily (18 months).

The Reed family had now worked in NSW for six and a half years, living cheek-by-jowl with the other soldiers of the regiment. They were deliberately separated from both the convicts who they guarded and the general population so that military discipline was not undermined. Nevertheless, they would have witnessed many unsavoury incidents where discipline and punishment was imposed on convicts; and where convicts reacted against that discipline.

But unsavoury incidents were not restricted to the convicts under guard; some of the regiment's soldiers were also involved in very troubling episodes. For example, in December 1837 a soldier of the 80th regiment attempted to rob an elderly man of his gold pocket watch just near the Barracks Gate in George Street.[118] Three months later, two of the regiment's soldiers attacked Luke O'Connor at the Brickfields in Bathurst, one bludgeoning him many times with a lump of wood nearly two metres long and the other hitting him multiple times with a garden rake. O'Connor never regained consciousness and Private White was subsequently found guilty of wilful murder.[119] Four months later, Private Thomas Smith deserted from the regiment's station at Windsor.[120] Later in the year, Privates Samuel Pike and J B Mills were sentenced to death for an armed highway robbery that had been committed with the assistance of several convicts that they were supposed to be guarding at Bowen's Hollow (between Hartley and Lithgow). The sentence was commuted to banishment to Norfolk Island with hard labour.[121] Private Joseph Slater was also indicted for a highway robbery committed on Ellen Jones at the Vale of Clwydd at around the same time.[122] In the same year Private John Sunderland was committed to trial for rape at Port Macquarie, but he was eventually discharged for lack of evidence.[123] Three years later, in January 1842, Privates Samuel Bradley, James Booth, Thomas Egan and Charles Brown of the 80th Regiment were all sentenced to four months imprisonment in Sydney Gaol with hard labour for their part in larceny, to which they had all pleaded guilty.[124]

The newspapers of the time also contain many good news stories about the regiment, mostly about the popular performances of its military band at public ceremonies and entertainment events. But many of James Reed's regimental fellows had become as bad as some of the worst-behaved convicts under their supervision. Indeed, the regimental diary specifically laments the adverse effects on military discipline that flowed from close association with convicts.

It is difficult to conceive any employment more calculated to destroy the discipline of a Corps; ... the

Guards, generally young Soldiers or recruits, were sent into the interior in charge of Road Gangs without ever having seen or been seen by the Major part of the officers of their Regiments. These Guards, with few Exceptions, were commanded by Subalterns, many of them without experience and who from want of other sources of amusement, gladly availed themselves of the society of such of the settlers as casually fell in their way and insensibly acquired their habits. (AJCP, 'Digest')

It may also be that soldiers became disgruntled when they realised that their lives and conditions were not that much better than the convicted criminals that they were guarding. They would have also seen that colonial society offered them opportunities that were not available back in England.

It was in this environment that James and Frances decided that he should resign from the regiment so that they could make a life for themselves in NSW. In making this decision, the Reeds may have had some foreknowledge of the next assignment for the regiment because, nine months after his discharge, the regiment embarked aboard four ships at Sydney bound for Calcutta, where it was to serve with distinction in the Sikh Wars.

Photograph 2 - Insignia of the 80th Regiment, Staffordshire Volunteers.
Image courtesy of the National Army Museum, London

The bulk of the regiment landed in Calcutta, India on the 16th of November 1844 where they camped at Fort William. Three Companies under the command of Major Bunbury did not arrive until March 1845 after the transports Briton and Runnymede were wrecked en route to India in the Andaman Islands, where they were stranded for 50 days. On the 8th of January the lead Companies of the 80th left from Calcutta for Agra, with the remainder following on the 12th of January 1844. The Companies that had been shipwrecked rejoined the regiment on the 5th of April 1845 after travelling by Steamboat from Calcutta. The 80th whole once more left Agra on the 20th of October 1845 to join the rest of the Army. The regiment was to see bitter fighting during the First Sikh War winning battle honours at Moodkee and Ferozeshah.[125]

No doubt James and Frances weighed all these factors before concluding that he should leave the army. It must have been a very difficult decision, because he would have been entitled to a small lifetime pension after a further three and a half years' service. No doubt they discussed the pros and cons in detail and at great length with other families in a similar position, including those of their future in-laws the Brennan and Bend families.

James gained his official discharge on 31 October 1843 after sixteen and a half years in the army, with nearly seven of them spent in NSW. All he and Frances had to show for this service was a gratuity of four pounds, eleven shillings and three pence, equivalent to about three months' pay. Nevertheless, now that they were free to forge their own path in life, they had plans for how they would make their living.

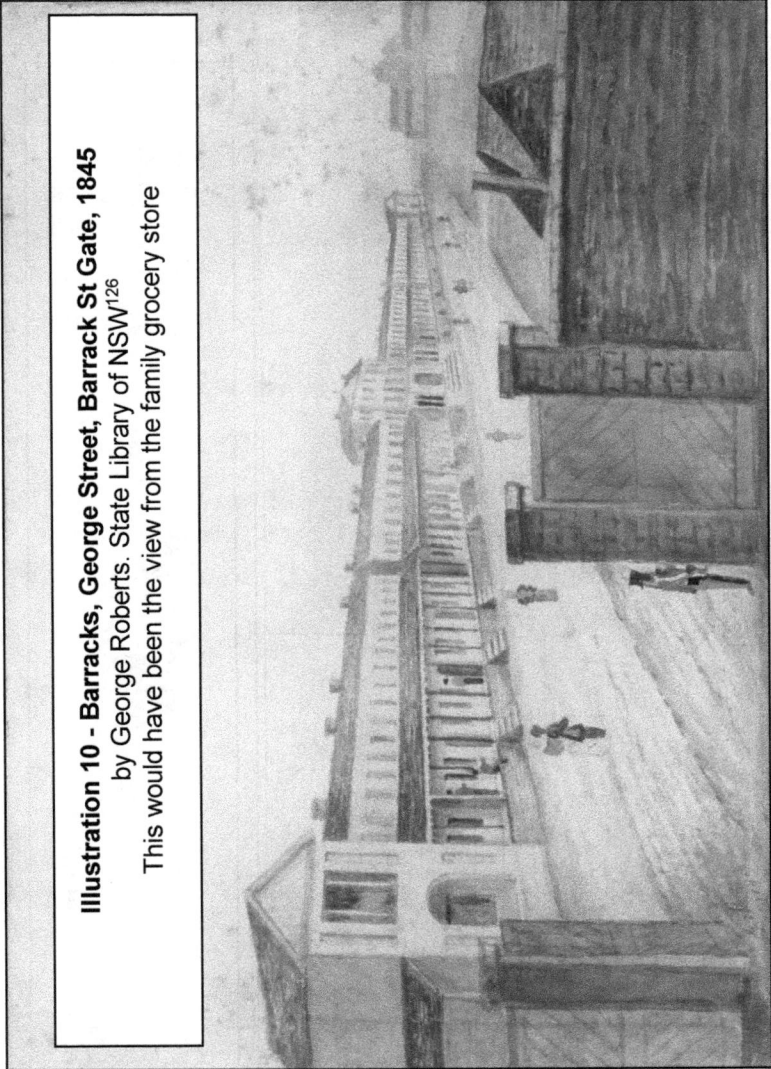

Illustration 10 - Barracks, George Street, Barrack St Gate, 1845
by George Roberts. State Library of NSW[126]
This would have been the view from the family grocery store

Illustrations 11 (top), 12 and 13 (bottom), previous page and 14 (top) & 15 (bottom), this page
Baptism records

11. Sarah Ann Reed on 26 May 1844 at St James church, Sydney.
12. Prudence Reed on 30 August 1846 at St Andrews church, Sydney.
13. Frances Reed on 2 July 1848 at St James church, Sydney.
14. George Charles Reed on 13 October 1850 at St James church, Sydney.
15. Mary Ann Reed on 27 February 1853 at St Philips church, Sydney.

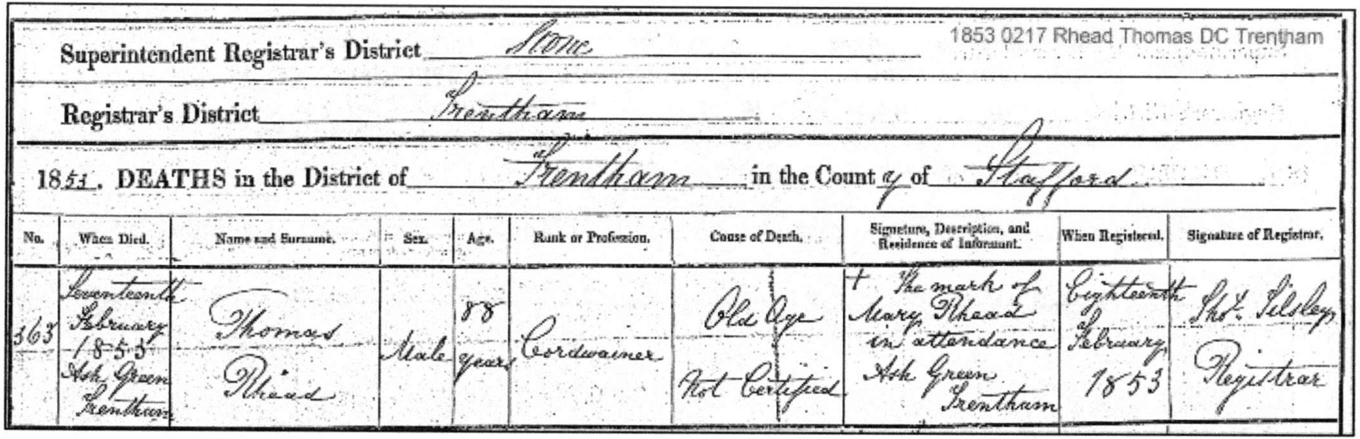
1853 0217 Rhead Thomas DC Trentham

Superintendent Registrar's District Stone

Registrar's District Trentham

1853. DEATHS in the District of Trentham in the County of Stafford

No.	When Died.	Name and Surname.	Sex.	Age.	Rank or Profession.	Cause of Death.	Signature, Description, and Residence of Informant.	When Registered.	Signature of Registrar.
363	Seventeenth February 1853 Ash Green Trentham	Thomas Rhead	Male	88 years	Cordwainer	Old Age Not Certified	+ The mark of Mary Rhead in attendance Ash Green Trentham	Eighteenth February 1853	Thos. Silsley Registrar

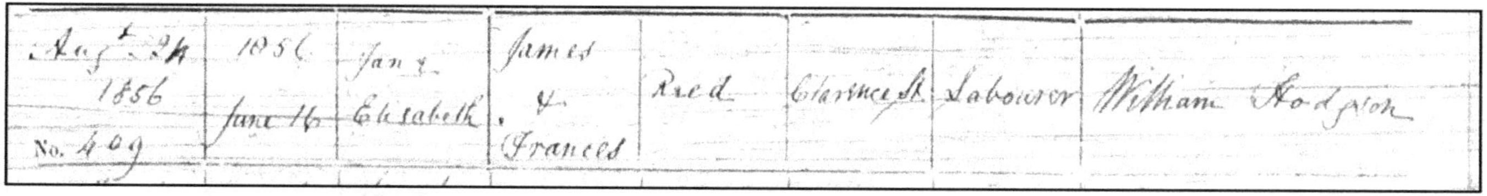

Augt 24 1856 No. 409	1856 June 16	Jane Elizabeth	James & Frances	Reed	Clarence St	Labourer	William Hodgson

Illustration 16 (top) - Death Certificate for Thomas Reed of Ash Green on 17 February 1853.
Illustration 16A (bottom) – Baptism of Jane Elizabeth Reed at St Philips church, Sydney on 16 Jun 1856

CHAPTER SIX

Turbulent years

The first decade of life after the army was a turbulent one for the Reeds due to business difficulties, while the family expanded rapidly despite the death of another child. Eventually, the gold rush would upend the society in which they lived, ushering in new opportunities for the family.

James and Frances used his payout money to set themselves up in a grocery business on the Barrack and York Streets corner.[127] They were living above the shop when **Sarah Ann Reed** was born on 21 March 1844. She was baptised two months later (see Illustration 11) in St James church by Mr Charles Kemp Esquire[128].

Charles Kemp had come to Australia as a child in 1825 with his father Simon (an employee of the Australian Agricultural Company at Port Stephens who was later Mayor of Newcastle). On reaching adulthood Charles became a journalist, working as the first Parliamentary reporter for the *Sydney Herald* (now the *Sydney Morning Herald*). He eventually bought that newspaper and later expanded his business interests into insurance, real estate and share investment. He was one of the founding directors of the Sydney Railway Company and would be appointed one of three Railway Commissioners when the government took it over in 1855. He and his wife would undertake a grand tour of Europe in 1856-7 before resuming his successful business career in Sydney. Kemp was one of the colony's leading Anglican laymen, serving on many church committees and was churchwarden at St James when he baptised Sarah Ann Reed. He later helped found St Paul's College within the University of Sydney and its neighbour, Moore Theological College. His writings reveal him to be both extremely religious and very pompous. He had a short political career during which he was viewed with distaste by liberal thinkers like Sir Henry Parkes, one of whom described him as the "most oleaginous parody on the great idea of Senator that has ever been perpetrated".[129] With such vitriolic rhetoric, is it any wonder that the NSW Parliament became known as "the bear pit"? Despite this, Kemp was later memorialised with an impressive marble monument mounted on an internal wall of the church where he had baptised Sarah Ann Reed. It describes him as "a kind friend, an upright citizen and a devout and benevolent Christian".[130]

Sarah Ann was the first of the Reed's children to be born outside a Military Barracks, although her family's recent home was only just across the road! She was named in honour of her late sister Sarah who had died just ten months earlier, aged about four years old.

The prospects for the family grocery business would have looked good, on paper. The shop was situated in the centre of Sydney and very near the Military Barracks, a ready source of customers who already knew the Reed family (see Illustration 10). Much of the business would have involved buying goods in bulk and selling them to customers in small batches, including flour, sugar, tea, coffee, oatmeal, cornmeal, cocoa, baking powder, tobacco, dried fruit, salt, pepper and other spices. In addition, there would have been staple foods like bread, butter, cheese and eggs. They probably also stocked other bulk goods such as wheat and pollen (for feeding poultry) and perhaps chaff for horses. The store may have also sold other household necessaries such as vinegar, soap, candles, matches and lamp oil. Neither canning nor the mason jar had yet been invented, but they may have sold preserved fruit and vegetables in jars that had tin lids sealed with wax.

James would have needed to visit the local produce markets on a regular basis to obtain these bulk goods as well as to stock up on seasonal fruit and vegetables like oranges, peaches, apples, grapes, potatoes, carrots, onions, turnips and pumpkins. The markets were two kilometres away, so he would have needed a horse and cart to bring his stock back to the store. The cart would also have been useful for making deliveries to regular customers. Their older children would have been roped in to assist with unloading the market produce, storing it in the shop and stacking shelves.

It seems likely that the older boys were tasked with driving the cart to make home deliveries. While Alexander was only 7 years old, James was nine and John Benjamin was twelve and it was normal for boys to start work around John's age. All of them eventually made a living as carriers for many years.

There was no such thing as customers serving themselves. Each one was served personally by the store attendant who had to source goods from shelves behind or underneath the counter, weigh them on scales and calculate the cost while wrapping them individually. As each item was selected, measured and priced, the attendant would write the price on a paper pad in pencil so that a grand total could be calculated at the end. This amount was then paid in cash, although many customers expected the grocer to offer them credit, kept on a "tab" that was meant to be paid at the end of the month.

Running a shop required a very different set of skills from those used in guarding convicts or going into battle. James Reed had been a brick maker before he joined the army, so he and Frances would have had a very steep learning curve in the grocery trade. Fifteen years before, James had signed the wedding register with his mark but Frances had signed her name. It is possible that Frances had learned to read and write while attending some school lessons as her family accompanied her father on his army postings. It was normal for the army to supply a schoolteacher for the officers' children and her father, Sergeant Heazle, may have had enough influence to have his children included as well. It is also possible that James Reed had learned to read and write at some time after his marriage. It would have been difficult, but not impossible, for an illiterate man to run a grocery business.

James and Frances would have had to use most of their savings to establish the business - obtaining a horse and cart, paying the initial rent and buying stock all before making a single sale over the counter. Furthermore, they would have been pressed to extend credit to their best customers. So, they would have needed to establish their store very quickly and then enjoy a good steady trade to keep the business afloat.

They must have been aware that a large part of their customer base would disappear as soon as the building of the new Victoria Barracks in Paddington was completed. Convicts had been working on the construction of the new barracks for three years already, so it was only a matter of time before the George Street Barracks were closed and all the soldiers moved to the new premises. Opening a grocery store that depended too heavily on trade from the barracks was risky, especially as the soldiers' meals were provided by the army.

The Officers Quarters at Paddington were completed in 1842 and the main Barracks Block four years later, but the Reed's grocery business must have failed before that, because the family had moved into new accommodation before Victoria Barracks was occupied. The City of Sydney council rates Assessment Books for 1845 record that the Reed family was living in a Clarence Street house of stone and shingles valued at 15 pounds and owned by Thomas Leary, rented weekly.[131]

Regret and grief caused by the failure of the business may have been one of the reasons for James' unfortunate behaviour one night in November that year.

FRIDAY.—James Reed, residing in Clarence Street, was charged by constable Tigh, with being drunk in that neighbourhood on the previous evening, and going through sundry evolutions with a knife, to the great danger of Her Majesty's lieges. Having professed contrition for his freak, together with a promise that he would "sin no more" backed by a good character, he was admonished and discharged.[132]

There were other people named James Reed in Sydney at this time, but the subject of this report probably was Frances' husband because the family address was to be recorded as Clarence Street several times over the next thirteen years. This incident was very much out of character and he was never again in trouble with the law. In fact, within a year he was employed as a constable.

Three months before James' drunken folly, the residents of NSW had been shocked to learn of the wreck of the *Cataraqui*, a British barque of 802 tons. The ship was carrying 369 emigrants and 41 crew when she entered Bass Strait during a storm and was wrecked on King Island. This was the exact route that had been taken by the *Earl Grey* when bringing the Reed family to Australia nine years earlier. Only eight crew members and one passenger survived the wreck and they retrieved 314 bodies, which they buried in five graves. The nine castaways were stranded on the island for five weeks before being rescued and taken to Melbourne. With 400 lives lost, this remains Australia's worst-ever maritime disaster.[133]

Before the birth of their new daughter on 3 July 1846, the family had moved again, this time to nearby Kent Street. She was baptised **Prudence Reed** on 30 August at St Andrews church by Reverend Thomas Wall Bodenham, headmaster of the Grammar School attached to St James church and a prison chaplain (see Illustration 12). He had officiated at the burial of Prudence's sister Sarah three years earlier. The baptism ceremony would not have taken place inside the church because St Andrew's cathedral was still under construction. The parish must have been using an alternative venue for services and ceremonies.

The baptism record states that James Reed was a Constable. He had commenced duties in that role on 1 April 1846 on a salary of 2 shillings and nine pence per day (more than double his previous salary in the army). The Police Salary Register for 1846 shows that he was paid at that rate for every day of the month, so he must not have had any days off.[134] His duties would have mainly consisted of patrolling the streets of the city in much the same way that he had patrolled the perimeter of the army barracks and stockades in his former career as a soldier.

James' new daughter Prudence was named after his sister, Prudence Reed, who would by now have been 43 years old. She had married Thomas Peak at Bolton le Moors (Lancashire) nine years earlier on 7 September 1837 and they went on to raise a large family there over the next four decades. Thomas had been a Finisher by trade but rose to become Manager of a Bleaching Works that employed 45 men, 16 women and 22 boys in 1871. Prudence Peak nee Reed died at Ramsbottom on 26 May 1873 and was buried at the church of St Michael at Great Lever, Lancashire.

On New Year's Eve, four months after Prudence's baptism, James and Frances celebrated ten years in Australia. They were, by now, very familiar with Sydney and the countryside around it, from Windsor in the north-west to 17 Mile Hollow in the west and Wollongong in the south. Their family had expanded from the two sons who had arrived with them to now include another son and three daughters, while another daughter lay in the graveyard at St Phillip's church. Having left the military life behind, 1847 heralded the start of a second decade in Australia with the promise of a better life for them and their children. Their eldest surviving sons, John and James, were approaching their 15th and 13th birthdays and were almost certainly already working in the carrying industry.

James Reed was dismissed from the Police Force in early May 1847 after just twelve months in the job. The records don't provide any hint of the reason.[135] Thereafter he worked almost exclusively as a labourer.

The NSW Registrar of Births, Deaths and Marriages online index of pre-1856 church baptisms includes registration number 2150 in 1847 for the baptism in St James Church of Frances Reid, a daughter of James and Frances Reid. But the microfilmed copy of the Baptism Register for that church does not contain any such record. It does, however, contain a record that matches this index entry in all but year (see Illustration 13). The register reveals that **Frances Reed** (mis-spelt as Reid) was born on 16 June 1848 in Clarence Street and baptised on 2 July 1848 by George Fairfowl MacArthur.[136] The Registrar's index does not have a record of that baptism dated 1848. I have concluded that the Registrar's index has incorrectly recorded the 1848 baptism as an 1847 baptism.

The minster who officiated at Frances' baptism had been appointed deacon of St James church just four months earlier. He was the 23-year old son of Hannibal MacArthur and Anna Maria King (daughter of Governor King). His uncle, the infamous John MacArthur, had been one of the instigators of the Rum Rebellion against Governor Bligh in 1808. In addition to his duties as a Minister, George Fairfowl MacArthur also took in pupils and, later, established a school at Macquarie Fields. Later still, when The King's School closed in 1864 for lack of funds, he was asked to revive it, which he did very successfully and the school continues to this day.[137]

Frances' baptism record indicates that the Reed family had now returned to Clarence Street. The Council rates Assessment Books specify that they were living at 68 Clarence Street in a house of brick and shingles valued at 13 pounds and owned by Thomas Whitney.[138]

James was listed in Brisbane Ward on the Roll of Electors for the Electoral District of Sydney. At forty years old, this would have been his first opportunity to vote, but Frances was still excluded because the franchise had not been extended to women. A year later, however, James was not listed on the Electoral Roll for 1849-50.

When another son was born on 23 September 1850 the family was still living in Clarence Street and James was still a labourer. The child was baptised in St James church (see Illustration 14) as **George Charles Reed** on 13 October 1850 by Charles Frederick Durham Priddle.[139]

Priddle was a 26-year-old Englishman who had arrived in NSW six years earlier with his parents and siblings. (His sister, Margaret Ann Priddle, was married to George Fairfowl MacArthur, who had baptised Frances Reed two years earlier). He had been admitted as a deacon at St James in 1848, was to be Priested in December 1850 and was later in charge of St Luke's church at Liverpool. He was to open the first Penny Bank in NSW and became their chief promoter. They aimed to encourage the less well-off to save by depositing very small sums 'to encourage and foster habits of regularity and frugal economy'. The Trustees of the Penny Bank then deposited a consolidated sum in a Savings Bank which would pay interest that was passed back to the Penny Bank depositors (as the Savings Banks would normally only accept a minimum deposit of one shilling).

This form of banking proved to be very popular.[140]

Two months after the baptism of George Charles Reed, his grandfather Benjamin Heazle died on 28 December 1850, aged 58 years. Since his retirement eighteen years earlier he had lived on his military pension.[141] It is unlikely that news of her father's death ever reached Frances Reed in far-off Australia.

It is also unlikely that James Reed knew whether his father was still alive. In fact, Thomas Reed was recorded on the 1851 English census as an 86-year-old widower who was still working as a shoemaker and living at Ash Green (where his family had been situated for at least 45 years). He was supported by his eldest child Mary and her husband John Grindley.[142]

Two days before Christmas 1852 Frances gave birth to a daughter in the family residence at Clarence Street. The council rate records show, however, that this was not the same house where they had been living in 1848. This new abode (recorded in both 1851 and 1852) was a brick and shingle house valued at 8 pounds and owned by the Trustee of R Wilson.[143]

Their new daughter was baptised (see Illustration 15) **Mary Ann Reed** in St Philip's church on 27 February 1853 by William Cowper.[144] The church was situated on the current site of Lang Park, opposite the site of the current St Philip's church which was to be opened three years later.

Sixty-five year old Reverend Cowper had been associated with St Philip's for forty-four years and was very well-known and respected in Sydney as a conservative, evangelical figure. He had been originally employed by Reverend Samuel Marsden during his trip to England in 1808. With Bishop Broughton overseas from 1852, Cowper was acting as his commissary for the diocese while continuing to direct the work at St Philip's. Throughout his ministry he was active in many church organisations, notably the Church Missionary Society which was working for the betterment and conversion of aboriginals. After his death in 1858 he would be succeeded at St Philip's by his son William who was made dean and archdeacon of Sydney. Another son, Charles, was (as detailed below) Premier of NSW on five occasions during the 1850s and 1860s.[145]

Ten days before the baptism of Mary Ann Reed in Sydney, her grandfather Thomas Reed had died in his home at Ash Green near Trentham, Staffordshire. His daughter Mary Grindley registered the death with the Registrar (Thomas Tilsley) the next day, 18 February 1853.[146] The death certificate records that he was an 88-year-old cordwainer (shoemaker) who had died of old age.

He had lived a very long life for someone born in rural England in 1765. Subsequent events show that he had passed those good longevity genes on to his son James and thence to Reed descendants in Australia, many of whom were also to live into their 80s and 90s. Thomas and his wife Elizabeth nee Sutton had produced a family of nine children before her death 44 years earlier. He was buried at Trentham on 20 February 1853.[147]

***

During the ten years following James Reed's discharge from the Regiment, he and his family had lived a relatively uneventful life in the very heart of Sydney. Having failed in the grocery store business he had found employment as a constable for a year or two but was now working as a labourer. Life would have been very busy for both he and Frances as they worked hard to feed, clothe and house a family of four sons and five daughters. No doubt the older children were a great support to their parents as they found their own employment and brought additional income into the household.

While the Reed family's lives were proceeding smoothly, the same could not be said for the city and the society in which they lived. Change abounded all around them in many ways as the city moved into the second half of the 19th century and approached its 65th birthday, having reached a population of 39,000 (out of nearly 300,000 in NSW). Queen Victoria had reached her mid-thirties and had been on the throne for fifteen years. NSW now had its tenth governor, Sir Charles Augustus FitzRoy, a veteran of the Battle of Waterloo and grandson of Augustus FitzRoy, 3rd Duke of Grafton, who had served as Prime Minister of Great Britain eighty years earlier.

On 2 July 1851, the colony of Victoria had separated from NSW, 26 years after Van Diemen's Land had achieved its independence. South Australia had become independent of NSW in 1834 and Queensland was to follow suit in 1859. Governor FitzRoy noticed that tensions were rising between the colonies in relation to trade and other issues, so he sought some means of fostering cooperation, uniformity and consensus amongst them. His solution was that a person should be appointed as a higher authority, to whom all measures passed by local legislatures should be referred for assent. The British government agreed, and supplemented Fitzroy's appointment as Governor of NSW by also appointing him as Governor of Van Diemen's Land, South Australia and Victoria, effectively the first Governor-General of the Australian colonies.

During FitzRoy's ten years as Governor of NSW, the colony made great strides. Transportation of convicts ceased, Sydney University was founded, a branch of the royal mint was established and responsible self-government was granted (explored further in chapter 8). But the rapid and well-managed advancement of the colonies was about to face major disruption following the discovery of gold in 1851.

Gold had been found many times in all the colonies before 1851, but the Governors had deliberately suppressed the news of each discovery out of a fear that it would cause workers to abandon their regular employment and so destabilise the economy. As early as 1815, convicts who were employed cutting the first road over the Blue Mountains were rumoured to have found small pieces of gold. In March 1820 a Russian naturalist named Stein claimed to have sighted gold-bearing ore while on a 12-day trip to the Blue Mountains. The first officially recognised discovery was made on 15 February 1823 by assistant surveyor James McBrien, at Fish River, between Rydal and Bathurst. In 1834 John Lhotsky travelled to the Monaro district of New South Wales and explored its southern mountains. On returning to Sydney in that same year, he exhibited specimens that he had collected that contained gold. In 1839 Paweł Strzelecki, geologist and explorer, found small amounts of gold in silicate at the Vale of Clwyd near Hartley. In 1841 the Reverend William Branwhite Clarke found gold on the Cox's River near Bathurst and the following year he found more on the Wollondilly River. He was later given grants of one thousand pounds from both the NSW and Victorian government for his contribution to the discovery of gold in those colonies.

There were gold discoveries in Victoria in 1841 and 1848 (Pyrenees Ranges and Plenty Ranges), 1844 (Bundalong), 1847 (Port Philip), 1849 (Woady Yaloak River) and 1850 (Clunes). There were also discoveries in Van Diemen's Land in 1840 and 1849 (Lefroy) and 1847 (Beaconsfield); and at Castambul (South Australia) in 1846.

It took the California Gold Rush of 1848 to change the government policies in Australia from suppression to encouragement. Many people had rushed to California from places throughout Australia causing a shortage of labour and disrupting the economy. To stem the exodus, the New South Wales government sought approval from the British Colonial Office for the exploitation of mineral resources and subsequently offered rewards for gold discoveries. Almost immediately, prospector Edward Hargreaves (a veteran of the California Gold Rush) claimed the reward for his discovery of payable gold near Orange, at a site that he called Ophir. He was granted rewards by the colonies of NSW and Victoria and the first gold rush in Australia began in May 1851.

Within a month there were more gold discoveries at Sofala in NSW and Warrandyte in Victoria. A month later there were finds at Bungoin, Hill End, Louisa Creek and Moruya in NSW and at the Clunes goldfield in Victoria. During the next month (August) there was a rush at Buninyong and in September at Yuille's Diggings (both near Ballarat). That same month there was another rush at Castlemaine, with Bendigo following in November.[148]

The effect of these discoveries was electrifying. Here at last was a chance for people to make a fortune that most could have only dreamed of in normal circumstances. This opportunity could enable them to gain some independence by relieving them of the necessity of lifelong labour. All over Australia men downed tools and left for the goldfields.

There is no evidence that any member of James and Frances Reed's family joined the rush to the goldfields. James himself was probably fit enough, at age 44, but could not leave Frances and the younger children to fend for themselves. Their eldest son John was nearly 20 years old and his brother James was nearly 17, so it is likely that their parents would have strongly opposed them trying their luck on the goldfields, which were lawless places. Nevertheless, with the general exodus to the interior, Sydney suffered a sudden and very severe shortage of labour, so it is likely that James and his older sons could now command very good wages in return for their labour.

The Victorian goldfields proved to be richer than those in NSW but nevertheless there were further finds at Araluen, Braidwood, Bell River, Tuena, Lake George, Monaro and Oakey Creek in NSW before the year was out! There were more sites discovered in NSW, Van Diemen's Land, South Australia and Victoria over the next couple of years.

The gold rushes were a huge catalyst for change throughout the colonies. Between 1852 and 1860, 290,000 people migrated to Victoria from the British Isles, 15,000 came from other European countries, and 18,000 emigrated from the United States. Australia's total population more than tripled over two decades from

430,000 in 1851 to 1.7 million in 1871.

This influx of free immigrants sped up the transformation from convict colonies into more varied and progressive societies. These new Australians, soon known as diggers, brought new skills and professions, giving a huge boost to the economy. Their comradeship was mixed with the ex-convicts' collective resistance to authority to produce a national identity based on fairness and self-reliance, finding expression in the concept of mateship. Although not all diggers found riches on the goldfields, many decided to stay in Australia and integrate into what were now prosperous cities and towns.

Between 1851 and 1861 Australia exported at least 30 million ounces (850 metric tons) of gold - more than one third of the world's total. The Victorian Gold Discovery Committee wrote in 1854:

> *The discovery of the Victorian Goldfields has converted a remote dependency into a country of world wide fame; it has attracted a population, extraordinary in number, with unprecedented rapidity; it has enhanced the value of property to an enormous extent; it has made this the richest country in the world; and, in less than three years, it has done for this colony the work of an age, and made its impulses felt in the most distant regions of the earth.*[149]

Life outside the army had started disastrously with the failure of the family's grocery business but, as the subsequent years wore on, they had gradually found a way to make a reasonable living through perseverance and hard work. Now they stood to profit from the gold rush as it brought a range of benefits to everyone in NSW.

CHAPTER SEVEN

Inexorable expansion

The enriching effect of the gold rush on colonial society in general must have trickled inexorably down to the Reed family because their accommodation after 1854 was somewhat more salubrious than in previous years. James and Frances were now entering the best phase of their life, during which they would produce their last child, toast the marriages of their oldest children and celebrate the arrival of grandchildren.

Since James left the army ten years earlier the family had lived in at least six different houses in the inner city, as detailed in the previous chapter. For the remainder of the decade, they continued to move regularly, but henceforth each new house seems to have been a little bit better than the previous one.

In 1854, after the gold rush had brought more wealth to the colony, they moved into a house at the back of 122 Clarence Street that was (given its higher ratable value) probably better than anywhere they had lived previously. It was a house of stone and shingle valued at 22 pounds and owned by Stubbs.[150]

Two years later they were living at 17 Clarence Street for the birth of their twelfth and last child **Jane Elizabeth Reed**[151]. She was baptised in St Philip's church by William Hodgson on 24 August 1856, aged 2 months (see Illustration 16A). The ceremony would have probably taken place in the second church building that was used by this parish from 1810 to 1856, with the current St Philip's church not completed until two years later.

Minister Hodgson was the youngest son of a London bookseller and had been ordained a priest twenty years earlier in Chester cathedral. Jane's baptism was probably the very first sacrament that he celebrated after arriving in Australia where he was to take up the position of Principal of the new Moore Theological College at the invitation of the newly enthroned bishop of Sydney, Frederick Barker. Both Barker and Hodgson were low-church evangelicals who emphasised biblical faith, personal conversion, social welfare and piety as they favoured the church's Protestant heritage over the Catholic legacy of the Anglican Communion. They were soon caught up in an acrimonious controversy that played out in the pages of the Sydney Morning Herald in November and December of that year. An anonymous letter-writer who signed himself as "Anglicanus" bemoaned that the Anglican church had been taken hostage by narrow-thinking leaders including William Cowper (who had baptised Mary Ann Reed in 1853 and was father of NSW Premier Charles Cowper), Bishop Barker and his protege Hodgson. The chief accusation was that the students at Moore College were being kept separate from ordinary parishes to the extent that they rarely attended Mass in a parish church.

Despite this brouhaha Hodgson soon won repute as one of the best classical scholars in Australia. By the time he resigned from Moore College and returned to England eleven years later, he had seen 46 of his students ordained, thus having a significant influence over the direction of the Anglican church in NSW for the coming decades.

Six months before Jane's birth, the NSW Parliament had passed legislation entitled An Act for Registering Births, Deaths and Marriages 1855. It required the parents of all children born after 1 March 1856 to register the child's birth at the Land Titles Office. Accordingly, in June 1856, Jane was the first and only member of her generation of the Reed family whose birth was registered with the civil authorities.

James and Frances were now 48 and 44 years old respectively and had produced twelve children over a period of twenty five years (see chart 5). Their eldest son, William Reed had died before the family emigrated to Australia in 1836. His sister Sarah who had been born in Sydney in 1839 had only lived for about four years before her burial at St Philip's church. But ten children had survived and all would grow into adulthood. As baby Jane Reed started the first of her 67 years, she joined her surviving siblings John Benjamin aged 24, James junior 21, Alexander 19, Eliza Emily 15, Sarah Ann 12, Prudence 10, Frances junior 8, George Charles 6 and Mary Ann 4.

At some time in the early 1850s, young James Reed junior had travelled more than 350 kilometres from the family home in Sydney to Wellington in the central west of NSW. This was a major journey that would have required him to travel firstly to Penrith via Parramatta and then onwards over the Blue Mountains, past his brief childhood home at 17 Mile Hollow and on to Lithgow. From there he could proceed to Wellington either via Bathurst or via Mudgee. How he made this journey is uncertain, as is the identity of his travelling companions, if any. In later years he was to work as a drover and in similar rural occupations, so he must have already been an experienced horseman and able to travel the long distance on horseback. Presumably he had gained experience with his father's horse and cart as a young boy and extended this by working with his older brother John, who long worked as a carrier and bullock wagon driver. In fact, Jimmy may have travelled with his older brother John and they may have been accompanied by their younger brother Alexander, now 19 years old, who was also to be recorded as a bullock wagon driver ten years later.

Bullock wagons were a very slow mode of travel in comparison to horse-drawn wagons, but they could reliably haul really heavy loads for long distances. When faced with difficulties, bullocks were less excitable and more dependable than horses. Furthermore, they were cheaper to purchase, equip and feed. Horses required complex, expensive leather harness that needed frequent repair while bullock gear was so simple that the yokes were sometimes made by the bullocky himself. For these reasons, bullock drays and wagons were used extensively during this period of Australian history to carry all sorts of bulk goods (including essential food, building materials and station supplies) from coastal ports to isolated country areas. On the return journey they would haul rural produce including wheat, wool, sugar cane and timber.

On a good day the bullocks could cover thirty

kilometres; much less when the route was sandy or wet or involved a long ascent or descent. At night the bullocky and his team would have made camp near a watercourse where he could water and feed the bullocks. He and his passengers would have slept under the stars except during inclement weather (when they would have erected tarpaulins or slept under the dray or wagon). Occasionally they would have been able to camp for a night or two near an established rural property and may have even got to sleep in a bed set up on a verandah or in a vacant shearer's hut.

The bullocky walked on the nearside (left) of the bullocks and could direct each bullock by name to adjust its pace and effort. He also carried a very long whip that was swung over his head, twirled a few times and then cracked or let fall upon the back of a specific bullock. Sometimes he had an apprentice who assisted in yoking up and caring for the team. He walked on the offside (right) of the team, the origin of the term "offsider", meaning assistant.

James Reed junior was generally referred to as Jimmy Reed to distinguish him from his father. His destination at Wellington was situated on the very edge of the nineteen counties in which settlement was permitted by the government. These counties extended from Taree in the north to Batemans Bay in the south and to Wellington in the west. The government discouraged settlement further out due to the risk that local aboriginal tribes might respond aggressively to incursions on their land and because of the dangers posed by fugitives who had fled beyond the normal reach of colonial law enforcement.

In accordance with this policy, the Governor had

discontinued the practice of granting land for free after 1831, so that the only way anyone could now obtain land was to purchase it within the nineteen counties. Despite this, businessmen could not resist the opportunity to make big profits by running large flocks of sheep and herds of cattle outside the nineteen counties. They ventured outside the allowed limits, found good land for their flocks and claimed it on the basis that possession was nine-tenths of the law. This practice of squatting illegally on good land led to these graziers being referred to by the disparaging term "squatters". Nevertheless, the government was relatively powerless to stop the practice, so in 1836 it had decided instead to regulate it by providing squatters the opportunity to pay an annual fee of £10 to lease non-surveyed land.

The wool industry, in particular, benefited from this more liberal administration of grazing land. The industry had been started in 1797 by John and Elizabeth Macarthur and the Reverend Samuel Marsden, but it had taken more than twenty years to build the flocks up to a sufficient size to make exports financially viable. Commercial quantities of wool were sent to Britain from 1821, but the wool industry was smaller than the fisheries, whaling and sealing industries for the next decade. From the 1830s, however, the wool industry thrived, increasing exports from 2.3 million kilograms in 1834 to 6.4 million kilograms by 1850. NSW replaced Spain and Germany as the main source of wool for the British textile industry and thus attracted more investment capital and more migrants.

Prior to 1815, the European colonists had been restricted to the coastal strip of NSW because they could not find a way of crossing the Great Dividing Range. But after Blaxland, Lawson and Wentworth found a way through the Blue Mountains in 1813, Governor Macquarie arranged for William Cox and his team to build a road to the Bathurst Plains, leading to the establishment of the town of Bathurst. The way was now open for the colonists to move inland; and that expansion process started almost immediately.

Two of the first people to be granted land in the Bathurst district were James Blackman (who was also superintendent of convicts for the district) and his brother John. By 1820 James had marked out a road northwards from Bathurst to Wallarewang and the following year he explored a route onwards from there to the Cudgegong River near Mudgee.[152] Blackman also played a leading part in opening the Orange district and the Wellington valley (where the government established a convict agricultural station in 1823).

Very soon other settlers followed in Blackman's footsteps and much of the best land in the area around Bathurst was taken up. Push back from the local Aboriginal population was led by Windradyne in the short-lived Bathurst War of 1824. Windradyne's counterparts from closer to Sydney had eventually lost the Hawkesbury and Nepean war of 1816 but now there was a new flashpoint as colonists from the coast moved inland. In response to the defence mounted by Windradyne's warriors, Governor Brisbane proclaimed martial law on 14 August 1824 to end "the Slaughter of Black Women and Children, and unoffending White Men". The conflict ended soon afterwards when Windradyne walked to Parramatta to meet the Governor. Peace was established when he, in effect, surrendered on behalf of his clan.[153] After Windradyne accepted that his warriors could not win, one of the restraints on further expansion was overcome, resulting in an influx of even more settlers and their employees.

As Map 3 shows, Europeans started to move inland from Newcastle and Maitland via the Hunter valley at about the same time. Thus, by the end of the 1820s there were significant numbers of Europeans living in the Bathurst, Mudgee, Wellington, Muswellbrook and Quirindi districts.

Europeans also started to move inland from the penal settlement at Port Macquarie that had been established in 1821. By the mid-1830s those moving westwards from there had reached Tamworth, Gunnedah and Narrabri while those moving northwards from Muswellbrook and Mudgee had reached Dubbo and Gilgandra. There were also several grazing runs on the Bogan River.[154]

From the 1830s onwards, the first Europeans to reach each of these inland districts were cattle graziers seeking new "runs" for their ever-expanding herds. While large stock owners sent their employees to seek fresh pastures further inland, virtually no-one else resided there because permanent settlement outside the nineteen counties was officially discouraged.

The runs were occupied primarily for speculation or of necessity to provide temporary pasturage for the increasing numbers of stock in adjoining districts. They were used only as out-stations. It was considered at the time that the climate was too harsh and the isolation too great for permanent occupation ... Licence holders or their superintendents visited the runs periodically but few resided on them. The stock usually were left in charge of emancipated convicts and ticket-of-leave men who lived in rough huts constructed of logs and bark near the more permanent waterholes.[155]

In these early days there were few sheep on these out-stations. Cattle required less work and supervision and there was a ready market for them in Australia, whereas the overseas market for sheep's wool was very hard to access from far inland. There was also a view that woolly sheep could not survive the hot summer conditions.

Soon enough these inland runs lined both sides of the most reliable water courses. Since cattle must drink daily, land further than a few hours walk from permanent water had little value for these early graziers. Hence the pattern of European settlement of inland NSW followed the Namoi, Castlereagh and Macquarie Rivers and their tributaries.

The stock owners took out annual leases on any land that they occupied. For ten pounds per year a lease entitled its owner to occupy as much land as they could stock. But without a freehold title or a long lease, they weren't inclined to invest in any long-term infrastructure. They purchased stock and supplies and paid wages but bore no other costs. The profits were huge.

At that time there were no dams, fences or buildings apart from the slab huts and cattle yards. Sometimes there was neither a horse nor a cart.[156]

During the 1840s the new arrivals moved inexorably downstream, establishing leaseholds near the sites of the future towns of Coonamble and Walgett. Many of the new runs were established by the same people who had been among the first Europeans in places settled earlier. For example, some of the earliest settlers in the Coonamble and Walgett districts had settled the Mudgee district twenty years earlier (or had worked for those Mudgee landowners). These included the Blackman, Lawson and Walker families and their employees George Gibson, Andrew Brown and John Angus.

The area around Adelaide had been settled in the 1830s and South Australia had been separated from NSW in 1836. Soon graziers were also making their way up the Murray River from South Australia into NSW and Victoria. By the 1840s some of them had moved up the Darling River and established runs as far north as Wilcannia (then known as Mount Murchison) – see Map 3.

The purpose of young Jimmy Reed's journey to the Wellington district was probably to obtain employment in the expanding grazing industry which now employed a large proportion of the population. In fact, he may already have received an offer of employment there from Mrs Eliza Atkins.

She was well-known to the Reed family because her late husband (Charles Bend) had served as a Private in the 80th Regiment with James Reed. The families had been co-located at the Sydney Barracks for a few months in both 1837 and 1840 and may even have had a connection back in the Old Country during the regiment's various postings throughout the United Kingdom.

Bend's widow Eliza had married secondly John Atkins whose family owned a large swathe of grazing country near Wellington. Reliable rural workers were hard to get following the gold rush, so it is probable that the Atkins family reached out to friends and acquaintances who may have had sons looking for paid employment.

So, it is likely that young James' destination when he left Sydney was Wellington and the prospect of a job. In the course of his employment on Atkins' properties nearby, he became reacquainted with Eliza Atkins' daughter Eliza Bend who he would later marry. His only memory of her would have been as a baby when the families were co-located in Sydney sixteen years earlier.

When the Reed family arrived at the Sydney Barracks in January 1837, they would have found Charles and Eliza Bend already there, along with their baby son John.

Charles Bend was said to be 40 years old at his death, implying a birth year of 1804-05. He may be the Charles Bend who had been baptised at Tamworth (Staffordshire) on 12 September 1806, a son of Joseph Bend and his wife Margaret.[157] This would be consistent with Charles later joining the 80th Regiment, a Staffordshire regiment. It is even possible that Charles Bend and James Reed were known to each other before joining the regiment, as Tamworth is just 50 kilometres from Trentham (where James Reed was born).

But a search for Charles Bend's baptism record between 1800 and 1810 reveals another possibility. This Charles Bend was born in Durham on 6 September 1806 and baptised at St Oswald's church on 28 September. The baptism register records that he was the fourth child of John Bend (a Private in the Durham Militia) and his wife Isabella Carr.[158] His father was a native of Bedworth, Warwickshire, where the family later moved.

Later English records for these two Charles Bends

are elusive, so either one could be our man who later came to Australia with the 80th Regiment. Nevertheless, the Durham origin seems marginally more likely than the Staffordshire one because Charles later named his oldest son John.

Some family historians have identified Charles's wife, Eliza Bend, as Eliza Huxley, presumably on the evidence of a NSW marriage between Charles Binn and Eliza Huxley in 1855. However, Charles Bend had been dead for ten years at that stage. The 1924 death certificate for her daughter Eliza Reed nee Bend gives her mother's maiden name as Eliza Hood[159].

A couple of months after the Reed and Bend families had cohabited in the Sydney Barracks in 1837, the Reeds had been assigned to 17 Mile Hollow, while the Bend family was a part of a contingent of the 80th Regiment that was assigned as the convict guard on Norfolk Island between 1838 and 1840.

Eliza and Charles Bend produced four children, with John, their oldest, baptised at St Philip's church, Sydney in 1836.[160] Since he was baptised in Australia less than six months after the first ships that carried the 80th Regiment had left England, his mother Eliza Hood must have come to Australia with her husband. They must, therefore, have been married in England, although the record of their marriage remains elusive.

Jimmy Reed's future wife Eliza was their second child, born and baptised on Norfolk Island in 1839.[161] Around the time of her birth a nasty incident occurred on the island. The soldiers of the regiment had been supplementing their rations and their income by growing food in gardens that they had built and tended themselves. In July 1839 their commanding officer, Major

Thomas Bunbury, ordered the demolition of one of the huts that they were using to store the harvest. He intended to have it rebuilt somewhere else but failed to effectively communicate this to his soldiers beforehand. When convicts and an overseer attempted to carry out the demolition order, they were forcibly prevented from doing so by the soldiers who owned it. Major Bunbury officiously intervened to enforce his order but his soldiers defended their hut with loaded firearms. Tempers cooled when a rainstorm intervened, but Bunbury was ordered to charge eight men of the 80th Regiment with mutiny.

This contingent of the Regiment returned from Norfolk Island to Sydney in 1840 so that the courts martial could proceed. Seven of the mutineers were later sentenced to transportation for life and were sent to serve their sentences at the notorious Port Arthur in Van Diemen's Land. Private Andrew Murray was sentenced to fourteen years transportation but this was remitted on the recommendation of the Court.[162] Fortunately, Charles Bend was not involved in the "mutiny".

The Bend and Reed families would therefore have been reunited at the Sydney Barracks for a few months in 1840 before the Bends were reassigned to Newcastle and the Reeds to Wollongong. In 1841 the Bend family welcomed another son into the family, who was baptised George at Hexham, Newcastle.[163] Their daughter Ann was born in 1843.

Later that year Charles Bend left the army and was granted 25 acres of land at Maroota (near Wiseman's Ferry). The Grant Register notes that the purchase price of 25 pounds was remitted, "authorised for him as a late Private in Her Majesty's 80th Regiment of Foot under the Regulations of 15th February 1840".[164] Presumably it would have been open to James Reed (who left the army at the same time) to also obtain a grant of 25 acres, given that his circumstances were the same as Charles Bend. But 25 acres of average land was nowhere near enough for a farm that could support a large family, so James and Frances Reed had chosen to open their grocery store instead.

Despite the land grant at Maroota, the Bend family chose to move to Wellington where Charles was working on *Nanima* Station when he died suddenly in 1845. A year later his widow Eliza married the station owner[165] John Atkins at Apsley Mission, Montefiore, Wellington. She was already pregnant with their first son who was baptised as Charles Atkins on 19 November 1846 at Montefiore.[166] He died in April 1848.[167] Three more Atkins children were born at Wellington - Mary in 1848,[168] John in 1851[169] and William in 1853.[170]

By 1855 the grazing industry was short of labour, due to the combined effects of the gold rush and the end of convict transportation to NSW. The Atkins family of *Nanima* Station would have cast their net wide in search of new employees. In this environment, one could well imagine John Atkins' wife Eliza contacting her old friends the Reeds who, she knew, had several sons who were the right age to enter the industry. So, it is likely that Jimmy Reed travelled to Wellington in response to an offer of employment from Eliza Atkins.

Six months after the birth of his baby sister Jane Reed, **Jimmy Reed** married **Eliza Bend** at the church of St John the Baptist in Wellington on 5 December 1856.[171] The groom was 21 years old and his bride was just 17, so her mother officially consented to the marriage.[172] Theirs was the first Reed family marriage to be registered with the civil authorities.

The marriage was performed by Reverend William Watson and witnessed by Eliza's stepfather, John Atkins. Jimmy was recorded as a bachelor of *Wambangalang*, which was a station situated on the Wambangalang creek about 50 kilometres west of Wellington. It had been used for sheep grazing for at least sixteen years.[173] The property was now owned by Duncan McKillop,[174] a Scotsman who had arrived at Sydney in January 1839 with his parents and siblings. His older brother, Alexander, had settled in Melbourne and produced a family of six children, the eldest of whom was to become Saint Mary MacKillop.[175]

Reverend William Watson had first come to Wellington in 1832 to set up an evangelical mission under the auspices of the Church Missionary Society that aimed to "civilize and Christianise" the aboriginal population. The mission used buildings abandoned by the defunct convict agricultural station that had operated there between 1823 and 1831. Reverend Watson attempted to gain control of any Aboriginal children he could, gaining a reputation among the Aboriginal women as an eagle hawk (kidnapper). The mission eventually failed due to drought and aboriginal disinterest and in 1839 the Church Missionary Society decided that Watson should be removed. He left and, taking the children with him, established a more successful private mission about four miles away (called the Apsley Mission). This is where John Atkins and Eliza Bend senior had been married in 1846.

***

Twenty-three year old **John Benjamin Reed** married **Eliza Jane Green** in Sydney in October 1857.[176] According to the Bourke Court House record of her death, Eliza Jane had been born in London around 1832; her parents were John Green and Jane Hutton; and she had arrived in Australia around 1844.[177]

Bachelor John Green had married spinster Jane Hutton in the well-to-do parish of St George, Hanover Square on 21 October 1828.[178] Their daughter Eliza Jane Green was baptised about 3 kilometres away in Christ Church, Southwark on 14 July 1830.[179] This is the only baptism record for an Eliza Jane Green in London around 1832. Other details of the family are difficult to establish because there were at least three couples named John and Jane Green living in inner London at that time.

The English census for 1841 did not record any child of the right age named Eliza Jane Green. There were many Elizabeth Greens around that age but only one lived in a London household with parents named John and Jane.[180] This family lived at Bedford Row in Islington, about two kilometres from the church where Eliza Jane's parents had been married thirteen years earlier. The census record also includes Elizabeth's siblings John (aged 15), Samuel (10) and Jane (6) as well as two female servants.

This record is problematic because the eldest son John was born three years before the marriage of John Green and Jane Hutton[181] and the second son Samuel was born at about the same time as Eliza Jane.[182] Nevertheless, it seems that Samuel was Eliza Jane's twin (but baptised separately) and that the family's oldest child was born out of wedlock.

Three other children of this couple had died before

the 1841 census was recorded. Anna Maria Green had been baptised in the parish of St Mary, Islington in Feb 1829 while the family was living at Northampton Place.[183] Her father John was described on this and other records as a gentleman. Her older sister, three year old Ann Lucy Green of Bedford Row, was buried in the same parish in May 1831.[184] The family was still living there when her sister Elizabeth Hannah Green was baptised in August 1832.[185] At the end of that year Anna Maria, aged four, was buried in the parish of St John the Evangelist at Lambeth while the family was living at Princes Street.[186] Soon afterwards the family abode was Harriet Street when her sister Elizabeth Hannah Green was buried in the same parish.[187]

The family was still at Lambeth when Jane Green was baptised in February 1836[188] but had returned to Bedford Row when the census was recorded five years later. Any record of their emigration to Australia is obscure.

Jane Green died suddenly at 82 Prince Street in the Sydney suburb The Rocks in June 1857, just 4 months before her daughter's marriage.[189] The Green family was then living just a few doors from the residence of John Reed's future brother-in-law Michael Brennan at 92 Prince Street.[190] According to the City of Sydney Rates Assessment Books, John Benjamin Reed and his wife Eliza Jane were living at 105 Prince Street four years later.[191]

John and Eliza Jane produced the first grandchild for James and Frances Reed during early June 1858.[192] It is interesting that, despite him being the first member of the next generation of Reeds, he was named **William John Reed** rather than a traditional family name. Perhaps he was named for his late uncle, the eldest child of James and Frances. His sister, who was also born in Sydney two years later, was named **Frances Eliza Reed** after her mother and paternal grandmother.[193]

John Benjamin and Eliza Jane Reed were not to produce any more children and, tragically, neither their son nor their daughter was destined to live into adulthood.

While Jimmy Reed had been beaten by his brother John in producing the first grandchildren for their parents James and Frances, he and his wife Eliza now started to make up for their slow start. In the decade starting in 1859 they produced six children (with four more to follow during the 1870s).

Their first three children were John 1859,[194] Eliza 1860[195] and James 1862[196], all born at Wellington. Like his brother John, Jimmy did not choose a traditional Reed family name for his eldest son, although his second and third children were both named after parents or grandparents.

By the time his son James was born, Jimmy had lived at Wellington for at least seven years and was now established in the grazing industry that would provide him employment as a drover and rural worker for the rest of his life.

As the 1850s drew towards a close, James and Frances had every reason to be happy with their situation. All members of the family were doing well and they had been blessed with the arrival of their first grandchildren. Most of their children were now working, giving the senior Reeds time to reflect on how far they had come and to consider what opportunities were on offer for the family during the coming years.

CHAPTER EIGHT

Impetus for change

For six decades after the arrival of Europeans in NSW, most of the benefits of colonisation had been reaped by a very elite group, despite the best intentions of several reformist Governors. Well-connected individuals had built large, profitable enterprises by securing substantial areas of the best land; working it with as much free convict labour as they could obtain; and averting their eyes from any damage caused to ordinary people or the environment. But the gold rushes had introduced significant changes in demography with consequent political implications that ultimately led to policy changes that benefited families like the Reeds.

The seemingly inexorable expansion of colonial graziers into north-western NSW (see map 3) had slowed very dramatically from the early 1840s in response to several factors. Firstly, the price of wool fell substantially because England experienced economic problems early in that decade. This downturn combined with a severe drought in NSW to cause a depression that affected all aspects of the Australian colonies and reduced the demand for grazing land as a consequence.

Secondly, the graziers' workforce was severely disrupted by the gold rush and then by the increased wages that flowed from it. The industry was very labour-intensive, so graziers could not expand their landholdings until they could secure the workforce for the task.

Another reason for the slower migration towards far western NSW during the 1840s and 1850s was its extreme isolation. Supply chains to this area were incredibly long, with all goods having to be carried overland for hundreds of kilometres by very slow bullock wagons from Sydney, Maitland or Port Macquarie. Not only was this a significant logistical problem, but it was also very expensive, making it much cheaper to exploit land that was closer to the coast.

> *The arrival of supplies, sent out to the runs by bullock wagon from the head station, was often delayed for months. The men then had to survive as the natives did - living off the land - eating mussels and fish from the river and creeks, the flesh of birds and animals and native berries, fruit, corms and herbage. Some of the workmen prevented the natives from using the waterholes and their traditional hunting grounds, stole their women and lived in fear of reprisals. Others befriended Aborigines and learned from them ways of coping with the loneliness and the harsh environment.*[197]

Finally, friction with the native population contributed directly to slowing the westward movement of the newcomers. While the major conflicts of the 1816 Hawkesbury and Nepean War and the 1824 Bathurst War were now in the past, new conflicts flared up regularly as colonists moved inland onto the land of previously unaffected tribes. The graziers at the forefront of the colonial pioneers saw Aboriginal people as a hindrance, akin to kangaroos, dingoes and emus: strange fauna obstructing the development of farming and grazing. They routinely took forceful steps to displace the local clans so that their grazing businesses could expand unimpeded.

Governors maintained that Aboriginal people should be treated with humanity and as British subjects, but they were hundreds of miles away and soon found that moral persuasion was completely ineffectual. Some of those at the forefront of colonial expansion developed an increasingly organised system of incursions and forced dispersal of the native population. If necessary, that system employed poisonings and massacres. The law itself, as well as the difficulties of enforcing it in outlying districts, favoured the settlers, so that these methods of depopulation usually went unpunished.

But in 1838 the Myall Creek Massacre had played out in a much different way. Newly arrived James and Frances Reed would have been shocked to learn the details of this incident, which were widely reported in detail. On 10 June, a group of eleven stockmen led by John Henry Fleming murdered at least twenty eight aborigines, mainly women, children and old men. Ten younger men survived because they were away on a neighbouring station cutting bark.

The indigenous Australians had been camped on *Myall Creek* station for a few weeks after being invited to do so by one of the convict stockmen, Charles Kilmeister. He was concerned for their safety and so offered protection from the gangs of marauding stockmen who were roaming the district harrying any Aboriginal people they could find. One day, Fleming arrived with his group of stockmen, tied all the aboriginals to a long rope and led them away. They were forced to run the gauntlet between a stockyard fence and a line of sword-wielding stockmen who hacked at them as they passed.

Eventually they were taken to a gully where all were murdered by sword blows except for one woman who they kept with them for the next couple of days. The bodies were later burnt and the remains removed from the site of the massacre.

A few days later a local squatter, Frederick Foot, heard about what had happened and was so incensed that he rode to Sydney and reported the matter to Governor Gipps personally. Gipps ordered that a thorough investigation be carried out and, eventually, twelve perpetrators were brought to justice. The only one to escape was the only free man involved, the leader, John Fleming.

The accused were tried before the Chief Justice of NSW and were defended by three of the colony's foremost barristers, paid for by an association of landowners and stockmen. Justice Dowling took care to remind the jury that the law made no distinction between the murder of an Aboriginal person and the murder of a European person. Nevertheless, the jury found all the accused men not guilty after deliberating for just twenty minutes.

The grazing interests had doubled down and won the day but the Attorney-General responded by bringing additional charges against seven of the accused. This time he managed to get a witness who gave detailed evidence that resulted in a guilty verdict and a sentence of death for each accused man. The seven who were hanged on 18 December 1838 included Kilmeister, the stockman who had initially offered protection to the indigenous group but lacked the courage of his convictions when faced with a mob of his peers who were determined to advance the interests of their squatter employers.

This was not the first, nor the last such massacre. It was probably not even the worst, as we shall see later in relation to the Hospital Creek massacre near Brewarrina. But it was the first time that any of the perpetrators were made to pay for their crimes. News of this case would have alerted James and Frances Reed to some of the realities of their new life in Australia.

[The Myall Creek massacre Supreme court trials were] the first place white man's justice done some good. Right across Australia, there were massacres. What makes Myall Creek real is that people were hanged, see. That was the difference. Gamilaraay elder, Uncle Lyall Munro, 2013.

Three years after Myall Creek, another incident put a brake on much of the speculative grab for western land for a period of ten or fifteen years. This area of NSW had been experiencing a severe drought since 1837, so grass on the river-side holdings had been depleted through grazing and lack of rain. Many graziers were forced to look for unexploited pasturage.

The savviest of the pioneer graziers, like George Gibson of the Coonamble district, had realised through their experience of earlier droughts that they could not rely solely on river-side holdings. They now knew that it was best to reserve the best land as a refuge for their breeding stock during times of drought. So, rather than rely solely on his main holdings on the Macquarie River (*Wallamgambone* and *The Molle*), he acquired other land (such as at *Mungerabambone* and *Carwell*) that was well-grassed in a good season but suffered from a lack of grass and water during drought years. During good seasons he exploited *Mungerabambone* and *Carwell* while resting his best land; and in poor seasons he sold stock early and moved his best stock back to *Wallamgambone* and *The Molle* where there was permanent water.

But many of the later-arriving graziers did not have the experience to develop this fundamental understanding of the land that they relied on. One of these was William Lee, an ex-convict who was supported by James MacArthur. He leased land in the Walgett district but had no backup plan for a long season of drought so, as the drought extended into a fifth year, he was forced to look much further afield for pasture or risk losing his stock to starvation. His men drove cattle southwards, past Mount Harris (near the later town of Nyngan).

In October 1841, William Lee's overseer, Andrew Kerr, with a party of stockmen were sent to establish a new station on the Bogan River beyond Mount Harris. One of the requirements of the licence of occupation of Crown lands was to leave water sources for the Ngiyampa people as it was a particularly dry spell. Establishing the new station breached these instructions. The Ngiyampa retaliated by killing Robert Roach, William Moreton and Abraham Fearnham 'and wounded three others' (SMH, August 24, 1842, p 2). A detachment of Mounted Police based at Bathurst led by Corporal Reilly and assisted by squatter Joseph Moulder, William Carr (stockman on squatter William Lee's run at the Bogan River), Andrew Kerr and other stockmen, avenged the death of the three men, killing 12 Ngiyampa and arresting three of the alleged killers, one of whom escaped 'and two were committed to take their trials' [later released] (SMH, August 24, 1842, p 2). Commissioner of Crown Lands William Allman investigated the case and charged the two Ngiyampa men with murder, brought them before the Circuit Court in March 1842, and secured their discharge for lack of evidence. Allman recommended that Lee's pastoral lease be withdrawn and not renewed, and Governor Gipps agreed. Outraged that a settler of Lee's standing should be treated in this way, a group of settlers at Bathurst petitioned Gipps to restore Lee's licence. The matter was raised by James Macarthur in the NSW Legislative Council on 22 August 1842 and in the debate on 23 August, Gipps justified his decision on the grounds that Lee had failed to observe instructions not to squat on the Bogan river and to leave water for the Ngiyampa. The debate was reported in full in the SMH on August 24 1842.[198]

This case was clearly the last straw for Governor Gipps. He was an experienced soldier and administrator who had governed NSW now for three years. Soon after his arrival he had been confronted with the outrages committed by squatters and their men including the Myall Creek Massacre. In that case he had acted decisively to punish offenders and ensured that their sentences of death by hanging were, in fact, carried out. Soon afterwards he reported to his superiors in England: *Your Lordship is, I am sure, well aware of the extreme difficulty of devising any measure, that shall effectually check the outrages, which, I regret to state, are now of frequent occurrence beyond the boundaries of location.*[199]

In the current case, the Circuit Court had discharged the aboriginal defendants from their murder charge because there was no way of adequately informing them of the nature of the charges that they faced, let alone providing them with a defence team with whom they could communicate effectively. Gipps identified this as a significant issue that undermined his efforts to educate the aboriginal population about the British law and its implications for them. Instead, he sought to rein in the squatters, but they were fighting him on several fronts.

It is worth noting that Lee's story that his men had been forced by drought to come to the area from Walgett in search of new pasture was probably a convenient excuse. The explorer Major Mitchell had recorded, six years earlier, that he had been followed down the Bogan by a couple of Lee's stockmen and saw some cattle.[200]

Governor Gipps made an example of Lee by tearing up the lease for his land at Walgett, thus signalling to all graziers that he was serious about ensuring that they observed the limits that his government had placed on them. Despite a concerted attack by grazing interests in the Legislative Council during 1842, he vigorously defended his government's policies and refused to concede to the Council's demands. He pointed out that the fault lay with Mr Lee's employees who had broken the law and noted that none of Mr Lee's defenders in Parliament had even mentioned the loss of fifteen lives that had resulted from this.

The Governor stated at this time that in 1840 positive orders had been issued forbidding the formation of stations lower down the Macquarie than 20 miles from

Mount Harris, and the ban also applied to the Bogan River. The ban against the occupation of the Bogan country was not lifted until 1858, but in spite of it, in 1843 a man named Gilmore put cattle on Lee's station.

Despite Gipps' decisive actions in response to the Myall Creek massacre and the incidents associated with William Lee, many graziers refused to reform their policies in relation to the aboriginal inhabitants, as remarked by Bishop Polding in 1845.

I have myself heard a man, educated, and a large proprietor of sheep and cattle, maintain that there was no more harm in shooting a native, than in shooting a wild dog. I have heard it maintained by others that it is the course of Providence, that blacks should disappear before the white, and the sooner the process was carried out the better, for all parties. I fear such opinions prevail to a great extent. Very recently in the presence of two clergymen, a man of education narrated, as a good thing, that he had been one of a party who had pursued the blacks, in consequence of cattle being rushed by them, and that he was sure that they shot upwards of a hundred. When expostulated with, he maintained that there was nothing wrong in it, that it was preposterous to suppose they had souls. In this opinion he was joined by another educated person present. Bishop Polding, 1845[201]

The gold rushes had by now transformed the Australian colonies into multicultural societies, although this did not come without friction. It was not just the native inhabitants who bore the brunt of discrimination. Non-European immigrants, especially the Chinese, were made to feel very unwelcome. The Chinese worked very industriously in teams, using techniques that differed markedly from those employed by Europeans. Their physical appearance meant that their difference was easily identifiable and fear of the unknown led to them being subject to racist bullying that would be repugnant in modern Australia.

More than 11,000 Chinese arrived in Melbourne in 1855 prompting the government to pass the Chinese Immigration Act 1855 which severely limited the number of Chinese passengers permitted to disembark from an arriving vessel. The Chinese immigrants cleverly evaded the new law by disembarking in South Australia and then walking more than 400 km across country to the Victorian goldfields, along tracks that are still evident today.

The Chinese diggers moved regularly from goldfield to goldfield within Victoria and New South Wales. These frequent moves attracted particular attention and local newspapers were quick to comment on their distinctive features, clothes, languages, habits, methods of transport, diligence, tirelessness and productivity. Any admiration of their work ethic was offset by envy and resentment when times got hard. They were often scapegoated, as seen in the violent anti-Chinese riots at Turon in 1853; Meroo in 1854; Rocky River in 1856; Tambaroora in 1858; Lambing Flat, Kiandra and Nundle in 1860 and 1861; and the Tingha tin fields in 1870. The Chinese were seen initially as oddities, later as rivals and then as threats to white Australians.

Among the European and American migrants attracted by the lure of the goldfields were many men and women who brought new political ideas to the young colonies. Initially, the colonial establishment resisted such progressive thinking as a threat to their authority and the resulting tensions culminated in the Eureka Rebellion of 1854.

This was the third rebellion in Australian history, following the Battle of Vinegar Hill in 1804 (when Irish rebels botched their coup attempt) and the Rum Rebellion of 1808 (when Governor Bligh was ousted by a military coup backed by wealthy vested interests). The Eureka Rebellion was a series of events involving gold miners who revolted against the government of Victoria. It started with several peaceful demonstrations and civil disobedience where miners voiced various grievances, chiefly the cost of mining permits and the officious way the system was enforced. The tin-eared response of the government caused an escalation of tensions that culminated in the Battle of the Eureka Stockade at Ballarat on 3 December 1854 between rebel miners and garrison forces of the Victorian government (British soldiers of the 12th and 40th Regiments of Foot). The fighting resulted in an official total of 27 deaths and many injuries, most casualties being rebels.

The subsequent Royal Commission into the Victorian goldfields was scathing in its assessment of all aspects of the administration of the goldfields, particularly the Eureka Stockade affair. Within 12 months, several reforms sought by the rebels were implemented, including legislation providing for universal adult male suffrage for Legislative Assembly elections and the removal of property qualifications for members of the Legislative Assembly.

Key members of the rebel side were later tried in Melbourne for high treason, but mass public support led to their acquittal. Rebel leader Peter Lalor was elected to parliament, later serving as Speaker of the Victorian Legislative Assembly.

It was not just the gold rush that was bringing great change to the people of NSW. Work on the construction of a railway line from Sydney to Parramatta had been underway since 1849, financed by private enterprise. This railway was by far the largest and most ambitious engineering project embarked upon anywhere in Australia up until that time. It commenced with clearing the right-of-way and included the erection of fencing; establishing a sandstone quarry at Lewisham; creating seven brickyards along the route; cutting tunnels under Cleveland Street and Parramatta Road; and building 27 bridges and 50 culverts, workshops at Redfern, stations at Newtown, Ashfield, Burwood and Homebush as well as terminal stations at Redfern and Parramatta.

British civil engineers William Randle and James Wallace, who had worked with George Stephenson and his Rocket twenty years earlier, had become leaders in railway construction in Europe and were contracted to oversee the construction of Sydney's railway. Their company was tasked with recruiting 500 artisans and navvies whose fares to Australia were paid by the Government. These included the author's GGG-grandfather, John Poulton, and his brother-in-law, John Ashworth who would both arrive with their families aboard the *Fitzjames* in 1860.[202]

But the soaring cost of labour caused by the gold rush had undermined the business case and the railway owners (not the construction company) went bankrupt just 23 days before the inaugural journey was scheduled to be made. The NSW government stepped in so that the project was completed on time and the line began taking traffic in September 1855. Nevertheless, Melbourne had beaten Sydney, running a service from Flinders Street to Hobsons Bay a year earlier. But the opening of the first passenger rail service was just the start. Soon work commenced to duplicate the single track and to extend the line westwards to Penrith.

After the first frantic months of the gold rush, most people had realised that it was only the lucky few who would strike it rich, so many thousands gradually trickled back into the towns and cities in search of employment. Sydney became the colony's principal port and was transformed into a centre of government. Manufacturing was finding a foothold and many other businesses were prospering. The rudimentary buildings that had served for a few decades were gradually being replaced by substantial buildings and gracious architecture. The population, permanently enlarged by the gold rushes, consumed much more food, clothing and housing than ever before, giving a significant boost to businesses and the economy in general.

The continuing growth in the grazing industries, the influx of new migrants and the growing number of convicts freed on expiration of their sentences was changing NSW rapidly from a convict colony into a free society. These demographic trends began to influence how the society was managed, as ideas on individual rights, egalitarianism and democracy found fertile ground among the rapidly growing working and middle classes. Those ideas led to significant political reform that benefited people like James and Frances Reed. One of the most important reforms was to land management across the state.

Despite two decades of restrictions on land sales to

within the nineteen counties, squatters had leased large grazing runs further out and were now controlling the best land. Eventually, new ideas that had been introduced with the changing demographics prompted a reformed NSW government to adopt policies that encouraged more intensive settlement and the establishment of country towns to service the newly settled areas.

From the early 1850s, influential politicians like Henry Parkes and Charles Cowper (third son of the Reverend William Cowper who had baptised Mary Ann Reed in 1853) had begun agitating for voting rights to be expanded to include citizens without property and for local legislatures to be given independence from Britain. In 1853 the NSW Legislative Council passed a draft Constitution for self-government and submitted it to the British government for approval. The British Parliament passed an amended version in 1855 that established two houses of parliament - an appointed upper house (known as the Legislative Council) and an elected lower house (the Legislative Assembly) of 54 members. Eligibility to vote for the lower house was extended to adult men who met a moderate property qualification.

This new constitution gave the parliament wide powers over domestic matters, including revenue raising and land, but Britain still retained the power to disallow colonial legislation. Significantly, power passed from the Governor to whichever political leader from the lower house could command majority support.

NSW had moved from representative government to responsible government and, for many of the early years, Charles Cowper was Premier of NSW. Nevertheless, the allocation of lower house seats was biased in favour of rural areas, so it heavily favoured established landowners. The governor-appointed upper house was even more biased towards the vested interests of the squatters. This situation fell short of Cowper's democratic ideals and he had the support of many people in the community. In practice, however, these shortcomings were eventually overcome because the Constitution could be easily modified by simple majorities in both Houses.

In 1857, Cowper proposed to increase the rents on graziers and to levy an assessment on their stock. This move was defeated in parliament and so Cowper called an election. He remained Premier after the election and convinced the new parliament to amend the Electoral Act to provide for secret ballot, universal manhood suffrage, representation primarily by population and more equal electoral districts. Each of these initiatives had the effect of making the government of NSW more democratic. The legislation also created 40 new municipalities, established district courts and prohibited grants to support public religious activity. The next item on the agenda was land reform.

In 1858, Sands Directory listed James Reed as living at 78 Kent Street[203] (a house that was valued at 24 pounds).[204] But, during that year, the family moved to 165 Clarence Street, a house of brick and shingle valued at 34 pounds and owned by Joseph Spinks.[205] The ratable value of their accommodation had gradually increased from eight pounds in 1851 to 24 pounds by 1858 and now up to 34 pounds. This may reflect an improvement in the family finances but it could also have been part of a strategy to cater to boarders by renting a bigger house. Indeed, on Wednesday 24 November 1858, James placed an advertisement on the front page of the Sydney Morning Herald newspaper.[206]

If Mrs Thompson does not come and pay me what she owes me for board and lodging within fourteen days from this date, her things will be sold to pay expenses. JAMES REED, Clarence Street.

The aftermath of the gold rush would have created an accommodation crisis in Sydney as disappointed diggers returned from the goldfields in droves. This sudden increase in demand for housing would have created a backlog of building projects and the resulting accommodation shortage would have provided a lucrative opportunity for any families that had a spare bedroom. Those who were particularly enterprising could create bedrooms by closing in a verandah or putting up a temporary partition in a larger room.

The Reeds were to spend many of their later years in the hotel business, as were all their younger children including Eliza, Sarah Ann, Prudence, Frances, George Charles and Jane. So, it seems that the family had probably taken a step in the direction of the hotel business by 1858, by taking in lodgers. It is not clear whether the family was running a boarding house or simply renting out a spare bedroom while James continued to seek employment as a labourer.

In return for a weekly "board and lodging" payment, the Reeds would have provided their lodgers with a bed, breakfast and dinner. This was a perfect business for them because all members of the family could assist in the provision of accommodation and meal services to their guests. Daily chores would have included providing fuel for the stove; shopping for provisions; preparing, cooking and serving meals; washing dishes; making beds; and sweeping floors. Each week floors would be washed; bedding would be changed and the used sheets and towels washed and dried. Other guest laundry could also be washed, dried and ironed, at additional cost to the guest. There was so much work that all members of the family would need to lend a hand, thus learning the skills that they would use in their own hotel businesses in years to come.

By 1861, the Reed family was living at 80 Kent Street in a large house of stone and shingles valued at 36 pounds and owned by John Glovett.[207] In the same year they were also recorded at 171 Clarence Street in a house of wood and shingle valued at 45 pounds owned by Mrs Jones.[208] So, the trend for them to rent more salubrious houses was continuing, possibly reflecting an expansion of their board and lodging business.

Now that the graziers' influence on government policy had been reduced, the grazing industry became the focus of much political discussion and maneuvering. John Robertson became Premier in March 1860 and appointed former Premier Charles Cowper as his Chief Secretary (head of the Public Service). Control of pastoral land became the key issue of government when they introduced legislation that was designed to free up the stranglehold that the squatters held over land in NSW. Robertson and Cowper wanted to terminate the leases of large landholders and break their holdings up into smaller farms for settlers. These reforms were opposed by conservative forces led by William Charles Wentworth, a self-made man who had become rich by obtaining large pastoral grazing licenses. Wentworth advocated for an hereditary upper house (controlled by squatters like him), a concept that was ridiculed by liberals as a "bunyip aristocracy".

The democratic reforms that Cowper had implemented meant that the conservative forces had lost ground to the urban middle classes who now had the vote and soon came to dominate political reform. Liberalism gradually gained the ascendancy based on the widespread view that society should offer opportunity to a wide cross-section of the community.

Accordingly, in 1861 the Robertson government succeeded in passing the Crown Lands Act that overturned the ban on the sale of land outside the nineteen counties and allowed for the free selection of crown land. This meant that the squatters' lands were now open to selection by ordinary citizens once the squatter's lease had expired. So-called "selectors" could then buy land at auction by paying a 25% deposit on a purchase price of one pound per acre. They had then to live on their land for three years and to make improvements worth one pound per acre.

Despite these changes, the existing graziers still held most of the cards. They retained the right to buy four percent of their lease in addition to any improved areas and could also pre-lease three times the area of the freehold. Furthermore, they could request the survey and auctioning of large parcels of their remaining lease, giving them the ability to bid for this land at short notice while other potential bidders were unaware that the land was on the market.

So, despite the intentions of the Robertson Land Reforms to create an industry of small farmers, the squatters mostly prevailed by buying the best land, building permanent homes and investing in improvements such as fences (which reduced their reliance on shepherds and herdsmen). Nevertheless, small holders did gain a foothold and established a dairy industry and intensive cultivation in the more fertile and better-watered parts of NSW.

In August 1860, eighteen-year-old **Eliza Emily Reed** made a decision that she would later come to regret; she married **Andrew Bufe** in Sydney.[209] Unfortunately, the marriage was over within three years because her husband had, by then, disappeared.

Bufe is a German surname. The only record of anyone with that surname in eastern Australia or New Zealand before the Bufe-Reed marriage of 1860 is for the arrival of two passengers from Hamburg aboard the *Australia* in September 1849. The immigration of JG and J Henry Bufe was not only reported in the *Adelaide Observer*,[210] but it was also specifically mentioned in the German-language newspaper *Die Deutsche Post fur die Australishen Colonien* (*The German Australian Post*).[211] Nevertheless, there are no records of them having married or produced children in South Australia. Had Andrew Bufe been born in Australia or arrived as a convict or an immigrant, there would be many more local records of him before his marriage in 1860.

Given this lack of earlier Australian records and that he subsequently disappeared, it is likely that Andrew Bufe was a mariner. So, he is probably the 26-year-old Andrew Buff who had arrived in Sydney three months before the marriage as the ship's carpenter aboard the *Minnie Ha Ha*[212]. This was an American ship with a mainly American crew that had sailed from Hong Kong with 97 Chinese passengers, arriving at Sydney on 22 May 1860.

While this implies that, during the subsequent three months, Eliza and Andrew probably enjoyed a whirlwind romance, other information suggests that they may have known each other for a little bit longer than that. Andrew Bufe is probably the same person as the Anders (also known as Andrew) Buff who had arrived in Sydney seven months earlier as a 25-year-old ship's carpenter aboard another American ship, the *Matilda*[213]. That ship had sailed from Manila with six passengers. The crew lists for both ships state that Andrew Buff was a citizen of the United States.

It is unlikely that James and Frances Reed would have approved of their 18-year-old daughter marrying an itinerant mariner just three months after meeting him; but more likely that they would have consented if he had returned to Sydney to resume an attachment from several months earlier.

Fortunately, the marriage did not produce any children because it is clear that Andrew Bufe had been missing from his wife's life for some considerable time when she placed the following advertisement in the Sydney Morning Herald on 26 and 27 August 1863.

Notice is hereby given that, if I do not hear from my husband, Andrew Bufe, within one month from this date, I intend to enter into another engagement, Eliza Bufe.[214]

Whether she really was considering another engagement is unknown, but she did not marry again until two years later. The newspaper notice reads like it was placed by a lawyer on Eliza's behalf, so it may have been an essential part of a formal legal process that she had to go through to have her marriage officially voided. It seems that this process may have resulted in her husband being declared dead, because she was recorded on her second marriage certificate two years later, as a widow.[215]

The Reed family had become more prosperous by the time that the calendar flipped over to the decade of the 1860s. The eldest sons, John and Jimmy, were now married and making their own way in the carrying and grazing industries respectively, as was bachelor Alexander. Daughter Eliza had recently married and her older sisters had now reached the age where they, too, would be looking for husbands. James and Frances were observing the fundamental changes in society and wondering what advantage they could obtain for themselves and their family.

Photograph 4
Portrait of James Reed
Probably taken in 1862 when he was 53 years old.
Source: Noreen Watts

CHAPTER NINE

Bourke

Following the gold rush, members of the Reed family were enjoying a better standard of living but, unlike many others, had not managed to accumulate much wealth. They needed to save some income to invest in long-term assets that could sustain the family into the future. The NSW government had recently implemented reforms to land laws designed to help families like the Reeds to do just that. This is probably what prompted James and Frances to start thinking seriously about making a big change in their lives with the aim of improving their situation and that of their children. Within two years of the passage of the legislation they had moved from Sydney to Bourke.

The Reeds had been providing lodgers with food and lodgings, probably involving just a room or two in their own rented house rather than a larger boarding house. Nevertheless, they apparently decided to improve their lot by seeking opportunities to invest further in boarding house and hotel businesses. It was difficult, however, to break into these industries in Sydney and other older towns, where the best spots had already been taken by well-established businesses. This could explain why they turned their attention to the areas of the State that had now been opened to new settlers because of the Robertson land reforms.

Their son Jimmy was now well established in Wellington and his experiences as a drover would have equipped him well to advise on the new areas opening further west. Their eldest son John Benjamin had also established himself as a carrier (his long-term career) and would therefore have also been able to provide advice on the areas that he had seen.[216] Third son Alexander, now in his twenties, was also later recorded as a bullock driver,[217] so he may have also been a source of information and advice.

The detailed reasons why they chose Bourke have been lost to history. It is possible that they were aware that a new town had been gazetted and that the first auction of land in the town was planned. This would have provided an incentive to get to Bourke as soon as possible to assess what opportunities it provided.

***

The first European to venture into the area around Bourke had been the explorer Charles Sturt (accompanied by the other well-known explorer, Hamilton Hume) in 1829. Sturt's party had travelled from Wellington, along the Macquarie River and the lower part of the Bogan River - much the same route that the Reed family would follow 33 years later. Sturt and Hume discovered Mount Oxley on 2 January 1829 and named it for John Oxley who had explored along the

Macquarie River eleven years earlier. Oxley had never reached the Bourke district because he had turned right at the Macquarie Marshes and made his way eastwards across the Liverpool Plains to the site of the future Port Macquarie.

Sturt's party briefly visited Mount Gundabooka before pushing north from Mount Oxley to the Dry Bogan, an anabranch that runs from the Bogan into the Darling during wet years. After crossing it they proceeded northwest for two days until *"we suddenly found ourselves on the banks of a noble river"*. Sturt named it the Darling River after Governor Darling. As graziers later moved into the Walgett district they adopted the Aboriginal name of the local stream, anglicising it as the Barwon River, without realising that it was the same waterway that had already been named the Darling. Even more confusingly, further upstream (above Barwon Junction near Mungindi) the same river is called the MacIntyre.

Sturt followed the Darling downstream for about 100 kilometres to a point just above its junction with the Warrego River. In that year of drought and heatwave, he and Hume concluded that the district was unsuited to grazing or settlement. The prevailing conditions forced them to abandon their exploration and return to Wellington. Later that year Sturt started on his famous exploration of the Murrumbidgee and Murray Rivers whereby he proved that they ran to the sea at Lake Alexandrina in South Australia.

Six years later, Major Sir Thomas Mitchell essentially retraced Sturt's course to the Darling before continuing much further downstream - as far as Menindee. About 13 kilometres downstream from the future town of Bourke he discovered a high point of land near the riverbank that bore many Aboriginal grave sites. He needed the high ground for a stores depot in case his party had to later retrace their steps, so he built a rough log stockade that could provide his party with *"stout resistance against any number of natives"* because they *"had not asked permission to come there"*. Even though it was quite a small enclosure, he gave it the grandiose name of Fort Bourke in honour of the Governor, Richard Bourke.[218] It was never needed for defence.

Surveyor Roderick Mitchell (son of Sir Thomas), who was Commissioner of Crown Lands for the western districts, visited the area around Bourke ten years after his father in 1845. He found that the stockade had by then been burnt down (although the temporary stockyards that had been built nearby were still secure).[219] Natives near the Culgoa River (north-west of Bourke) told him that they had never seen a white man before but they had heard about the killing of two white men near the Narran River, another near the Birrie River (both near Brewarrina) and two more on the Ballonne River (in southern Queensland).[220]

During the early 1840s there were some attempts at introducing grazing in the Fort Bourke district but they were abandoned, probably because of the restrictions imposed by Governor Gipps as well as the practical difficulties that the graziers faced. Push back from the original owners would have been one of those practical difficulties. Even though Fort Bourke had survived for less than ten years and had never been anything more than a palisaded depot, the name stuck to the district and was later adapted for the town that was established nearby.

In 1847 the explorer Edmund Kennedy passed through the district en route to Queensland where he had been commissioned to trace the Victoria River in the hope of reaching the Gulf of Carpentaria. Surveyor George Boyle White (who must have been a part of that expedition) later reported that, in the area 110 to 130 kilometres north-west of Fort Bourke, the land had been previously taken up but was now deserted; and he frequently fell in with old huts.[221]

The following year a Mr Raye led a large party with 2,000 cattle plus horses and drays down the Namoi, Bogan, Darling and Murray Rivers to Adelaide. A year later the Surveyor-General of NSW (Walter Davidson) was in the district and noted the presence of several stations, but these were upstream of the site of Bourke.[222]

If it hadn't been for the determination of Governor Gipps to slow the expansion of the grazing industry, the far western district of NSW would have been settled at least ten years earlier than it was. In response to frontier flashpoints on the Liverpool Plains and elsewhere in the early 1840s, he had placed a moratorium on graziers settling on the Bogan and Barwon-Darling Rivers; and when that directive was later flaunted, he acted decisively to enforce it. Consequently, the inexorable expansion of grazing into the Bourke district was delayed from the early 1840s until the late 1850s. Nevertheless, his governorship ended in late 1846 and the subsequent impact of the gold rushes led to many changes in policy which allowed graziers to eventually resume their expansion towards the Bourke district from about 1857.

Volume 1 of the History of Bourke journal includes an article entitled *"Some early settlers"* that was written by WK Glover. It reports that

Active settlement commenced on the Upper Darling in 1857; in rapid succession the district witnessed the arrival of Messrs. Colless and Colin McKenzie (Weilmoringle); Mr Gerald Spring (Gundabooka); Mr T.A. Smith (Yanda); Mr P. Boyce for Hugh Glass (Winbar); Mr McGilvery for Mr Youall of Melbourne (Kallara); Mr Joe Smith (Mertie); Mr Field (Mara); and Messrs Kay and Butcher at Nelyambo.[223]

Aside from Weilmoringle (which is over 200 kilometres from Bourke), the other stations listed are all well to the southwest of the town - much closer to Wilcannia and Tilpa than Bourke. The nearest, Yanda and Gundabooka, are 50 to 60 kilometres downstream.

Volume 2 of the History of Bourke journal includes a range of research by William (Bill) Cameron on early surveying work that was carried out in the Bourke district. On page 67 he notes that a surveyor named Berry produced a map in 1858 that showed several stations on both sides of the river near Bourke, including Dunlop, Toorale and Fort Bourke.[224] In that same volume there is another article entitled *"Robert Biggart Gow"* that outlines an 1861 journey that Gow made to the area around the Paroo and Warrego Rivers (southwest of Bourke). The only stock that he mentions seeing was a flock of sheep owned by the Bogan River Company. Gow noted that *"this is the furthest out settlement in NSW"*[225].

Clearly graziers had by now realised that sheep were, in fact, well suited to the hot, dry climate of the Bourke district. Furthermore, sheep numbers had boomed in NSW and overseas demand was very strong. Many western graziers had shifted from cattle to sheep.

So it was that, just five years before the arrival of the Reed family, the first Europeans came to the Bourke district with an intention of settling. The earliest stations spread upstream from the southwest (near Wilcannia) pioneered by people like Vincent Dowling, William Sly, Edward Bloxham, Thomas Andrew Mathews and John Kelly.

Some of the men who did much to establish the town at Bourke around this time were associated with these stations. William Sly was an American who came to the district as a representative of Jeffrey Bros of the Murrumbidgee district who originally owned *Toorale* Station[226]. Sly quickly established a timber mill at the site of the future town, with much of the timber that it produced being used on *Toorale*[227]. He later built the *Bourke* hotel, the first building in the town and is often referred to as the Founder of Bourke.

Jeffrey Bros soon sold *Toorale* to the Bogan River Company which sent one of its partners, Edward John Bloxham, to manage the station in about 1860. He lived in Bourke for the rest of his life and was its first Mayor in 1879. He is often referred to as the Father of Bourke.

Another early *Toorale* employee and pioneer of the Bourke district was blacksmith Thomas Andrew Matthews (later the founder of Louth).[228]

The proprietor of the other early hotel in Bourke was John Edward Kelly who had come to the Bogan district at the age of 14 as a ration carrier and storekeeper. Three years later he had full charge of a station on the Namoi and at 18 he was head stockman for Vincent Dowling on *Fort Bourke* station.

The rapid development of the Bourke district after 1859 was greatly aided by the new-found ability of paddle steamers to reach the area. A steamer and its barges could carry vastly more cargo than a bullock wagon. Even though travelling on a very winding river was a lot further than the overland distance, the journey was mechanised and therefore much easier and faster. The age of the paddle steamer therefore overcame many issues of isolation, supply chain and expense that had restrained development in the district hitherto.

Pioneering river navigator Captain Francis Cadell had brought his steamer *Albury* to Wilcannia early in 1859. But it was his rival, William Randell, who first managed to get further up the Darling, bringing his steamer *Gemini* past the future site of Bourke and as far upstream as the aboriginal fish traps at Brewarrina.

Captain Randell, with his steamer Gemini, has just come up the Barwon as far as the rocks … It was quite a surprise to all of us to see to see a steamer sailing, or rather steaming, up the river in such a wild out-of-the-way place as this. It will double the value of the runs on this part of the river, as we shall be able to get up our rations at a comparatively low rate. Mr Randall says that he met with no obstacles on his way up. When the river has a fresh he can go higher.[229]

Randell himself later supplied particulars of his trip to the Sydney Morning Herald newspaper, as follows.

The Gemini arrived at the Mount Murchison station (Mr. Jamieson's), the highest point attained by the Albury, on the 16th February. On the following day passed Mr. Sutter's station, the highest up supplied from the Junction. Mr Spence's station at Fort Bourke was reached on the 20th. This station has hitherto been supplied from the Sydney side, the next station passed before reaching the Barwon was Gunnawarra (Mr. T. Dangars), on Wednesday, the 23rd February. On the following day the highest point attained by the Gemini, which is on the Barwon, was reached. This is called the Falls, or the blacks' fishing-grounds, and includes a rapid, with a fall of seven or eight feet in 200 or 300 yards.[230]

The correspondent of the *Goulburn Herald and County of Argyle Advertiser* described the fishing grounds in an article published on 30 April that year.

The blacks have contrived at the falls a multiplicity of cellular formations of rude stonework, with apertures towards the up stream and lesser openings of intercommunication. When the river is low the several tribes suspend their hostilities, and assembling at a point about eight miles above the Falls, they come down the stream in a body, causing a great commotion in the water, and making very loud and peculiar noises, which have the effect of driving the fish towards the cellular contrivances, where they are speared in some of the numerous cells by a succession of dexterous assailants. Drayloads of fish are thus taken, and a season of festivity and gluttony supervenes.[231]

The local tribes knew the fish traps as Baiame's Ngunnhu. According to their ancient tradition, the Ngunnhu had been designed and created by Baiame, a great ancestral being who is respected by numerous cultural groups in western NSW. The structure is now listed on the NSW State Heritage Register and is thought to be one of the oldest human constructions in the world, having been maintained by the local population for tens of thousands of years.

On returning from his journey in the *Gemini*, Randell commented that

The country from Mount Murchison to Fort Bourke is taken up, but quite unoccupied, although the banks of the river are covered with luxuriant grass, and the land generally is lightly timbered. The Darling country is admirably adapted for wool-growing, and fit for pastoral purposes generally.

This confirms that the first leaseholders in the Bourke district had not installed significant numbers of stock until late 1859 at the earliest, although the official Statistics of NSW published by the Registrar-General later that year recorded that *"the whole valley of the Darling, from Fort Bourke downwards, is now partially occupied with stock"*.[232]

The NSW government recognised the rapidly growing population of the Bourke district in December 1859 when it awarded a contract of 350 pounds per annum to James Keating to run a fortnightly mail service between Walgett and Fort Bourke.[233] This was *Fort Bourke Station*, as the town of Bourke had not yet been established.

While graziers were moving up the Darling from Wilcannia towards the Bourke district, others were approaching from the opposite direction. Regrettably, the spread of grazing downstream from the Walgett district involved one of the worst massacres of native people in Australian history, just 120 kilometres from Bourke. Several hundred Aboriginals were murdered near Hospital Creek (20 kilometres north of Brewarrina) in 1859. The perpetrators knew that the government would have no choice but to prosecute them if the story came out, so they disposed of the evidence and kept all knowledge of the massacre under wraps for many years. Consequently, the details of exactly what happened (and why) are not entirely clear. It is likely that the version that was recorded by GM Smith in the *Sydney Mail* of 12 September 1928 is close to the truth because he recounts what he was told by Con Bride who was quite open about having organised the massacre.[234]

Bride was a cattleman and station manager employed by squatters to open new land for grazing. To "open up" land, Bride was expected to ensure that the original inhabitants did not get in the way. In 1857 he left *Tullaba* station on the Namoi River with 200 head of cattle to stock *Bunnawanna* station (now called *Warraweena*).[235] He later "opened up" huge tracts of land on the Barwon, Darling and Warrego Rivers from Cunnamulla to Brewarrina. An Irishman, he called one of his huts Erin's Gunyah, which later became Eringonia and is now called Enngonia.

According to Smith's account, Bride became aware that a large group of Aboriginals were spearing and eating his employer's cattle on *Quantambone* station, so he asked them to move on. They replied "baal" meaning no, so he sent for reinforcements. When the natives maintained their answer a few days later in the face of twenty armed station hands, Bride had his men fire over their heads. The natives quickly grabbed their spears and woomeras and prepared for battle, so Bride, realising he was outnumbered, ordered his men to open fire.

"When they made a move forward I feared a rush on our small force by their hundreds; so we fired a volley into them and a dozen or more fell."

Bride alleged that the remainder then ran away across the plain towards the Culgoa River. Another account depicts the massacre as retaliation for the murder of a stockman and his de facto Aboriginal wife by Aborigines. Yet another account says that the massacre was led by Mr J McKenzie who found an encampment of 300 of whom only one or two escaped.[236]

Despite the lack of exact detail about this incident and others, there is no doubt that the arrival of grazing in the Bourke district had the same effect on the Aboriginal population that it had had in other parts of NSW; it took from them their means of making a living in their traditional ways. Instead, those that survived the introduced diseases and the massacres were forced to seek employment from the graziers and to accept handouts from the government.

It is hard for modern Australians, 160 years later, to understand how the likes of Bride and his mates could perpetrate such an atrocity, let alone get away with it. Their society viewed Aboriginals as obstacles to progress that had to be dealt with. With Governor Gipps gone, the government (controlled by pastoral interests) was complicit in such massacres by conveniently turning a blind eye. Worse still, from 1848 it funded the NSW Native Police Force which employed aboriginal men in a mounted and armed force that was charged with "protecting" graziers. These men were often coerced into service and always employed away from their local area. Always led by a white officer, the Native Police were active in moving local aboriginals off their land, by force where necessary. Over the subsequent decades they were responsible for the deaths of a great many people of their own race in NSW, Queensland, the Northern Territory and Western Australia.

In 1845 the Aboriginal population around Bourke was estimated to be about 3,000. This was further reduced after the establishment of Bourke in 1862 and by 1863 it had shrunk to around 1,000. Government blankets were distributed in the town or within the district from 1865 indicating increasing contact between settlers and the land's traditional owners. Settlers were relying on Aboriginal labour while Aboriginal people, with decreasing access to traditional resources, were becoming reliant on non-traditional food and materials. Station records show that numerous Aboriginal people were employed on stations, working as timber cutters, shearers, stockmen and domestic workers.[237]

Over the following few decades, the number of Aboriginal people in the Bourke district continued to decline significantly. Dr Max Kamien, a Bourke General Practitioner in the early 1970s who implemented several programs aimed at improving Aboriginal health, concluded that

By 1884 the Aboriginal population had plummeted to 80–25 men, 35 women, 10 girls and 10 boys. Contact between the two cultures clearly had a devastating effect on the Ngiyampaa people as it had on all Indigenous people.[238]

It was not just the native population of humans that suffered adverse effects from the influx of commercial graziers onto their land; many of the native animal species were also devastated. One example is that of the Lesser Stick-nest Rat (*leporillus apicalis*) whose image was incorporated by John Gould in volume III of his Mammals of Australia in 1863.[239]

It was a moderately sized native rodent (body mass 60 g) that differed from its larger relative, the Greater Stick-nest Rat, by the narrow brush of white hairs near the tip of its tail. During the years 1852-1862 Gerard Krefft studied the animals of the Lower Murray and Darling Rivers. On 10 October 1862 he read his paper *The Vertebrated animals of the lower Murray and Darling* to the Philosophical Society of NSW,[240] which contained a description of this little animal that, he noted, was called *tillikin* by the natives.

Illustration 17
Leporillus apicalus by John Gould, 1863.
Public Domain

I observed the first specimens in the neighbourhood of Euston and found it in great numbers upon Sir Thomas Mitchell's old track on both sides of the Murray. It also occurs on the Darling; and I have no doubt that the late lamented explorers called Rat Point, in the neighbourhood of Fort Bourke, after this [animal]. Gregarious in their habits, I have often dislodged as many as fifteen specimens from a single tree and kept large numbers in captivity. They become quite tame; and many which escaped would invariably join my frugal supper at night, and help themselves to damper, in particular. This is a very graceful animal, strictly nocturnal in its habits, and its flesh white, tender and well tasted.[241]

The *tillikin* built nests of sticks that accumulated over the years into a mound of up to three metres in length and a metre high. After the arrival of cattle and sheep its numbers declined rapidly, to the extent that there has not been a confirmed sighting since 1933 and it is now officially extinct.[242] No doubt the hooves of the cattle would have devastated the stick nests, making breeding difficult and exposing the rats to predation from owls and eagles. The subsequent arrival of apex predators like feral foxes and competition from feral rabbits would have applied the *coup de grace*.

Bourke was one of the last towns to be established in NSW because of its great distance from the nineteen counties where land purchase was available and where the NSW government provided some level of security for new settlers. Other factors that slowed the advance towards Bourke were a severe drought in the early 1840s; disruptions to the graziers' labour force caused by the gold rushes of the early 1850s; the huge expense associated with very long supply chains to the area; and government action in the 1840s that was designed to protect the Aboriginal population of the area. But all of that was about to change.

Photograph 3
Portrait of Prudence Reed
Probably taken in 1862 when she was 16 years old.
Source: Noreen Watts

CHAPTER TEN

Life on the frontier

By 1862 the Reeds had decided to join the inexorable colonial expansion into western NSW so that they could obtain land on which to establish their own businesses. While they would have had a general awareness of the adverse impact on the aboriginal population that colonial expansion was having, they were nevertheless, like most of the newcomers, focussed on their own daily lives and prospects. Accordingly, it was easy to leave curly ethical questions to others while confining any discussions with their adult children to practical matters associated with implementing their plans.

The ink was still drying on the Bourke Town Plan completed by the Surveyor-General in February 1862, so there were opportunities available there that could not be found elsewhere. To early arrivals would go the chance to obtain a site that was very well-positioned to attract future custom. Boarding houses and hotels in Bourke could theoretically be more lucrative than those in older towns because they would serve a much larger district due to the town's isolation. It was imperative, therefore, to arrive at the site of the town as soon as possible so that they would have the time to consider the available town allotments and decide their buying strategy prior to the earliest land sales.

There was much to be planned and organised before James and Frances could take their family to Bourke. They would need to sell most of their belongings, downsizing to whatever could be hauled 800 kilometres on a couple of bullock wagons. They also needed to obtain a horse and cart, essential in setting up and operating any new business.

In the last few months prior to their departure, James and Frances moved from their residence at 171 Clarence Street to temporary accommodation at 37 Cambridge Street in the central Sydney suburb of The Rocks.[243] Their son John lived next door at number 39 with his wife and children. No doubt all the adult members of the Reed family were working as hard as they could to save the money that would be needed to set the family up in the boarding house or hotel business soon.

Sarah Ann Reed was now 18 years old and contemplating marriage to Michael James Brennan, son of William Brennan of the 50th Regiment, who lived less than 100 metres away at 110 Princes Street.[244] Her older sister Eliza Emily was 21 and married to Andrew Bufe, but he had probably disappeared by this time. Their younger sister Prudence was 16 and Frances was 14.

The Reed family journeyed to Bourke in two separate groups, with the first arriving in the district by November 1862 while the second did not arrive until about two years later. For many reasons it made sense to separate into two groups. It was wise not to put all their eggs into the Bourke basket until after they had obtained a complete understanding of what this new life would entail. By arriving earlier, the first group would be able to learn about their intended new home and to gauge whether the venture was indeed practical before the second group committed to the arduous journey. If James and Frances had struck unforeseen obstacles they could have warned the others not to make the journey. On the other hand, if their reconnaissance proved that the plan was practicable, the advance party could then spend the next few months purchasing land and making a host of other arrangements before the remainder of the family arrived.

It is clear that the first group included James, Frances and their daughters Prudence and Frances while it is highly likely that George Charles, Mary Ann and Jane were incorporated in this advance party. Jimmy and his wife were living at Wellington, about halfway between Sydney and Bourke, so they were well placed to provide the weary travellers with some hospitality and a brief respite from the road, but they chose to remain behind in Wellington for another two years before travelling to Bourke in 1864 with the second group of Reed family members.

There were several different routes that James and Frances could have chosen for their journey to Bourke. The easiest of these would have been to travel south and west by sea from Sydney to Adelaide and then to proceed northwards up the Murray and Darling Rivers by paddle steamer (the first of which had reached the Bourke district three years earlier). But this route carried the very significant risk that the Darling would be un-navigable due to a low water level. In fact, during 1862 the Darling was perfectly dry in places, so this route would not have been feasible at that time.

Alternatively, the Reeds could have sailed north from Sydney to Maitland before continuing north-west with an overland journey along the Hunter Valley through Muswellbrook, then onwards through Gilgandra and Coonamble, before approaching Bourke from the East. The overland part of this trip would have been about 740 kilometres, at least 50 kilometres less than their actual route (and it would have involved much less climbing and descending). But it would not have passed through Wellington, thus robbing James and Frances of the chance to reunite with their son Jimmy and to meet their grandchildren John and Eliza.

So, the Reeds chose an all-overland route that took them westwards on a very difficult climb and descent through the Blue Mountains before heading north-west to Lithgow and on to Mudgee. From there they headed west to join their son Jimmy and his family at Wellington, where they would have rested for a few days (see Map 4).

During the journey, the family would have had all their remaining goods and chattels piled high on a dray or wagon that was pulled by a team of bullocks. (It is probable that the bullock dray was driven by one of their sons, most likely Alexander who was now 25 years old.)

Sixteen-year-old Prudence Reed posed for a studio photograph at some point on the journey (see Photograph 3). Fellow Reed descendant Wendy Mayes provided a copy of the picture in 2010, having obtained it *"from another distant cousin on the Whye side who lives in Dubbo"*. She noted that *"on the bottom of the photo it says*

J.T. Gorus SYDNEY (perhaps the person who took the photo)".
Subsequently Noreen Watts (who descends from
Prudence through her son George Charles Reed Murphy)
provided a much better copy. Prudence wears her best
clothes - a dark dress with a ruffle at the neck beneath a
choker that supports two beads that match the earrings
dangling from pierced earlobes. She has very long
flowing hair and the confidence to pull off a fashionable
and flamboyant tall bowler hat, too small to provide any
practical shade, and featuring an unusual white pom-
pom thingy on the very top.

Jan Tangelder Gorus ran a photography studio at
101 King St Sydney from February 1863[245]. He was later
Mayor of St Peters and was to photograph Prince Albert
in 1881. He is known to have worked as a photographer
at Sofala and other places on the NSW goldfields from
about 1854. Since Prudence Reed had reached Bourke
before he opened his studio in Sydney, she must have
posed for him somewhere on the Reed family's trek
towards Wellington; perhaps at Mudgee.

Gorus may also have taken the picture of James
Reed at the same time (see Photograph 4). If so, it is a 53-
year old James who gazes fixedly at the camera, having
no doubt been instructed not to move! He too is sporting
his Sunday best, a grey suit with waistcoat and bow tie.
He wears his hair long enough to amply cover both ears
although he needs a comb-over on the top. A thin grey
beard is confined to below the mouth only.

They would have reached Wellington about three
months after departing Sydney. After a brief rest, the
journey continued, once again heading north-west. From
here the going was easier, without too many significant
climbs or descents as they moved inexorably

downstream, initially following the Macquarie River via Ponto and Dubbo to Warren. Since the Macquarie then veers more to the north, the next phase followed the Gunningbar creek before moving on to the nearby Duck Creek. They would have stayed overnight on the squattage property of Mr John Brown at Canonba before continuing along Duck Creek to its junction with the Bogan River. From there the route followed the Bogan north-west towards Gongolgon and Bourke - see Map 4.

The drought of 1862 meant that conditions for the journey were good. The creeks would have been dry and even the Darling River was dry in places. James and Frances had arrived in the Bourke district by 27 November because on that day Frances assisted Mary Wright and her husband William during the birth of their son William.

While the original record[246] names William's birthplace as "*Gralger No. 17* Station on the Bogan", there are no other surviving references to this place. It is very likely that this should read "*Cowga* Station", which comprised blocks numbered 16 and 17 on the East Bogan. Perhaps the scribe misheard the name of the station. According to a list of early Bourke District births published on page 30, volume 7 of the History of Bourke journal, William Wright was the ninth child of European origin born in the Bourke District. The first had been born at *Fort Bourke* station two years earlier.

It is possible that the Wright family had accompanied the Reed family on the journey from Wellington. William Wright senior had been born near Bathurst in about 1837 and his wife Mary Sloey had been born at Wellington in about 1843.[247] William may have been the father of Mary's daughter Sarah[248] who was born in the year before their marriage at Orange on 6 September 1859.[249] When the young couple moved to the Gongolgon district they brought Sarah and her younger brother, John Thomas Wright, who had been born at Orange in September 1860.[250] So, while they may have accompanied the Reeds on the journey, it is also possible that they had arrived a year or two earlier.

William and Mary Wright were to live in the Gongolgon district for the rest of their lives, producing a total of twelve children. William was soon to witness the marriage of Prudence Reed and Joseph Whye and was later the undertaker for Joseph's burial. He was a stockman who, by 1878, was managing *Nidgerie* Station,[251] a post that he still filled fifteen years later[252] when he was buried in Byrock cemetery on 6 April 1893.[253] Mary was to survive her husband by seventeen years before she died from abdominal cancer and was buried at Brewarrina on 7 November 1910.[254]

Their son, William Wright, who Frances Reed assisted into the world in November 1862, lived out his life in the western districts, working as a bullocky and as a coach driver. He and his brother Robert were based in Brewarrina when they drove the Cobb and Co runs between that town and Bourke and Byrock in the early years of the twentieth century.[255] William died from heart failure on his 50th birthday following a one-punch attack at Wilcannia by Henry Nolan, who was later charged with manslaughter.[256]

When James and Frances arrived in Bourke in late 1862 they may have started to doubt their sanity in coming so far, because the town was virtually non-existent. The Fort Bourke correspondent of the *Empire* newspaper of Sydney reported in March 1863 that

Nine months ago there were two bark huts in the place and a store in the course of erection.[257]

But, over the course of those nine months the store was finished, two hotels were erected, a house was built for the police magistrate and there were *"one or two other small places in the course of erection"*.

So, despite a paucity of stock in 1858, the fledgling town at Bourke was about to bloom. While there had been just two bark huts and a half-built store in mid-1861, just two years later the town had a large goods warehouse, a police force, a post office and two pubs that had done a thriving business at the end of the 1862-63 shearing season. In June 1862 a Bourke court had tried a case of highway robbery.[258]

Edward Readford recorded in his reminiscences, written in 1903, that he had stayed in William Sly's *Bourke* hotel for two days in 1863.

The only buildings then erected in that town were Sly's hotel (not long opened), police magistrate's residence and police quarters. The late J. E. Kelly at the time was camped in a tent, preparing to build what was afterwards the second hostelry in Bourke. Becker and Co. were carrying on a store in a large tent, and making preparations to commence erecting the first general stores in that town.[259]

Becker and Co is a reference to Joseph Becker who had come to Bourke as manager for Alexander Ross and Co for whom he built the first warehouse and store in the town. A German whose real surname was Baedecker, he was a quintessential entrepreneur who had a finger in every pie. A glance at the earliest town plan reveals his name on many of the choicest blocks of land and he financed the establishment of many of the earliest businesses. While the hotelkeeper and later grazier, William Sly, has been referred to as the "Founder of Bourke" and Edward Bloxham (the first Mayor) as the "Father of Bourke", businessman Becker became known as the "King of Bourke".

So, on arrival the Reeds would have found a village of tents with only one or two completed buildings. Nevertheless, they had probably arrived too late for the first sale of town land, which took place on 23 and 24 September 1862 and where 33 town lots were sold. They would now have to continue camping in the open for a few more months, just as they had been doing during their journey from Sydney.

Soon after their arrival, the Reed family would have learnt that the Bourke environment was extreme. While they had no doubt become used to the heat of an Australian summer while living in Sydney, nothing could have prepared them for Bourke heat. In her story *Of Henrietta, Marooned*, Bethia Foott wrote

> *There were days when the temperature soared to 115 degrees in the shade; when hot winds seared their way through the tent by night, and when the scorching sun by day made the sand under their feet feel like red-hot ashes.*[260]

The environment brought with it other challenges too, from burnt skin to dehydration. For example, glare from the huge sky with its wide horizons when coupled with long Summer days often caused eye problems such as ophthalmia, the symptoms including congestion of the eyeball, watery eyes, redness, swelling, itching, burning and a general feeling of irritation under the eyelids.

We were all for weeks feeling our way like blind people, and were unable to sleep for pain at night. The only relief for this distressing complaint ... is an eye-water composed of a small quantity of sugar of lead and a few drops of laudanum.[261]

In addition to the extremes of climate, there were other challenges for these early settlers. Food staples and other necessary goods were always very expensive and in short supply. The conditions in the town at that time were summarised by the *Empire* correspondent.

A considerable amount, I will not say of suffering, but inconvenience, has been experienced for the last few months, from the want of rations, such as flour, sugar, tea, and tobacco, &c. This is attributable partly to the difficulty of travelling the latter part of last year, arising from the drought, and partly the non-arrival of the steamers up the Darling.

In some situations, these staples ran out completely and people had to make whatever arrangements they could. In March 1862 the *Empire* newspaper had published *The Modern Crusoe*, a doggerel poem that was reputedly "written by an ex MP during his solitary abode at Fort Bourke".[262]

The blackfellows laugh at my sway,
    And of whites there are none to dispute
I have puffed all my 'bacca away,
    And have dined off a starved bandicoot.
I long for a nicely cooked dish -
    That 'possum was shocking to me -
I am scaly with living on fish,
    And damper I seldom now see.

I am out of both sugar and tay,
  And my flour is fast failing me too;
I fear that at no distant day,
  I shall have to depend on nardoo[1];
When I think of my own Wollongong,
  In a moment I seem to be there,
But alas! Recollection, too strong,
  Soon hurries me back to despair.

The extreme conditions led to many stockmen giving up and leaving, thus abandoning their employers' sheep and cattle to fend for themselves. This became such a problem for the large grazing companies that they had their former employees arrested and charged with abandoning their contracted posts. In October 1862 the Fort Bourke correspondent for the *Bathurst Fee Press and Mining Journal* reported that

There have been several cases recently before the Police Court under the Master and Servants Act - this week no less than four. This would seem to be the staple of our police business just now. And it was high time that something should be done, for our flock-owners are at the mercy of their men. Instances are numerous of flocks being left unprotected and abandoned without notice; shepherds sometimes telling their owners, in not very choice terms to go to a certain place - them and their sheep; presuming on the circumstance that redress was not to be obtained. Now, however, we have got a court at hand, it is to be hoped that a change for the better will take place.[263]

---

[1] Nardoo is a traditional Aboriginal food made from the spores of the nardoo fern.

The writer's hopes were dashed as further cases were still being brought before the court a couple of months later.

The Police business of this month has consisted wholly of cases under the Master and Servant Act. There are several cases pending. Two of the Bogan River Company's men were sentenced to fourteen days hard labour, which labour has been expended in stumping and clearing a part of the township reserve.[264]

By early 1863 James and Frances were working hard to establish their family at Bourke. Not only were they tackling the day-to-day problems of procuring a living and finding shelter, but they also needed to scout for suitable blocks of land to buy while also endeavouring to secure the materials that they would need to build a house and a business premises. But it was not only these practicalities that occupied their minds, because their daughters Prudence and Frances had both received and accepted proposals of marriage. In addition, as mentioned above, back in Sydney, **Sarah Ann Reed** was engaged to marry Michael Brennan.

Sarah Ann and her older brothers had not travelled to Bourke with their parents in 1862. She had remained behind because she did not want to leave her fiancé **Michael Brennan**. Presumably James and Frances had consented to her staying behind under the care of her married older brother John Benjamin.

Michael Brennan had a similar background to his new wife having been born in NSW about a year before her. His parents, William Brennan and his wife Ellen[265], had given him a Catholic baptism in 1843.[266] Given their surname and religion, it is likely that the Brennan family was Irish.

1863 was a big year for marriages in the Reed family. Sarah Ann married Michael Brennan in Sydney on 6 January;[267] her younger sister Prudence married Joseph Whye at Bourke on 28 April;[268] and Frances married James Tobin junior at Bourke on 25 November.[269]

At the time of their marriages, Sarah Ann was 18 years old, Prudence was not quite 17 and Frances was just 15, so it is surprising to our modern sensibilities that James and Frances had consented to their marriages at such tender ages. This is particularly the case when we consider that their daughter Eliza had married at just 18 and this marriage had failed (although James and Frances may not have known about that failure yet because Eliza was still 800 kilometres away in Sydney). While people generally married young in nineteenth century Australia, even in 1863 less than 10% of NSW brides were younger than 18 years old when married.[270] And yet the early-marriage pattern continued in the Reed family, with Mary Ann later marrying at 19 and Jane at 15. Their brothers, on the other hand, were 21 (Jimmy), 25 (John Benjamin), 27 (George Charles) and 40 (Alexander) on their wedding days.

The main reason for the large difference in the age at first marriage between the Reed sons and the Reed daughters was probably the nature of the frontier society that they lived in at Bourke. They had chosen to live in a place that had a huge disparity between the number of men and women, with very significant consequences for the atmosphere and mores of the local society. It was a very macho culture where men were men and women were, of necessity, extremely careful.

The balance between men and women was

somewhat lopsided in NSW generally at this time. There had been a huge preponderance of males over females in the convict arrivals prior to 1842. For example, between 1830 and 1842 more than 5 male convicts arrived for every female convict.[271] By 1851 there were nearly 70,000 men in NSW but only 45,000 women.[272] In the country districts, however, the imbalance was far more pronounced.

> *In the squatting districts of New South Wales, beyond the defined boundaries of settlement, there were 38 single males aged 14 and over for every single female of similar age at the time of the 1841 Census. By 1851, this ratio had fallen to 13.5 males per female.*[273]

The gold rushes exacerbated this imbalance, but by 1861 government policies to promote and assist the immigration of unmarried women had largely redressed the situation. Nevertheless, because the grazing industry in far western NSW employed mainly men, there was still an extreme disparity between the sexes at Bourke in its early days. This had the effect of reducing the inhibitions that would normally constrain the most extreme male behaviour in civilised society; many of them felt free to indulge the whim of the moment, particularly when they rolled into town after spending many months working on an isolated grazing property.

For example, when the *Gemini* paddle steamer arrived in Bourke for the first time in 1859, it brought stores that had been lacking for several months, including alcohol. The sudden availability of liquor led to a Bacchanalian grog-on that lasted for three days.

> *There were two hotels in Bourke at that time, one kept by a man called Sly and the other by John Kelly. Sly asked*

for an Axe. He knocked in a case of pannikins and a quarter cask of rum and said "Boys, help yourselves – this is my shout." Within an hour Bourke was a perfect pandemonium and the jubilation lasted three days.[274]

In this frontier society, women had to rely on the presence of a reliable police force to deter men from any extreme violence against them. Unfortunately, the local force had recently proved itself to be anything but reliable. Just a few months before the arrival of the Reed family, Sergeant George Bell of the Bourke police had been murdered by Constable Francis Elliott due to Bell's clandestine relationship with Elliott's wife. Elliott was found guilty of murder at the Bathurst Assizes in March 1862 and sentenced to death by Mr Justice Wise.[275]

James and Frances soon realised that the disproportion between the number of men and women in rural NSW was even more pronounced in Bourke, its furthest outpost. They had brought their family to a frontier town with all the resultant problems of lawlessness. In these circumstances they seem to have taken the pragmatic decision that the best way to protect their teenage daughters was to put rings on their fingers.

Life on the frontier

CHAPTER ELEVEN

Reunited

When the Reed family arrived, Bourke was a town in name only, consisting of one or two roughly finished buildings with nearly everyone living in tents or under tarpaulins. Household supplies were extremely expensive and everything about the place was rudimentary, including the food, sanitation and interpersonal relationships. The Reeds entered this new phase of their life with nothing but their life experience, some meagre savings and a spirited family resourcefulness.

The first of Bourke's buildings to be completed was **William Sly's** *Bourke* hotel, closely followed by **John Kelly's** *Fort Bourke* hotel (later called the *Old Fort*). Both were issued with their first trading licenses on 21 April 1863.[276]

Like other early Bourke buildings, they were constructed from slabs of split timber topped by a roof of bark, a style known as a slab hut. The builders felled selected trees, sawed the trunks into suitable lengths that were then split into flitches using a maul and wedge. Rafters were fixed above the walls and a pitched roof was covered with bark that had been stripped from living trees in sheets between two and four feet wide and about six feet long (a roofing technique learned from the Aboriginals). The sheets of bark were tied onto the rafters with cords or wire while the framing of the roof was secured by wooden pins. In Australia's harsher conditions, buildings constructed this way lasted much longer than the English system of wattle and daub.

In the absence of a ready supply of affordable bricks, the chimney was also built from wood using chunky green shingles, then lined internally with a thick layer of fireproof clay. Chimneys butted up to the end walls so that they could be quickly knocked away to save the main building in the unlikely event of a chimney fire.

Sly's hotel can be seen in the earliest known Bourke photograph (Photograph 5). It is on the far right of the picture, an L-shaped slab-hut building behind the newer Tattersall's hotel (constructed in 1868 of brick with a corrugated iron roof).

The Reed's first few months in Bourke were a whirlwind as the family sought to establish themselves in this isolated frontier community. Not only were they busy with the practicalities of finding food, shelter and employment but two more of their daughters were about to be married.

While it seems likely that Sarah Ann had been engaged to Michael Brennan before her parents left Sydney almost two years earlier, the engagement of sixteen-year-old **Prudence Reed** was much shorter. Exactly a week after the first two pubs in the Bourke district were licensed, she married Joseph Whye[277] in just the second marriage celebrated at Bourke.[278] He was recorded as a 26-year-old stockman on *Nidgerie number 15* station while she was a 17-year-old servant on *Gongolgon number 17* station, having put her age up by a couple of months. The marriage was witnessed by Margaret Tobin and William Wright (father of the child whose birth Frances Reed had assisted at five months earlier).

Joseph Whye had been born at Waterbeach in Cambridgeshire (England) in 1836, the sixth child of **William Whye** and his wife **Hannah Headland**. His parents had married there on 2 October 1821.[279]

The spelling of both the Whye and Headland surnames is inconsistent across the various historical documents where they are recorded. A cleric in the parish of Waterbeach had recorded the marriage of Joseph's parents as Wey and Headley, but on the same page of the register he recorded the marriage of Elizabeth Why to Thomas Darling. The Bourke marriage register spells the maiden name of Joseph Whye's mother as Hedlin.

On the English census of 1841, Joseph was recorded as a five year old living with his parents William (an agricultural labourer) and Hannah Whye at Church End in the parish of Waterbeach. He had six siblings: Johannah aged 18, William 17, Elizabeth 11, James 8 and Frederick 1[280]. He also had a 14-year-old sister Jane who, on the night of the census, was living with her uncle Joseph Headland and his wife Sarah 15 kilometres away in Cambridge Road at Trumpington, Cambridgeshire.[281] Joseph Headland was a 40-year-old gardener.

Ten years later the census recorded Joseph as a 14-year-old labourer who was still living with his parents at the same address. Also residing there were his siblings

Elizabeth aged 19, James 17 (labourer), Frederick 11, George 8, and David 5. His 24-year-old sister Jane was now employed as a house servant in the nearby Waterbeach household of John Stacey Youngman (a merchant and miller) who had a wife and four children.[282] Also in this household was an 18-year-old apprentice miller named George Haylock.

A year later an unmarried Jane Whye gave birth to George Haylock's son, Alfred Haylock Whye. When this young nephew was three years old, Joseph Whye emigrated to Australia but, as we shall see below, they would be reunited twenty years later.

Joseph arrived in Sydney on 18 October 1855[283] aboard the sailing ship *Gilmore*. She was a 31 year old ship of 500 tons that had been built in India and about a third of her crew were Chinese. The ship carried "mostly English agriculturalists", including Joseph. She had previously brought settlers to Australia in 1829 and convicts in 1832, 1839 and 1843.[284] During the slow passage of 127 days the passengers were terrified on 31 August when a heavy sea suddenly broke over the ship causing severe damage. The lifeboat and cutter were "smashed to atoms", the front of the poop driven in, the berths in the hospital knocked to pieces and the port rail and bulwarks carried away. Some immigrants were severely cut and bruised, but no-one died.[285] The passenger manifest recorded that Joseph's parents "William and Anna" were still living in Waterbeach; that he had no relatives in NSW; and that he could both read and write.

He would not had had any trouble finding employment because experienced agricultural workers had been in high demand ever since the gold rush.

Evidently he was soon working for a squatter who had land on the Bogan, but there are no specific records of him during the period between his arrival in 1855 and his marriage in 1863, by which time he was working on *Nidgerie* station. This station, on the western side of the Bogan just above Gongolgon, was owned by John Patrick O'Sullivan who had stocked it from about 1860 and who also owned *Cowga* station on the other side of the river.

Life on these stations would have been very hard, repetitive and boring, with nothing to occupy a stockman other than work and alcohol. A traveller named Thomas Luke passed this way in 1866 and was forced by floodwaters to linger at *Nidgerie* for a week. He commented that there were no candles or kerosene for lighting at night. On his return journey a few months later, he stayed just an hour because both the cook and the manager were "in a terrible state of intoxication". He found it to be a "badly conducted station".[286] In 1874 another traveller recorded a similar impression of *Nidgerie* as he

> entered the miserable hut and rested on an adze-planed sofa for half an hour. Finding this state of things unprofitable I "explored" for provisions, but could not find any.[287]

Nevertheless, it seems that Joseph Whye saved his money rather than drinking it during the years he spent working on grazing properties. Like other stockmen, he would have received much of his wages in the form of a percentage of the increase in the herd that he was working with. Over the years this would have expanded into a valuable asset, hence his occupation description as "stockowner". This does not imply that he owned the land that the stock was on. Instead of aspiring to become a grazier, he had an entrepreneurial spirit and was planning to establish a hotel at Gongolgon.

The first child of Joseph and Prudence Whye was born in 1864 and baptised as **Frances Anna Whye** in honour of her grandmothers, Hannah Headland and Frances Reed.[288] During the following year a brother was born and named William for his paternal grandfather, William Whye.[289] Unfortunately, little **William Whye** died at *Nidgerie* Station on 9 July 1865.[290]

Seven months after Prudence's marriage, her fifteen-year-old sister **Frances Reed** married **James Tobin junior** at Bourke on 25 November 1863.[291] The marriage record shows that, like Prudence, she was a servant at Gongolgon, had raised her age by a year and the marriage was witnessed by Margaret Tobin (her new sister-in-law). Frances' husband James was recorded as a stockowner of Marra Creek who had been born at Hunter's River twenty two years earlier to stockowner James Tobin senior and his wife Catherine Maloney.[292]

James Tobin junior had been working for his father, a grazier at Marra Creek (upstream of Gongolgon). Unfortunately, just a month before the marriage, James Tobin senior had been declared bankrupt with liabilities of 600 pounds and assets of just 517 pounds.[293] Hence his occupation was recorded as a "stockowner" rather than a grazier.

James Tobin junior had been born at Wybong (near Muswellbrook NSW) in 1842, two years after his parents' marriage at nearby Whittingham.[294] Since his father was a convict, he had required permission to marry, which was granted by the Reverend Irving Hetherington of Patrick's Plains.[295]

James Tobin senior had arrived in Sydney in 1830 aboard the convict ship *Dunvegan Castle*[296]. The indents state that he was then only sixteen years old and describe him as 4 feet 9 inches tall with brown hair, hazel eyes and a ruddy complexion. He must have served a significant portion of his sentence on a prison hulk because he didn't arrive in Australia until three years after his trial.

He had been convicted on 5 April 1827 at London's Old Bailey court of stealing a handkerchief from barrister Philip Tattersall who gave sworn evidence and was supported by eyewitness Thomas Peregrine Turner. The court records estimated that James was just twelve years old on the day of his conviction. Nowadays the law deems that such a young boy cannot be tried in an adult court but in 1827 James was sentenced to be transported for life[297] for the unspeakable crime of stealing a barrister's handkerchief!

Some researchers have concluded that he was the James Tobin who had been admitted to Castle Street Workhouse at Westminster in London just two months before the court case at the Old Bailey, but that boy was said to be just 8 years old.[298] Furthermore, he was admitted to the workhouse as one member of a family of six headed by Richard Tobin, but James' 1901 death certificate states that his father's name was William.[299] For these reasons, the workhouse inmate was almost certainly another boy with the same name.

On arrival in 1830 he was assigned to Archibald Bell junior whose father had discovered Bell's line of road across the Blue Mountains seven years earlier. For this discovery he had been granted 1000 acres of land near Singleton that he called *Corinda,* which is where his son sent James Tobin.[300]

James' wife, Catherine Maloney, had arrived in Australia on 7 February 1836 as a free emigrant from Ireland aboard the *James Pattison*. A year after their marriage, their first child Amelia was born at Wybong,[301] followed by James Junior in 1842,[302] Margaret Mary 1844,[303] William Patrick 1846,[304] Ambrose Bede 1848[305] and twins Edward[306] and Henry[307] in 1852.

James Tobin senior was granted a conditional pardon on 2 March 1846, after serving 19 years of his life sentence.[308] According to his obituary, he had brought his family to the western district in 1854. That would mean that the Tobin family was one of the very first to move down the Bogan.[309] Fifteen years later in 1869 his wife Catherine died at just 54 years old,[310] but James senior survived her by 32 years. At the age of 80 he was admitted to hospital on the recommendation of the Police Magistrate at Bourke, suffering from senile debility and hernia.[311] He died at Bourke eight years later on 28 August 1901.[312] His obituary reported as follows.

On Monday last Mr James Tobin Snr, of North Bourke, died in the Bourke Hospital, at the great age of 88 years. Mr Tobin was one of the pioneers of the western district, first coming to it about the year 1854. Twenty-six years later he disposed of his property on the Marra and came to North Bourke to reside. ... We understand that two of [his] sons reside in another State, while Mr James Tobin and Mr WP Tobin live in Bourke and North Bourke respectively. Mrs D Sullivan, of Wellington, and Mrs F Clarke of Marra Creek, are the daughters. ... the coffin was taken to the Union Hotel and the funeral, which was very largely attended, took place next day, Father Killian officiating at the cemetery.[313]

Within a year of their marriage, James Tobin junior and his new wife Frances produced a daughter whose birth was registered at Dubbo in late November 1864.[314] Even though there is no known direct evidence of her death or burial, it is likely that she died soon afterwards because she was not given a name at birth and there are no subsequent records of her. Frances Tobin was just 16 years old and her youth may have caused complications with the pregnancy or birth. This could explain why the child was born at Dubbo rather than at Gongolgon or Bourke. It is notable that James and Frances Tobin did not produce any more natural children, which could indicate that complications with this pregnancy had long term implications for Frances' fertility, although family lore attributes the fault to James Tobin having been gored by a bull soon after their marriage.[315] As we will see in chapter 17, fourteen years later they would adopt Eliza Emily Tobin Maxwell, the fifth child of Frances' sister Jane Reed and her future husband Joseph Maxwell.

Bourke was, in its very earliest years, generally referred to as Fort Bourke due to its proximity to the stockade that had been built by the explorer Sir Thomas Mitchell in 1835. The so-called fort was no longer there, having been destroyed by fire before 1845, but its name had been memorialised in the name of a later grazing property, *Fort Bourke* Station. Since some of the town's earliest infrastructure and founders were associated with that station, the name was colloquially appropriated for the town as well and stuck for a few years.

Eventually the Bourke correspondent of the *Empire* newspaper expressed his exasperation at the town being consistently referred to in that newspaper by the wrong name: Fort Bourke.

I am quite at a loss to discover the reason of your persisting in calling this place Fort Bourke, although I uniformly call it Bourke. I must tell you the original Fort Bourke is on a station six miles below this, besides which, the Government have named this town Bourke; therefore, the sooner you drop the word "Fort", the better.[316]

He was quite right. The official gazetted name of the town was simply Bourke; and it had been named not for the Fort but in honour of the former Governor, Sir Richard Bourke. This column seems to have had the desired effect and the town was subsequently given the correct moniker.

By the end of 1863, James and Frances had finished their reconnaissance of the opportunities that the fledgling town had to offer and were ready to make a commitment. To a large extent, the marriages of their daughters Prudence and Frances had rendered the decision inevitable. During the next year they bought four out of the five allotments of land along the southern side of Darling Street between Glen and Wilson Streets. The other allotment (later subdivided into housing blocks numbered 19 and 21 Darling Street) was purchased by John Kelly, publican of the *Fort Bourke* hotel. A decade later this fifth allotment would be acquired by their son George Charles Reed, so that the Reed family eventually owned the whole block of five allotments. One of these would remain in family hands for sixty years and another three for forty years.

The first allotment was purchased for nine pounds in Frances' name at the town auction on 18 December 1863.[317] It was on the north-eastern corner of Darling and Glen Streets and comprised 2 roods of land that was later subdivided into housing blocks numbered 15 and 17

Darling Street. It is very likely that James and Frances quickly built one or more houses on this allotment and lived there with their younger children for at least the next six years.

But no-one in the Reed family had previously built a house, so James would have needed an experienced person to plan and oversee construction. The best available person was the "Founder of Bourke" himself, William Sly. He had recently finished erecting his hotel, had previously constructed buildings on *Toorale* Station and owned the local sawmill.

There is some circumstantial evidence that Sly may indeed have been involved in building the Reed's house because, on 6 January 1864, a month after buying her land, Frances Reed was joined by him in witnessing the marriage of Charles May and Mahalath Witmarsh.[318] May, a sawyer, was probably one of Sly's employees and may have been working on the construction of the Reed's house.

The Reeds had now been living in Bourke for a year and were, no doubt, keen to get a roof other than canvas over their heads before the winter of 1864. They had clearly decided to prioritise this over any preconceived plans to establish a boarding house or hotel.

All their plans were interrupted by nature as Bourke experienced a large flood in early 1864. Huge quantities of water flowed down the rivers and flood plains from Queensland and north-eastern NSW towards the fledgling town.

The early explorers had noticed that the river often flooded because the lowlands were covered in grey silty soil while the higher land had sandy red soil. It is surprising, then, that the NSW government surveyors foolishly chose a flood-prone spot for the town when there was a higher red hill right on the river only a few kilometres away. The *Empire* newspaper described the location in the following terms:

> *Township at Fort Bourke ... The locale of this township is about six miles above the original Fort Bourke of the late Sir Thomas Mitchell, called by the natives Mortumertie; or the Eighteen-mile Point by the settlers.*[319]

The correspondent may have got the spelling of the Aboriginal name wrong, as this name was memorialised in naming Wortumertie Street in Bourke. While the surveyors should have laid out the town on the higher red land where the bridge was later built, politics got in the way. That higher land had already been claimed by a settler so, rather than waiting for his lease to expire or, better still, re-possessing the land, the surveyors simply plonked the town on one of the few pieces of unclaimed riverfront land.

The townspeople of 1864 were the first to pay the price for this short-sighted decision as the Darling rose rapidly, sometimes by a metre in a day. By the middle of March floodwater entered the town and remained for seven weeks.

> *The whole of the inhabitants of Bourke ... including villagers and travellers (about 130) with the exception of one or two families, are all located in the two inns, which are, and have been since the commencement of the floods, kept habitable by a wall or dam thrown up all around each of the premises, and which was made by degrees as the floods rose, by using the earth inside the walls - the water being three feet deep outside. Messrs Ross and*

Co.'s stores were defended in the same way from the water but unluckily their embankment gave way, and the store has three feet of water in it; but fortunately the precaution was taken to remove all perishable goods to places of safety before the water broke in, and but little damage will be sustained. All other houses and places of habitation have more or less water in them. The court house (a temporary one, which was built of mud) is a perfect wreck - the walls having given way and the roof fallen.[320]

It is very unlikely that James and Frances had quite finished building their house in Darling Street but the building site would have been inundated. They and their younger children would have been included amongst the 130 townsfolk forced to seek refuge behind the temporary levees around the two hotels. Even after the water receded, they would have remained behind the levee while the ground outside dried out.

Unlike many Bourke floods, the 1864 floodwaters remained high for an extended period because it was a long wet season across a wide area of the river catchment. The water reached a peak on 28 March but had not fallen much before the town endured a ferocious storm.

On Saturday night about 8 o'clock, we were visited by a terrific thunderstorm, accompanied with heavy rain and a gale of wind from the south. The effect of this wind upon the water was such that you might fancy yourself on salt water in some cove in a gale of wind instead of a plain 600 miles from Neptune's abode. I will not say the rollers were mountains high, but they were high enough to wash over the dams, and it needed the utmost exertions of some twenty men to keep the water out.[321]

While James, Frances and the younger children were flood bound in Bourke, their married daughters Prudence Whye and Frances Tobin were upstream at Gongolgon. Meanwhile, the other half of the family had left Sydney and was making slow progress towards them.

Michael and **Sarah Brennan** had a very difficult journey to Bourke. Her obituary later reported that:

> She came westward at the age of 20 with her husband and brothers in a bullock wagon. From Wellington to Bourke the means of travel was in a bullock spring dray and from the time the party left Sydney until their arrival in Bourke was just on six months. It was a strenuous trek and before reaching town the whole of the country westward from Mount Oxley was a sea of water, indicating a big flood on the river at that period.[322]

The reference to "brothers" (plural) suggests that her party included **Alexander Reed, Jimmy Reed**, his wife Eliza (Bend) and their three children (John, Eliza and James). Presumably Sarah Ann's sister **Eliza Bufe** was also a part of this second group because she was to re-marry in Bourke a year later.

John Benjamin Reed, his wife and daughter must have remained behind at Ponto for several months. Presumably he had been previously operating his bullock wagon carrying business in that general area because there were four unclaimed letters addressed to him at Forbes NSW (140 kilometres away) in June 1863.[324] According to a newspaper report, they were still living at Ponto in October 1865,[325] although they were to later join the family at Bourke. Nevertheless, their son **William John Reed** accompanied his aunts and uncles to Bourke.

The demands of the trip would have been exacerbated for Sarah Ann because she was in an advanced state of pregnancy. Her first child was baptised **Sarah E Brennan** at Ponto (near Wellington) on 24 July.[323] Presumably those who had travelled from Sydney were able to linger here for a few days while her brother Jimmy packed up all his family's belongings before they joined the travelling party for the second leg of the journey to Bourke.

Bourke's enduring flood slowed their progress.[326]

Lower Macquarie District. - The long continuance of rain in the hill country at the head of the Macquarie has of course caused a succession of freshes in that stream, which, breaking over the banks low down, has flooded the country from Duck Creek to a point far away down the Bogan. Creeks, swamps, and lagoons are full to overflowing; and many places, submerged only in excessively wet seasons such as this, are covered with water. Some carriers, just returned from the Darling, report the track to be most difficult to travel, as the ground has been so thoroughly soaked that it is quite rotten, and sometimes long reaches of water must be gone through. Loaded teams have to keep wide from the river to head the flood, so that they may obtain ground solid enough for travelling purposes. The unsettled state of the weather in the range districts sends down flood after flood; one is hardly by before another "banker" comes down on its heels, causing much delay and inconvenience to travellers. A large quantity of this water, finding an outlet through the banks of the lower rivers, stretches away for miles back, and, owing to regular additions from fresh floods, the country has no chance to clear itself. It will probably be some months before the Bogan and Darling districts resume their ordinary appearance. On this side of Fort Bourke, even where the water has drained off, all kinds of bush work are suspended, it being impossible to obtain timber, because trees that are felled on the river banks bury themselves in the soft earth by the mere force of their fall.[327]

So, the Brennan and Reed families with their sister Eliza Bufe would have had a difficult time coming down the Macquarie, Duck Creek and the Bogan and would have been stopped completely at Gongolgon to wait until the final approaches to Bourke had dried out. This delay would have given the newcomers a wonderful opportunity to reunite with their married sisters Prudence and Frances and to meet their brothers-in-law Joseph Whye and James Tobin junior.

Within a year, **Eliza Emily Bufe** nee Reed, now aged 24, had also found a new husband. Like his new wife, **Henry Johnson** had been born in NSW, although both of his parents, William Johnson and Bridget Caton (or Keating) had been convicts.

Henry's father, **William Johnson,** had been arrested at Nottingham in March 1818 and charged with stealing from George Adcock two deal boxes, three brushes, a pair of stockings and other articles. He was tried at the Nottingham Assizes on 13 March, aged 20, where he pleaded guilty and was sentenced to seven years transportation. Two weeks later he was put aboard the *Justicia* Hulk at Woolwich to await a ship that would transport him to NSW. The prison records indicate that he had previously used two aliases: Goodman and Hutton. After five months aboard the hulk, he was transferred aboard the convict ship *Lord Sidmouth* which departed on 27 September. William arrived in Sydney on 11 March 1819, a year after his arrest.[328]

Upon disembarkation he was sent to Parramatta to work as a labourer and was soon assigned to William Lawson, an explorer and pastoralist who had (six years earlier) been one of the three men who found a way across the Blue Mountains.[329] Lawson owned a 500 acre property at Prospect on which he had built a fine 40 room mansion in early colonial style. William Johnson may have proved unsatisfactory because Lawson listed him as "turned in" (or returned to the government) in 1820.[330] However, William was a shoemaker and his skills would have been in high demand, so he may have been recalled by the government to make best use of those skills.

Very soon after arriving at Prospect, William met fellow-convict **Bridget Caton (or Keating)** who had been assigned to Lawson 18 months earlier. They clearly began a de facto relationship almost immediately because Lawson recorded in 1820 that Bridget was married.

She had arrived in NSW three years before as a 20-year-old convict who had been tried at Kilkenny, Ireland in August 1816 and sentenced to seven years transportation. She was included amongst 89 female convicts placed on board the *Canada* on 21 March 1817, arriving in Sydney on 5 August.[331] More than half of the prisoners on the *Canada* were forwarded to Hobart aboard the *Pilot*, but Bridget was sent to the Female Factory at Parramatta, from where she was assigned to William Lawson.[332]

Bridget Caton/Keating and William Johnson were given permission to marry on 7 February 1820 by the Reverend Samuel Marsden[333] and were married three weeks later by George Middleton at St John's church,

Parramatta. The marriage witnesses were **James Stinson** and Mary Martin.[334] A year earlier, Stinson had been given permission by the Reverend Samuel Marsden to marry **Magaret Cayton** (an alias of 17-year-old **Sarah Keating** who had also arrived aboard the *Canada*).[335] Since Margaret/Sarah Cayton/Keating had (like Bridget Caton/Keating) been tried at Kilkenny, they were almost certainly closely related, possibly sisters.

Later that year William and Bridget had their first child, who was baptised as Sarah Johnson. Another daughter, Mary, was born two years later, followed by sons William in 1824 and James in 1826.

William's sentence expired in 1825 and he was therefore issued with his Certificate of Freedom on 17 March. It indicates that he had been born at the Isle of Ely (near Cambridge).[336] When the NSW census was taken in 1828, the family was living in Cambridge Street Sydney where William was working as a shoemaker.[337]

Thirteen years later, when the 1841 census was recorded, the family had moved to Richmond NSW. Unfortunately, only the statistical summary has survived, but it reveals that the household consisted of a married couple, each aged between 21 and 45, with five boys. One child was over 14 years old, 3 were aged between 7 and 14 and one was less than 7[338]. The oldest boy would have been James (born 1826) and the youngest was probably Henry (who was born about 1838 according to his death record).[339]

Henry would have been about 16 years old and was probably already employed when his father died at Richmond on 23 July 1854 aged 56.[340] In later years Henry's occupation was recorded as a stockman,[341] so he may (although this is far from certain) be the Henry

Johnson who was charged with drunkenness at Bathurst on 7 January 1858[342] and again on 23 June 1858.[343]

Henry Johnson and Eliza Bufe nee Reed were married at Bourke on 12 September 1865, about a year after Eliza had arrived in the district[344] . Clearly she had obtained evidence that her former husband, Anders Bufe, was now dead; or a court order to that effect. Over the next five years she and her new husband Henry produced four children, all born at Bourke: **Frances Eliza Johnson** in 1866,[345] **James Henry Johnson** in 1868,[346] **Alexander George Oxley Johnson** in 1869[347] and **Sarah Jane Heazle Johnson** in 1871.[348]

A month before the birth of Sarah Jane, a person named Henry Johnson faced the Brewarrina Police Court as the defendant,[349] but this was another man with the same name. He had been charged on 30 September 1871 with stealing a horse belonging to Robert Elliott of *Milroy* Station and a saddle and bridle belonging to Henry Coppard of the same station. This other Henry Johnson was committed to trial at Bourke at the next Quarter Sessions and, on 9 November was tried there before Judge Josephson and found guilty on all charges.[350] He was sentenced to 12 months gaol with hard labour for the saddle theft and a further two years for the horse theft, these terms to be served cumulatively in Darlinghurst Gaol.[351] He would serve a total of 32 months in confinement, but the Gazette Notice about his early release gives his birth year as 1851, so he was 13 years younger than Eliza's husband.[352]

If any further proof were needed that Eliza's husband was not the Henry Johnson who was gaoled between November 1871 and April 1874, it came in the form of their fifth child, **John Benjamin Linley Johnson,** whose birth was registered at Bourke in October 1873.[353]

While **John Benjamin Reed** and his wife were still living at Ponto, a horrible incident occurred at Bourke that would blight their lives forever. Their seven-year-old son, **William John Reed**, who had been living with his grandparents for about six months, was drowned in the Darling River on 7 October 1865.

> *Boy Drowned - On Saturday last (7th), a boy of the name William John Reed was drowned in the Darling while bathing with some other children. Some eight or ten minutes elapsed before the body was recovered ... For several hours efforts were made to restore life, but with no avail. The boy's parents live at Ponto, near Wellington, but he was stopping with his grand parents, at Bourke, for the last six months. A gloom was cast over the whole community by this melancholy accident, he being an interesting little fellow of seven years of age.*[354]

The sudden loss of their eldest grandchild would have dealt a devastating blow to James and Frances and the rest of the family, especially as it came just a few months after the death of the little fellow's cousins **William Whye** and the unnamed baby Tobin.

About a year after **Sarah Ann Brennan** had given birth to her first child at Ponto while en route to Bourke, she produced a second daughter. **Frances Brennan**[355] was born at Bourke in the same month as her cousin drowned and was named in honour of her grandmother Frances Reed and her aunt Frances Tobin. In about July 1867 a third daughter was born and named **Emeline Brennan**.[356]

During their first couple of years in Bourke, James and Frances Reed had bought land, been flooded out, endured drought, reunited the family, suffered the tragic loss of three grandchildren and celebrated the marriage of three daughters. As they entered a third year in their new hometown, they now had time to reflect that, despite the sadness and difficulties, they had successfully transplanted the Reed family sapling into Bourke; and to imagine it flourishing there for many decades to come.

Photograph 5
Mitchell street looking southeast from Tattersall's hotel, ca 1871.
Source: Cameron, Bill. *Bourke, A Pictorial History, volume 1.* Bourke Wool Press 1982

Original photo: Mrs Joan Joyce

Photograph 6 - The port of Bourke, 1871.
Source: Australian Town and Country Journal, 28 Oct 1871, p 16

Photograph 7 - Mitchell Street looking southeast, 1871.
Source: National Library of Australia

An etching of this photograph was published in the Australian Town and Country Journal on 8 June 1872, page 24.

Photograph 8 - Commercial hotel, ca 1871.

Photograph 9 - Commercial hotel and Mitchell Street looking southwest, ca 1871.
Source: Cameron, Bill. *Bourke, A Pictorial History, volume 1.* Bourke Wool Press 1982

Original photo: the late Ted Harrod

Reunited

CHAPTER TWELVE

Work, save, invest

The key objective of the move to Bourke was to build wealth by taking advantage of the government's new land policies. The Reed family planned to capitalise on this opportunity by working hard and saving money for use as deposits on their chosen land. They started by establishing a timber business run by James, his sons and sons-in-law, while they worked towards the erection of a boarding house to be run primarily by Frances and the teenage children.

Surviving documents record that James Reed worked as a labourer for several years, but don't provide specific details. He may have found ad hoc labouring work with several employers while preparing to set up his own businesses. This would have provided a good income while allowing him to spend his downtime on the many tasks associated with establishing the family in Bourke. His sons and sons-in-law would also have taken any employment that they could secure during their first few months in Bourke. For example, according to the obituary of Sarah Ann Brennan,[357] her husband Michael *"was employed as back-storeman by the late Mr August (sic) Becker, 'King of Bourke' in those days"*.

A year after Frances bought the family's housing block in Darling Street, her husband purchased at auction three of the four remaining allotments on the southern side of that street between Glen and Wilson Streets[358]. He paid a total of twenty-six pounds and twelve shillings, the equivalent of about nine months' income as a labourer at that time. The middle allotment (later subdivided into housing blocks 23 and 25 Darling Street) would pass out of the Reed family fourteen years later but the other two blocks were retained for much longer. They were on the Corner of Darling and Wilson Streets where George Charles Reed would later establish the *Bourke* hotel (subsequently transferred to his sister Prudence Reed and her future husband James Murphy who would change the name to the *Family* hotel).

Two months later, James was fined one pound in the Police Court for using obscene language to constable Hashan![359] Since this was quite out of character for him, it could signal that he was experiencing significant anxiety about their future. If, as seems likely, they had gone to Bourke with a plan to build a boarding house or hotel, they must have been feeling frustrated that two years had now passed without realising their dream. In fact, they had clearly decided to delay the implementation of that plan for a few years. While they would establish a hotel at Mount Oxley six years later, they made their living in other ways in the meantime.

This delay may have been caused by the fact that two hotels were already established in Bourke before the Reeds were able to obtain any land and another was under construction. They may have been concerned that opening a fourth hotel in the still-small community could involve too much risk. If so, it was an unfortunate miscalculation, because those three hotels and other early businesses made money hand over fist in these early years.

Nevertheless, as we shall see later in this chapter, it seems likely that the family started a hotel-like business at this time: a boarding house. This would have been a safe initial step towards a later hotel business.

By August 1865 James Reed was also running a timber business in conjunction with his sons and sons-in-law. He held a timber licence in 1865[360], 1866,[361] 1867[362], 1868[363], 1869[364], 1871[365] and 1874[366]. His sons **Jimmy**[367] and **Alexander**[368] and son-in-law **Michael Brennan**[369] also obtained timber licenses around this time, so they probably all worked together in this business.[370] The inspiration for it may have come from William Johnson (father of James' son-in-law Henry Johnson) who had been granted a timber license at Bourke in 1864.

The business did not supply building timber; it delivered timber to homes and businesses for use as fuel. Oil-based fuels were still in their infancy, with coal-based kerosene the main liquid fuel available. In western NSW this was used primarily for lighting, while the staple fuel for cooking, heating houses and powering steam engines was wood.

The Reed men would initially have driven a horse and cart into the bush around the town in search of fallen timber that had dried out in the sun. The chosen trees and branches were then sawed into lengths suitable for domestic stoves or steam engines. The sawn logs would be stacked onto the cart and transported to the customer. Those customers would place their orders verbally and then pay cash on delivery at the going rate for a cartload of wood.

The best clients would have been the paddle steamers that plied up and down the river bringing supplies upstream and then returning with cargoes of wool and other primary produce. Timber supply businesses maintained wood piles at many places along both sides of the river for this purpose. Any steamer could pull up to the bank nearby and take aboard a load of wood to power the steam engine providing propulsion to the boat through the paddle wheel. The Reed family maintained a wood pile for this purpose. After taking wood aboard, the steamer's captain would send to the supplier of that pile an order for the appropriate quantity of wood accompanied by payment in the form of a cheque.

But the steamers could not always reach Bourke and Gongolgon due to low water levels. For months at a time, they could only come upstream as far as Wilcannia, more than 300 kilometres southwest of Bourke. This created another business opportunity for Bourke-based carriers like John Benjamin Reed and his brothers Jimmy and Alexander, all of whom were bullock wagon drivers. They would have found regular work on the Wilcannia-Bourke run carrying wool to Wilcannia for export via Adelaide. Carriers could always find a market in Bourke for any household supplies brought from the steamers at Wilcannia as a back load, thus creating a good business model.

Some of the timber licenses that the Reed clan obtained in these years were for the Warrego district, southwest of Bourke. This makes sense as part of the Wilcannia-Bourke shuttle run that passes through the

Warrego district on both legs. James, Jimmy, John Benjamin, Alexander and Michael Brennan may have travelled together in small teams with one or more horse-drawn carts as well as a bullock wagon so that they could gather a load of timber from the Warrego district for sale at Wilcannia; and then pick up another load of timber while en route back to Bourke, thus making efficient use of their journey time. Other family members, such as James Tobin junior and George Charles Reed, may have joined such trips to assist in timber-getting and to drive one of the carts.

By the middle of 1865 the flood of twelve months earlier was a distant memory. The rains had eventually dried up and the district moved into drought. Given the huge influx of sheep and cattle over the preceding few years, any grass that sprang up as the floodwaters receded was quickly consumed. Suddenly there was a significant shortage of forage, particularly near the town with its many horses and bullocks. James Reed saw an opportunity, so he expanded his business into the supply of animal feed. A correspondent of the Maitland Mercury newspaper reported from Bourke:[371]

> *A rather amusing scene occurred here last night, illustrative of our sad condition relative to forage. I had procured from Mr. James Reed a bundle of grass, which he informed me he had carried for more than twenty miles; going to the boat my hay was suddenly set upon by some hungry kine coming in to water …*

James and Frances, now probably living in a new house on Frances' land, most likely established a boarding house soon after James acquired the additional blocks. This would have been a logical move because they had previous experience in providing board and lodgings in Sydney; and a well-designed boarding house could, conceivably, be later converted into a hotel without much difficulty.

The Bourke correspondent of the Sydney *Empire* newspaper reported in October 1866 that the town continued to increase in both buildings and population.

> *We have two stores, three public-houses, one baker, three butchers, saddler, wheelwright and blacksmith, two lodging houses, a branch of the Commercial bank* [and steps were being taken for the erection of a public school].[372]

One of those two lodging houses was run by Matthew Good on land he owned on the northern side of Mitchell Street (between the billabong and Sturt Street)[373] where he would later open the *Telegraph* hotel. The owner of the other boarding house has not been identified, but it was probably James and Frances Reed. We know that they owned several land allotments and had experience in running a boarding house. It is hard to imagine any other reason why they would have needed so much land. Furthermore, it was a natural step from running a boarding house to running a hotel, a step that was later taken by Matthew Good.

An incident occurred five years later that lends credence to the hypothesis that the Reed family had opened a boarding house. By that time, James and Frances had acquired land at Mount Oxley and were focused on building their hotel there. In these circumstances, it would make sense for them to arrange for another member of the Reed clan to take over the boarding house.

There is evidence that their daughter Eliza and her husband **Henry Johnson** were doing just that. In April 1869 their lodger, **Alex Ramsay**, sued Henry Johnson for 8 pounds and 16 shillings for non-payment of wages for work done on Johnson's cottage. After hearing the case, the Bourke Police Court bench noted that they had heard a vast amount of words and some very hard swearing but had managed to cut through the hyperbole to ascertain the heart of the dispute. In summary, Ramsay had been engaged by "a third party" to do some work on Johnson's cottage on the understanding that his wages were to be deducted from his rent, so Ramsay's suit was dismissed. The third party was probably Henry's wife, Eliza, or her mother, Frances Reed. At the same hearing, Johnson counter-sued Ramsay for five pounds, twelve shillings and sixpence for board and lodging. He was successful but was awarded a pound less than he claimed.[374]

So, most members of the Reed family were probably employed in the carrying, timber and boarding house industries during their first few years in Bourke.

There had been a very heavy flood in February 1867 but the climate quickly produced a drought and by 1868 the river could be crossed by stepping from stone to stone in some places, so steamers would not have been able to reach Bourke from mid-1867.[375] Around this time, **James Reed** visited Wilcannia with his son Alexander. They had probably taken a load of wool from Bourke for transport by steamer to Adelaide; and they probably also brought a load of wood from the Warrego district to Wilcannia for the steamers.

James left Wilcannia before his son and returned to Bourke, leaving behind instructions for Alexander to sell James' bay mare. Six months later James noticed the same horse in the company of **John French** outside the newly established *Royal* hotel, Bourke's third inn, run by George Harris on the corner of Glen and Mitchell Streets. When challenged over the mare's ownership, French replied that he had come by her honestly and had a receipt but refused to show it. So, James called the police and Constable McElligott promptly arrested French.

On December 27, James charged French in the Bourke Police Court with the theft of his mare. He explained to the Police Magistrate (Mr Garrett) that he had last seen the horse six months earlier at Wilcannia where he had instructed his son Alexander to sell her. The prisoner then produced his receipt for purchasing the mare from Alexander, which was accepted by the bench as clear proof that he had come by her legally. French was nevertheless cautioned that he had been foolish to take a receipt without witnesses, especially as Alexander Reed had only signed it with a cross.

As soon as French was discharged on the stealing charge he was arraigned on a charge of assaulting Constable McElligott during his arrest for the alleged theft of the horse! He pleaded guilty to having inflicted the Constable's shiner and was fined four pounds or three months in Dubbo Gaol. He was then fined a further 3 pounds and ten shillings (or another month of gaol) for damage caused to the constable's uniform. No doubt he reflected ruefully as he paid the fines that it would have been a lot cheaper to have produced his receipt to James Reed when asked.[376]

While the timber business was keeping James busy, Frances seized an opportunity to bring a modicum of sophistication to the town. Having now made their home in Bourke for five years, she understood there remained a significant imbalance between the sexes, as illustrated by the fact that adult women comprised only 7 of the 176 deaths recorded so far in the district.[377]

This preponderance of boofy males tended to foster a less civilised society, so Frances Reed, with the assistance of George Harris's wife, organised a charity tea party that would appeal to some of the more genteel townsfolk. A detailed report on the tea party was published in the *Maitland Mercury* newspaper on 26 November.[378]

At first the idea was laughed at as utopian by those for whose benefit it was mooted. However, in spite of the ridicule, these two earnest ladies went about the work and succeeded admirably. Not only were their own friends appealed to take tickets, but the rough bushman handed out his money, until a sum of 25 pounds, nine shillings and sixpence was actually raised. This done, the court-house was obtained from Mr Garrett and the manual part of the affair was commenced; huge tables were taken from the Royal, the residence of Mrs Harris, with other necessary appliances, and on Monday the 11th instant, a superb repast was ready for the subscribers. All passed off with wondrous glee and satisfaction, and at its conclusion Mr Garrett, in behalf of the ladies, thanked the company for their attendance, and the movers of the affair for the energy and charity displayed by the two above-mentioned ladies, and I think they richly deserved their tribute.

No doubt the "superb repast" would have also provided a practical advertisement of the superior hospitality available to lodgers in the Reed family's boarding house.

A month or so later, in January 1868, three of the four unmarried children of James and Frances Reed attended the latest town land auction and bought a total of four acres of land on the northern side of Anson Street. **Alexander** (who was now 30 years old) paid four pounds for one-acre in the centre of the block between Richard and Glen Streets (marked 9 on Map 8). His younger sister **Jane** (just 11 years old) paid five pounds for the next allotment, also one acre, on the corner of Richard Street (marked 8 on the map). Their 17-year-old brother **George** paid a total of ten pounds for two adjacent one acre blocks next to the billabong (marked 6 and 7 on the map).[379]

It seems unlikely that teenagers Jane and George were self-motivated and entrepreneurial enough to be investing in land. Perhaps this was part of a plan by their parents to provide each of their unmarried children with a solid financial start in life by purchasing them an acre of land in the town. And perhaps George used some of his own savings to purchase an additional acre for himself. John and Jimmy may have been given money previously to buy bullocks, horses, wagons and carts for their businesses and Eliza, Sarah Ann, Prudence and Frances may have been given money on the occasion of their weddings. But this hypothesis does not account for the fact that 15-year-old Mary Ann Reed did not acquire any land at this time.

The four acres in Anson Street were on the southern edge of the town and may have been intended for use by Alexander and John (for their carrying businesses) and by all members of the family involved in the timber-getting business. The land would have provided some grass for horses and bullocks plus storage space for wagons, carts and harness.

Around this time, Jimmy Reed went to Queensland, probably on a carrying job with his brother Alexander. As we shall see in chapter 14, during the trip he selected land at Springsure and subsequently moved his family there. Alexander later selected land nearby and their families lived out their lives in this area.

Michael Brennan called the police in April 1868 to report the theft of a light grey gelding of 15.5 hands. Horse theft was a relatively common crime at this time and consumed a significant portion of police resources. Michael offered a reward of three pounds to anyone who recovered his horse and a further three pounds if the thief was subsequently convicted[380], but the outcome of this case has been lost.

Two months later, Michael took the first step towards implementing his plan to move the growing Brennan family to North Bourke. He paid 5 pounds and ten shillings for 2 roods of land on the corner of Bogan and Culgoa Streets (marked 1 on Map 6) in the fledgling town (then known as West Bourke).[381] The blocks marked 2 and 3 were owned by Joseph Lunn. The block marked 4 would be acquired from Joseph Becker by George Charles Reed in 1881.

There wasn't much there at this early time, not even a hotel. It is possible that Michael Brennan was taking his family there because he had been engaged to work for Joseph Lunn, who was, at this time, engaged in building the *West Bourke* hotel. Two years later Brennan was working as a house painter,[382] but he may have started in this line of work as early as 1869 having been tasked by Lunn with painting the new hotel.

The government surveyor had completed a plan for

a town at North Bourke a few months earlier. The *Maitland Mercury's* Bourke correspondent reported on his inspection of the site in November 1867.

> *Over the river at last I proceeded along the road to the newly-laid out town - West Bourke. A magnificent site it is too, for a town, being some eight feet higher than East Bourke, as I presume we will have to call this town ere long. There are, and always were, arguments as to which was the right side of the river to have the town so; but now that we have Bourke on either side I presume all parties will be satisfied.[383]*

On his way to the new town site, this correspondent had met with an accident when attempting to cross the river, for which he blamed the NSW government which had built a punt at Bourke but then left it to lie idle.

> *I succeeded in getting across the river, after drowning one of my best horses, an animal worth £30. This being the second valuable horse I have lost, owing to the Government punt not being at work, I think it high time the boot pinched me. What in the name of all that is good and holy did the Government build this Bourke punt for? Was it to be looked at, or to be tied up in the sun, and allowed to shrink and warp into all shapes, while the public are compelled to endanger their property in a little puntoon, about 12 feet by 8, strung round with casks to keep it afloat?*

He added more rhetoric in this vein before concluding with the observation that Bourke businesses were losing a great deal of trade because travellers were being diverted away to *Beemery* Station where another punt was operating successfully. He had made a good point that is well illustrated by the events of 11 October

1868, when three members of the extended Reed family suffered separate mishaps.

Last Friday was, as is supposed by many, an unlucky day. George Kelly, in crossing the river, overturned his dray, smashing it and seriously injuring two bullocks; shortly after Mr. Brennan, whilst crossing to Reedy corner, upset horse and dray, making splinters of a lot of furniture. ... Mr. G. Reed's horse towards evening ... fell in a hole, and, to wind up, the camp of Mr. James Reed at West Bourke got on fire while the men were away, and consumed a tarpaulin; luckily a person saw the flames in time, or the whole effects must have been destroyed.[384]

So, on this rather calamitous day for the Reed clan, Michael Brennan's dray overturned while attempting to bring the family's furniture across the river to the new abode at North Bourke; his father-in-law James Reed, also camped at North Bourke, lost a valuable tarpaulin to fire; and George Charles Reed's horse fell into a hole!

Five months later, Sarah Ann Brennan gave birth to the couple's fourth daughter, **Isabella Maude Mary Brennan** (who was to be generally known throughout her life as Maude).[385] According to her biography,[386] published as part of a series on "Women of the West", Maude Brennan was *"the first white baby born at North Bourke"*[387].

Presumably the Brennans built a house on their block of land at North Bourke, but the family had moved back to Bourke two years later when their fifth daughter **Victoria Prudence Brennan** was born[388]. A further two years later, in August 1872, the birth of their son **William J Brennan** was registered.[389] In 1874 they finally sold the land at North Bourke to Joseph Lunn.[390] The *Occidental* hotel was built there about ten years later.

***

In 1867 William Sly had decided to move to Queensland. On 26 March he placed his hotel into the hands of **Joseph Becker** for auction and it was knocked down to John Kelly, the highest bidder, for 2100 pounds.[391] This sale must have fallen through, because Sly subsequently sold the same land to **the Colless brothers (Henry and George)** on 27 April 1868.[392] They immediately started work to construct a new hotel on the site which was named *Tattersall's* hotel. (There was a chain of hotels with the Tattersall's name across Victoria and NSW that were all associated with the members-only Tattersall's Club in Sydney that offered high-end accommodation and dining services for travellers.) A correspondent of the *Maitland Mercury* newspaper reported in July 1868 that

> *Bourke is progressing very satisfactorily; many brick buildings are in hand. The Tattersall's Hotel (Colless's) is to be a very fine building.*[393]

A few photographs have survived that give us a good impression of the Reed's hometown at that time. As we saw in chapter 11, Photograph 5 depicts on the right the newly completed *Tattersalls* hotel with Sly's old *Bourke* hotel building behind it. The far left of the picture shows another new building that had replaced the *Old Fort* hotel. Briefly known as the *Commercial* hotel, it was soon renamed the *Royal* hotel. Ross and Company's Bourke Store is in the centre of the picture.

I show, in Appendix 1, that John Kelly sold his *Old*

Fort hotel to Henry Nancarrow in 1869 and that Nancarrow held the license to that hotel in 1870. Nancarrow demolished the original *Old Fort* building and constructed a replacement in brick and iron. A year later he sold it to WW Davis who renamed it the *Commercial* hotel and installed his brother-in-law Joseph Maxwell as licensee. In 1872 Davis sold it to George Harris who took over the license and renamed it the *Royal* hotel (a name that he had also used for his former premises on the north-eastern corner of Mitchell and Glen Streets). So, this photograph must have been taken in 1871 or later.

Photograph 8 was taken at about the same time and depicts the new *Commercial* hotel with a cart bogged out front and an outbuilding at the rear, built in slab hut style. The left-most wing is brick and iron while the right-most wing is weatherboard and iron and has a streetlamp at the front.

Photograph 9 was taken a little time later, as the bogged cart has gone. The *Commercial* hotel is on the far left with Ross and Company's Bourke Store just right of centre. There may be a vacant block of land between them. Beyond a gap (Sturt Street) is *Tattersall's* hotel followed by one or two more vacant blocks before a building on the far right on land owned by Ross, Becker and Green (lot 2, section 1).

Photograph 7 dates to 1872 when an engraving of it was published in the *Australian Town and Country Journal*. It depicts the same street from the far distance looking back. So, the Ross, Becker and Green building is in the foreground on the right (with another building half cut off nearer the camera). Next comes a brand new brick building with twin-peaked roof on another block owned by Ross, Becker and Green (lot 4, section 1). Partially obscured behind it is *Tattersall's* hotel. On the far left is Ross and Company's Bourke Store, now featuring a large flagpole with flag.

These four pictures give a good sense of Bourke's rapid progress and demonstrate the frontier nature of the town at that time.

After all members of the Reed family were reunited at Bourke in 1864, they had worked together and supported one another as planned in establishing a life in the fledgling town. In addition to some paid employment and opening a boarding house, they expanded their carrying business by supplying timber fuel to paddle steamers, businesses and households. The objective of building wealth through the acquisition of land and buildings was achieved, with family members erecting houses and business premises on several allotments that they had bought in Bourke and North Bourke. The carrying business took both Jimmy and Alexander to Queensland where they eventually both selected land and built their own small farms.

COMMERCIAL BANK, BOURKE.
Photograph 13
Commercial bank on the Northeastern corner of Mitchell and Richard Streets, 1872.
Source: Australian Town and Country Journal, 8 June 1872, page 24.

Photograph 10 – Study of *Tattersalls* hotel, ca 1871.
Source: Cameron, Bill. *Bourke, A Pictorial History, volume 1*. Bourke Wool Press 1982
Original photo: Mrs Joan Joyce, cropped by the author

← ===== **Photograph 11 - *Tattersalls* hotel graphic.**
Highlighting differences with the building in Photograph 12

Gable ended

No chimney

L- shaped

Photograph 12 - The *Lame Horse* hotel at Gongolgon, ca 1871.
Source: Noel Butlin Archives, Australian National University.

Work, save invest

CHAPTER THIRTEEN

The Lame Horse and the Mountain Home

When **Prudence Reed** married **Joseph Whye** in 1863 (see chapter 11), he was working on *Nidgerie* Station, but the young couple soon implemented his plan to transition out of the grazing lifestyle by establishing the *Lame Horse* hotel at nearby Gongolgon. Four years later her parents also entered the industry when they opened the *Mountain Home* hotel at Mount Oxley.

Joseph had already bought the land where they planned to build the hotel but kept working at *Nidgerie* for the next two years as they worked and saved to acquire everything necessary for the new venture. Unfortunately, as mentioned in Chapter 11, their infant son **William Whye** died and was buried at *Nidgerie* in July 1865.[394]

The Robertson land reforms had given selectors the right to acquire a "living area" (between 40 and 320 acres) of any Crown land regardless of its current leasehold status. The purchase price of £1 per acre was payable by a deposit of 25 percent with annual instalments on the balance, plus interest at 5 per cent. The selector had to live on the property for at least three years and make improvements worth £1 per acre. Title was secured upon payment of the final instalment provided that the conditions had been met.

Joseph and Prudence had cannily selected land near the Bogan River ford where the town of Gongolgon was subsequently established. This was an excellent place to cross the river because it had a smooth rocky bottom that could support heavily laden wagons. That made it an ideal place for a hotel, given that it was on the main road to both Bourke and Brewarrina from Wellington and Dubbo in the southeast.

Their third child was born in July 1866, just a couple of months before the hotel was first licensed. She had not been given a name at the time her birth was registered but was subsequently named **Jane Elizabeth Whye**.[395]

On 17 September 1866 the NSW Treasury published a notice in the NSW Gazette that a publican's license had been issued to Joseph Whye for the *Lame Horse* hotel at Gongolgon.[396] It is likely that he had employed someone with building experience to erect it for him while he continued earning an income.

There is a significant amount of circumstantial evidence indicating that Joseph may have employed William Sly to build the hotel. We saw in Chapter 11 that Frances Reed and Sly had witnessed a marriage in January 1864. Furthermore, there are many remarkable similarities between Sly's 1863 *Bourke* Hotel and the *Lame Horse* hotel building erected three years later. These commonalities led Bourke historian Bill Cameron to conclude in his book *Bourke: A Pictorial History, volume 1* that Photograph 12 depicts Sly's hotel, but the evidence outlined below suggests that it is, in fact, the *Lame Horse* hotel at Gongolgon.

A caption on the picture itself describes the subject as "Bourke's First Hotel 1866", but does this mean that the picture was taken at Bourke in 1866; or that the hotel was first licensed that year in the Bourke Licensing District? Since the picture is a much higher quality than the 1870s Bourke photographs (numbered 5 to 9) discussed in chapter 12, it is unlikely to pre-date them. For this reason, 1866 probably refers to the hotel's original license date, not when the picture was taken.

Sly's hotel was first licensed in 1863, not 1866. It is shown in Photograph 10 with only one chimney, unlike the "1866 building" that has one on each end. While Sly's building appears to have had a gable end near the chimney, the "1866 building" has a sloping roof there. Furthermore, Sly's building is L shaped rather than the simple oblong of the "1866 building".

Cameron bolsters his case by noting that *the horse sign indicates that it may have already received its later name, "Tattersall's"*.[397] (This claim is based on the fact that Tattersall's was a name that had long been associated with racehorses in England and had recently been similarly associated in Australia.) On the contrary, there is no record of Sly's hotel ever being called Tattersall's or any horse-associated name. All the surviving records prior to its purchase by the Colless brothers in 1868 refer to it as *Sly's* hotel, the *Bourke* hotel or *Bond's* hotel. The first reference to *Tattersall's* hotel is the one quoted in chapter 12, which dates to the Colless ownership. Furthermore, it is unlikely that the Tattersall's Club would have consented to its name being applied to a hotel built in the slab hut form. This club marketed itself as a refined establishment for refined people who could demand the best available accommodation.

There are surviving pictures of many different NSW hotels with the Tattersall's name from that period (and later) but none of them feature the picture of a horse, despite the association with the racing industry. In any case, were they to have a horse picture, it would almost certainly have been a racehorse, but the horse on the sign outside the "1866 building" is standing still; probably because it is meant to depict a <u>lame</u> horse.

There is no record of Sly's hotel ever having a sign of any kind, but there are two contemporary records that prove that Joseph Whye's hotel at Gongolgon did have a sign that featured a horse. It was first noted by a correspondent for the *Maitland Mercury* newspaper in August 1867 who wrote:

> *I paid a visit to the little township of Gongolgon … The situation is remarkably pretty, being open box forest, with a fine red soil, well grassed; but I am sorry to see that the axe has been too freely at work, and wide desolate patches are seen which should be beautified with trees. There is a comfortable inn kept by Mr Joseph Whye, which bears the unusual sign of the "Lame Horse", though the painter has failed to convey a just copy of the afflicted animal. Whye's hospitality, however, is quite sound.*[398]

The sign was later noted by a correspondent of the *Town and Country Journal* newspaper who stayed at Whye's hotel in October 1874.

> *Gongolgon is a clean and very nice little township, built on land high and dry, on the western bank of the Bogan River. There are two public-houses, two stores, police station, public school, and a pound in the township. The first hotel, on entering Gongolgon from the Sydney side,*

is the Royal, kept by Mr. John Hawthorne, who distinguished himself by the capture of Dunn, the bushranger, some years ago. The other hotel has the remarkable sign of "The Lame Horse." This is also a comfortable building, carried on by Mr. Joseph Whye.[399]

Based on the evidence outlined above, it is clear that the 1866 picture depicts the Bourke Licensing District's *Lame Horse* hotel at Gongolgon (first licensed in 1866), not William Sly's *Bourke* hotel that was licensed three years earlier.

***

A month after Joseph and Prudence started to operate their hotel, a correspondent of the *Empire* newspaper reported that

Gongolgon is the best crossing-place on the Bogan, it being a flat rock bottom. At this place there is a public-house recently opened, kept by a free selector, Joseph Why.[400]

Joseph may have employed his father-in-law, James Reed, as a labourer during the building phase. He had, like Joseph, selected land at Gongolgon and both were mentioned by name on Surveyor Campbell's map of the area on 6 July 1867[401] (see Map 5).

Campbell visited Gongolgon to draw up a town plan so that the government could auction off town allotments. He soon realised that Joseph Whye had already secured the best site for the town with his selected conditional purchase. Rather than look elsewhere for a town site (as Surveyor Glen Wilson had done in choosing a site for Bourke when faced with a similar dilemma), Campbell decided to work around the fact that some of the planned town's land was already owned. While ensuring that the town was on the best possible site, this decision also benefited Whye (and others who had already selected portions of the town site). Otherwise, his hotel may have become redundant if a town had been established elsewhere.

Campbell secured an agreement with the existing selectors to resume their land in exchange for a guarantee of specific lots in the new town (see Map 5). This was a practical way to please almost everybody, but it resulted in a rather eccentric town plan, with the two main streets (River and Colayne Streets) meeting at an acute angle; and a large section in the centre of the town not completely subdivided into allotments.

The government did not actually have any existing legislation that authorised a process for resuming land, so it had to pass a special Act through the NSW Parliament just for the Gongolgon resumption. Joseph Whye became one of the first people ever to be specifically named in an Act of the NSW Parliament. *An Act (number XVII) to authorise the Sale of certain improved Lands* was given assent on 23 December 1867.[402] In relation to Joseph it provided that

> [whereas his land] *is contained within an area which has since been duly declared to be set apart as the site of a town and whereas [he had] agreed to relinquish the land ... in consideration that he was allowed to purchase the five acres ...* [being lots 4 and 5 of section 3 and 4 of section 30 in the Village of Gongolgon].

Section 30 was a misprint; it should have read section 33. The two one acre lots in section 3 were the prime land in the village, being closest to the river ford (lots E and F on the map). Lot 4 in section 33 (map lot H) was three acres of riverfront land near the ford that Whye would have selected as a good source of water and forage for the horses and bullocks of future hotel guests. He paid a total of twenty-four pounds and fifteen shillings for these five acres.[403]

A fourth child was added to the family in January 1868 and named **Frederick Whye,** but unfortunately he died within the same month.[404]

A year after his death, Prudence gave birth to a daughter who was named **Emily Maud Mary Whye**[405]. Her sixth child was born at Gongolgon two years later 26 February 1871[406] and baptised **Albert George Henry Whye** at Bourke on 23 April.[407]

When the unallocated town lots came up for auction in September 1868, Joseph paid sixteen pounds and ten shillings for another four and a quarter acres as lots 4, 5 and 6 in section 2 (map lots B, C and D) on the other main corner of the village, opposite his hotel site; and another acre behind his hotel (and facing Colayne Street) as lots 1 and 2 of section 2 (map lot G).[408]

At the same auction, James Reed paid seven pounds six shillings and sixpence for just under two acres as lot 1 in section 33 (map lot A), fronting the river.[409] This is probably the spot where he maintained a pile of sawn timber for sale to passing paddle steamers. He and Frances had two daughters (Prudence Whye and Frances Tobin) living at Gongolgon at this time and may have also started to think of basing themselves there, hence the purchase of land in the village. It is notable that Frances' husband, James Tobin junior, paid eight pounds at the same auction for two half-acre lots (1 and 3 in section 2) near Whye's blocks in River Street.[410]

This was a year of drought, worsening as the months drew on and culminating in several of the dust storms that have blighted the district during subsequent droughts. During December the *Maitland Mercury* published a vivid account of one of them.[411]

Yesterday, Tuesday, we were again visited by millions of acres of dust. About 10 am the wind came in soughing angry gusts from the west, increasing up to 3 p.m., when the climax of the scene was reached. Some time before this a vast dense ocean of lurid red came rolling in upon the town; when a mile or so from the place it had the appearance of a volcano's fires under a terrible eruption; the heat at the time was 108° in the shade, heightening the simile. On came the rolling, wrestling, pyramids of sand, making as it were a palpable road from earth to sky; and men as it neared them looked forth with a feeling of awe, the same which they experience when gazing on Martin's pictures. Now it crushed in upon us; the sun was hid, or struggled through the suffocating mass; darker and fiercer it poured onward, till the scene was nearly as gloomy as midnight. Lamps were lighted, making the confusion more ghastly. It seemed as if nature was expiring, and the smoke of her dissolution covered the world. Lashed by the hurricane, the innumerable columns, mid the crashing of trees, and the rattle of falling brickwork passed, and the rain, not in drops, but sheets, fell, as though the flood-gates of heaven were unhinged. This was succeeded by a pulse less calm, as if the elements had wearied themselves by their violence. During the night the winds were again unloosed, and the deep diapason of the thunder crashing among sable clouds, caused us to hope for rain: a little fell, the thunder ceased, and morning dawned as tranquil as a dream.

Earlier in the year residents of the Bourke district had been distressed by an alarming incident that took place at Enngonia. **Frank Pearson**, a serial impostor and conman, had been posing as a doctor in the Walgett district when he teamed up with a young stockman named **Charlie Rutherford**, stole some horses and embarked on a crime spree. They headed north and robbed several properties in both NSW and southern Queensland. Pearson, ever the egotist, started to call himself **Captain Starlight** as he and his accomplice continued their dangerous exploits.

Only three years had passed since the police pursuit of Ben Hall's gang in the Bathurst district that had ended when Hall was shot dead by police at Goobang Creek in May 1865. The general community remained very concerned about the depredations of bushrangers and consequently there was significant political pressure on police forces to bring them to justice. Accordingly, **Senior Constable John McCabe** of NSW Police and **Constable Hugh McManus** of Queensland Police were soon on the trail of Captain Starlight and his offsider.

During their patrol the policemen stopped for supplies at Shearer's Inn, Enngonia (about 100 kilometres north of Bourke). Almost immediately the two bushrangers entered! Pearson yelled "Bail up!" with the obvious intention of robbing those present. The police fired several times, hitting Pearson in the wrist and right arm. The bushrangers returned fire, wounding Constable McCabe in the chest before escaping.

After rallying for almost a month, McCabe died because of his infected wound and was buried in the Bourke cemetery where his grave is marked with a very prominent memorial.[412]

The bushrangers split up and Bourke's **Constable Cleary** was quickly on Pearson's trail near *Toorale* station. Assisted by Aboriginal trackers, he caught Pearson and, after shooting his horse, chased him up Mount Gundabooka on foot. Despite losing him in the darkness, Cleary later found Pearson in a cave and arrested him on Christmas Day.

The pathological liar at first pretended to be his accomplice Rutherford but was later properly identified. He eventually admitted to having shot Senior Constable McCabe, was convicted of murder at Bathurst and sentenced to hang. Surprisingly, this sentence was commuted to life imprisonment and, after faking rehabilitation, he was released 16 years later. He was subsequently gaoled in Queensland for a time. Upon his release he went to Western Australia and assumed the identity of Major Patrick Francis Pelly, eventually conning his way into a responsible position with the Geological Survey of Western Australia. He died on 22 December 1899 when, while drunk, he accidentally swallowed cyanide, having mistaken it for his medication.[413]

His offsider Rutherford managed to evade capture for almost a year, committing property crimes across a large area of NSW. On 5 September 1869 he attempted to rob at gunpoint the publican at Pine Ridge, between Warren and Canonbar. After a brief struggle, the gun went off and Rutherford was shot in the head, dying the next day.[414]

The death of Senior Constable McCabe brought home to the people of Bourke that, for all their recent advances, they were still living in a frontier society. Only six years had elapsed since the murder of Sergeant George Bell at Bourke; and another bushranger, Captain Thunderbolt, was also rumoured to have been active in the district during 1868. (He was to be shot and killed by police near Uralla two years later.) Prudence and Joseph Whye would have now been made aware that the risks posed by bushrangers were real, particularly for those running inns in isolated villages like Enngonia, Pine Ridge and Gongolgon.

The drought wore on, as did the flowery prose of the *Maitland Mercury's* correspondent.[415]

Yesterday, after an eclipse of dust, which came as usual from Gundabooka, the clouds rolled up from the same quarter, and anyone would have sworn that our cruel drought had broken up; but we thankfully received about thirty drops of rain to the acre; and today the fierce sun is smiting everything with pain - sheep are crawling about in thousands more dead than alive, while the river is lined with dead and dying horses and cattle; the poor brutes go for drink, get bogged, and die. It would move the icy heart of a Nero to see the terrible state of things out here; each man and woman talks of nothing else but rain. Three years have elapsed since we had rain to supply our wants, and each month passes with vain promises, and we seem as far away from it as ever. Men are actually afraid to go from the river; there is such an awful danger in the waterless wastes. James Brown, of Bourke, bullock-driver, was brought in very nearly dead from Oxley's Table-land; he went out cutting grass, the water cask got upset, and he was alone with the grim terror. He was found, I am informed, by some of Barton's men, in a fearful state; he is slowly recovering.

On 4 March 1869, James and Frances Reed selected 80 acres of that waterless waste land at the northernmost tip of Oxley's Tableland where they intended to finally build their hotel. The site was well chosen as it was on a road that had a regular flow of traffic in both directions and the nearest hotel was 30 kilometres away in Bourke, so competition was non-existent. It provided an ideal overnight resting place for people travelling between Gongolgon and Bourke, allowing them to split the 110 kilometre trip into two legs. The 80 kilometre leg from Gongolgon to Mount Oxley could be done in a day or two, leaving just the remaining 30 kilometre leg to Bourke to be completed on the following day; or vice versa. It would also have been possible for travellers between Brewarrina and Bourke to rest there overnight, although this was not the most direct route. Another advantage of the site is that it was above the flood plain, so that travellers coming from the southeast could still reach it during a flood, even though they could not then proceed through a vast expanse of floodwater to Bourke. Nevertheless, during later floods the hotel became a de facto post office where Bourke's incoming and outgoing mail was brought by boats rowed across the floodplain.

The site also facilitated access for visitors who wanted to explore Mount Oxley and enjoy its extensive views, although tourists would have been few and far between in those days.

The main problem with the site was access to water because run-off from the mountain would have been extremely unreliable. They must have installed corrugated iron tanks to store rainwater from the building's roof, because the hotel was to flourish for several years. They were fortunate that the drought broke around the time that the land was acquired.

The Reed family, having now assisted in the erection of buildings on several properties, would probably have done most of the construction work on their new hotel themselves. According to Cameron's *History of Bourke*, it consisted of two sitting rooms and three bedrooms (but presumably these were in addition to the private rooms set aside for use by the publican and his family.)[416] Unfortunately no photograph of it has survived, so it is impossible to know whether it was built in the slab hut style that Joseph Whye had used for the *Lame Horse* hotel at Gongolgon three years earlier or whether the Reeds had managed to secure a supply of the timber necessary for a weatherboard design. Given the water problems at this location, it seems likely that the building would have needed a roof of corrugated iron to facilitate the collection of rainwater.

James Reed was first issued a license for the *Mountain Home* hotel at Mount Oxley during February 1870[417] and the license was renewed for twelve months on 25 January 1871[418].

The Whye's hotel business at Gongolgon was doing very well. In July 1870 they took out a mortgage on two acres of their land, presumably to finance an expansion of the business. Joseph was also granted a timber license in the Warrego district (between Bourke and Wilcannia) at this time[419] (which was renewed in 1871[420]), so the loan may have been required to finance the purchase of a horse and cart that could be used for that purpose and for general use in support of the hotel business. The loan was repaid and the mortgage discharged within just seven months.[421]

Since Joseph could not simultaneously saw timber

in the Warrego district and run the *Lame Horse* hotel at Gongolgon, it is likely that these timber franchises were actually worked by his brother-in-law John Reed (with Jimmy and Alexander having by now moved to Queensland). It is notable that **James Tobin junior** also held a Warrego District timber license at this time, so both sons-in-law may have been cooperating in the expansion of the family timber business.

In June 1871 Joseph and Prudence purchased 48 acres of land adjoining the southern boundary of Gongolgon, possibly to meet the needs of hotel guests who needed a secure area for their grazing animals to forage.[422]

No doubt James and Frances were fully aware that their business was very isolated and therefore at high risk from bushrangers, but it was a risk that they had to take to earn a living as publicans in this area. They may have felt more relaxed after running the hotel for 18 months, but their remnant fears were about to be proven justified.

In about April 1871, William Reed (alias Willis, alias Mason) and John Thomas stuck up and robbed several stations on the Lachlan River including Owen's station (where they fired shots at the overseer), Paterson's Inn, *Roto* Station, Crawford's at Crowie Creek and Lynch's station. From each place they took either money, valuable articles or horses which they used to effect their escape northwards towards the Bogan district.

Less than three years had passed since Captain Starlight had murdered Senior Constable McCabe at Enngonia. In this environment, Sub-Inspector James Stephenson of the Forbes police gave chase with support from Constable Maloney. This was bad luck for the bushrangers, because Stephenson had successfully led a team in pursuit of bushrangers eight years earlier,[423] which had resulting in him shooting Fred Lowry (who later died) and capturing the notorious murderer Lawrence Cummins at Thomas Vardy's public house at Cooks Vale Creek (near Crookwell).

At Obley, the police party was supplemented by Constables Parker and Shilling and, as they tracked the bushrangers towards the headwaters of the Bogan River, Constable Slack of Dandaloo also joined the pursuing party.

Several times they lost the trail and, at Monkey, the black trackers reported that the case was hopeless, but Stephenson persisted and was able to pick up the trail once more. When the police party reached Gongolgon they conscripted local Senior-Constable William Murphy and, shortly afterwards, were also joined by Brewarrina's Constable Rixon.

They kept on until reaching Handcock's public-house at the Oxley Table Land (about three o'clock p.m.). They then heard that the bushrangers had been there the previous evening. They also knew that the rascals had field glasses with them by which they could watch from a distance the movements of the police without being seen themselves.[424]

Stephenson suspected that the bushrangers had camped near Mount Oxley, giving them a good view of anyone approaching, so he wisely detoured his men about ten kilometres so that they could approach unseen, below the brow of the hill. Stephenson, Rixon and a tracker were in the advance party and saw their quarry first. They immediately charged towards them, firing guns to scare off the bushranger's horses; successfully.

Thomas and Reed/Willis/Mason took aim at the police but, observing the approach of the other policemen from different directions, soon realised that there was no escape and surrendered without firing a shot. Stephenson, having pursued them for nearly a thousand kilometres, now had the pleasure of handcuffing both prisoners. It took his party a further nine days to return them to Forbes where they were charged on 19 July with robbery under arms and were committed for trial. The reporter for the *Dubbo Dispatch* opined

> *This is certainly one of the most brilliant achievements the police have performed for many a day, and every one concerned in it deserves more than mere commendation.*

It is interesting that the newspaper reporter attributed the "public house at Oxley Table Land" to "Handcock". John Hancock was listed in the 1872 Greville's directory as a Selector (not an innkeeper) who had 80 acres of land at Mount Oxley, a few kilometres east of the Reed's land.[425] It seems likely that the bushrangers had camped on or near his selection on the night before the police arrived; and that they were captured further west near the hotel at Mount Oxley. The reporter may have conflated these two events.

Despite this alarming occurrence on their doorstep, James and Frances Reed soldiered on with their hotel on the mount. Later that year they hosted the correspondent of the *Western Examiner* newspaper who was most impressed by Frances' method of preserving butter in the hot climate. He wrote an article about it that was syndicated across several newspapers in NSW and Queensland over the following few days. For example, the *Australian Town and Country Journal* reported:

A few days ago, Mr James Reed, of Mount Oxley, 20 miles from Bourke, showed me some butter made on the Yankee system, recommended by the Town and Country Journal. Three pints of cream was placed in a cloth and buried in the garden about two feet, but before the three days allowed, curiosity compelled them to see what it was like; it was found to be nearly all good butter. I am using some of it now, and it is superior to the churned butter, being firmer and sweeter. I would advise all parties living in warm climates to adopt this plan.[426]

Rather than learning this plan from the newspaper, it is much more likely that Frances had been aware of it since her childhood or early adulthood. This method of preserving butter (known as bog butter) had been used in Ireland and other parts of the world for centuries. She may have learned it from her Irish father, Benjamin Heazle, or observed it herself during the time that she and James had been stationed in Ireland with the 80th Regiment between 1832 and 1834, nearly forty years earlier.

The hotel license renewals for 1872 were not published in the gazette, but James Reed was listed as an innkeeper at Oxley's Tableland in Greville's Official Post Office Directory of NSW for that year, so it is safe to assume that his license had been renewed. It was renewed again in January 1873.[427]

While the Reeds had made a success of their hotel, its isolation is illustrated by a discovery that was made nearby on 16 January 1873.[428]

A human skull and other ones were found by Henry Nancarrow in a secluded spot near Mount Oxley, Bourke District. The bones are believed to be those of a white man who, most probably, was lost in the bush and perished for want of water. Deceased's death is supposed to have taken place more than five years ago.

Five years later, in June 1878, there was a similar discovery in the same area.[429]

On the 5th instant, some human bones, supposed to be those of a white man, were found in the bush five miles southeast of Mount Oxley and thirty five miles from Bourke. The following is the result of a Magisterial inquiry, ... "That deceased most probably died from thirst." A pair of moleskin trousers, elastic sided boots and an old white felt hat were found with the bones.

By the early 1870s Prudence and Joseph Whye were running a successful hotel at Gongolgon and James and Frances Reed were doing likewise at Mount Oxley, while other family members continued to run the established boarding, timber and carrying businesses. The family was prospering in this frontier town with even the Reed's youngest children having, by now, entered the real estate market. Over the next few years more family members would also move into the hotel industry so that, by 1876, they were running four of the ten hotels in Bourke, North Bourke, Gongolgon and Mount Oxley.

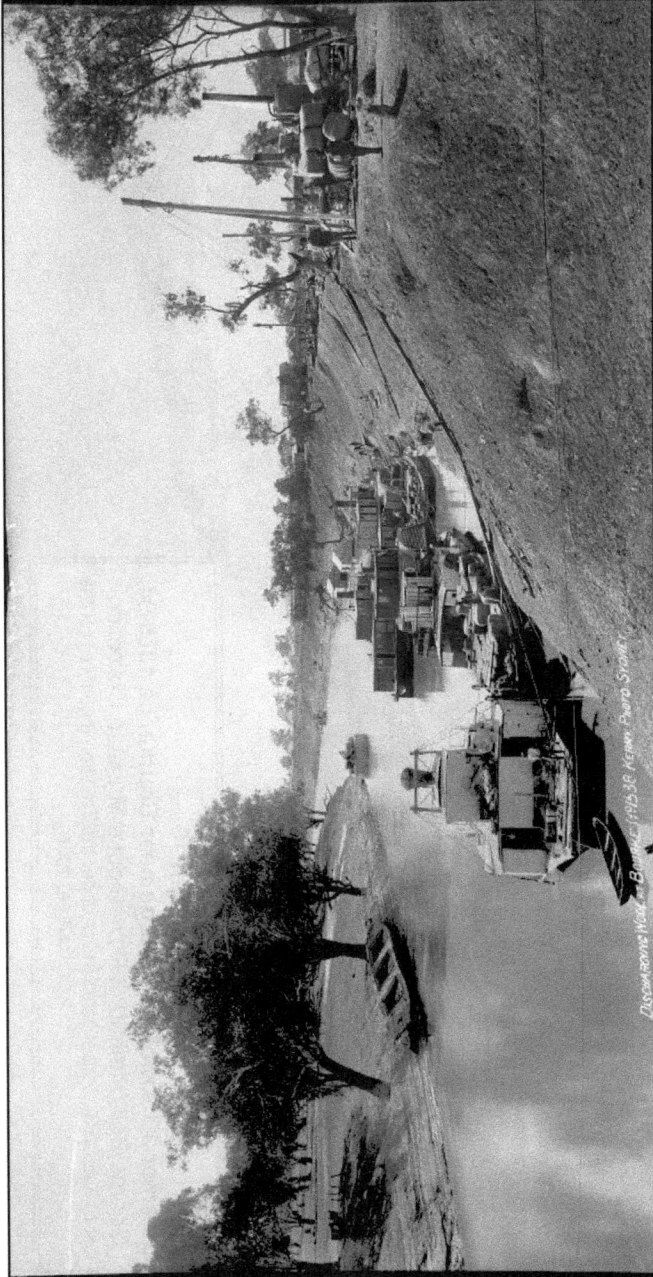

Photograph 14 - Steamers discharging wool at Bourke, ca 1885-94.
George Bell (attributed) Powerhouse Museum Collection.
Gift of Australian Consolidated Press under the Taxation Incentives for the Arts Scheme, 1985.
This is two photos stitched together by the author.

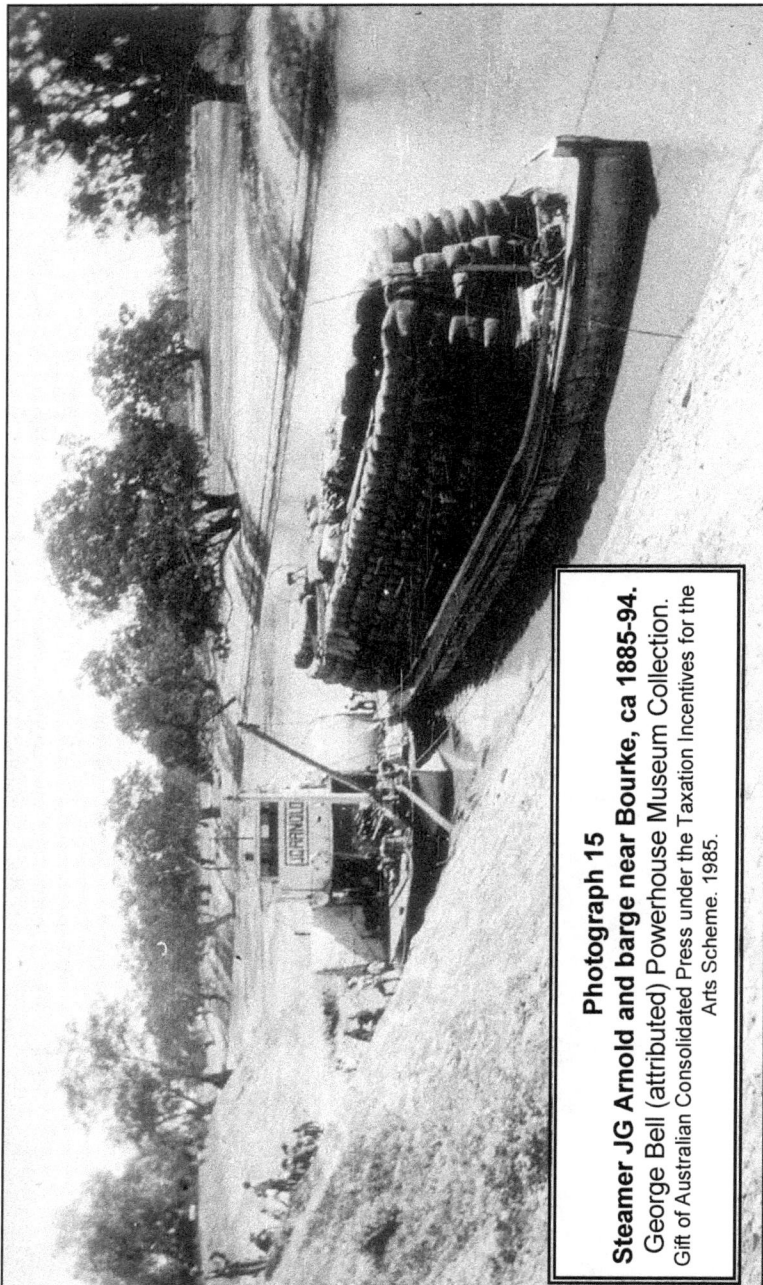

Photograph 15

Steamer JG Arnold and barge near Bourke, ca 1885-94.

George Bell (attributed) Powerhouse Museum Collection. Gift of Australian Consolidated Press under the Taxation Incentives for the Arts Scheme. 1985.

CHAPTER FOURTEEN

Jimmy, Alexander & Jane

By 1871 **James and Frances Reed** were well respected pioneers of the Bourke District, having already lived there for nine years. Eight of their ten children had also established homes in the area and the extended family was now running carrier, timber supply, house painting, boarding house and hotel businesses.

John Benjamin Reed, their eldest surviving son, was operating his bullock wagon business (with the possible assistance of his 21-year-old brother, George Charles). He and his wife Eliza Jane had one surviving child, Frances Eliza, now 11 years old. Alexander Reed may have also been working as a carrier with John Benjamin, but it is more likely that he had, by this time, moved to Queensland along with the family of his brother Jimmy. Sarah Ann now had seven children and her husband Michael Brennan was working as a house painter. Eliza Emily had four children and her husband Henry Johnson was now employed as a stockman. Prudence had four surviving children and she and her husband Joseph

Whye were operating a very successful hotel at Gongolgon. Frances and her husband James Tobin junior had not produced any more children since their first-born daughter had died seven years earlier. James Tobin had probably been working in the family timber business but was now planning to establish a grazing property near Gongolgon. Finally, the two youngest daughters, Mary Ann (aged nineteen) and Jane (aged fifteen) were both unmarried, as were their brothers Alexander and George Charles. The only member of the family who was definitely not in Bourke was Jimmy Reed who had by now taken up farming at Springsure in Queensland along with his wife Eliza.

With six of the second generation now married, a clan was starting to flourish. James and Frances had already welcomed twenty-five grandchildren into their family, although four of these had died in infancy or childhood.

Jimmy and Eliza had been among the second group of Reed family members to arrive at Bourke during 1864, but they remained for only about four years before moving permanently to Queensland. While living in Bourke their family had grown with the arrival of two more sons. Following his siblings John, Eliza and James (who had all been born in the Wellington district) **Charles A Reed** was born around October 1865,[430] within the same month as his cousin, Frances Eliza Brennan. Unfortunately, these happy events would have been overshadowed by the drowning death of their cousin (William John Reed) on 7 October.

A year later, his brother **George Reed** was born at Bourke and named in honour of his uncle who was now 16 years old.[431]

Their father Jimmy had worked in the timber business while living in Bourke and would have also worked with his brothers Alexander and John in the carrying business, requiring them to be away from home for much of the year. But Jimmy may have also taken work as a drover because he went into Queensland on at least one occasion. Alternatively, he may have accompanied his brother Alexander on a bullock wagon trip north. Some of the stations to the north of Bourke found that, rather than sourcing supplies from the south, it suited them better to bring supplies from Queensland, so bullock wagon drivers from Bourke were employed to venture as far north as Rockhampton, more than 1130 kilometres away.

Once at Rockhampton, Jimmy may have accepted local droving jobs to parts of the Fitzroy River catchment that was, at this time, opening up for cattle grazing. Somewhere along the line he found himself at Springsure, in the Central Highlands, about 66 kilometres south of Emerald.[432] This area of the country clearly appealed to him much more than Bourke because he decided to select land there and settle down. On 18 April 1868 he applied for selection 81 of 640 acres at Springsure, where he would establish Sandy Creek Farm and live out the remainder of his life.

Jimmy was probably aware that, six years earlier, the Springsure area had been soaked in blood in one of the bitterest incidents of the frontier confrontations between colonists and indigenous owners. In October 1861 a party of Victorian graziers led by squatter Horatio Wills had arrived nearby with an enormous settlement train of bullock wagons and 10,000 sheep to establish a property named *Cullin-la-ringo*. The group included

Wills' son Tom, the celebrated cricketer who had captained the Victorian team to repeated victories in matches between the colonies. Just three years earlier Tom Wills had codified the laws of a new sport that is now called Australian Rules Football.

Their sudden arrival in such large numbers on traditional Gangalu country was always going to attract a reaction from the local indigenous population, but the situation was exacerbated by an incident that had recently occurred nearby.

Jesse Gregson, manager of the neighbouring *Rainsworth* Station, had murdered Gayiri tribesmen who he accused of stealing his cattle. Two weeks after the large group of new arrivals had set up their camp at *Cullin-la-ringo*, they were the target of a revenge attack by the Gayiri. Nineteen settlers were killed,[433] including Horatio Wills, in the largest massacre of Europeans in Australian history.[434] Soon the survivors and nearby colonists had enlisted the help of Queensland Native Police to seek revenge for that revenge. On 27 November 1861 an encampment of about 300 tribespeople was attacked at 2:30 am by a party of men comprising both Queensland Native Police and a militia of local colonists. The *Sydney Morning Herald* reported two weeks later:

A note of the editor of the Rockhampton Bulletin states that the police overtook a tribe of the natives who committed the massacre ...; that they drove them into a place from which escape was impossible; that they shot down sixty or seventy and ceased firing only when the ammunition was expended. One of the blacks who was shot cried out, "Me no kill white fellow!" showing that they comprehended the proceedings.[435]

Having reported the facts, the *Sydney Morning Herald* editor went on to opine in defence of the indigenous victims.

Among the hundred human beings who in all, we are told, have fallen in vengeance for the ... massacre, how many were there young children? How many who had nothing to do with the white murder? The fundamental idea of a Christian Government is that the innocent shall not be confused with the guilty; that even the guilty shall escape rather than that the innocent should perish. ... The only justification of this wholesale destruction is that which justifies the policy of extermination. But is extermination the policy that a British Government ought to proclaim or assist? ... Whatever excuses may extenuate the conduct of the police, we cannot have the least doubt that in the eye of the British law they are guilty of murder.

Views such as this had formed the basis, more than twenty years earlier, of the Letters Patent that had been formally adopted by King William IV in 1836 to establish the Province of South Australia. The Letters Patent reflected the policies of the Secretary of State for War and the Colonies, Charles Grant, 1st Baron Glenelg. This founding document for South Australia guaranteed the rights of "any Aboriginal Natives" and their descendants to lands they "now actually occupied or enjoyed". Unfortunately, no heed was paid to those words as colonisation proceeded. No treaties were signed. The South Australian government (controlled from the outset by Squatters) sold, leased and granted land to colonists, thus effectively dispossessing the original inhabitants of their land. Those who held progressive views against such dispossession were shouted down and outvoted by those with a vested interest, just as had happened in NSW. The same process was now occurring in 1860s Queensland as the frontier moved inexorably northwards; and would continue into the twentieth century as it moved westwards towards the Kimberley.

Tom Wills survived the massacre and returned to Melbourne in 1864. Ironically, in 1866-7 he led an Aboriginal cricket team on an Australian tour as its captain-coach.[436] This was a prelude to the famous Aboriginal Cricketers' tour of England of 1868 that included several members of Will's team under the captaincy of Englishman Charles Lawrence.[437]

Jimmy Reed and his family had still been living in Wellington when people were massacred near Springsure in 1861. By the time he applied for his selection in 1868 the area was completely under colonial control and a town plan had been drawn up. He and Eliza then lost no time in establishing themselves on their new selection. A great deal of work would have been required to clear land and to erect a house, huts and fences.

Their sixth child, **Henry Reed**, was born on 16 January 1869 in Queensland;[438] with his brother **Frank Edward Reed** born two years later.[439]

When their sister **Frances Reed** was born on 4 February 1874,[440] her oldest brother John was 15 years old, Eliza was 14 and James was 12. They would no doubt have been helping to establish the farm by undertaking various chores and helping around the house.

Another son was born on 21 May 1876 and named **Thomas Reed**.[441] The family was completed two years later with the birth of **Mary Jane Reed**.[442]

Three months earlier, her oldest sister Eliza married

George Henry Horsfield at Rockhampton, the first of James' and Frances' grandchildren to marry.[443] Her husband was, like her father Jimmy, a carrier. While George had worked between Rockhampton and the Barcoo, Jimmy had worked between Rockhampton and the Gulf country before both settled on either side of Sandy Creek at Springsure. George was later licensee of the nearby *Shearers' Arms* hotel. According to an obituary of their daughter, Mary Ellen Kavanagh nee Horsfield, Eliza and George produced a family of nine children.

Jimmy and Eliza Reed's 26-year-old son James married Alice Elizabeth Foote seven years later on 12 June 1885,[444] followed a year later by their 21-year-old son Charles' marriage to Margaret "Agnes" Maguire.[445] Unfortunately, another son George died a year later in 1887, aged 21 years.

Jimmy and Eliza almost certainly had assistance in setting up their new farm from his brother Alexander, for whom there are no surviving records between 1868 and 1877. It is clear, however, that Alexander went to Queensland at some point during those years, because he married **Mary Eckel** at the residence of the Wesleyan Minister in Rockhampton on 5 December 1877,[446] just four months before his niece Eliza wed George Horsfield in the same town. Alexander, still working as a carrier, was now 40 years old but his new bride was only 18. She had been born at Dalby[447], 550 kilometres further south, the eldest of six children of Henry Eckel and Christine nee Erskine[448] (formerly Tomb or Thom).

A year and a half later, Mary gave birth to their first child, **Margaret Reed,**[449] probably named for Mary's maternal grandmother, Margaret Campbell. Their second child was born eighteen months later and named

Eliza Jane Reed,[450] in honour of two of her Reed aunts.

Alexander must have undertaken a carrying trip to Bourke during the following year because he sold his one acre of land in Anson Street to Cavendish Lister Nevile on 11 October 1881.[451] He had obtained a replacement deed from the NSW Land Titles Office two months earlier. Both he and his brother (George Charles) supplied statutory declarations that the original deed had been destroyed by fire. (Details of this fire are provided later in chapter 16.)

He must have returned to Queensland soon afterwards because there was a new addition to the family on 1 February 1883 with the birth of **Christina Wingfield Reed**.[452] Her brother **Henry James Reed** (also known as James Henry) was born about three years later on 5 December 1885.[453]

Eliza and Alexander had clearly been working towards the goal of obtaining their own farm because they chose Selection 23 at Springsure on 1 August 1887,[454] near the farms owned by Alexander's brother Jimmy and Jimmy's son-in-law George Horsfield.

Alexander's family would have been barely settled on their new farm when their fifth child was born on 28 November 1887 and named **George Charles Alexander Reed**[455] (after his uncle and father). Over the next four years the family was completed with the addition of two more sons, **William Edward Reed**[456] (born on 6 April 1890 and also known as William Frederick) and **Ernest John Reed**[457] (born on 19 July 1891). As we will see in the Epilogue, three of Alexander and Mary's sons would fight in World War I.

***

Six years before Alexander's marriage in Rockhampton, his youngest sister Jane had beaten him to the altar, becoming the second Reed daughter (after Frances) to be married at just fifteen years old. In her case, James and Frances would have felt significant pressure to approve the marriage (or may have actually insisted on it) because **Jane Elizabeth Reed** was seven or eight months pregnant when she married **Joseph Maxwell** at Bourke in July 1871.[458] Fortunately, unlike her sister Eliza's ill-fated nuptials with Anders Bufe eleven years earlier, the Maxwell union was to prove successful and very fruitful.

The first fruit of the union, **Alexander Maxwell**, was born two months later, even though his birth was not registered with the authorities until July 1872.[459] It is clear that he had been born before 25 September 1871 because, on that day, he paid 7 pounds and 15 shillings for 2 roods of land at lot 3, section 8 in Oxley Street Bourke.[460] Obviously a one-month-old child could not have initiated this purchase, so it was probably a wedding gift to his mother from her parents. James and Frances Reed may have insisted on the land being in their grandson's name rather than that of their new son-in-law, just in case the marriage had later failed.

Part of this block of land was to remain in the extended family until at least 1948. The other part passed out of the family in 1920 but was subsequently purchased on 9 July 1958 by my parents, **Reginald Bruce Fleming** and **Halvene Therese nee Kessey** (a GG-grand-daughter of James and Frances), and our family lived there, at 56 Oxley Street, for four years before selling it to finance a new house in Mertin Street.[461]

Jane's new in-laws, the Maxwell clan, were, like the Reeds, one of the earliest pioneering families in Bourke. Her new husband, Joseph, was related by marriage to other significant early families including that of William Walter Davis (who had married his sister Kate Maxwell a year earlier) and Joseph Lunn (whose daughter Emma later married his brother James Maxwell). The Maxwell clan was also allied with the Farrell family that would later be linked by marriage into the Reed family.

Joseph Maxwell had been baptised at Montefiore (near Wellington NSW) in 1846,[462] the fourth of seven children of **Richard James Maxwell** and his wife **Ann Cross**. Harvey Barnett (husband of their granddaughter Elizabeth Laura Maxwell) was later to be an important contributor to recording the early days of Bourke. He had a prodigious memory and wrote a wide-ranging memoir that was published in the History of Bourke journal in 1972. According to his memoir,[463] Richard Maxwell and Ann Cross originated in the north of Ireland, where they were married in about 1836-40.

He was sent out to Australia as General Manager of the Bogan River Company with headquarters on a large property at Kelso, near Bathurst. ... There were seven children of the family, four girls and three boys: Sarah, Jane, Kate, Joseph, James, Alec and Margaret. ... When the Bogan River Company extended its operations to the Bourke district [Richard] Maxwell came with it as General Manager and built the first homestead on the Warrego and named it Karney. Later he brought the remainder of the family but not until [even] later did the girls come to live at Karney when their education was finished. Maxwell continued to manage Karney until the Bogan River Company sold it to Sam McCaughey ...

At no time did [Richard] Maxwell live in the town of Bourke until he went to live with his daughter Jane, Mrs. James Brown.

It seems that Richard James Maxwell was commonly known as Joseph and his second son was therefore often referred to as Joseph junior. Other sources indicate that his role with the Bogan River Company was as a Station Overseer, not as General Manager of the whole company.

On arrival in Australia in about 1843, Richard and Ann must have brought two children: Sarah and Alexander (generally known as Alec). Catherine (Kate) was baptised in 1844 in the Church of England parish that included Gundaroo, Gunning and Yass.[464] Joseph, Jane and James were baptised at Montefiore near Wellington in 1846,[465] 1848[466] and 1850[467] respectively. Their youngest sibling was baptised Margaret Hellenore Maxwell at Carcoar in 1852.[468]

The family had reached the Bourke district before June 1863 when Edward Farrell, who worked for Richard Maxwell on *Cockerline* station, drowned in the Culgoa River.[469] (Since there was no such station, this is probably a reference to Collerina.)

[Farrell] *had a family of seven children and Maxwell allowed the widow and family to remain in the cottage and employed the boys, Tim, Tom and another boy on the station.*[470]

Richard Maxwell must have employed his son Joseph Maxwell junior as a stockman. According to the latter's obituary, he came to the Bourke district as a 19-year-old in 1864 from *Buttabone* Station on the Macquarie (60 kilometres from Nyngan) and returned there with a draft of bullocks.[471] Around this time he was tracking some missing stock on *Milroy* Station on the Culgoa River when he accidentally discovered a swamp surrounded by an abundance of feed. His employer was so pleased that he gave the young stockman a reward of 25 pounds.

The following year, according to the obituary, he was a stockman on *Boonawanna* Station (across the river from *Beemery*) and two or three years later he went to *Warraweena* Station where he worked for a few years. By 1870 he had gone into business as a butcher with **William Walter Davis** (who was also his brother-in-law).

Davis had been born at Bathurst on 5 July 1840 and Catherine Maxwell was his third wife. He was commonly known as "baldy" because one side of his head was hairless due to his being scalded as a child, so he always wore a wig. He was the basis for Henry Lawson's character Baldy Thompson, described as "rough squarish face, curly auburn wig, bushy grey eyebrows and moustache, and grizzly stubble … a squatter of the old order".[472] In the outback way, he pretended to have little sympathy for rural workers and swagmen but was generous in practical ways. He was a real entrepreneur who took large risks. According to one of his sons his overdraft was so great at one stage that he needed to shear 50,000 sheep to be able to simply pay the interest on it.[473] During the 1890s he was elected as the Member of the Legislative Assembly for the Bourke District on three occasions. At his death in 1923 he was survived by his fourth wife and 16 of his 19 children.[474]

Soon after Jane Reed married Joseph Maxwell, a correspondent of the *Australian Town and Country Journal* visited Bourke and published a very extensive report in the October edition of 1871, including a well-drawn etching of "The Port of Bourke" (Photograph 6).[475]

> *Bourke has about 500 inhabitants. The Commercial*
> *Banking Company of Sydney have a commodious and*
> *elegant building. There are several stores, the principal*
> *one being A. Ross and Co.'s, who have also branches at*
> *Menindee and Wilcannia. ... The vine has been*
> *cultivated to perfection by Mr J Horsfall (sheep*
> *inspector). Vegetables of every description grow here*
> *(with irrigation) as well, if not better, than in many other*
> *parts of the colony ... The hospital is an excellent*
> *building and is a blessing to many poor destitute and*
> *afflicted wanderers, who, under the skilful treatment of*
> *Dr Roberts, and the humanity of Mr Louis, the warden,*
> *have reason to bless such an institution. A gaol, capable*
> *of holding over thirty prisoners, is now in course of*
> *erection.*

The journalist had over-estimated the size of the town, as the 1871 census recorded 318 people of whom 204 were males.[476]

The same article mentions that Joseph Maxwell was now managing the *Commercial* hotel (although the official licensee was WW Davis). No doubt Joseph was running it on a day-to-day basis as an employee of his brother-in-law. A year later Maxwell was recorded in Greville's Post Office Directory as an innkeeper in Mitchell Street, as were Henry Colless (Tattersall's) and George Harris (Royal), while WW Davis was an auctioneer in Mitchell Street.

Their son, Alexander Maxwell died in July, around the time of his first birthday.[477] In July 1873, a year after Alexander's death, Jane gave birth to a second son who was named **Richard James Oxley Maxwell**[478]. While his first two Christian names were undoubtedly chosen in honour of his paternal grandfather, the Oxley part is more mysterious. It may have been a reference to the street where the family now resided on land that had probably been a wedding gift from Jane's parents. In any case, the name stuck and Richard was generally known as Oxley Maxwell throughout his long life.

According to Joseph Maxwell's obituary,[479] *"he was on an off butchering with Alf Hickles ... It was shortly after this that he took to teamstering and made several trips to Cunnamulla"*. This was probably during the mid-1870s. He may have been inspired to take up this business by his brothers-in-law John Benjamin, Jimmy and Alexander Reed.

The town of Bourke produced its first newspaper in January 1872, the *Central Australian and Bourke Telegraph*. Its debut was welcomed with short tributes in several existing newspapers throughout NSW, including this article published in the *Bathurst Free Press and Mining Journal* on 10 January.[480]

Newspapers are stretching into the far interior. We have received No. 1 of vol. 1 of a new weekly (Wednesday being the day of issue) intitled "The Central Australian and Bourke Telegraph". It is the same size as the Free Press, and is a very, fair sample of a country newspaper as respects workmanship and the rest. The editor says — "We hardly feel called upon to particularise extensively our future line of thought;" but a more sufficient representation for the interior, the Border duties, a customs house at Bourke, the navigation of the Darling, and the speedy completion of the telegraph are under promise to be discussed in due time. The undertaking is certainly a spirited one and deserves success.

These best wishes have since been realised. The new paper was to survive competition from the short-lived *Bourke Watchman* between 1882-1886 before welcoming a new competitor, *The Western Herald*, from October 1887. Following a takeover in 1898, the Telegraph changed its name to the *Bourke Banner*. After coexisting for twenty years these two Bourke papers were amalgamated in 1918 into *The Western Herald* masthead that has continued to this day[481] (totalling more than 150 years of continuous publishing in the town).

By late 1872, the Reed family had called Bourke home for ten years and had observed many rapid changes in the district. The town was now the centre of a booming rural economy and could boast some impressive buildings as well as a growing feeling of community. Some of the rough edges had been polished from its earlier heavy-drinking, frontier culture, transforming it into a much more hospitable and friendly oasis. Undoubtedly Mrs Harris, Frances Reed and her daughters had continued to play an important role in enriching the town in this way.

The *Town and Country Journal* followed up the comprehensive October 1871 report of Bourke's progress with an even more detailed and complimentary report in June 1872, this time accompanied by engraved sketches[482] of Ross's Store, the Commercial Bank building (see Photograph 13) and *Tattersall's* hotel. After outlining the town's physical attributes, the reporter turned his attention to the attitudes of its people.

The residents of Bourke and surrounding stations look with much more favour on their dealings with Adelaide and Melbourne than with Sydney ... and when one speaks of local representation in the Parliament of New South Wales, the subject is treated as a good joke.

It was easier to reach Adelaide and Melbourne (by paddle steamer) than Sydney and consequently many residents thought that Bourke would fare much better if the district was incorporated into South Australia. They deprecated the NSW government because it had failed to build a bridge over the Darling and the town lacked a Public School (although a private school was well attended). The journalist noted drily that the government was only providing six mails a week, a resident police magistrate, a sub-Collector of Customs, a commissioner of Crown lands, a clerk of petty sessions and registrar, a sheep inspector, a new gaol, a district court and bailiff, a court of quarter sessions and a police force!

The town now boasted two shoemakers, two blacksmiths and wheelwrights, two boarding houses, a chemist, cordial factory, baker, saddler, tailor, watchmaker, vineyard, large orchard, several Chinese-run vegetable gardens and a floating public baths. A Catholic church was in the course of erection but the Anglican congregation was yet without one. Mails ran twice a week to Sydney; Maitland (via Brewarrina and Walgett); and the Paroo and Bulloo Rivers. They also ran weekly to Melbourne and Adelaide (via Wilcannia) and to Queensland. A dozen steamers plied the river between Adelaide and Bourke during periods of high water (see Photographs 14 and 15) but there was discontent about the customs duties payable on goods moving between the colonies.

Take the townspeople socially and you will find them hospitable, ever ready to promote, by their liberality, a charitable object, and singularly jealous of maintaining, not only individual character, but the regulation of their town.

Bourke was developing rapidly and now boasted its own newspaper, but recent events initiated by James and Frances Reed's next son-in-law were about to supercharge the growth rate. A copper mining boom was in full swing and was the main topic of conversation in Bourke. Ten pound shares were trading for 160 pounds each!

Jimmy, Alexander & Jane

CHAPTER FIFTEEN

The mining boom

Following a chance discovery in 1870, Bourke businessmen quickly established a mining industry at Cobar that has, over the subsequent 150 years, unearthed huge quantities of minerals and continues up to the present day. **Mary Ann Reed** soon married the man chiefly responsible but he would die tragically less than four years later.

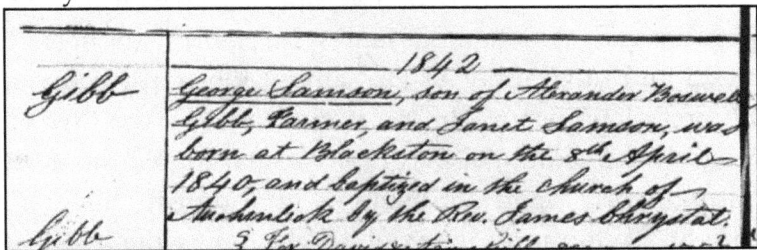

Illustration 18 - The 1842 baptism record for George Samson Gibb at Auchinleck in Ayrshire, Scotland. ScotlandsPeople

Nineteen-year-old Mary Ann married 32-year-old **George Samson Gibb** in Bourke on 25 April 1872. He came from a Scottish farming family but, through his good fortune and good management, both he and the town of Bourke were now on a fast track to prosperity. Born at Blackston in Auchinleck, Ayrshire, he was the second son of Alexander Boswell Gibb and Janet nee Samson[483] whose antecedents had lived there for generations. George's siblings were John Howie Gibb (1838-1861), Andrew Alexander Gibb (1842-1848), Jessie Murray Gibb (1845-1849) and Charles Gibb (1847-1870).

He was ten years old and living with his parents on the family's 65 acre farm at Blackston in 1851.[484] The census scribe recorded his father's occupation as both farmer and "factor for Lady dowager Boswell", clearly the source of his middle name. Alexander's household included his wife Janet; their sons George (aged 10, scholar) and Charles (aged 4); Margaret Howatson aged 14; and farm labourer James Gibb aged 23. Since he was not Alexander's son, he may have been a much younger brother or cousin.

The Auchinleck family held a barony of the same name from the thirteenth century or earlier. In 1504 King James IV bestowed it on the husband of Sir John Auchinleck's daughter and heiress, Thomas Boswell.[485] By 1851 it was owned by James Boswell whose grandfather (also named James Boswell) had been a friend and biographer of Dr Samuel Johnson (editor of the first dictionary). Johnson is described by the Oxford Dictionary of National Biography as "arguably the most distinguished man of letters in English history". Boswell's biography is widely regarded as the greatest biography written in the English language.

Alexander Gibb's role as factor was to manage the estate on behalf of the Laird of the Boswell family, including collecting rents from tenant farmers and ensuring that farm infrastructure was well maintained. This role was traditionally passed down to the factor's eldest son. Indeed, Alexander's father, Andrew Gibb

(1768-1839), had been appointed factor by James Boswell (the biographer) in November 1790.[486] Alexander had inherited the role after his father's death in 1839, by which time the estate was owned by Lady Boswell, widow of James Boswell's son Andrew (1775-1822) who had been killed in a duel. She was referred to as dowager because she (rather than her eldest son) now held title to the estate. By 1851 she had been running the estate, with the factor's assistance, for nearly thirty years.

When the 1861 census was recorded, twenty-year-old George was working as a ploughman in the household of William Lennox at Brentwood in Galston, Ayrshire (16 kilometres north of Auchinleck).[487] His parents were living in the Main Street at Ochiltree (near Auchinleck) with their son Charles (now 14). Alexander Gibb was now "Estate and House Factor", indicating that his responsibilities had expanded to include managing both the estate and the Boswell family's home, Auchinleck House, built about 1760. This house has, since 1986, been managed by the Scottish Historic Buildings Trust.[488]

George's older brother John Howie Gibb died that year, so George could now have expected to inherit the job as factor on his father's death. Instead, he decided to seek adventure in Australia, although if he intended to later return to Scotland, fate had other plans.

His decision to travel to Australia was almost certainly influenced by his first cousin, John Gibb who was eight years older, a son of George's uncle Andrew Gibb and Agnes McMinn. He had arrived in Melbourne as a 22-year-old aboard the *Bloomer* in August 1854. Six years later he returned home aboard the *Great Britain* but did not remain for long. He married Fanny Johnston on

July 18 1860 in Convoy, near Belfast (Ireland) before embarking with his new wife aboard the *Lord Raglan* bound for Melbourne. Accompanying them were Fanny's presumed siblings Ann (aged 17) and John Johnston (22) as well as John Gibb's siblings Alexander Boswell (23), James (19) and William Gibb (16). This group disembarked at Melbourne on 25 November and settled at Ballarat. Alexander Boswell Gibb (who had been born at Auchinleck in 1837 and named after George's father) died in Victoria in 1872 aged 35.[489]

It is not clear how or when George Samson Gibb joined his cousins in Australia, but he is probably the George Gibb who was robbed by John Duff of a watch, chain and pocketbook as he slept near the *Plough and Harrow* hotel at Ballarat on 23 August 1862. Duff had form and was eventually sentenced to two years' imprisonment for his crime.[490]

George seems to have spent at least part of the next several years working as a miner, because he was later reputed to have experience in this field. He was also closely associated with other men who had mining experience, so he had presumably tried his luck on the Ballarat goldfields.

By the end of the 1860s he was working as a tank sinker south of Bourke, along with his German business partners Ferdinand Kempf (known as Charles Campbell) and Thomas Hartman (who had both arrived in Melbourne aboard the *Olympia* in 1859).[491] In the Spring of 1870 they were all travelling from Louth to Gilgunnia (near Nymagee) with the help of aboriginal guides Frank and Boney, who led them to a waterhole named *Kubbur* where they camped overnight. The next morning, they noticed bright green and blue staining in the kaolin on the walls of the rock hole and decided to investigate. Their previous mining experience prompted them to take specimens for later analysis.

The following day they showed the specimens to Henry Kruge and his wife Sidwell who operated a shanty further south. This proved to be serendipitous because Mrs Kruge had worked in Cornish copper mines as a "balgal" (a traditional Cornish name for female mine workers) and was able to immediately identify the samples as copper ore. Her assessment was confirmed when her husband smelted some of the ore samples in his blacksmith's forge.[492]

The three men immediately took their remaining samples to Bourke where they looked for a backer to finance a more thorough mining feasibility study. On 6 October 1870, in partnership with Bourke businessman Joseph Becker, they took up a mineral conditional purchase of 40 acres.[493]

With equipment financed by Becker, they returned to the site and extracted a three ton sample that was transported to Louth by bullock dray and then by paddle steamer to Adelaide. The assay results, received in February 1871, showed 33 percent fine copper.

So, Campbell, Hartman and Gibb had discovered copper at what was later the town of Cobar, named after the waterhole. Mining of these resources (and other metals including silver, lead, zinc, antimony and gold) has continued on and off ever since, with the mines still producing more than a million tonnes of copper ore annually.[494] There is now a stele monument to them and "the balgal" near the mining museum at Cobar.[495]

Within a few months, the 40 acre mining lease had been transferred to the Cobar Mining Company, formed with 200 shares priced at ten pounds each to obtain the finance necessary to set up a mine. In addition to the three discoverers and Joseph Becker, the other shareholders were all from Bourke: Rusell Barton, William Bradley and James Smith. The company called for tenders from people interested in building the mine infrastructure and let the contract to Captain Thomas Lean, an experienced mine manager, who started work with six Cornish miners on 4 November 1871.

By that time, the Melbourne Herald reported that the price of the shares had *"rushed up from £15 to £70 and £80 per share"*, thus providing the discoverers with a 700 percent capital gain in a couple of months.[496] If we assume that the three discoverers owned just 25 percent of the company (with the financiers owning the rest), then their share would have been worth 4,000 pounds, with George Gibb entitled to a third of this.

Within a year the company had re-financed and now boasted 74 shareholders with nominal capital of twenty thousand pounds at one pound per share. Among the original backers, Becker (and his family) held 3850 shares, Bradley 3450, Barton 400 and Smith 300. Big new investments had been made by the Nancarrow family (2450 shares) and Edward Good 1000. Well over half of the shares were owned by residents of Bourke.[497]

No members of the Reed family had invested in the new mine, although WW Davis (brother-in-law of Jane Reed's husband Joseph Maxwell) had 175 shares. He may have met George Gibb (a future business partner) at this time and may be the connection that brought George into contact with Mary Ann Reed. Before long they were planning to get married.

Two of the original discoverers, Hartman and

Campbell, sold their shares to Becker, thus turning their chance discovery into considerable personal wealth. George Gibb retained only 200 shares, so he must have also sold most of his shares and realised more than a thousand pounds. He nevertheless retained a small stake in the company that was to become the Great Cobar Copper Mining Company (Limited) following a merger with the adjacent South Cobar mine in 1876.

George and others suspected that there might be other rich deposits awaiting discovery nearby. Some, such as Joseph Becker, took out claims around the site of the initial find but George Gibb decided to use part of the proceeds from the sale of most of his shares to take a more scientific approach. In late 1871 he and his business partners (John Connelly, Henry Nancarrow and Richard Nancarrow) started to search the area around the *Kubbur* waterhole for other mining prospects. In January 1872 the *Bourke Telegraph* newspaper published an article about their activities.[498]

> *Some short time since Mr George Gibb ... equipped a prospecting party for the purpose of testing new country. ... They have been prosecuting their researches with some success. ... We have no doubt that Mr Gibb's perseverance, combined with his practical knowledge as a miner, will result in the discovery of other fields for labour and enterprise.*

Soon afterwards the Gibb party discovered a large boat-shaped gossan of brick-red iron oxides on a low rise (later called Eloura Hill) eleven kilometres north of Cobar. They were understandably keen to lay claim to this site before any of the other mining enthusiasts in the area got wind of it.

They departed for Bourke very quietly in the hope of securing the ground without opposition, even muffling the hoofs of their horses with bags so that their movements might not be heard in the clear night air. ... The claim was lodged on the 1st of February 1872. On the 27th of February a well-equipped party including Henry Nancarrow and John Connelly revisited the discovery to further evaluate the find. They returned to Bourke around the 21st of April with fine specimens of grey and ruby oxide of copper. The four lease holders decided to put the venture into 1,000 shares and call the mine the Cornish, Scottish and Australian copper mine after their respective nationalities, Nancarrow (Cornish), Gibb (Scottish) and Connelly (Australian).[499]

The name Cornish, Scottish and Australian has since been shortened to the CSA mine and it remains one of Australia's highest grade copper mines, now owned by Glencore Australia.

It was in this heady atmosphere of discovery that George Samson Gibb and Mary Ann Reed were married. There were great expectations of success for the two mines in which he held shares and his prospects were, therefore, exceedingly good. No doubt the honeymoon was kept very brief as the demands on his time were growing by the day. Between February and July 1872, George was a member of partnerships that claimed leases on ten blocks of land in the mining district, totalling 400 acres.[500]

A month later the *Australian Town and Country Journal* reported on the progress of the mine.

The finders of this mine have been subjected to great hardships, having to contend against the want of water and often food, notwithstanding they have persevered most assiduously, and are at length rewarded. The copper ore is of a soft malleable nature, the same as Cobar, and a continuation of the same lode.[501]

Copper fever suddenly gripped the people of Bourke. In mid-June the local courthouse was besieged by sixty eager land applicants before it had even opened for business, all keen to claim a forty acre block near one of the two mines under construction.[502] By July, everyone had an opinion about the relative merits of the two mines, while the naysayers were predicting that the sky would soon fall on both. But the first mine was working well, with more than 500 tons of ore already having been carried by horse teams to Louth for shipment to Adelaide by paddle steamer. Another 100 tons of ore was sitting on the riverbank at Louth awaiting the next steamer[503] while the horse teams returned to Cobar with mining supplies and water. The value of George Gibb's 200 shares in this mine had risen rapidly, reaping him a tidy capital gain with the prospect of healthy dividends to come in due course.

Meanwhile, the CSA mine had been put into the hands of a company with a capital of forty thousand pounds. Soon another company was set up for a mine on an adjacent block with a capital of fifty thousand pounds. Demand for the shares was very strong and in August they were selling in Bourke for eighteen pounds each! If George Gibb had sold his share of the mine at this stage he would have pocketed thousands of pounds.

By September a shaft had been sunk to 27 feet on the CSA mine with good results, but speculators were selling and shares were now down to thirteen pounds. A month later the shaft was down to 38 feet but the ore was assayed at just 11 percent copper.

The owners of the CSA mine continued to experience real trouble in getting it established, with the main problem being a lack of water. With claims pegged all around the mine, it was soon proposed to simplify matters by amalgamating them all. But, in conveying this proposal to shareholders, those in Bourke seemed to get a different message to those in Sydney, leading to confusion and tension. George Gibb, Henry Colless and WW Davis were chosen to represent Bourke interests at a shareholders meeting in Sydney.

Around this time, Gibb and Davis embarked on a separate business partnership. Presumably they spent a lot of time together during the journey to and from Sydney, so there would have been plenty of opportunity to discuss business options; and Baldy Davis was never short of ideas and opinions. With their shares still well-priced but with uncertainty over the mine's progress, it made sense to cash up at least some shares and diversify into other ventures.

They must have liquidated some of their mining assets so that they could invest in the grazing industry because, on 23 August 1873 they bought *Kerribree* station from Mr McAulliffe of Ford's Bridge, along with 620 sheep and 46 head of cattle.[504] They soon registered a new cattle brand for the partnership:[505] D.G (for Davis and Gibb).

Two months later, in October 1873, Mary Ann gave birth to the couple's first child who was named **Jannet Frances Gibb** (in honour of her two grandmothers).

By March 1874 the shaft was down to 150 feet and the mine manager was "positive that the mine will be profitable". But, in the short term, his confidence was unrewarded and no significant body of rich copper ore was found. By the end of the year the shareholders' money had run out and, with assay results underwhelming, no one was prepared to invest additional capital. The company was officially declared insolvent[506]. Among the biggest losers were Joseph Becker, the Nancarrow brothers, WW Davis, Matthew Good and Henry Colless. Gibb's brother-in-law, 24-year-old **George Charles Reed**, was also numbered among the losing shareholders, holding 80 shares.

We now know that there was a wealth of copper ore that ran down from the surface to great depths, but the part of the lode that was nearest the surface had been leached of the precious minerals by weathering over millennia. If those intrepid early investors had procured the money, water and technology to get a bit deeper, they would have been richly rewarded.

The insolvency of the company that he had played such an important part in establishing and leading must have come as a devastating blow to George Gibb's ego. Nevertheless, he would have been very relieved that he had diversified some of his new-found wealth into the grazing industry. At the end he still held 240 shares, but this was almost certainly a lot less than he had possessed earlier, as one of the four discoverers of the site. And he would probably have still retained his 200 shares in the other mine which was now progressing very nicely.

Eventually the company that owned the other mine also took over the CSA mine site and much success was later achieved. The Great Cobar Copper Mine became the largest in Australia and, at its peak in 1912, boasted 14 smelters, a 64 metre chimney stack and over 2000 employees. But long before then, most of the investors and speculators of the 1870s had lost their money.[507]

As we shall see in the next chapter, George Gibb's brother-in-law, George Charles Reed, had opened a hotel in Bourke during 1873. Soon afterwards he was offered an opportunity to start another new hotel at North Bourke. Since he could not hold the license for two hotels simultaneously, when he opened the *Overland* hotel at North Bourke he relinquished the license on the *Bourke* hotel and arranged for it to be taken over by his brother-in-law, George Samson Gibb. Following the collapse of his CSA mining company, George Gibb was no longer actively involved in the mining industry, but he had retained his partnership with WW Davis in *Kerribree* Station near Fords Bridge. He was basically a "silent partner" because Davis had extensive experience in the grazing industry and was managing the station on a day-to-day basis. So, it made sense for George to take over the license of the *Bourke* hotel from his brother-in-law. They published an advertisement in the local newspaper, the *Central Australian and Bourke Telegraph*, on 2 August 1875[508], two weeks before the official transfer of the license was notified in the Gazette.[509]

Notice. I have this day authorised Mr GS Gibb of the Bourke Hotel to receive all Monies due to me, and his receipt will be held a sufficient discharge. GC Reed

Four months earlier, Mary Ann Gibb had given birth to their second child. At his baptism on 1 June, he was named **Alexander James Boswell Gibb** in honour of his paternal grandfather.[510] The ceremony that day was an extended Reed family affair with two first cousins baptised together. Michael Brennan (painter) and his wife Sarah Ann Brennan also presented their new daughter for baptism. **Mary Jane Heazle Brennan** had been born almost a year earlier on 23 July 1874.

A month after the double baptism, Michael Brennan was a central figure in an incident that was undoubtedly the worst tragedy suffered by the Reed family. It occurred on Tuesday 6 July 1875 at the nearby home of his in-laws John Benjamin and Eliza Reed, where their 15-year-old daughter **Frances Eliza Reed** had returned from school for her lunch. The town's *Central Australian* newspaper recorded a vivid report of the subsequent events, later republished in the *Maitland Mercury*.[511]

> *On last Tuesday afternoon, between the hours of one and two o'clock, Frances Eliza Reed, the only daughter of Mr John Reed of this town, while standing before the fire preparatory to going to school, her clothes accidentally took fire. Mrs Reed, the mother of the girl, was sitting outside in the verandah at the time quite unconscious of the peril of her daughter. When the girl saw that her clothes were on fire, and thinking there was no one in the house to assist her, she rushed out into the street screaming, and made for the Bourke Hotel, close by, running through the various rooms in a frantic state and into the bar, where she was seen by several persons with her clothes all in flames about her. She was thrown down by Mr Michael Brennan, who with difficulty extinguished the fire. Dr Grant, who was close by, and saw the girl on fire, quickly prescribed the proper remedies. The unfortunate girl (who was the only surviving child of her parents, and beloved by all who knew her) was fearfully burnt, and lingered in dreadful agony till Thursday afternoon, when death terminated her sufferings. The grief of the bereaved parents is*

inconsolable, this being the second catastrophe which has bereft them of their only children, as, it will be remembered by old residents of Bourke that the son of Mr Reid was accidentally drowned in the Darling river some seven years ago.

James and Frances and all members of the extended Reed family would have been immensely saddened by this, the seventh death among their 36 grandchildren born thus far, but the blow to John Benjamin and Eliza Reed, who had now lost both of their children, was immense. Each of them was so devastated as to almost lose their will to live.

Unfortunately, just a few months later (and following a brief illness), George Samson Gibb died suddenly on 9 December 1875, aged just 35 years.[512] It was a very premature end for the man whose life story testifies to his adventurous spirit supported by significant skills and knowledge all reinforced with large reserves of perseverance. He had dared to leave Scotland (despite the reliable prospect that he would eventually succeed his father and grandfather as factor to the Boswell family's Auchinleck estate) for a life of escapade and enterprise in Australia. He had capitalised on his luck on that fateful night camping at the Kubbur waterhole through his subsequent endeavours and consequently founded one of Australia's most important mines. His death was reported in both the *Evening News*[513] (Sydney) and the *Australian Town and Country Journal*.

On Tuesday ... news came that Mr George Samson Gibb, one of the discoverers of Cobar Copper Mine had passed away; he had been ailing, but being a young, strong giant, no one thought that death would have struck him thus soon. He was at one time proprietor of the Central Australian, and from his modest unassuming nature, was respected by all classes. He was buried on Monday, attended by a large train of true friends.

It seems that the term "Central Australian" was almost synonymous with Bourke in those days, so the *Bourke* hotel must have been colloquially called that at the time, thus explaining the reference in the article. In fact, the first license issued for a hotel with that official name did not occur until 1885 when William Gale chose the name for his new hotel on the corner of Anson and Richard Streets.[514]

George was survived by his 22-year-old widow Mary Ann and two children, Janet Frances Gibb (aged 2 years) and Alexander James Boswell Gibb (9 months). Even though he was a partner in *Kerribree* Station and owned shares in the Cobar mine, he had neglected to make his will. In applying for letters of administration for his estate,[515] Mary Ann was supported as executrix by her brother-in-law James Tobin junior (who was described as a teamster and grazier of Gongolgon) and Michael McAuliffe (who held the license for the *Salmonford* hotel at Fords Bridge). McAuliffe had sold *Kerribree* Station to Gibb and Davis a year earlier, so he may have held a mortgage, thus explaining his involvement in the administration of the estate.

Following the untimely death of her clever and entrepreneurial husband, Mary Ann faced an uncertain future. While she was now in need of practical support, her parents were both in their sixties and starting to slow down, her brothers Jimmy and Alexander were far away in Queensland and John Benjamin was consumed by the grief of losing both his children. It would fall to the younger members of the family to help Mary Ann.

Her immediate concern was the fate of the *Bourke* hotel license. Her brother George Charles had only relinquished it to George Gibb four months earlier and was now publican of the *Overland* hotel at North Bourke, so he could not take it on. Nevertheless, he would have provided her with great support over the next few months, so that Mary Ann was successful in her application to take over the license from 1876.[516]

Almost four years later, Mary Ann gave birth to a daughter who was baptised as Hazel May Gibb in St Stephen's Anglican church on 5 October 1879.[517] The register refers to Hazel as an "illegitimate child" and to Mary Ann as a "hotel keeper". She would continue as publican of the *Bourke* hotel until 1881 when it was briefly taken over by her second husband, Timothy Farrell.[518]

While the copper boom had brought very significant wealth to many enterprising Bourke residents who possessed the financial resources required to capitalise on the nearby discoveries, that did not include many members of the Reed family. George Charles Reed had acquired some shares but would probably have lost money in the end while his sister Mary Ann eventually inherited a relatively modest estate from her husband, the chief discoverer, George Samson Gibb.

CHAPTER SIXTEEN

The Bourke and the Overland

The Reed's youngest son, George Charles, celebrated his 21st birthday in 1871. He had, no doubt, been earning his own living for several years already, starting with chores in the boarding house and later assisting his father and older brothers in their carrying, timber, fodder and hotel businesses. He now moved into the business world and saw immediate success but would soon be called upon to assume de facto leadership of the family in Bourke.

George Charles bought shares in the CSA mine at Cobar around the time that his sister Mary Ann married its founder George Samson Gibb in April 1872 and enjoyed early fortune as the mine progressed and the prospects for his shares looked promising. Around this time, he would have learned from another brother-in-law (Joseph Maxwell) that the *Commercial* hotel in Mitchell Street (owned by Maxwell's brother-in-law WW Davis) was about to be sold to George Harris, owner of the *Royal* hotel. Closure of the old *Royal* hotel would leave Bourke with just two inns, so George Charles decided to seize this opportunity by opening his own.

He immediately set to work making all the necessary arrangements, including engaging a supplier of alcoholic drinks and applying for a publican's license. In September 1873, to raise some capital for the new business, he sold to James Moloney, a local Customs Officer, the two acres of land in Anson Street that he had bought at auction six years earlier.[519] That same month, the *Australian Town and Country Journal* reported that George Charles' new hotel had opened for business.[520]

> *A new place of entertainment was opened last week by Mr G Reed - the Bourke Hotel - making three inns now in Bourke. A supper of unusual goodness was spread before the guests, who did justice to it.*

No doubt his mother Frances, who was now well known in the district as an experienced and reliable caterer, had produced the sumptuous repast, with assistance from her daughters.

The gazette notice for George Charles' new license on 24 October 1873 specifies that his hotel was in Darling Street.[521] Since there is no record of George purchasing land in that street, the hotel must have occupied one (or more) of the allotments already owned by his parents. In later years the *Bourke* hotel would be run by his sister Mary Ann Gibb, her second husband Timothy Farrell and ultimately by his sister Prudence and her husband (who were to change the name to the *Family* hotel). It is, therefore, very likely that George Charles had transformed the family's former boarding house on the north-western corner of Darling and Wilson Streets into a hotel, thus fulfilling his parents' intentions in coming to Bourke eleven years earlier. Thirty years later, in 1904, the building would be completely gutted by fire.

In volume 4 of the *History of Bourke* journal, Bill Cameron's article about the *Jolly Waggoner* hotel[522] (on the corner of Mitchell and Glen Streets) states that it had been first licensed as the *Victoria* hotel to Donald McDonald on 30 October 1873 (a week after George Reed's *Bourke* hotel was first licensed). In fact, the *Jolly Waggoner* did not open for business until eight years later when its first gazetted license was issued to Edward Dugan.[523] McDonald's license was for the old *Royal* hotel premises that he renamed the *Victoria*, but his business did not last and these premises were unlicensed in 1874. The gazette for late 1873 therefore lists only the (new) *Royal*, *Tattersall's* and George Reed's *Bourke* hotel, thus confirming that the town had just three hotels, as reported in the newspaper article quoted above.[524] The old *Royal* premises would be re-licensed as the *Shakespeare* hotel two years later in 1875.

There were two more at Gongolgon (owned by Joseph Whye and John Hawthorn), one at Mount Oxley (owned by James Reed) and one at North Bourke - the *West Bourke* hotel owned by Joseph Lunn who had opened it in 1869.[525]

Despite the early optimism, George Charles' 80 shares in the CSA mine would have become worthless when the company went into receivership in December 1874. Nevertheless, his business confidence remained high because the new *Bourke* hotel was doing well, with solid bar sales and a steady demand for short-term overnight accommodation in addition to a few longer-term boarders in residence. In February 1875 a boarder named Mr Murchland (a building contractor working on a new house for Mr O'Shanessy) died in his bedroom from an ailment that he had incurred three months earlier in a site accident.[526] Despite this unfortunate incident, the hotel continued to do well and George Charles was gaining a reputation as a good businessman.

He expanded the land associated with the hotel when he purchased lot 2 in section 11 from fellow-publican John E Kelly on 18 June.[527] The Reed family now owned all five allotments on the northern side of Darling Street between Glen and Wilson Streets.

Three months earlier, in March 1875, a man named Henry Hackley had stolen George Charles' horse and saddle, but they were quickly recovered by Constable Prior.[528] Hackley was committed for trial at the Bourke Quarter Sessions Court on 7 May where he was found guilty and sentenced to 4 months hard labour in the new Bourke Gaol.[529] Hackley may have been in cahoots with Thomas Collins who was also arrested by Constable Prior for a similar offence against Joseph Lunn and faced the same session of the Bourke Court. Collins was sentenced to twelve months hard labour in Bathurst Gaol.

Joseph Lunn and George Charles Reed went into business together at this time. Lunn's *West Bourke* hotel at North Bourke must have also had very good custom. It was safe from floodwaters, the only Bourke hotel on the northern bank of the river. It would have been getting business from teamsters, drovers and other travellers using the river ford nearby, seemingly more business than it could handle. So, Lunn had built a second hotel on land that he owned nearby, facing Macquarie Street (on lots 3, 6, 7 and 8 in section 6) and must have approached George Charles to run it for him.

As we saw in the previous chapter, George Charles relinquished the license of the *Bourke* hotel to his brother-in-law George Samson Gibb so that he could transfer to the new hotel at North Bourke. He was granted a license for the *Overland* hotel on 21 January 1876[530] and was to run it successfully for six years (although he sub-let it for two of those years).

***

Prudence and Joseph Whye had settled into a routine in running the *Lame Horse* hotel at Gongolgon and were also involved in the family timber business, with Joseph obtaining a timber license for the Warrego District in October 1871.[531] They disposed of two blocks of land in Gongolgon that were surplus to requirements. Firstly, in November 1871 they sold a triangular block facing Colayne Street opposite their hotel (lot 6 in section 2) to Thomas Davis of *Milroy* Station.[532] Then, a year later they sold the other triangular block (lot 5 in section 2) to William Cleaver, a carrier from Dubbo.[533]

Their seventh child was born in April 1873 and baptised at St Stephen's church in Bourke as **Kate Whye** on 10 May. Her sister **Josephine Hazel Whye** was born two years later and baptised at St Stephen's on 7 October 1875 by Samuel Edward Marsden, Lord Bishop of Bathurst.[534]

Bishop Marsden's father (Thomas Marsden) had been a storekeeper at Windsor and Sydney before founding the wool-buying firm of Marsden and Flower in about 1829. The bishop's mother was Jane Catherine Marsden, fourth daughter of the Reverend Samuel Marsden, his father's second cousin. So, the bishop was a Marsden on both his paternal and maternal sides.[535]

After leaving the King's School at Parramatta, he had gone to England for further education at Gloucestershire and Trinity College, Cambridge. He was ordained and served as a deacon and curate there for several years while writing an unpublished biography of his grandfather. On 29 June 1869 he was consecrated as Bishop of Bathurst at Westminster Abbey before returning to Australia to take up that appointment. Despite working hard and travelling extensively throughout the Diocese, his administration became unpopular with both the laity and the clergy. This could explain why Josephine Whye was the only child that he baptised during his visit to Bourke in 1875. His popularity declined even further after the Bathurst denominational school closed in 1879 and he was forced to resign as bishop in 1885. After returning to England, Marsden served as assistant bishop of Gloucester and Bristol before ending his career as canon at Gloucester and later at Bristol.

Around the time of Josephine's birth, her cousin Alfred Haylock Whye turned up at Gongolgon to re-join his uncle, Joseph Whye. They had not seen each other since Joseph left England twenty years earlier when his nephew was just two and a half years old.

Alfred's mother Jane was eleven years older than her brother, Joseph. We last heard of her in chapter 11 when she was recorded on the 1851 census as a 24-year-old house servant in the Waterbeach household of John Stacey Youngman (a merchant and miller) who had a wife and four children[536]. Also, in that household had been George Haylock, an 18-year-old apprentice miller. A year later Jane had given birth to Haylock's son, who was baptised as **Alfred Haylock Whye** on 19 November 1852. Eight years later Jane had married Charles Doggett at Chesterton in Cambridgeshire[537].

Twenty-one-year-old Alfred sailed from London on

3 June 1874 as one of 460 passengers aboard the *Zoroaster*, arriving in Brisbane on 25 September[538]. He must have spent a couple of months in Queensland, getting acclimatised to Australia and earning some income before sailing aboard the steamship *City of Brisbane* to Sydney arriving on 2 January 1875[539]. From there he would have travelled to Gongolgon to be reunited with his uncle. He may have worked for Joseph for a while before moving on to other employment in the grazing industry.

Two years later, in January 1877, Prudence bore a son who was named **Joseph Headland Whye** in honour of his father.[540] This happy event came at the start of a tumultuous four years for Prudence, during which she would mourn the deaths of four members of her family interspersed with the joy of yet another baby.

When her new son was just four months old, his father became ill with pneumonitis (lung inflammation) that may have been caused by a respiratory infection like asthma or bronchitis. The disease can also be caused by exposure to airborne irritants emanating from mouldy hay (farmer's lung) or from mouldy bird feathers and excrement. (Joseph may have, like many contemporary hoteliers, kept pigeons for the table and for shooting sports.) Severe cases can come on suddenly, with wheezing, shortness of breath, chest pain and coughing. In modern times it is treated with anti-inflammatory or immuno-suppressant drugs, although it can sometimes require surgery, but none of these treatment options were available to Joseph and he died after five days of suffering, aged just 41 years. He was buried in Gongolgon cemetery on 8 May 1877 by William Wright, witnessed by his brother-in-law, George Charles Reed.[541]

It was a premature, abrupt and sad end for a man who had achieved a great deal since arriving in Australia twenty-two years earlier as a 19-year-old agricultural worker. He had worked and saved hard, enabling investment in land at Gongolgon and the establishment of a very successful hotel business; and had earned the admiration of the local community. He was survived by his wife Prudence, seven of their nine children and his recently arrived nephew Alfred.

Joseph's demise had come so suddenly that he died without a will. Probate in his estate was granted to his thirty-year-old wife Prudence as Administratrix[542] on 2 August 1877 with the support of dual executors William Wright (a station manager of Gongolgon and her husband's undertaker) and James Tobin (grazier of Gongolgon and her brother-in-law). The value of the estate was estimated at less than one thousand pounds, still a significant amount that included the hotel business, several acres of land in Gongolgon and a larger land holding on the outskirts of the village.

Prudence now had to assume Joseph's role in running the business as well as taking on the responsibilities of both parents in raising their children, including two toddlers and a baby. Before the year was out she had been granted the license as publican of the *Lame Horse* hotel that she had helped her late husband establish.[543] Despite the hard work, heartache and stress that would have been involved, she was to thrive on the responsibility and eventually survived Joseph by 64 years.

Four months before Joseph Whye's death, George Charles Reed had married Mary Ann Peters on New Years Day 1877.[544] Details of her early life are opaque, obscured by apparent inconsistencies in the official records. According to the Bourke Court House record of her death, she had been born at Windsor in about 1860 and her parents were William Peters and Sophie Smith.[545] The only birth registration for a Mary Ann Peters at Windsor between 1855 and 1865 relates to a girl born in 1856, but her mother's name was Mary Ann, not Sophie[546].

By the end of 1877 two of George Charles Reed's sisters held publican's licenses. Mary Ann Gibb had been managing the *Bourke* hotel in Darling Street since the death of her husband two years earlier; and now Prudence Whye was doing the same at the *Lame Horse* hotel at Gongolgon. It is likely that George Charles had been kept very busy supporting Mary Ann while also trying to establish his new *Overland* hotel at North Bourke. Now he was called on to support Prudence as well, as she tried to work through her grief, run her hotel, raise a large family and administer the estate of her late husband.

George Charles must have been a very capable and hard-working individual. At just 26 years old he was the junior male in his generation of the Reed family and yet it was to him that his sisters turned in their hours of need. Their father, James Reed, was now nearing his seventieth birthday and probably no longer had the energy necessary to provide much practical support. George's older brother John Benjamin Reed was only in his forties, but he was a broken man due to the tragic deaths of both his children, while both Jimmy and Alexander now lived in Queensland. In these circumstances, George decided to hand over the reins of his *Overland* hotel so that he could better support his sisters with practical advice and assistance. So, he gave up the licence for two years during 1877-78. In his absence, the *Overland* was run in 1877 by his brother-in-law Joseph Maxwell and in 1878 by David Neale, before George returned from 1879.

Following Joseph's death, Prudence was seemingly beset with the dark hand of fate. While she and her brother George Charles acted quickly to ensure that her hotel business remained on a sound footing, her family would endure much more loss of life.

Her youngest son, Joseph Headland Whye, died from a "continued illness" on 21 March 1878,[547] less than a year after his father's demise. Three months later his sister Kate succumbed to whooping cough on 14 July.[548]

While Prudence was managing to run her hotel business successfully, the effort and stress was adversely affecting her family. Four of the nine children that she and Joseph had brought into the world over the previous fifteen years were now dead. She needed help to nurture into adulthood her remaining five children (aged between 3 and 14 years). She found that help in the person of a second husband, James Murphy, who had been working as a butcher at Gongolgon for a couple of years.

James was three years older than Prudence, having been born at Kilnabrack near Glenbeigh in County Kerry (Ireland) on 12 November 1843. It appears that he was baptised on the day he was born, although the register is too faint to reproduce here. It states that his parents were John Murphy and Mary nee Shea while his baptism was sponsored by Michael Lynch and 21-year-old Honora Shea, his mother's younger sister[549].

Nine years before James' birth, his grandfather (Denis Shea) had been arrested on a charge of sheep stealing, found guilty at Tralee on 13 March 1834 and sentenced to transportation for life.[550] After arriving in Sydney aboard the convict transport ship *Blenheim* on 26 October that year,[551] he was assigned to serve Joshua Kinghorne[552] at Goulburn Plains.

Denis must have behaved very well because he was granted a ticket of leave after just eight years,[553] by which time he was living in the Irish Catholic enclave at Campbell's River in the Bathurst District. Five years later, he was granted a conditional pardon[554] and celebrated by applying to the Governor for permission to bring his wife and family out from Ireland.[555]

Denis' wife, Mary nee Horgan, arrived at Sydney aboard the *Panama* on 14 September 1849,[556] along with their three youngest children. Her oldest daughter Mary had married John Murphy at Kilnabrack[557] just two years after her father had been sent to Australia and now had five children. When she and her family rejoined her parents in Australia four years later, she had been separated from her father for nineteen of her 32 years. He paid 16 pounds under the Remittance Regulations for her family's emigration.

The Murphy family arrived in Sydney on 15 August 1853 aboard the *Talavera*[558] and were immediately offloaded at the Quarantine Station on North Head where they lived for a short period before continuing to Campbell's River. John Murphy's father Jeremiah (Darby) Murphy had died, but his mother Johannah was still living at Glenbeigh.

James Murphy was literate by the time he arrived in Australia as a nine-year-old. He helped his parents establish their farm at Campbell's River and later found work as a farm labourer before creating his own farm nearby. When he married Ann Malcolm on 28 December 1864[559], she was three months pregnant with their second son James[560], his older brother Bernard having been born and died a year earlier.[561]

In February 1866, James was charged by the police at nearby Rockley with stealing a saddle belonging to Dennis Clifford.[562] His father (or brother) John Murphy was later acquitted on a charge of conspiring with Henry Neale to defeat the ends of justice by attempting to induce Clifford to refrain from pressing charges[563]. Found guilty in the Bathurst Circuit Court, James was sentenced to one year's hard labour in Bathurst Gaol[564].

Six months after he returned home from gaol[565], Ann gave birth to twin girls[566] named Abbey and Mary, but they were premature and died within a few days[567]. Despite the impossible timeline, James accepted Ann's assurances that he was their father and they produced three more children during the next six years[568] (another Mary, Catherine and John). However, in April 1874, under James' dogged questioning, Ann eventually admitted that he was not the twins' father. He immediately left the family home, never to return. This was a somewhat hypocritical reaction to her admitted adultery given his own role as the father of her illegitimate son Bernard, two years before their marriage[569].

He later recalled that he then "travelled about to many places, taking any employment that offered"[570]. After four years, in July 1878, he returned to Bathurst and engaged a solicitor to file for divorce[9], which had only been available in NSW since 1873.[571]

His divorce petition accused Ann of adultery with Henry Herring while obscuring some of his own awkward truths. He described himself as a carrier of Bourke, even though he was working as a butcher at Gongolgon, 100 kilometres away[572]. This neatly hid his current whereabouts and prospects from Ann while giving credence to another fallacy that was designed to hide his prison sentence - that his absence from home when the twins were conceived was due an extended carrying trip.

Although Ann knew that he had been in gaol, rather than absent on business, she chose not to contest the divorce.[573] It suited her by enabling her later marriage to Herring.[574]

Within two weeks of signing the divorce petition, James had returned to Gongolgon and conceived a child[575] with Prudence Whye. His divorce decree became absolute on 7 June 1879.

***

In addition to his moral support and practical assistance, George Charles Reed may have provided some financial help to his sister Prudence during the first year of her widowhood. That could explain why she transferred most of her landholdings at Gongolgon into joint ownership with him on 15 November 1878[576]. Another possible reason for this arrangement may have been to protect her assets from the control of any future husband by placing them under the legal ownership of her trusted brother. After all, Prudence had recently discovered that she was carrying James Murphy's child.

Prior to the passage of the NSW Married Women's Property Act in 1889, wives were legally subordinate to their husband. Upon marriage, husband and wife became one person under the law and the property of the wife was surrendered to her new husband. After years of political lobbying by English women, their parliament changed the law in 1882 to give women the same right to own property as men, with NSW falling into line seven years later.

Whatever the reason, Prudence's brother would transfer all these landholdings back into Prudence's sole name on 16 December 1886.

In September 1878 George sold lot 2 in Darling Street to Edward Warmoll, land that he had bought just three years earlier[577]. Warmoll was to lose it in a mortgagee sale ten years later, when it would return to a member of the extended Reed family.

Warmoll was one of several new publicans in Bourke. After George Charles Reed opened Bourke's third hotel in 1873, competition had increased dramatically as four additional hotels were licensed over the next four years. The first of these was Matthew Good's converted boarding house at the western end of Mitchell street, licensed as the *Trafalgar* hotel in 1875.[578] Seven years later Good renamed it as the *Telegraph* hotel.[579] Also in 1875 Ephraim Smith was granted a new license for the original *Royal* (later *Victoria*) premises, now renamed the *Shakespeare* hotel[580]. It would continue in business on the north-eastern corner of Mitchell and Glen streets for many years to come. A year later new licenses were issued to Edward Dugan for the *Carriers Arms* hotel (on the northwestern corner of Mitchell and Tudor streets) and to Edward Warmoll for the *Turf* hotel[581] (on the northern side of Mitchell Street between Glen and Wilson Streets). Map 11 shows the location of these hotels.

The *Carrington* hotel may have also opened about this time.[582] It was situated about four miles out of Bourke on the Brewarrina road and was generally referred to as the *Four Mile*.

So, by 1877 there were seven hotels operating in Bourke, two at North Bourke, one at the four mile, two at Gongolgon and one at Mount Oxley. In addition to these, an Ebenezer Timothy Smith was granted a license for the *Criterion* hotel in the Bourke District in 1874.[583] This license was re-issued in 1875 and 1876 but then the establishment disappears from the records, so its location remains obscure. It may have been a roadside inn somewhere near the town.

The first child for George Charles Reed and his wife Mary Ann was born on 14 December 1878 and baptised as **Edward John Bloxham Reed** by Charles Dunstan at St Stephen's Anglican church on 10 March 1879.[584] This was a very clear tribute by his parents to Edward John Bloxham (the Father of Bourke) who was elected as the town's first mayor at this time. George Charles Reed and his brother in law Michael Brennan had both been signatories to a petition that had recently been submitted to the Colonial Secretary, successfully calling for the establishment of a municipality at Bourke.[585] Bloxham is commemorated with streets named after him in Bourke, Cobar and Louth and his final resting place in Bourke cemetery is marked by an impressive obelisk.

When Mary Ann gave birth to another son on 28 February 1880, George memorialised his late brother-in-law Joseph Whye by naming the child **Gilbert George Joseph Whye Reed**. He was baptised by EG Wright at St Stephen's on 16 May 1880.[586]

George Charles Reed had successfully assumed a

leadership role in the extended family from the mid-1870s with sound handling of the establishment of the *Bourke* hotel in Darling street and the *Overland* hotel at North Bourke. He had then provided able support to his widowed sisters Mary Ann Gibb and Prudence Whye and, no doubt, also to his brother John Benjamin Reed and sister-in-law Eliza Reed, grieving the accidental deaths of both their children. He had provided an opportunity for his brother-in-law Joseph Maxwell (who ran the *Overland* hotel for a year) and his parents were probably relying on him more and more. But the blow that fate was about to land on George demonstrates that the vicissitudes of life can be manifestly unfair.

On Tuesday 7 September 1880, he lost his business when the *Overland* hotel at North Bourke burned to the ground. The events of that night were reported in the *Maitland Mercury* on 18 September.[587]

> *On Tuesday night a fire occurred at West Bourke, by which the Overland Hotel, owned by Mr. George Reed, was completely destroyed. A little after tea time, Mrs. Carr, a lodger in the house, went to her room and lit a candle. On leaving her room she blew the candle out, everything seemingly being safe, but five minutes afterwards she saw a glare of light, and returning found the mosquito curtains of the bed on fire. There was no supply of water handy to stop the flames and the building being weatherboard with calico partitions, was quickly destroyed with all its contents. Mr. Reed who was not insured, is a considerable sufferer, there having been, according to his statement, over £50 and some valuable deeds in the cash box, which was destroyed.*

There is no record of George ever owning the land

that the hotel was built on, so he probably rented the building from Joseph Lunn. But, in addition to the contents of the cashbox, he would have lost a large amount of furniture, bar fittings, equipment, stock, manchester and more. Furthermore, he lost his livelihood and was never able to start again as a publican.

One of the valuable documents in the cashbox was the deed to an acre of land in Anson Street that belonged to his brother Alexander. Both he and George Charles had to provide statutory declarations to the NSW Land Titles Office so that Alexander could obtain a replacement deed before selling the land to solicitor Cavendish Lister Neville on 11 October 1881.[588]

By June 1881 Charles had opened a store and was engaging in some wheeling and dealing with land. He bought 2 roods of land on the corner of Darling and Narran streets at North Bourke from Joseph Becker. This purchase was financed with a mortgage loan but, within two weeks, George Charles had on-sold the land to Alfred Kirkpatrick.[589] A month later the license for the *Overland* hotel was transferred to Thomas Willoughby, who must have erected a new building, as he retained the license for over a decade thereafter.[590]

Around this time George Charles opened a boarding house at North Bourke.[591] Clearly he was doing whatever he could to start again after losing everything in the disastrous fire, but the wheel of fortune still had further heavy blows to rain upon him. On 4 November 1881 his eldest son Edward died at just three years old.[592]

George Charles' eldest daughter was born three months later and, when baptised at St Stephen's on 1 May 1882, was named **Frances Hazel Reed** in honour of her grandmother.[593]

George Charles and his young family continued to battle on, running both a store and a boarding house, but creditors were continuously knocking on their door. The final twist of fate's knife came on 29 September 1882 when he surrendered to insolvency.[594]

Four days before marrying James Murphy on 18 May 1879[595] Prudence gave birth to his son and named him **Daniel Reed Murphy**[596] (in honour of James' oldest brother). Three months later his half-sister Mary Murphy died of pericarditis at Bathurst.[597] Prudence was probably not yet aware of James' first family as he had claimed to be a bachelor.

The demands of child-rearing were soon consuming most of Prudence's energy, so her new husband took over the running of her *Lame Horse* hotel[598] before the birth of their second son on Christmas Eve 1880. He was named George Charles Reed Murphy[599] after Prudence's beloved younger brother who had so recently lost his North Bourke hotel business to fire.

A few months later, on 31 May 1881, Prudence's eldest child Frances Anna Whye (who had witnessed her mother's marriage two years earlier) was herself married to Augustus Sullivan.[600] At 26 years old he was nine years senior to his new wife.

Unfortunately, Daniel Reed Murphy died from diphtheria on his younger brother's first birthday, Christmas Eve 1881.[601] This disease is caused by infection with a bacterium that releases a toxin that attacks the upper airways. The victim experiences great difficulty in breathing and eventually the windpipe is completely blocked by a membrane, resulting in death by suffocation. On Christmas Day he was interred into the same grave that already contained the remains of Joseph

Whye, Joseph Headland Whye and Kate Whye. During the burial ceremony, prayers were read by his new brother-in-law, Augustus Sullivan. Prudence later erected a gravestone (see Photograph 16) with the following poignant verse.

A loving Husband, a Father dear,
A faithful friend, that lieth here.
In Peace he lived, in Peace he died.
His life was craved, but God denied.

This sudden spate of deaths in Prudence's household hints at a common cause. It could not be poverty-related because the family was running a very successful business. At least three of the four had died from lung problems while the cause of young Joseph's death was recorded opaquely as "continuing illness". His father's pneumonitis probably resulted from exposure to mould while Kate's whooping cough and Daniel's diphtheria were caused by different bacteria.

Even though these causes of death were different, all could have stemmed from a general lack of hygiene in the household. They probably kept a cow, sheep, chickens, pigeons and pigs to supply the hotel with fresh food. There was probably also a vegetable garden and fruit trees that would have been fertilised with animal manure. It would have been commonplace to slaughter an animal on site and to hang it in a meat-house nearby the hotel until it was time to cook the meat. Toilet facilities would have been a long-drop hole in the ground under a roughly built wooden outhouse that was used by both hotel guests and family members. It is very unlikely that running water was plumbed in, with wash water probably provided from a large jug and basin used by everybody. The handle of the jug would have been a crucible for disease if not disinfected regularly, as would the door handles for the outhouse and meat house.

For these reasons, infectious diseases were much more common in the nineteenth century and there was no effective treatment for severe disease because antibiotics would not be discovered until forty years later. Those afflicted had to rely solely on the body's immune response but it could be overwhelmed if it was immature or had been weakened by earlier contaminations.

George Charles Reed had been a tower of strength for his widowed sisters Prudence Whye and Mary Ann Gibb while continuing to run his own businesses very successfully - until the cruel hand of fate had intervened. Now he was a broken man who would have to lift himself up again, but other members of his family were also experiencing very tough times.

Photograph 16
The gravestone of Joseph Whye, Joseph Headland Whye,
Kate Whye and Daniel Reed Murphy in Gongolgon cemetery.
Author's photo

Photograph 17
John Benjamin Reed and his wife Eliza (nee Green) pictured
with Frances Reed in about 1879.
Shared by Biles Family Group on Ancestry.com.

CHAPTER SEVENTEEN

The worst of times

It was not only the families of George Charles Reed and his sisters Mary Ann Gibb and Prudence Whye who had to cope with a series of dreadful events during the late 1870s and early 1880s. Most of their siblings also faced very unwelcome trials.

Jane and Joseph Maxwell suffered as much misfortune as anyone during this period. As we saw in chapter 14, their oldest son Alexander had died in 1872, but they were soon to suffer business failure and the death of two more children.

Three years after Alexander's death his father Joseph was employed as Bourke's pound keeper, charged with securing stray livestock (including pigs, cattle, horses, sheep and goats) in a fenced area set aside by the Council. Wayward animals could also be placed under his care by police constables or private citizens. He was then responsible for providing feed and water and notifying the owner who could claim their animal after payment of a fine and any associated fees (such as for feed or to repair any damage it had caused). Unclaimed animals would eventually be sold at auction.

On 26 September 1875 Jane produced their first daughter who was baptised as **Kate Hazel Maxwell** at St Stephen's Anglican church on 2 November.[602]

A year later Joseph was surprised when, upon answering a knock at his door, he was greeted by a young aboriginal man who was lying prone on the ground.[603] The lad worked for Joseph at the pound but had taken a severe fall from his horse two days earlier, breaking his leg. He had since laid in the bush without food or water but, when no help came, had managed to splint the leg himself by binding two stout pieces of wood to it using strips of cloth torn from his waistcoat. Thus patched up, he had crawled for two miles to reach the house. Fortunately, Joseph was able to quickly secure medical aid and the lad made a good recovery.

While pound-keeping was a steady job, Joseph harboured an ambition to run a hotel as licensee, which would afford him an opportunity to expand a customer base into a thriving and profitable business. He got his opportunity[604] when his brother-in-law (George Charles Reed) asked him to take over as publican of the *Overland* hotel at North Bourke in early 1877. Joseph had managed the *Commercial* hotel six years earlier on behalf of another brother-in-law WW Davis, but this was his first chance in the role of licensee. As manager he would have been paid a risk-free wage, but as licensee he had to pay rent to the owner, invest in stock and pay wages to any employees. It was a riskier proposition but the rewards would be significant if he could improve the hotel's custom.

While the family was working in the hotel at North Bourke they welcomed another daughter into the world. **Frances Annie Maxwell** was born on 3 December 1877 and baptised in St Stephen's church a month later.[605] Sadly she died at just five months old.[606]

Unfortunately, business at the hotel fell away and left Joseph with no means of paying the debts that he had incurred in setting himself up as licensee.[607] A year after taking on the job he was financially unable to continue and was replaced as licensee by David Neale[608].

Joseph returned to his former job as a stockman and the Maxwells moved to Gongolgon to be closer to the stations where he found work. Soon afterwards, the family expanded with the birth of **Eliza Emily Tobin Maxwell** on 11 December 1878.[609]

His income as a stockman was nowhere near enough to meet the debts that had been run up during his period as hotel licensee. In February 1879 we was sequestered into bankruptcy with liabilities of 218 pounds and assets of just 30 pounds[610] and he was finally declared insolvent a year later.[611]

Worse was to come in 1881 when their son **Augustus George Maxwell** was born in April[612] but died in the same month.[613]

As the family endeavoured to leave these troubles behind, they faced a continuous financial struggle while raising their surviving children Oxley, Kate and Eliza. In normal circumstances they could have relied on the strong support of their parents and siblings, but most of them had been similarly afflicted. In these circumstances the Maxwells accepted an offer from Jane's childless sister, Frances Tobin and her husband James, to permanently adopt their youngest child, Eliza Emily.

***

Even though Frances had only been 15 years old when she married **James Tobin** junior, they would have a very long and successful partnership of 55 years. The loss of their only child within the first year may have bound them together during the intervening eighteen years as their desire for children went unfulfilled.

Back in 1868 she and her husband had paid eight pounds for two Gongolgon town allotments - lots 1 and 2 in section 3 totalling 4 roods[614]. It is likely that they then lived in a house that they built on this land while James pursued a career in the grazing industry.

On his marriage record James had been described as a stockowner, indicating that he was working as a stockman who had been paid in new-born stock, rather than in money. He aimed to build up a herd on his employer's land so that he could later acquire his own land and stock it. That time came six years into the marriage when he applied successfully on 5 August 1869 to buy 320 acres near Gongolgon under the Conditional Purchase scheme.[615] Those 320 acres of freehold land were part of a 960 acre run in County Clyde (north and east of the village) on which his lease was extended in 1875.[616] Around this time he was granted a timber license in the Warrego District,[617] so it seems that he also had a stake in the Reed family timber business.

In December 1870 he reported to the Gongolgon police that George Bell had stolen his mare and wagon along with six sets of harness.[618] The police issued a warrant for Bell's arrest. Four months later, however, James was himself arrested by Constable Benton and charged with stealing a bullock from the Richardson brothers of Duck Creek[619] (probably grazier neighbours near his property in County Clyde). He was allowed bail of 200 pounds. Unfortunately, the outcome of both cases has been lost in the mists of time.

In June 1871 he acquired another property on the East Bogan run in County Cowper (south and west of Gongolgon). Like the County Clyde property it comprised 960 acres, of which 320 acres were held freehold.[620] Having thus established himself with two modest holdings, he was to continue in the grazing industry for two more decades, using the skills that he had learned since arriving with his parents in the Gongolgon district at the age of twelve. He later expanded into the stock trading[621] business while continuing to graze animals on his own small holdings.

James Tobin was not the only western grazier who was doing well. A reporter for the *Sydney Morning Herald* briefly noted on 4 February 1875 the rapid development that had recently occurred in this area of the State.[622]

A stranger, absent for some years, visiting the northwest now would hardly recognise it. Not only have towns sprung up where only stockyards held the pride of place, but on the stations the improvements and changes made are something surprising. The principal sheep establishments are fenced, the sheep being housed out in paddocks. The "shepherd" will soon be a thing of the past. Three boundary riders do now what fifteen shepherds used to accomplish in the pre-fencing days. Every place you go you see the ominous "poison" placard - a warning to all mongrels and vagabond tame dogs. The wire fences are not so liable to be destroyed by fire as dog-leg or three-rail, so they are in more request.

As the decade wore on his wife Frances must have started to wonder how she and her husband could assist the struggling members of the Reed family, as successive misfortunes were added to the family's sorrows. She watched on seemingly helplessly as the Maxwells suffered the death of two children and bankruptcy. When Joseph Maxwell was forced to resume his former occupation as a stockman and to move his family back to Gongolgon in 1878, Frances Tobin was closer at hand to offer her sister practical assistance. No doubt this included child-minding duties, as Jane Maxwell now had to establish a new home while probably taking on whatever employment she could obtain. Her son Oxley was now 6 years old, Kate was 4 and little Eliza was just a baby, so it is likely that the children spent lengthy periods in the care of their aunt Frances. That would explain why it was eventually agreed that Eliza would remain with and be raised by her aunt. This decision must have been taken before 27 October 1879 when the child was baptised as Eliza Emily Tobin Maxwell.[623] She was generally known as Lila in later life.

***

James and Frances Reed had run the *Mountain Home* hotel for just three years after it was first licensed in February 1870. By mid-1873 James was almost 65 years old and Frances was in her 62nd year. No doubt the hard, constant work involved in running a hotel was starting to wear them down, particularly as their children had left home and found their own employment. They were by no means decrepit, with both having more than two decades left to live, but it made sense to slow down since they could afford to do so.

They now owned an established hotel business and

its land at Mount Oxley plus several blocks of land in Bourke. One of these was the site of their boarding house which would soon be leased to their son George Charles for conversion into the *Bourke* hotel. The other blocks probably contained residential houses used by members of the extended family.

They also had an interest in the family timber business. James Reed did not stop working completely because he was again granted a timber license for the Warrego district on 23 December 1874. Nevertheless, it seems that he and Frances decided that they had finally amassed enough wealth to allow them to move into semi-retirement. So, they sold their hotel business to their neighbour John Hancock who successfully applied for a license for the *"Mount Oxley"* hotel in February 1873.[626]

While Hancock then ran the hotel business, he did not own the land or buildings associated with it, which were retained by James Reed. The editor of the *History of Bourke* journal concludes, based on the slight difference in name, that the *"Mountain Home"* hotel of James Reed was different from the *"Mount Oxley"* hotel of John Hancock,[627] but there is no evidence to support this. On the contrary, Hancock would have rented the existing premises from James Reed who retained ownership for another 14 years.

A year after they leased the hotel at Mount Oxley to Hancock and moved back into Bourke, Frances was asked to provide refreshments for the congregation that had gathered on 26 August 1874 to celebrate the laying of a foundation stone for the new Church of England building on the corner of Mitchell and Richard Streets.[628]

After the ceremony there was a tea meeting in the Public School, for which Mrs Reed, senior, kindly provided the tea, eatables, etc. The room was crowded. There was a programme after tea of music, recitations and short speeches.

A year later James and Frances transferred lots 3[629] and 4[630] in section 11 (in Darling Street) to their sons-in-law Joseph Whye and Michael Brennan respectively. Two years later when their daughter Frances and son-in-law James Tobin were looking to move into a house in town, they transferred lot 1 to them[631]. While these transfers may have been gifts, it is much more likely that they were sales that would have provided the older couple with some cash to fund their semi-retired lifestyle. James and Frances nevertheless retained ownership of lot 5, on which their son George had recently established the *Bourke* hotel. In their later years they lived with the families of their married daughters, particularly that of Michael and Sarah Ann Brennan.

***

In chapter 11 we learned that **Eliza Emily Bufe nee Reed** had married **Henry Johnson** at Bourke in 1865 and that they had produced five children by 1873: Frances Eliza (1866), James Henry (1868), Alexander George Oxley (1869), Sarah Jane Heazle (1871) and John Benjamin Linley (1873). In chapter 12 we learned that they had almost certainly been running the Reed family's boarding house in Darling Street Bourke in 1869.

By May 1872 when his daughter Sarah Jane was baptised, Henry was working as a stockman.[632] Later that year he was granted timber licenses at both Brewarrina[633] and Bourke,[634] so he clearly also had a stake in the family's timber business. Three years later he was granted a timber license for the Warrego District.[635]

John Hancock renewed his lease on the *"Mount Oxley* Inn" during May 1874[636] but did not remain in the business for the full twelve months. By August 1875 the license had been transferred to Henry Johnson[637] who published the following advertisement in the *Central Australian and Bourke Telegraph* newspaper on 2 August.[638]

Henry Johnson begs to inform the Public that having taken the above Hotel [The Mount Oxley Hotel] he is prepared to afford the best accommodation. Only liquors of the best brands are kept in stock. Travellers will find this an excellent stopping place and will be afforded every convenience. The Hotel being situated in country completely fenced in and an abundant supply of water being on the premises, affords advantages not usually to be had from wayside Inns. NB Cobb and Co's Coach passes by twice a week.

Johnson retained the license of his father-in-law's hotel for four years[639] and bought at least 40 acres of Hancock's nearby selection[640] at this time. His wife Eliza gave birth to their sixth child who was baptised as **George Johnson** in St Stephen's Anglican church on 28 September 1876[641].

When young George was 18 months old his father suffered a severe injury to the index finger of his left hand when the barrel burst as he pulled the trigger of a double-barreled shotgun while aiming at a hawk in the sky. He was brought to Bourke on the mail coach where Dr Brown speedily treated his injury and dressed the wound. The lock of the gun was found 70 yards from where the shot had been fired and the second (unburst) barrel was found on the roof of the house.[642] Henry was extremely lucky to have received only a relatively minor injury from such a large explosion near his head and other vital organs. The fate of the hawk was not recorded.

Three months later his wife bore a son who was named **Henry Sampson Johnson** as a tribute to his late uncle, George Samson Gibb. Young Henry (who was generally known as Sampson) was approaching his second birthday when his sister **Emily Jane Johnson** was born on 15 October 1879. They were baptised at St Stephens in a triple-ceremony with their cousin Eliza Emily Tobin Maxwell on 27 October 1879[643].

Henry Johnson gave up the Mount Oxley hotel license in 1878, soon after the incident with the gun, and it was taken over by Patrick Welden for three years.[644] But Welden's license application for another year was refused on 16 August 1882[645] and the premises ceased to operate as a hotel from that time, thus eliminating the rental income that flowed from it to James and Frances.

Despite the hotel's closure, the Johnson family remained nearby on the land previously purchased from John Hancock and Henry was described as a "selector" when the family welcomed another son into the world. He was baptised as **Albert William Johnson** at St Stephen's on 25 September 1881.[646]

A year later, Henry applied for a license to operate a wine bar at *Mooculta* Station but the hearing was postponed.[647] He must have been refused because he was employed as a labourer on that Station when a tenth and last child was added to the family with the birth on 8 March 1885 of **Mary Ann Maud Johnston** (who was to be known as Maud throughout her life). Maud was baptised at St Stephen's two and a half months later.[648]

While Henry was employed on *Mooculta* Station for

several years, it seems likely that his wife and family continued to live on their selection near Mount Oxley. In August 1887 James Reed transferred his two 40 acre blocks there into the ownership of the two eldest Johnson sons (James Henry Johnson[649] aged 19 and Alexander George Oxley Johnson[650] aged 17).

***

When the Brennan family had sold its land at North Bourke to Joseph Lunn in 1874 the family included six children ranging in age from ten-year-old Sarah down to two-year-old William with another on the way. They then moved back into Bourke where, it seems, the family lived at or near the *Bourke* hotel while Michael continued to work as a painter. Their daughter **Mary Jane Heazle Brennan** was born in July 1874 but it was not until nearly a year later that she was baptised at St Stephen's church in a joint ceremony with her cousin Alexander James Boswell Gibb who was nine months younger.[651]

A year after their niece Jane Eliza Reed was burnt to death, the Brennan family endured their own tragedy when their four year old son William died on 14 August 1876[652]. Two years later Michael Brennan decided to give up his painting business and become a publican. He established the *Native Dog* hotel at Native Dog Springs, 44 miles north of Bourke on the Enngonia Road.[653] Three days after Christmas 1878, Sarah Ann gave birth to a daughter at this new home. She was baptised **Annie Brennan** at St Stephen's church three months later[654] but unfortunately died just five days after her baptism[655].

***

Four years after the tragic death of her daughter, Eliza Jane Reed nee Green died at Bourke on 23 November 1879 at just 47 years old.[624] Her widower, John Benjamin survived her for less than two years before his death on 15 September 1881 at 49 years of age.[625]

In the months before Eliza's death, she and John had been joined by Frances Reed in a photograph that depicts them staring at the lens, each with a look of joyless resignation in their eyes. Despite the coldness of the image, it is the best depiction of Frances that has survived - see Photograph 17.

***

It wasn't just the Reed clan that experienced the worst of times during the 1870s. While the town of Bourke had made some huge strides forward during its first two decades, the stresses and strains of the frontier society occasionally burst forth into extreme violence, as they did in September 1877. A man named Getting, who was employed by George Harris as a barman in the *Royal* hotel, shot three members of Bourke's police force, killing two, before drowning himself in the river.[656]

Constable Costigan, a hotel resident, had paid his board to Getting shortly before the incident. They were reportedly friendly and had planned to take a walk together on the following Sunday. But Getting then went to his room, changed his clothes, loaded his double-barreled gun and immediately shot Costigan on the hotel verandah where he died instantly.

A minute later Trooper Armitage passed by, unaware of Costigan's fate, and was himself shot and badly wounded in the shoulder. He died five hours later.

Getting was pursued to the riverbank by Inspector Keegan. After unsuccessfully trying to reason with the agitated murderer, he eventually rushed him to secure the gun but lost his footing on the slippery bank. This allowed Getting to take careful aim and shoot him in the chest before raining blows on his head with the gun. Heroically, Keegan continued the pursuit before Getting rushed to the river and drowned himself. Keegan later recovered from his wound.

The whole town turned out the following day to honour the two policeman as they were laid in their graves in the Bourke cemetery.

A year later, there was a similar incident in the district, but this one played out over several weeks. It started when the very effective Senior-Sergeant of the Gongolgon Police (James Murphy) led a raid on a cattle duffing operation on a property north of Brewarrina. (He had participated in the capture of bushrangers at Mount Oxley seven years earlier but is not the James Murphy who had recently married Prudence Whye at Gongolgon.) The gang had for years stolen cattle in NSW and sold them in Queensland before stealing more in Queensland for sale in NSW. Murphy and his team disturbed them while they were altering the animals' brands. On seeing the police team approaching, the gang dispersed and Murphy followed its leader, Alick (or Thomas) Law, one of many aliases. After a long chase and clever tracking, Murphy surprised Law and captured him before setting off for Brewarrina with his prisoner handcuffed to a horse.[657]

As they neared Brewarrina, Law hit Murphy over the head with a stirrup iron, badly injuring him, before making his escape. Murphy managed to return to

Brewarrina and telegraph details of the incident to his superiors before gamely resuming his pursuit, but this time Law got away. The NSW Police force announced that Law was wanted for the attempted murder of Senior-Sergeant Murphy and launched a major manhunt.

A few days later, a team consisting of Senior-Sergeant Wallings and Constables Souter and Walsh of the Dubbo Police challenged Law at the Wombobbie Inn near Warren. To avoid arrest, Law shot Wallings through the heart and made his escape.

Now wanted for both murder and attempted murder, Law soon affected the name "Midnight" as he fled north towards Queensland. The police theorised that he would probably pass through Enngonia on the way, so Troopers Hatton and Grey led by Sub-Inspector Duffy of the Bourke police went there and lay in wait. Before long they challenged a rider who had turned up at dusk but he galloped off into the night. Nevertheless, Constable Hatton fired at him and he was forced to abandon two other horses that he had been leading.

Midnight was then tracked and pursued with great determination by the three Bourke policemen, assisted by an Aboriginal tracker named Jimmy. They finally caught him three days later at Barringun, on the Queensland border. After an exchange of gunfire, *Midnight* was shot and brought down. Constable Hatton's shot three days earlier had wounded him and he had since lost a lot of blood. After placing him under arrest they acquired a cart to carry their prisoner who was, by now, very weak. They set off for Bourke post haste but *Midnight* died of his wounds soon after and was buried on the Irara run.[658] It later turned out that he had frequently visited Bourke where he was known as Harry Wilson.

***

As we have seen, an extended tale of woe had afflicted the Reed family during the decade leading up to 1882. Frances Tobin and her husband James had been unable to have any more children after their eldest daughter died soon after birth. Mary Ann Gibb's husband had been intimately involved in the failed CSA mine at Cobar; and she had then been unexpectedly widowed. Prudence Whye/Murphy had lost her children William, Frederick, Kate and Joseph Headland Whye plus Daniel Reed Murphy; and been suddenly widowed. Henry Johnson had narrowly escaped serious injury when his gun exploded. Michael and Sarah Ann Brennan had lost their son William and their daughter Annie. Jane and Joseph Maxwell had lost their children Alexander, Frances Annie and Augustus George; and been declared bankrupt. George Charles Reed and his wife Mary Ann had lost their son Edward John Bloxham Reed and seen their *Overland* hotel burn down, thus losing their livelihood resulting in bankruptcy. But the family members who suffered the most were John Benjamin Reed and his wife Eliza whose only daughter had been burnt to death (adding to the pain caused when her only brother drowned in 1865, before the start of this calamitous period). The only clan members who had not suffered seriously during this time were the Queensland contingent of Jimmy and Alexander Reed. Nevertheless, this series of misfortunes included at least one tragedy per year for a decade and would have therefore blighted the lives of all members of the Reed clan.

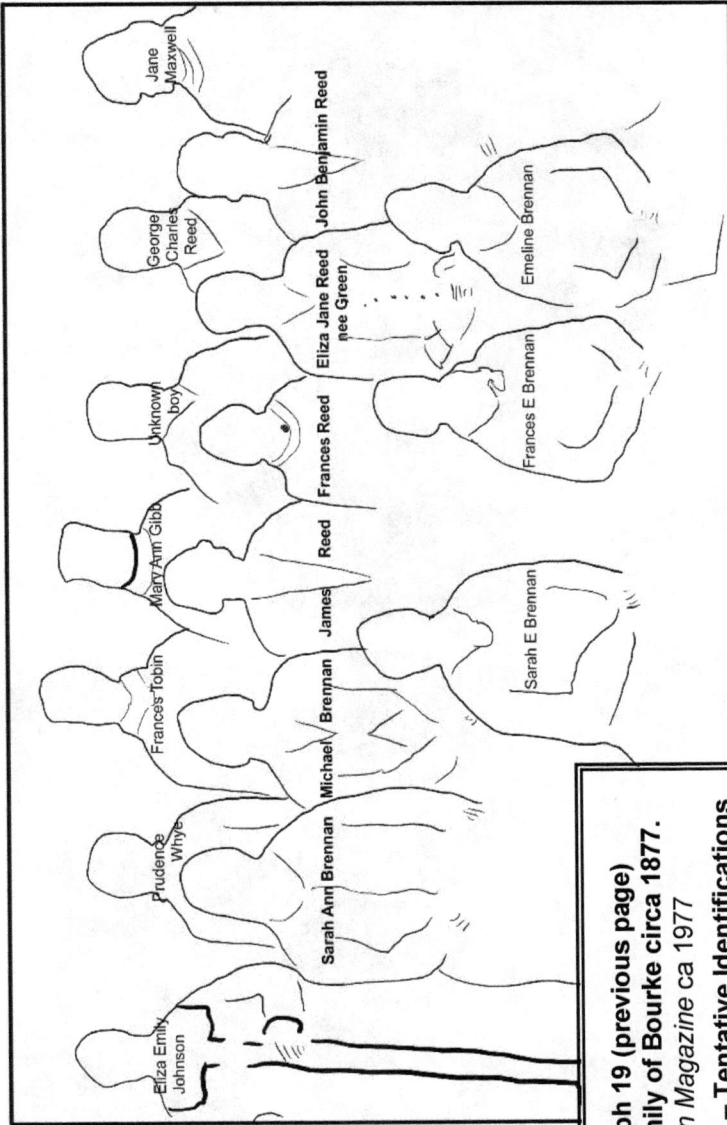

Jane Maxwell

George Charles Reed

John Benjamin Reed

Emeline Brennan

Eliza Jane Reed nee Green

Unknown boy

Frances Reed

Frances E Brennan

Mary Ann Gibb

James Reed

Frances Tobin

Michael Brennan

Sarah E Brennan

Prudence Whye

Sarah Ann Brennan

Eliza Emily Johnson

Photograph 19 (previous page)
The Reed family of Bourke circa 1877.
Western Magazine ca 1977
Photograph 20 – Tentative Identifications

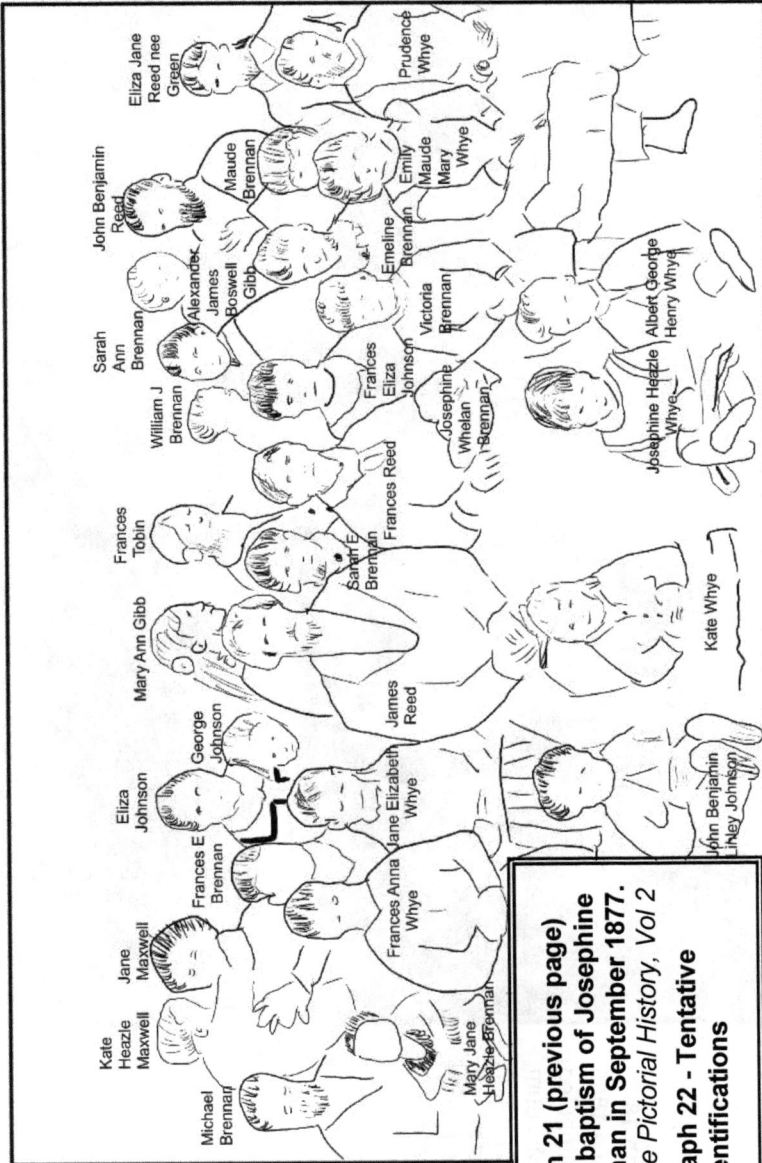

Photograph 21 (previous page)
Probably the baptism of Josephine
Whelan Brennan in September 1877.
Source: *Bourke Pictorial History, Vol 2*

Photograph 22 - Tentative
Identifications

Photograph 18
Bourke punt, ca 1885.
George Bell (attributed)
Powerhouse Museum
Collection.
Gift of Australian
Consolidated Press under the
Taxation Incentives for the
Arts Scheme, 1985.

CHAPTER EIGHTEEN

Life goes on

Even during the family's "worst of times" decade there was plenty of good news to leaven the bad. George Charles and Alexander were both married for the first time while Prudence and Mary Ann remarried. James and Frances welcomed more than thirty new grandchildren into their lives and, towards the end of the decade, some of their eldest grandchildren married. So, the family had many opportunities to focus on their blessings while acknowledging the tribulations outlined in the previous chapter.

One of the happier events during the trying years was the baptism of four month old **Josephine Whelan Brennan,** been born at Bourke on 28 May 1877. She was baptised in September at the new St Stephen's church[659], her second name a tribute to her father's mother, Ellen Whelan. Like most baptisms, it was attended by all members of the family who weren't required to work on the day. It may have been at Josephine's baptism that two photographs were taken that have survived the succeeding century and a half.

A close examination of the two pictures suggests strongly that both were taken on the same day. Photograph 19 was taken in a tent: the corner is clearly visible on the right where a white seam or cord runs down while there are seams at regular intervals along the back. Both the tent corner and the seam/cord are also visible in Photograph 21 which captures Frances Reed with a grandchild on her lap who appears to be dressed in a baptism gown. The date of Josephine's baptism is consistent with the tentative identifications set out below.

Photograph 19 was published in the *Western Magazine* about a century after Josephine's baptism. Unfortunately, the original remains elusive but given the importance of the picture for the descendants of James and Frances Reed, it is reproduced here, albeit at low quality.

The identity of the six people seated in the centre row and named in **bold text** in the identification graphic (Photograph 20) is certain. Comparison to Photographs 4 and 17 shows conclusively that the central couple is James and Frances Reed. The couple to Frances' left were pictured with her two years later in Photograph 17 that was shared by the Biles Family Group on Ancestry.com. It identifies them as John Benjamin Reed and his wife Eliza. Frances' image was later cropped from that photograph and used on her memorial card, reproduced in the next chapter. The couple seated on the opposite end are Sarah Ann Brennan and her husband Michael. Sarah Ann is readily recognisable when compared to several later pictures of her, particularly Photograph 33 that was shared by Sarah McKibbin on the Ancestry website. Given that two of the girls in the front row look very much like Sarah Ann, it is probable that all three are her eldest daughters: Sarah, Frances and Emeline.

Identification of those in the back row is less certain. The woman in white (second from the left) is probably the recently widowed Prudence Whye, given a good resemblance to known photos of her from 1862 (Photograph 3) and ca 1890 (Photograph 24). The older woman next to her (on the end) bears a good resemblance to Eliza Johnson in a photo from about 1909 (Photograph 37). The woman in the centre back (behind James Reed) may be Mary Ann Gibb because she wears a black band around her neck, possibly a sign of mourning for her husband George Samson Gibb, who had died nearly two years before. The surviving Reed sons-in-law (James Tobin, Henry Johnson and Joseph Maxwell) are not pictured; they may have been unable to attend on the day for work reasons.

The tall boy in the back row could be James Henry Johnson (who was nearly 10 years old) or his younger brother Alexander George Oxley Johnson.

Twenty-odd years after Photograph 19 was published in the *Western Magazine*, Photograph 21 was published in volume 2 of *Bourke Pictorial History* (compiled by Bill Cameron on behalf of the Bourke and District Historical Society). The accompanying text states that it depicts "Michael Brennan and his wife Sarah Ann (Reed) surrounded by various descendants and other relations". It also notes that the original photo has "Maude Johnson 1907" written on the back. Maude would be born seven years after the photos were taken, the youngest child of Eliza and Henry Johnson.

A close examination shows that the same couple is seated in the middle of both photos, so the central male is not Michael Brennan but James Reed. His wife Frances wears the same hat in both pictures while Eliza Johnson is clearly wearing the same dress. The woman in the centre back who is looking distractedly to her left in both photos clearly has a flower in her hair in Photograph 21 and there is a faint glimpse of this in the other picture too. Sarah Ellen Brennan and her sister Emeline are distinctive in both photos. Eliza Jane Reed (nee Green) wears the same dress in both pictures as does Prudence Whye, who also tilts her head slightly in both.

A month after Josephine's baptism, her father Michael Brennan reported his horse stolen and Senior Constable Prior of the Wilcannia Police soon apprehended Edward Palmer (alias Henry Wilmot Davis[660]) and charged him with both this crime and the theft of another mare belonging to James Cumerford. While Palmer was discharged on the latter charge, he was committed for trial in relation to the former, subsequently found guilty in the Bourke Quarter Sessions court and sentenced to 12 months hard labour in Bathurst Gaol.[661]

On 5 December two Bourke gentlemen, Valentine Edward Browne and Cavendish Lister Nevile, presented a Petition to the Governor praying that His Excellency would declare a Municipality at Bourke. It was signed by George Charles Reed and Michael Brennan along with another 76 of the town's businessmen including Joseph Becker, Edward Bloxham, Matthew Good, Edward Wormall and George Harris.[662] The government soon acceded to this request and Bloxham was elected as the town's first mayor a few months later.

One of the new council's first actions was to ban cesspits to reduce the transmission of disease by flies and mosquitoes. For twenty years every house and hotel had been serviced by a toilet building situated above a long-drop pit. A sewerage system would not be built for another seventy years. In the meantime, Bourke houses were now to be serviced by the pan system, whereby each toilet was fitted with a large bucket (or pan) that was replaced weekly by council employees. The foul contents of each used pan were transferred into a large portable tank that was later emptied outside the town limits.

After Annie Brennan was born and died at Native Dog Springs in 1878, her father's license for the *Native Dog* hotel was renewed in September 1879[663] and 1880[664] but it had been transferred to Arthur Desment by September 1881.[665]

Given the competition from so many hotels in the district, it is unlikely that the Brennans had been able to build a successful business or to sell it profitably as a going concern. It is more likely that their business struggled and they were forced to cut their losses. This could explain why they chose to sell the block of land in Darling Street acquired from James and Frances Reed six years earlier.[666] It was bought by Edward Warmoll, licensee of the short-lived *Turf* hotel in Bourke. This block would return to a member of the extended Reed family four years later.

The Brennan's tenth child was born in Bourke on 6 October 1881 and baptised four months later as **Michael James Brennan**, the same name as his father who was now working as a labourer[667]. The new baby was baptised on the same day that his sister Sarah Ellen, the Brennan's eldest child, married **Edward James Freeman** in Bourke.[668]

The Brennan's next daughter, Frances Eliza married **Frederick Jackson** at Bourke on 5 March 1883.[669] (The

Registrar of Births, Deaths and Marriages has indexed this marriage wrongly, recording the bride as "Francis" the groom; and the groom as the bride "Fredk".) They produced their first and only child, **Frederick George Jackson**, a year later on 27 April.

Michael and Sarah Ann Brennan were probably struggling, financially, at this time having failed to make a success of their hotel business at Native Dog Springs. Michael was granted a hardwood timber license at Bourke in June 1883.[670]

Early in the new year their family was completed with the birth of **Alfred John Brennan**[671] on 28 February 1884. He was not baptised until after his first birthday when he was included in the same ceremony as his nephew Frederick George Jackson and their cousin Mary Ann Maud Johnson at St Peters Anglican church on 8 March 1885.[672] By this time Michael Brennan had returned to his former employment as a house painter. Unfortunately, Frederick's mother Frances Eliza Jackson died just three weeks later[673] at just 19 years old, becoming the third of Michael and Sarah Ann Brennan's children to predecease them.

Two years later, in July 1887, the Brennans' third daughter Emeline married John S Harding at Bourke.[674]

***

Bourke's population had nearly quadrupled during the prosperous 1870s. An impressive Post Office building was opened in 1880 and the river was finally spanned by a bridge at North Bourke three years later, reducing the workload on Bourke's punt (see Photograph 18). The 1881 census recorded 718 males and 420 females in the town, part of the 5743 males and 2382 females in the Bourke Electoral District. Twenty years after its foundation, the town was still 63% male while the district was 70% male. The mining boom had seen Cobar grow even faster than Bourke, to the point where it was now bigger, with 1301 males and 558 females. Brewarrina had 210 males and 134 females while Gongolgon was at its peak, with 56 males and 49 females.[675]

An idea of the growth in Bourke can also be gauged by the increases in revenue collected by the sub-Collector of Customs at Bourke. In 1874 he had collected 1,698 pounds but five years later revenue had grown to 12,067 pounds and this would reach over 20,000 pounds in 1889 and 1890 and nearly 30,000 pounds in 1891.[676]

***

In 1881 Joseph Maxwell (who had, as next of kin, inherited from his late son Alexander a block of land in Oxley Street) transferred it in two portions, one to his sister-in-law Sarah Ann Brennan and one to his wife's brother-in-law James Tobin junior.[677] The Brennan family was living at this Oxley Street address a decade later.[678] James Tobin would transfer his portion into his wife's name in 1888 (as well as a block in Darling Street).[679]

***

Mary Ann Gibb was now well established as licensee of the *Bourke* hotel. As we saw in Chapter 15 she was probably assisted by her brother George Charles Reed during the immediate aftermath of her husband's death in December 1875 but by the end of 1876 had successfully acquired the license in her own right. Her daughter Hazle May Gibb (whose father is unknown) had been born three years later but Mary Ann nevertheless managed to continue the success of the hotel's accommodation and bar services. During six years of widowhood, she had also raised her children Jannet (now 8 years old), Alexander (aged 6) and Hazel (2).

In the first week of 1882 she married **Timothy Farrell**[680] who, at 28 years old, was a year younger. They were undoubtedly brought together by her brother-in-law Joseph Maxwell, who was Tim Farrell's oldest friend.

As we saw in Chapter 14, the links between the Maxwells and the Farrells had been strong ever since Joseph Maxwell's father Richard had employed Tim Farrell's father Edmund in the Culgoa River district more than twenty years earlier. Edmund Farrell and his wife Eleanor nee Ryan had emigrated from Tipperary (Ireland) with their eldest son Timothy born during the voyage[681] on 10 May 1853. The family later expanded to include Edmund junior (born 11 October 1855), Thomas born 1856, Mary Ann and Patrick (who was born in March 1863 and died the same year).

After Edmund Farrell accidentally drowned in the Culgoa two days before his son Tim's tenth birthday, Richard Maxwell had supported his widow and children with employment opportunities. He hired Tim, Edmund and Thomas Farrell as station hands and arranged for his daughter Kate Maxwell to hire their younger sister Mary Ann as a maid. Lifelong friendships were forged between these two pioneer Bourke families. (Barnett Memoirs, page 10)

When Tim Farrell was fifteen years old, he and his two brothers were caught in a thunderstorm some distance from the homestead. As they rode homeward, three abreast, a bolt of lightning struck the middle one, Edmund, killing him instantly but leaving his brothers untouched. (Barnett Memoirs, page 10)

Almost immediately after their marriage, Mary Ann handed over much of the responsibility for running the *Bourke* hotel to her new husband and he became the official licensee in April 1882.[682] Within a month he was fined five pounds for "permitting liquor to be consumed in his licensed premises during prohibited hours".[683]

Tim and Mary Ann added to her existing family of three children with seven more over the next seventeen years. The first of these, **Thomas James Edmond Farrell**, was born on 14 September 1882[684] and baptised in St Stephen's Anglican church on 22 October.[685]

The *Bourke* hotel was soon in financial difficulty, although it is not clear whether this was caused by debts that Mary Ann had run up before her marriage or by a shortage of business acumen in her new husband. In any case, they sold the business to Mary Ann's brother-in-law (James Murphy) in April 1882[686]. As part of the deal, Murphy bought the land that the hotel sat on from Mary Ann's father, James Reed. The Murphys now owned lots 3 and 5 in section 11 on Darling Street while Edward Warmoll (who was publican of the nearby *Turf* hotel in Mitchell Street) owned lots 2 and 4. Warmoll agreed to swap lot 4 for lot 3 so that he now held adjacent lots 2 and 3 while the Murphys held adjacent lots 4 and 5.

Within a year,[687] Murphy had changed the business' name to the *Family* hotel and become the new licensee. To take over this license, he had been required to relinquish his license (but not the ownership) of the *Lame Horse* hotel at Gongolgon. It seems that the family had arranged a swap, as Tim Farrell took over the license of the *Lame Horse* at that time.[688] The Murphys would retain ownership of both hotels for the next 21 years.

The Farrell's second child was born in 1884 and named **Lila Rose Farrell**[689]. Unfortunately, the money acquired from the sale of the hotel business was not enough to pay all the family's debts and Tim Farrell was placed under sequestration of insolvency on 5 March 1884.[690] James Murphy was consequently forced to return to Gongolgon and resume the license for the hotel, which he re-named the *Commercial*. He leased the *Family* hotel in Bourke to Joseph Donohue[691] (who would hold the license for the next four years).

It seems very surprising that the wealthy future that had beckoned for Mary Ann on her marriage to the mining entrepreneur George Samson Gibb had turned to ashes in her mouth within just twelve years. Calamity was then heaped upon adversity when her nineteen-month-old son Thomas died on 6 April.[692]

Tim Farrell was forced to return to the station work that he knew best and was soon working as a drover, stock rider, shearer and eventually as overseer on *Winnalabrinna* Station.[693] By the end of the decade the family had grown again with the birth of **Victoria K Farrell** in 1887[694] and **Timothy Oxley Farrell** in 1889.[695]

***

James and Prudence Murphy were now running two hotel businesses, one in Gongolgon and one in Bourke. It seemed that their fortunes had changed for the better, making James confident and forthright enough to impound a bay colt that had strayed onto his land from nearby *Belmore* Station[696], just as he had done 5 years earlier with a grey horse.[697]

Like their businesses, their surviving son George Charles Reed Murphy was thriving and he was soon joined by three healthy sisters, **Nora Lillian Murphy** in 1882,[698] **Mary Ethel Murphy** on 4 September 1884[699] and finally **Lila Kate Murphy** on 13 November 1886.[700]

Also in 1886, Prudence's 20-year-old daughter Jane Elizabeth Whye married Thomas Ralph at Brewarrina.[701] This new son-in-law immediately took over the running of their *Commercial* hotel at Gongolgon for two years, but it was a losing battle. A few months beforehand the railway to Bourke had opened for business, running in a straight line for 204 kilometres across the plains from Nyngan to Bourke. A new direct road was built along the railway line, thus significantly reducing the number of travellers traversing the old road to and from Bourke that followed the curve of the rivers through Gongolgon.

The main road from Sydney had been along the Macquarie River, Duck Creek and the Bogan, but moved to the railway route after 1885, reducing the two pub town of Gongolgon to a hamlet.[702]

Both the Bourke and Gongolgon hotel buildings were now ageing and trade at Gongolgon was severely reduced by the railway,[703] resulting in its closure for the next few years, but James Murphy responded by diversifying into mail delivery.[704] He had successfully tendered 400 pounds per year for the Nyngan, Monkey and Gongolgon mail contract in 1884,[705] requiring him (or his employee) to complete the 141 kilometre run weekly in a two horse buggy. He was also hatching ambitious plans to expand the family's commercial interests by leasing land and dealing in stock and would later take on work as a trustee of both the local cemetery[706] and the common.[707]

During 1886 James and Prudence bought a block of land at lot 5 in section 10 in Darling Street East Bourke from the London Chartered Bank of Australia in a mortgagee sale. Two weeks later they transferred it to Prudence's sister-in-law Mary Ann Reed nee Peters, wife of George Charles Reed.[708] It was now four years since George Charles had surrendered to insolvency, so this may explain why the land was put into his wife's name. This block was on the southern side of Darling Street on the corner of Monomeeth Street. At the same time, the six blocks of land that Prudence had inherited from her first husband (Joseph Whye) were transferred from joint title with her brother George into her sole ownership.[709]

At about this time James took steps to move into the stock trading business by applying for land in the resumed area of *Mooculta* Holding.[710] He was granted a special lease on portion 68 of 320 acres in the parish of East Bourke on 11 August 1888.[711] In 1890 his neighbour was ordered to pay 13 pounds as his share of the costs of a boundary fence.[712]

Joseph Donohue must have decided not to renew his *Family* hotel lease after four years because John Lennon became licensee during 1888 and 1889. During this time, it was sometimes referred to as "*Lennon's* hotel" despite being still owned by the Murphys.[713]

Around this time, Prudence Murphy posed for a photograph that would later be published in a *Sydney Sun* story celebrating her ninetieth birthday.

In 1891 Murphy successfully lobbied his local Member of Parliament (Mr Wadell) to get a road cleared between Gongolgon and the new railway station at Byrock.[715] No doubt he saw a business opportunity to revive the hotel at Gongolgon, because the railway would not reach Brewarrina for another ten years. Until then, there would be a good business ferrying people and goods between Brewarrina and the train at Byrock, with Gongolgon strategically situated between the two. The hotel was soon re-licensed to Prudence's son-in-law Thomas Ralph.[716]

Photograph 24
Portrait of Prudence Murphy taken around 1890.
Source: Sydney Sun[714]

There is no record of James' mail run contract being renewed, so he continued to seek other means of making money. For example, he was employed by the North Bourke Jockey Club as Starter for their race meetings from 1887.[717] This is undoubtedly where his eight-year-old son George Charles Reed Murphy first got a taste of the racing industry. Within a few years he became a champion jockey and would later make the sporting news across Australia when he rode the winning horse in all six races on the program at North Bourke on 18 October 1905, his wedding day[718] (see Photograph 25).

***

Frances Reed had turned 70 in 1882 and her husband James was four years older. They were now firmly into their retirement years and seem to have left the running of the various businesses to younger members of the family. There are very few records of their activities during the next few years as they quietly lived their day to day lives.

During these years, the most successful family member was their son-in-law James Tobin junior whose stock dealing business was progressing well. In 1879 he had mortgaged 2 roods of land in Darling street to Matthew Good[719] but was able to discharge the mortgage within two years. In August 1882 he transferred part of this same block to his sister-in-law, Mary Ann Farrell. In November 1885 he obtained a lease on the 34,000 acre property known as *Mulga No 4*[720] with an annual rental of 155/18/- and was issued with a rental assessment for that amount a year later. In May 1888 he sent 470 bullocks to market in Albury.[721]

Jane Maxwell and her sister-in-law Mary Ann Reed (George Charles' wife) both produced children in 1883, 1885 and 1887. **Albert Charles Maxwell** was born on 7 February 1883,[722] his sister **Frances Prudence Maxwell** in May 1885[723] and their brother **Joseph Henry Maxwell** (who was to be known as "Harry") in September 1887.[724] Their cousin **Ethel Mary Ann Reed** was born on 27 July 1883,[725] her sister **Emily Beatrice Reed** on 1 July 1885[726] and their brother **Bertie Augustus Reed** on 17 December 1887.[727] Unfortunately Frances Prudence Maxwell died on 4 November 1888, aged just three and a half years.[728]

George Charles Reed and Joseph Maxwell had

more than their children's birth years in common because in 1885 both were employed on *Charlton* Station (midway between Gongolgon and Mount Oxley). While George Charles worked as a cook (presumably a skill that he had mastered through years of working in boarding houses and hotels), Maxwell was employed as a stockman and drover. In July he was put in charge of droving 3000 fat wethers the 800 kilometres from *Charlton* Station to Sydney.[729] George Charles also held a hardwood timber license in 1884[730] and was described as a contractor when his son Bertie was baptised in 1888.[731]

As rural workers, George Charles and Joseph would have witnessed firsthand the start of one of the most significant developments in Australian history, the formation of an effective union movement. By the 1880s the various rural industries employed huge numbers of agricultural workers as boundary riders, bore sinkers, butchers, carriers, cooks, dam builders, drovers, fencers, fruit pickers, gardeners, hunters, jackaroos, land-clearers, rouseabouts, timber-getters, wool scourers and shearers. Local station owners had begun to experience income shrinkage due to lower produce prices and the reduced grazing yields that resulted from the long term degradation of their land.

When graziers first arrived in western NSW they benefited from abundant native vegetation that had only ever been grazed by native animals. As the introduced sheep and cattle feasted, their numbers grew quickly but this led to overgrazing which was exacerbated after the first bores were sunk in formerly unwatered paddocks. Grazing land was further degraded by introduced feral species including rabbits and goats and widespread infestations of the invasive species prickly pear.

Two dozen rabbits had been released near Geelong in 1859 to provide sport for hunters. Initially they were predated upon by quolls but these were systematically exterminated by settlers, leaving the rabbits free to breed unimpeded. By 1886 the rabbit plague had reached Queensland, further devastating the grazing land around Bourke in the process. In subsequent decades, rabbit numbers crashed during extended droughts but mushroomed to plague proportions in good seasons. It was only the release of the *myxoma* virus in 1950 that finally reduced the problem, while further success was achieved with the release of the *calicivirus* in 1995. The prickly pear problem also proved intractable until the introduction of the *cactoblastis cactorum* moth from Argentina in 1925 eventually solved the problem.

In addition to falling yields, graziers were experiencing falling wool prices. During the 1870s wool had averaged 11 shillings and tuppence per pound but this had fallen to 9/4 during the 1880s and would fall further to 8/6 during the 1890s. Graziers across NSW, Victoria, South Australia and Queensland responded to rapidly falling yields and prices by moving to cut labour costs. In April 1886 Bourke graziers unilaterally cut the amount that they paid for each sheep shorn, thus provoking a furious reaction from shearers. The Bourke Shearers' Union was among a few similar bush unions that quickly sprung up around the country to protect their members' incomes and to seek better working conditions. This caused great controversy as the pros and cons of unionisation were widely debated, but slowly membership grew.

Shearers at *Dunlop* Station near Bourke went on strike in 1886 after their demands were rejected. They withdrew to a camp a few miles from the homestead and held out for nine weeks, with shearing then proceeding on their terms.[732] They had won a battle, but the real war was still to come.

In January 1887, the Australian Shearers' Union (which claimed 5000 members in Victoria and NSW) amalgamated with the Bourke and Wagga Shearers' Unions to form the Amalgamated Shearers' Union of Australasia. A year later this organisation amalgamated with the South Australian Shearers' Union and additional branches were formed at Young, Moree and in New Zealand. Eventually the shearers would combine forces with other rural workers to form the General Labourers Union of Australasia. By 1894 further mergers would form the Australian Workers Union which continues in operation to the present day. Pressure was starting to build towards the 1891 shearers' strike which would bring upheaval to Bourke and district.

The Reed family's home of nearly 30 years continued to change rapidly as the decade of the 1880s drew towards a close. While some of these changes were localised, Bourke was also affected by a range of more widespread developments and trends, including widespread land degradation due to overgrazing, the rabbit plague and the prickly pear infestation. The coming decade would see further changes in the Reed family's hometown with industrial strife; the arrival of the Afghan cameleers; the challenges of flood, disease, heatwave and drought; and the growing movement towards Federation.

Photograph 26 - Floodwaters flow from the northern to the southern side of the railway embankment.

Photograph 27- Dr Side's dog finds a dry spot, main street.

Photograph 28 (opposite top) - Mitchell Street looking west from Richard Street.

Photograph 29 (opposite centre) - Railway station refuge.
Numbers 26 to 29: State Library of NSW, Helen Dash, 1890.

Photograph 30 (opposite bottom) - Central Australian hotel.
Arthur Laycock Collection, 1890, State Library NSW.

Photograph 18
James Murphy, ca 1890
Source: Noreen Watts.

CHAPTER NINETEEN

Flood and strife

At the start of the 1890s, James and Frances entered their eighties while their surviving offspring were now middle-aged grandparents. They probably shared in the widespread patriotic feelings that were moving the colonies towards Federation but, despite this optimism, Australia would soon experience a severe economic depression. Both city and country areas would experience widespread unemployment leading to the collapse of financial institutions and the loss of savings. Industrial trouble would break out, more serious than previously, with one of the most noteworthy being the long-running shearers' dispute that was to come to a head in Bourke. Locally, the Reed family would, like all residents of the district, also face major challenges, including flood and epidemic.

Early in 1890 Bourke residents were aware that a big flood was imminent. Conventional wisdom told them that Darling River floods were caused by "the Queenslan' rains" which sent huge volumes of water from its tributaries downstream towards Bourke and eventually to the sea in South Australia.

In the twelve decades after Bourke was settled there were thirteen significant floods (in addition to many lesser high river events). Five of these were high enough to have inundated the town: 1864, 1890, 1950, 1974 and 1975.[733] We saw in chapter 11 how the Reeds and other residents had been forced to live for several weeks on the higher ground at North Bourke in 1864. In 1950 the town would be saved from inundation by a massive community effort that built levees from scratch using motorised lorries and graders. In 1974 those defences would be enhanced and made permanent by modern road-building machines supplemented by a large volunteer workforce, trucks, sandbags, corrugated iron and pine tree branches. But sophisticated machines were not available in 1890 and, despite attempts to organise levees, the town was swamped. Twenty-six years after 1864, the Reed, Brennan, Maxwell, Farrell and Johnson families were among the few original residents who experienced a flooded town for the second time.

On 17 March, Mayor Daniells hosted a public meeting of 550 residents, all worried about the approaching floodwaters. Edward Good moved *"That if the river ... rose 6 ft from the embankment erected in 1879, steps should be taken to erect a dam; in the meantime all available steamers be kept in readiness for an emergency"*. James Murphy moved an amendment *"That immediate steps be taken to complete the dam in town"*, which was passed unanimously.[734]

Clearly James Murphy had been successful in his business dealings during the sixteen years since his marriage to Prudence, giving him the confidence to address and gain the support of this large meeting of his peers. His portrait and biography had recently been published in volume 2 of *Australian Men of Mark* which described him as a stock dealer who owned land in both Bourke and Louth as well as 3600 acres at Gongolgon.[735]

It added that he had recently joined the Order of Oddfellows, Manchester Unity, and was an avowed supporter of the free-trader position in politics. Some of this may have been hyperbole, as I have found no evidence that he ever owned land near Louth. The hagiography made no mention of his wife Prudence's contribution nor of the fact that his business dealings had been founded on the wealth she had accumulated with her first husband, Joseph Whye.

Illustration 19 - James Murphy Esquire, ca 1890.
Source: Australian Men of Mark volume 2.

Before the flood meeting ended, former Mayor Edward Bloxham sponsored a popular motion that the town apply to the NSW Government for a grant of 750 pounds for "erecting earthworks to keep back the flood waters". The gathering concluded on a sombre note after he opined that the railway embankment would impede the water's flow across the floodplain and "throw a large body of water directly into Bourke". He recommended that the Railway Commissioners construct some culverts immediately.

In fact, the railway embankment already had culverts[736] and therefore this advice was ignored for too long. Unfortunately, those existing culverts only amounted to a total of one mile in 13 miles of embankment and would prove to be insufficient.

The NSW Premier, Henry Parkes, sent a party of unemployed from Sydney to do the necessary labouring with pick and shovel, but they proved to be more trouble than they were worth and most of the work to build the town embankment was eventually done by local volunteers. Within a month it had been built and was successfully holding back the rising waters.

The Premier also sent an engineer from Sydney but he proved to be less popular than the navvies. When the townspeople suggested that the railway embankment was diverting flood water towards the town, he assured them that this was not the case, even though it could be plainly seen that the water was much lower on the Southern side of the line.

The Mayor was informed by telegram on 15 April that the Governor of NSW was coming to cheer the stout hearts of Bourke. The following day, Lord and Lady Carrington disembarked from the train to be met by the Mayor, Aldermen and two Members of Parliament. After a reception at the *Central Australian* hotel, the Vice-Regal party was driven in buggies and cabs to inspect the town embankment. The next day they travelled to North Bourke aboard the paddle steamer "Saddler", where they inspected the arrangements made for refugees in case

Bourke was inundated. Lady Carrington visited many tents already occupied by women and children, afterwards recording in her diary:[737]

Some 600 people are camped out in tents to be out of danger. I went to see a poor woman who had her first baby a few minutes after she was landed, & gave her two pounds & asked her to call the baby after me. They all seemed comfortable.

She had reportedly placed a gold sovereign into each hand of the newborn baby who was, indeed, later christened Lily Carrington Anderson[738] (afterwards known in Bourke as "the flood baby").

In the meantime, the engineer had agreed to make another inspection of the railway embankment. As soon as the Governor's train departed, this embankment was cut in several more places, but it was too late; too much water had accumulated behind it and now threatened the stability of the town's eastern embankment see Photograph 26). This "eastern sea" rose rapidly that evening and the next day it became clear that it would soon start to flow over the top.[739]

The flying gang had been hastily summoned ... to assist on the eastern bank and on arrival there we found the water level with the top of the embankment for at least half a mile. In an incredibly short space of time a layer of earth was run along the top of the embankment about a foot high raising it there to about 5 feet. One of the smartest bits of work performed throughout the whole fight was done there that afternoon.

Soon after, however, the journalist observed hundreds of men running along the embankment in the direction of the hospital.

On arrival ... we saw that about 15 yards of the embankment had been cut clean away and the water was pouring through in a roaring surging torrent. A row of men ranged along the fast increasing water, and shovels plied as they never plied before, and an immense amount of work was done in half an hour, but all in vain, all hope was over and the word was passed around to "knock off" ... The water was creeping along slowly in places, rapidly in others and in a very short time it was as far as the Oxford Hotel. By 9 o'clock the writer rowed a boat from the billabong to Tatts Hotel via Oxley, Sturt and Mitchell Streets. About midnight full river level had been reached.

The town was now swamped and many houses had two feet of water through them. Fortunately, the town's leaders had planned for this eventuality by providing sanctuary places at the railway station and North Bourke. Soon the railway waiting rooms were serving as a *de facto* hotel but filled quickly (see Photograph 30). In an ingenious solution, some "lucky" families were allocated their own covered railway wagon! Within a few days, 700 people had been moved by boat to higher railway ground 14 miles away. Eventually most of these moved to Byrock to await the ebb.

All night the steamers plied busily between the town and North Bourke and were speedily filled as they pulled into the wharves. Uprooted people brought blankets, bedding and pets, while officials stowed these guests wherever they could. Soon the village's three hotels and two stores were transformed into a soggy mass of humanity, with over a thousand people taking shelter there. Some may have reflected that night on the short-sighted political decision taken back in 1863 to position the main town at Wortumertie bend rather than on the higher ground at North Bourke, now christened "Noah's sand hill" by some wag.

Word of this calamity spread quickly, prompting the broader community to spring into action in support. The Master Bakers of Sydney forwarded 400 loaves of bread per day, carried free by the railway; money poured into a collection in Melbourne; benefit concerts were staged in Sydney.

The town's businesses pulled their weight, soon organising a daily supply of meat that was brought into town on rafts pulled by horses. The outer districts were not forgotten, with several policemen and six other men embarking aboard the steamer "Cato" with three smaller boats to bring emergency supplies of flour, sugar, tea and other essentials to the Culgoa. Among other experiences, they would encounter a large family who had been living for weeks on makeshift rafts and another living on a timber stage rigged up between trees. The steamer "Sturt" was sent to assist at Brewarrina. Everyone battled mosquitoes, spiders and the occasional snake. Several people drowned, as did thousands of head of stock.

Eventually, after weeks spent in primitive temporary accommodation, the floodwaters gradually flowed past and the town emerged from under the briny to reveal a vast expanse of deep, stinking, sticky black stuff. Mere mud would have been bad enough, but the floodwaters had filled every cesspit in town causing filth that had collected for twenty-odd years to float out. This then settled in the soil as the water receded, a crucible of disease that would haunt the town both immediately and for many years into the future.

Dr Samuelson published a very detailed letter of

advice to the townspeople about sanitation. He advised people to boil both water and milk and to avoid contact with mud (whether wet or dry) where possible, but this was impossible. Rubber gloves would not be invented until four years later. He went on

> No house should be re-entered until the pathway and the ground intervening them be dry. When a house is not elevated, a week should elapse before reoccupation and as far as possible, the ground under the house, vacant plots, pools, pits, closets and pipes should be disinfected. For this purpose chloride of lime is the cheapest and best.

He suggested removal of the soil to a width of six feet from the walls of each house to alleviate the adverse effect of future rainfall. He predicted that the community would face an immediate problem with low fevers, diarrhoea, dysentery and other intestinal conditions of catarrh; and he feared a later epidemic of typhoid.

Specific details about how James and Frances Reed fared during the flood have not survived. A year later, when the census was recorded in April 1891, they were living in a household of two at North Bourke, but it is difficult to know whether they had already been living there before the flood. One census record has them in Culgoa Street and another has them in Darling Street,[740] so they probably lived on the corner of those two streets (where the Enngonia road meets the Wanaaring road). William Murphy would build a new hotel on this spot[741] two years later.

Eliza and Henry Johnson's family of 4 males and 3 females was recorded on the next consecutive census return, also living in Culgoa Street. Since the Johnson family was bigger than that, it seems that some of the older children had left home. The family may have moved to North Bourke a year earlier as floodwater gradually overran their selection near Mount Oxley.

All members of the extended Reed family welcomed two new grandchildren during the flood year: George Charles' son **James Reed** was born at Bourke[742] and Jane's son **Edward H Maxwell** was born at Brewarrina.[743]

The census recorded James Murphy as the head of three different households in Darling Street, Bourke.[744] One of these included eleven males and six females while the premises next door had one male. Since his family comprised three males and six females, these extra people must have been tenants at the *Family* hotel. His third premises was a stable with no human occupants. He was also recorded as owning a produce store in Wilson Street.[745] With business slack at Gongolgon since the opening of the railway, he had clearly elected to move back to Bourke and resume his former occupation as licensee of his *Family* hotel.

He may also be the J Murphy recorded as head of a property on the Wanaaring Road comprising two males and five females;[746] and possibly also the J Murphy who headed a property in the Brewarrina district encompassing six males and two females[747]. We cannot know for sure because the detailed census returns were destroyed (after deriving their statistics) in accordance with a longstanding but doctrinaire government policy that, unfortunately, remains in force to this day (albeit that people can now opt in to have their returns preserved for posterity). Australia is the only country in the world that invests significant sums to gather census information only to then destroy most of it.

Around this time James Murphy was joined in Bourke by his younger brother Daniel, who held the license for the *Carrington* hotel (four miles out along the Brewarrina road) in 1891[748] and 1892[749] before taking over from his brother as licensee of the *Family* hotel in 1893.[750] By 1894 Daniel had returned to Orange where he held the license for the *Green Gate* Inn.[751]

Also in Darling Street was a household headed by Emmaline Harding, third daughter of Michael and Sarah Ann Brennan. Now widowed, she was recorded as E Brennan with her household comprising two females and one male.[752] She had married John Harding in 1887[753] and they had produced two sons, Arthur in 1888[754] and Alfred in 1889.[755] Unfortunately, her husband had died before the birth of his second son.[756] She was almost certainly occupying a house on Frances Reed's original 1863 purchase of lot 1 in section 11, now owned by her aunt, Frances Tobin. Emmaline's father, Michael Brennan, was recorded as the head of a household of five males and five females in Oxley Street (opposite the Cobb and Co Coach Factory).

The family of George Charles Reed was listed on the same page as four males and four females (as expected) living in Darling Street.[757] It seems that this family lived on the corner of Darling and Monomeeth Streets on land that had been transferred to his wife by Prudence and James Murphy five years earlier. George's wife, Mary Ann, had sold part of this block to Henry John Kay a year earlier, so her family now lived on the residue.[758] She would be given notice over the non-payment of rates in 1900[759] but must have managed to pay these taxes and retain the land because she would eventually sell it to Elizabeth Rogers in 1927.[760]

Jane and Joseph Maxwell were recorded at the *Commercial* hotel on *Tarcoon* Station, 23 kilometres from Gongolgon and 44 kilometres from Brewarrina. Their household comprised six males and two females.[761] Joseph had been granted a license for these premises (officially known as the *Exchange* hotel) a month earlier[762] and it would be extended a year later.[763] Unfortunately, this business was not a success and Joseph Maxwell would be subject to a sequestration order in bankruptcy two years later, thirteen years after his first bankruptcy.[764]

The census recorded three families of Reed descendants at Gongolgon.[765] James and Frances Tobin had a household of two males and two females in Bridge Street while Mary Ann Farrell headed another household of two males and five females in that same street. Her husband Tim must have been working elsewhere at the time. Thomas Ralph was head of a household of five males and six females in Bogan Street, no doubt the *Commercial* hotel owned by his mother-in-law Prudence and her husband James Murphy.

The Tobins also sought to move into the hotel business at this time, but James' application for a conditional license at North Bourke must have been refused.[766] Later that year his application for homestead lease number 59 of 2560 acres was also refused.[767] Nevertheless, he would have retained plenty of his many business interests.

The total population of the Bourke Municipality in 1891 was 3154[768] (of whom 59% were male), including 88 Chinese. Bourke had grown by 2016 people (or 177%) since the previous census in 1881. Only twelve males and eight females[769] were recorded at the "Aboriginal Camp", but this is clearly an under-count. Many Aboriginal people must not have cooperated with the census-takers, because 177 had been issued with blankets just two years earlier.[770] Nevertheless, their numbers had clearly plummeted in the thirty years since settlers had arrived in the District and it was apparent to local poet Jock Foley that their former lifestyle was forever lost.[771]

Lost between the Dreamtime and Armageddon,
They know not where to go, nor how, nor when.

They see their elders sit around in misery and shame,
Aimless, sick, the poorest amongst the poorest.
How have they fallen, these people, from the proud state
Where, lordly, they bestrode this land since time began?
Three hundred centuries of dreams, then sudden nightmare
Has left the Murri people dazed, almost destroyed.

What future for the brown children of Bourke?
No chance of tribal renaissance .... too late.
The forests gone, game extinct, the lore forgotten,
They needs must come to terms with modern life.
But where to start, and how to build the chain?
They wait in limbo for the work or deed or sign.

Who will aid, the politicians? Byamee[1] or Christ?
Help them to learn to help themselves. Help find them.

Unfortunately, Foley's sentiments apply as much today as when he penned them a century and a half ago.

---

[1] Byamee = Biame, the creator or sky father in the Dreaming traditions of several Aboriginal peoples of south-eastern Australia.

Around this time "Afghan" cameleers came to western NSW in growing numbers. The Victorian Government had imported 24 camels and their handlers from India as early as 1860 for the ill-fated Burke and Wills expedition. In 1866 Samuel Stuckey went to Karachi and imported more than 100 camels as well as 31 men. During the rest of that decade more cameleers came to Victoria and South Australia from Afghanistan and the Indian sub-continent (along with more camels) to provide a carrying service to the inland pastoral industry.

While bullock wagons could haul bigger loads, they were much slower than camels and could not travel far from water sources. Horse were faster but camels could carry much heavier loads over longer distances, easily handled sandy terrain and were less prone to getting bogged in wet weather. Camel trains serviced the pastoral industry by bringing supplies from rail heads, steamer wharves and towns and then returning with loads of wool and other primary products. Thus, they worked in conjunction with the railways and steamers, not in competition. Graziers favoured them because the camel team owners, very canny businessmen, paid the camel drivers low wages and were thus able to offer lower haulage rates. The cameleers soon captured a significant slice of the haulage market in the far west, creating friction with the traditional horse and bullock carriers.

The first report of Afghan cameleers in Western NSW, however, is not until 1880 when an Afghani named Surbeland captured three camels at Wilcannia said to have belonged to the Burke and Wills expedition from twenty years earlier.[772] In 1889 the arrival of a caravan of 63 camels driven by Faiz and Dost Mahomet into

Tibooburra was a rarity worthy of mention in the *Sydney Mail* newspaper.[773]

> *Messrs. Faiz and Dost Mahomet's caravan of 63 camels arrived on Tuesday. They were laden with goods for local storekeepers, and some for Queensland. They formed quite a procession through the town, each fastened by a gaily-coloured cord in single file, the Afghan drivers being gorgeously attired in many-coloured silks, shawls, gold lace, and turban. The whole procession was so brilliant as to be almost a show.*

During the 1891 Queensland shearers dispute, the Teamsters' Union (i.e. carriers) supported their striking comrades by refusing to carry any wool. The graziers took advantage of this opportunity to undermine both unions by employing camel teams protected by mounted troopers to bring supplies to Queensland from Bourke and to return with bales of wool.[774]

In the 1891 census, Gunny Khan was recorded as head of a household of seven male Afghans at "Billabong" in Bourke.[775] Abdul Wade established a camel stud farm on *Wangamanna* Station and built his Bourke Carrying Company into an Australia-wide business during the next few years. The camel industry would prosper in the Bourke District for more than twenty years, even after the arrival of the first motorised trucks (see Photograph 31).

Camels were valuable working animals. In 1912 Morbeen Perooz was leading a team past Paka Tank when a ten-day-old camel became "knocked up" and could not keep up, so he gifted it to Norman Harold Maxwell, the 16-year-old youngest son of Joseph Maxwell who was working nearby. Two years later young Norman gave the animal to RJ Bradshaw but, eighteen months later, Morbeen Perooz sued Bradshaw for the return of his camel which was valued at twenty pounds. He admitted leaving it at Paka Tank but denied gifting it to anyone. The Police Magistrate declined to make a ruling in the case, so Bradshaw got to keep the camel.[776]

In July 1891 the shearers' dispute flared up in the Bourke district. Graziers attempted to reduce wages and impose unacceptable conditions into employment contracts, so rural workers withdrew their labour and were forced to live for weeks in makeshift camps near big shearing sheds and near the town. The graziers had set up their own organisation, the Pastoralists Union, which set out to break the strike by hiring unemployed men in the cities and bringing them to the area as so-called "free labourers".

To the unionists they were scabs and when a second tranche of them arrived in Bourke by special train they received a hot welcome. The railway station was blockaded by several carriers and the platform was overrun by a large crowd of unionists vociferously urging disembarking passengers to join their cause. While some did, a large body of new arrivals was led by the manager of *Fort Bourke* Station (Mt Nutting) towards a steamer moored on the western side of Horsfall's Billabong. Unionists blocked the Oxley Street bridge and a melee ensued, with Mr Nutting dealt several nasty blows, sustaining a deep wound on his left temple. When a mounted policeman drew a revolver the crowd rapidly fell back, which allowed Nutting's remaining workforce to cross the bridge, board the steamer and get away. By then more of his men had deserted to the union's side and he managed to retain only about a third of those who had arrived on the train.

The Pastoralists' Union had left nothing to chance, also bringing non-union workers upriver by steamer to Wilcannia, where a similar clash took place. While the unionists had some success in these altercations, the Pastoralists' strategy was nevertheless effective. As the shearing season wore on with no work, the union shearers were forced to agree terms. The graziers won their "freedom of contract" policy whereby union and non-union labour would work together in the same shed. The shearers were guaranteed that that no Chinese or Kanaka labour would be employed, a key policy plank of the Australian Labor Party that was founded at Barcaldine in Queensland around this time.

Members of the Reed family would have been involved in these political issues as they were argued back and forth at most gatherings in Bourke. They were also directly affected as George Charles Reed, Henry Johnson, Tim Farrell and Joseph Maxwell were all employed in the pastoral industry while both James Tobin junior and James Murphy were landholders who dealt in stock. Given their backgrounds, their sympathies likely lay with the shearers. The only evidence of this, however, is the following account of a meeting held at Gongolgon in October 1893.[777]

A very large and enthusiastic meeting was held at Gongolgon on the 21st inst. Mr Tolless occupied the Chair. Mr James Murphy, late of Bourke, moved the first resolution, and spoke very strongly against alien labor. All the motions were carried unanimously, and the petition is being very largely signed.

In 1892 three more grandchildren were added to the Reed clan, with **George Charles Reed junior**[778] born at Bourke and both **Blanche Olive Maxwell**[779] and **Edwin Albert (Eddie) Farrell**[780] born at Gongolgon.

The Bourke weir and lock, built that year, was for many years the only one on the Darling. Many people thought that the river could be transformed into an Australian Mississippi if only the abundant flood waters could be prevented from draining away to the sea so quickly. A system of weirs and locks, they proposed, could achieve this and would bring untold improvements by facilitating permanent navigability. The necessary infrastructure was, however, never built. In Bourke's case, the weir solved the problem that the existing waterholes near the town had not held sufficient water for the town's needs during dry times.

In September the writer and bush poet, Henry Lawson, stepped down from the train at Bourke on an outback trip financed by the *Bulletin* magazine. He was a rising star of the booming literary scene, having recently engaged in a poetical sparring match with Banjo Paterson. He was a vocal advocate of the burgeoning Federation movement recently launched by Sir Henry Parkes' Tenterfield Oration of 1889 that was gaining impetus from patriotic sentiments expressed in popular poems like Paterson's *The Man from Snowy River* (1890) and his forthcoming *Waltzing Matilda* (1895).

Lawson spent the next two months in the town (working as a house painter) before walking 70 kilometres down river to *Toorale* Station where he was employed as a shearers' rouseabout for a month. After returning to Bourke for Christmas he walked northwest with Jim Gordon, a new mate that he had met in Bourke and who became a lifelong friend. After spending New Year's Day at Fords Bridge on the Warrego River, they arrived at Hungerford (180 kilometres from Bourke) a fortnight later. This journey was described by journalist Bruce Elder as "the most important trek in Australian literary history" as it informed Lawson's subsequent work and contributed to his reputation as Australia's greatest short story writer. Lawson acknowledged this in the first verse of his 1902 poem *Bourke* (see the title derivation page at the front of this book).

Within three weeks he was back in Bourke where he spent a few more months before returning to Sydney. He wrote prolifically at this time, both officially for the *Bulletin* and under a pseudonym for Bourke's *Western Herald*. Up until this point the local newspapers had tended to avoid writing about the district's biggest issue, the battle between the shearers and the Pastoralists, but Lawson's influence managed to change that.

Bourke was at its peak in 1892, boasting 5 doctors, 3 solicitors, 3 customs officers and 200 businesses including a meat preserving company, a soap factory, two carriage works, a wagon factory, a cordial factory, a sawmill, a brickworks and a brewery. There were 18 hotels in town and 4 at North Bourke and, in the judgement of one surprised visitor, none of them were second class. In addition, there were a wide range of government offices, a water works and the steamers competed with six train services per week in an electorate of 6,540 voters represented by three Members of Parliament. The town enjoyed two bands, football and cricket as well as a popular rowing club. The people were serviced by 2 market gardens, several orchards and the wealthy could keep food fresh using ice brought by train daily from Nyngan. Drainage had been improved by kerbing streets with wooden sleepers, while streetlights glowed on every corner.

But the foundations for this boom were weaker than they seemed, based as they were on an unusual succession of good seasons, good wool prices, overstocking and widespread land degradation. When the seasons returned to normal, the economy went into recession, grazing yields fell and the town's decline began. And further tribulations would soon follow.

Economic conditions worsened rapidly during 1892 and 1893, leading to a major recession caused mainly by disastrously low wool prices coupled with widespread drought and the rabbit plague. Unemployment grew rapidly in both city and country and the now-struggling graziers seized the opportunity to further reduce the wages that they offered to shearers. The rural unions responded with strikes in the Bourke district.

Shearers endeavoured to impede the arrival of non-union labour at *Killara* Station by stretching rope and fencing wire across the Darling but this failed to hold the steamer *Mundoo* as it came upriver.

Soon after, the Pastoralists' Union loaded 45 strike breakers aboard the *Rodney* at Echuca despite union attempts to prevent them. The steamer proceeded upstream, despite warnings that violence was increasing along the river. At 4 am on the night of 6 August 1894, long after she had moored for the night, 150 men boarded her. To avoid identification their faces were smeared with river mud and their clothes worn inside out. The sleepy crew and passengers were forced ashore, the *Rodney* was set alight and burnt to the waterline. Subsequent conspiracy theories suggested that this was the work of *"inner city larrikins ... anxious to prove they were no longer scabs"* rather than unionists; or even that it was initiated by police spies who had infiltrated union camps. The disguises were effective, because only one man was ever convicted of this crime, and he was probably innocent.

Several other steamers were involved in strike-breaking and were also attacked in various less effective ways. Ashore, guns were drawn at *Killara* Station as tempers frayed; thirteen jaws were broken in fighting at Bourke in a single day; and two unionists were actually shot at *Grassmere* Station, with one dying from his injuries several months later. His assailant was commended by Mr Justice Stephen and awarded a medal and seventy pounds by the Pastoralists' Union!

The graziers had won and the shearers had lost. In defeat, the union would change tactics, reducing its reliance on industrial disputes and instead use political strategies to work systematically towards its goals through affiliation with the newly established Labor Party.

The 1890 flood came back to haunt the town in 1894 by way of a significant typhoid epidemic. Contaminated soil was everywhere and the market gardens used night soil from the sewage pans as fertiliser.[781]

The symptoms are of fever, a rash, and diarrhoea. The method of spread from the stools of the carrier to the patient is either by drinking polluted water, or milk, or eating contaminated vegetables; or by flies transmitting the bacillus from stool to food.

It was a deadly disease, with 15% of those infected dying. It would become endemic in Bourke, with a fresh outbreak every summer for many years.

Another Reed grandchild, **Jane Maxwell**, was born in Gongolgon during September 1894[782] but unfortunately she died at Bourke later in the year.[783] Her brother **Norman Maxwell** was born there in 1895.[784]

Their father Joseph Maxwell had found a new means of earning some money, being appointed as a trustee of both the Gongolgon Common[785] and the local Burial Ground.[786] This may have been initiated by his sister-in-law Prudence Murphy whose husband James and son-in-law, Gus Sullivan were both also appointed trustees.[787]

Soon after, the Reed family gathered around their matriarch who was now feeling every one of her 82 years. Frances was living with her daughter Sarah Ann Brennan in late March when she suffered apoplexy (stroke). She was attended by Dr Richard Sides but, after a week of suffering, passed away on 5 April 1895. She was buried in the local cemetery two days later and her obituary was published in the *Western Herald* on April 10.[788]

Another old identity has passed away. On Friday evening last Mrs. Frances Reed, wife of Mr. James Reed, died at the residence of her son-in-law, Mr. M. Brennan, Oxley street, at the ripe old age of 82 years. Mr. and Mrs. Reed were married in England in 1830, and came to the colony three years later, in the ship 'Earl Grey the First." They came to Bourke in 1862, and have resided in the district ever since. The old couple had 12 children, and at the present time have 85 grand children and 40 great grand children. Mr. Reed is still living, being 87 years of age, but, we regret to say, is in feeble health. He belonged to the 80th regiment. The funeral of the late Mrs. Reed took place on Sunday afternoon last, when a large number of residents followed her remains to the grave.

Frances' had started life as a child of the 55th regiment and, later, the 80th regiment as she and her mother (Elizabeth Wilson) followed her father (Serjeant Benjamin Heazle) in his postings throughout the United Kingdom and the Mediterranean. She had witnessed the deaths of her younger brothers Benjamin and James and probably that of her mother and sister Eliza too, at some stage.

At age 18 she had married a young soldier from her father's regiment, a partnership that would endure for almost 65 years. Three sons were born before the family came to Australia in 1836 while another two sons and seven daughters were added during postings at Linden, Windsor, Wollongong and Sydney.

Frances was 50 years old when she and James brought the whole family to Bourke in 1862. She had employed her life experience and resourcefulness in assisting at the birth of William Wright in November 1862, just the eighth birth recorded in the district and was probably the first woman to buy land in Bourke. She earned a good reputation in the district as a hostess who did what she could to bring some feminine charm to a male-dominated town. In 1871 she unwittingly hosted several bushrangers in her hotel at Mount Oxley, shortly before they were captured by the police. Three years later she provided supper for the congregation after the opening of the new Anglican church.

Frances Reed was one of a few strong, brave, pioneer women who helped to tame the challenges of the frontier and to found the town of Bourke. Her family memorialised her with a poignant mourning card.

In Memoriam
In loving remembrance of
Frances Reed
Beloved wife of James Reed
Died April 5, 1895. Aged 82 years.
Farewell, my husband dear, farewell,
Adieu to thee, Adieu. I
and you my dearly love ones all,
Farewell, farewell to you.
Though I am gone and you are left
To tread this vale alone,
We'll hope to meet again in Heaven,
With Christ before God's throne.

...

Deeply Regretted

Photograph 32
Mourning card for Frances Reed.
Source: Jennie Hull, Dubbo.

Photograph 33
Sarah Ann Brennan nee Reed, circa 1895 aged 51.
Source: Sarah McKibbon.

**Photograph 31
Camel caravan near
Bourke, ca 1885-94.**
Powerhouse Museum
Collection.
Gift of Australian Consolidated
Press under the Taxation
Incentives for the Arts Scheme,
1985.

Photograph 34
James Reed, ca 1896
aged 87
(seated on right end)
Source: Ena Kessey
collection preserved by
the author

Photograph 25
Marriage of George Charles Reed Murphy and Ellen Ruby
Bowen, Bourke 18 October 1905.
Ena Kessey collection preserved by the author.

CHAPTER TWENTY

Brassy skies and bare plains

After experiencing flood, recession, epidemic and the death of their matriarch during the first half of the 1890s, the Reed family of Bourke was due a change of fortune, but it was not to be. The following few years saw the start of an extended drought, a devastating heatwave and the death of the family patriarch.

One of the few family photographs to have survived from the mid-1890s depicts Sarah Ann Brennan, recently turned fifty, standing behind an elaborate cane studio chair while dressed in her best clothes (see Photograph 33). She faces the camera directly with a resolute expression.

During the following year she welcomed two new nephews into the world. Her brother George Charles' youngest child **William Reed** was born on 8 August 1895 and was baptised in St Stephen's church seven months later.[789] As well, her sister Mary Ann Farrell produced her penultimate child, **George Charles Reed Farrell**, whose was probably born at Gongolgon as his birth was registered at Brewarrina.[790]

In June, James Tobin and his family moved into Bourke and took over the license of the hotel on the southeastern corner of Sturt and Mertin Streets. It had been originally licensed eleven years earlier to Bernard Deignan as the *Commercial* hotel but was generally known as *Deignan's* hotel. During 1890-1, while licensed to Edward Dorrington it had been known as *Dorrington's* before Clementina Dugan resumed the *Commercial* name in 1894. James Tobin immediately renamed it the *Union* hotel (perhaps a tribute to the union office across the road), a name that it retained thereafter. He improved the hotel's facilities for horses and promoted it to racegoers.[791]

Henry Lawson had experienced Bourke a few years earlier during a fairly average summer but was nevertheless able to depict the ruinous turn-of-the-century drought in indelible terms in his 1899 poem, *The Song of the Darling River*.

The skies are brass and the plains are bare,
Death and ruin are everywhere -
And all that is left of the last year's flood
Is a sickly stream on the grey-black mud;
The salt-springs bubble and quagmires quiver,
And - this is the dirge of the Darling River:

For those in the Bourke District depending on the river, the hard times started before the drought began due to the impact of overstocking, land degradation and invasive plants and animals. The outcomes were described by Pastoral Inspector WA Baker, seventy years later.[792]

In 1894 there were 56 million sheep in NSW, in 1902, 27 millions, and just as the Western Division, relatively speaking had led the expansion of flocks in the eighties and early nineties, so too, did it lead their reduction between then and 1902. For in the west the impact of the great drought of 1895-1902 was the outcome not merely of paucity of rain events, but practices of earlier days had established conditions in which any falling away of rainfall would be disastrous. Overstocking, rabbits and the encroachment of noxious scrub, had done permanent damage to pastures.

The drought was heralded by a dreadful heatwave, the savagery of which can scarcely be imagined. January 1896 was probably the hottest month ever experienced in Bourke causing forty-seven people to die in a population of 3000. Of these, forty-one perished from heat exhaustion, comprising 35 males and 6 females.

New Year's Day was relatively cool - 98 degrees [36.7 degrees Celsius]. The temperature climbed daily to 118 degrees on January 6th, slowly descended to 108.5 degrees by 10th January, raised daily to a peak of 119 degrees on 14th January and remained over 115 degrees with one day's exception until 25 January when it dropped to 91 degrees.[793]

The daily average maximum temperature during the worst fortnight was 116.6 degrees Fahrenheit (47 degrees Celsius). After four deaths on 12 January and three more the next day, the Sydney Morning Herald headlined "Great Heat at Bourke". After five more deaths in the next two days the Herald's headline was "Terrific Heat at Bourke". The next two days brought another ten deaths. The Herald reported:[794]

A man named John Ryan, a boundary-rider on Fort Bourke station, was found in a dying condition by the overseer. He was in terrible agony and complained of shooting pains in the back of the head. The overseer stayed with him for two hours, when the sufferer became light-headed. The overseer then went for assistance to bring him to the station, but when he returned Ryan was dead.

A day later the Herald reported that there had been 22 deaths at Bourke in a week; the heat was continuous day and night with a scorching wind; and that residents were worn out. Its reporter noted that *"horses are dropping from sunstroke, and birds are falling dead from the trees"*.[795]

Mothers with babies, such as Mary Ann Reed and Mary Ann Farrell, must have had a particularly trying experience. The unrelenting heat would have also tested the general fitness and resilience of old people, like James Reed.

As the heat and deaths continued, the NSW government finally came to the town's aid with the Railway Commissioner reducing train fares on 20 January to allow residents to escape to the southeast. On the following day the Herald reported that *"Large numbers left by train this morning and the cheap excursion train which leaves tomorrow will be largely availed of"*[796]. Despite this, five more people died the next day as a terrific wind blew several verandahs down as well as several ornamental street trees.

Almost all business, except in the hotels, was practically suspended. Heavy clouds are now hanging about, and great hopes are entertained that a good rain will fall ... A large number of residents have availed themselves of

the opportunity of leaving Bourke cheaply this morning,
by the special cheap excursion train. Many persons are
ill, and the hospital is so crowded that five extra beds have
been ordered.[797]

Day followed day with no relief and the deaths continued to mount. After a Mrs Honeysuckle died, her son-in-law travelled to Bourke to arrange for her body to be sent by rail to Mudgee for a family burial. But, after soldering the lid of her coffin closed, he was himself taken ill and died within the hour. The railway carriage that he had ordered ultimately carried his own body as well.[798]

Two days later a man named Frederick Forbes, maddened by the heat, took an axe and felled three telegraph poles before being apprehended by the police. He was later acquitted on medical advice that showed that he had been adversely affected by the sun at the time.[799]

Relief finally came on the evening of 25 January with a good downpour of rain following a heavy dust-storm. The Herald reporter wired:[800]

Now raining steadily. We are all out in it. Nobody cares
to be inside, actually delighting in getting a soaking to
the skin. ... The temperature is down to 75. The people's
gratitude knows no bounds.

The records currently available don't reveal for certain whether the recently widowed James Reed, now 86 years old, was evacuated from Bourke on one of the special trains. Nevertheless, one piece of evidence hints that he may have left the town for a time. It is a photo that shows him seated with crossed legs, holding a hat on his lap, alongside a large group of (presumed) family members (see Photograph   34).

I date the picture to about 1895-6 based on its non-professional format and size (slightly smaller than cabinet card but larger than the photo postcard introduced from 1898); hairstyles; clothing; and accessories. The leg-o'-mutton sleeves, in particular, date it to after 1892.

The picture was included in the collection of my grandmother, Ena Kessey nee Murphy, but unfortunately no one has been able to identify any of the family members. My analysis rules out all branches of Ena's ancestors except the Reed family.

Ena was not born until 1908, so she must have obtained the photo from her grandmother, Prudence Murphy, with whom she lived in Sydney in 1927. (Prudence also gave her Frances Reed's mourning card at that time.) James Reed is clearly identifiable by comparison to earlier photos, which means that this picture was likely taken after Frances' death in 1895. Since most of the men are sporting boutonnieres, the picture was probably taken at a wedding.

There were three family weddings in Bourke between 1895 and James' death in 1898. His grand-daughter Josephine Brennan married James Costello in 1895;[801] another grand-daughter Hazel Farrell (Gibb) wed Daniel Power in 1897;[802] and John Murphy (a stepson of his daughter Prudence) married Honorah Rawson in 1896.[803] But neither Prudence nor her husband James Murphy appears in the picture. Nor do Sarah Ann Brennan or her husband Michael. In fact, aside from James, the picture does not seem to include anyone from the 1877 pictures of the Reed family at Bourke.

The two males in the centre of the front row look similar enough to be brothers and they bear a striking resemblance to James himself. Could it be that he had journeyed to Springsure in Queensland and that the picture depicts the combined families of his sons, Jimmy and Alexander Reed? If James Reed had travelled to Sydney by train to escape the Bourke heatwave, the onward journey to Springsure would have been comfortable enough, with most of the distance from Sydney to Rockhampton sailed aboard ship. But, while this intriguing hypothesis could help to explain the photo, there is no evidence in shipping lists, newspaper reports or elsewhere to support it. Notably, the Henry Reed who married Alice Magdalena Schmidt in Brisbane on 24 June 1896 was an English immigrant, not James' grandson. The Henry J Reed who married Anne Lawler in Bourke in 1897 was also unrelated.

Around this time, Henry Reed's father Jimmy chose a new selection at Springsure[804] but, unfortunately, he was to lose it ten years later.[805]

Despite the good fall of rain that ended the heatwave, Bourke now entered a long period of drought, one of the worst of the many that the district has ever endured. From 1897 until 1905 the town's rainfall was well below average. High winds moved great quantities of sand and dust, loosened by an exploding population of rabbits. By 1903 sheep numbers in the district had dropped to about a quarter of what they had been at the peak.[806]

Members of the Reed family battled on with their declining businesses as best they could. Henry and Eliza Johnson were now working a small property near Byrock that they had named *Hazlewood* Selection in honour of

Eliza's late mother, Frances. During the winter of 1897, Henry placed a notice in the local newspaper warning people against cutting timber on this property.[807] Three months later their son Alexander George Oxley Johnson married Maria Mary Mapstone in Queensland.[808]

Jane's husband Joseph Maxwell tendered successfully for a three year contract worth 38 pounds and ten shillings per year to run the weekly Gongolgon to Tarcoon mail run using a four-wheeled carriage drawn by a single horse.[809]

Earlier in the year his daughter, Kate Heazle Maxwell, had married William Alexander Peter at Brewarrina.[810] Her new husband was a son of David Peter and his wife Elizabeth Dugan, both from Bourke pioneer families. The Peter family had built and run the Bourke Cordial Factory in Tudor Street for many years before later selling it to the Rice family in 1909.[811] The Dugan family had owned a hotel on the northern side of Mitchell Street (between Glen and Wilson) since about 1877, known variously as the *Commercial*, the *Caledonian*, the *Royal Exchange*, the *Golden Stairs* and the *Harp of Erin*. While the Dugan family seems to have retained ownership, the license was held at various times by (amongst others) Edward Dugan, David Peter, Nicholas Dugan, Donald Shaw, Richard Green and Mrs Elizabeth Peter (nee Dugan). Three years after his marriage to Kate Maxwell, William Peter would hold the license for this hotel for a year in 1900.

Like Joseph Maxwell, James Murphy had decided to diversify his business interests further by tendering for a mail contract. His businesses were facing increasing difficulties with a significant decline in trade in the Gongolgon hotel exacerbated by the multitude of problems faced by all graziers. This had led to a cash flow shortfall which resulted in the cancellation of his lease on 320 acres at East Bourke in 1893 for non-payment of 45 pounds in rent.[812] Fortunately, his tender of 118 pounds annually to run a four-horse covered coach twice weekly on the 103 kilometre long Byrock to Brewarrina via Gongolgon mail run was accepted in 1896,[813] 1897,[814] and 1898[815] but the payment had dropped to only 100 pounds for 1899.[816]

On 14 December 1897 James Reed celebrated his 89th birthday, but he was not in good health. His "feeble health" of three years earlier had continued to deteriorate. Six weeks later he was seen by Dr Charles Henry Scott who was treating him for senile decay but he died on the same day. He was buried on the following day in Bourke's cemetery.[817] An obituary was published a few days later in the local newspaper.[818]

In April last it was our melancholy duty to record the death of Mrs. Frances Reed, the wife of one of Bourke's oldest residents, Mr. James Reed, of North Bourke. To-day it falls to our lot to announce the death of Mr Reed himself, who at the ripe old age of 88 years, has gone to rejoin the faithful sharer of his life's pilgrimage during an uninterrupted partnership of 67 years. Mr. Reed was naturally in failing health at the time of his wife's decease and never recovered from the shock of her loss. On Sunday he passed quietly away, having attained his 88th year, and was buried on Monday, the funeral being attended by a large concourse of his numerous descendants and friends. Mr. Reed was born in 1810, in Staffordshire, and during his early youth had been a soldier in the 80th regiment. In 1833 he came with his wife (whom he had married three years previously) to

New South Wales in the "Earl Grey," and after various experiences reached Bourke in 1862, and here he remained till the day of his death, covering a period of 36 years. Twelve children were born to him, nine of whom still survive and are held in high esteem, while his other direct descendants number 86 grand children and over 40 great grand children.

Three more grandchildren were born within a few years of James' death, bringing the total number to 89. **Ena Elsie Marie Farrell** would be born in Cobar in 1899.[819] The penultimate child for Jane and Joseph Maxwell was born in 1898 at Bourke and named **William Walter Maxwell**[820], five years before his brother **John S Maxwell**.[821] A complete list of the 89 grandchildren is provided at the end of this chapter.

Having started life in 1808 as the youngest of nine children born to Elizabeth (nee Sutton) and Thomas Reed at Ash Green near Trentham in Staffordshire, he had lived a long and eventful life. His mother had died when he was just a few months old, leaving her baby to be raised by his much older sisters, especially the eldest, Mary. She had worked long and hard in her mother's place, not marrying until she was 32 years old, by which time James was 15 years old and probably already working in the local brick-making industry.

At the age of 18 he had journeyed 315 kilometres from his hometown to Newcastle upon Tyne where he joined the 35th Regiment. Within six months he had transferred to the 80th Regiment (stationed nearby at Sunderland Barracks) where he met his future wife Frances, the eldest daughter of his training officer, Sergeant Benjamin Heazle. They married two and a half years later in the local church.

Their eldest child William was baptised in April 1831 at Portsea but he must have died soon afterwards. Sons John and Jimmy were born before the family sailed to NSW in 1836 aboard the *Earl Grey* where the regiment had been assigned garrison duty. Alexander was born at Linden, Sarah at Sydney and Eliza at Wollongong before James and Frances took the life-changing step of resigning from the regiment to remain in Australia.

Their four year old daughter Sarah had died just before James left the regiment in 1843 and so it was natural that their next child was named Sarah Ann in her memory. Five more children completed the family over the next twelve years: Prudence, Frances, George Charles, Mary Ann and Jane. During these years James had run a grocery business and worked as a constable before becoming a labourer. The family may have run a boarding house for a period.

His eldest sons soon started in the carrying business as bullock wagon drivers. Once Jimmy moved to Wellington and got married, James and Frances could envisage the family becoming scattered, which may have prompted their decision to move with their younger children to Bourke in 1862. The older children and their families followed them in 1864 and, for a time, the whole extended family lived in Bourke.

Jimmy and Alexander later moved much further north to settle at Springsure in Queensland, but the rest of the Reed family remained in the Bourke district for the remainder of James' and Frances' lives.

The Reed men worked mostly in the carrying and timber industries in the first few years after their arrival in Bourke while the women probably operated a boarding house in the building that was eventually licensed to George Charles Reed as the *Bourke* hotel in 1873. In the meantime, James and Frances had built the *Mountain Home* hotel at Mount Oxley, first licensed in 1870, while their daughter Prudence and her husband Joseph Whye had built and licensed the *Lame Horse* hotel at Gongolgon by 1866. George Charles was also the first licensee of the *Overland* hotel at North Bourke in 1876.

The success of the various Reed businesses had enabled James and Frances to gradually hand over the reins and ownership of their assets to family members as they eased gradually into a fairly comfortable and well-earned retirement. Their extended family, grateful for the solid start in life that their parents had provided, made sure to look after them well as their health gradually failed in old age.

James and Frances endured much tragedy during their lifetime, burying two young children, one adult son and his wife, three sons-in-law and seventeen grandchildren. Perhaps the bitterest blows were the drowning of their 7-year-old grandson William John Reed in the Darling River at Bourke on 7 October 1865 and the death of his only sibling, 15-year-old Frances Eliza Reed, when her clothes caught alight at Bourke on 8 July 1875.

Despite these sorrows, James' and Frances' life story is one of a devoted, resilient and resourceful couple whose initiative and enterprise helped to forge a better life for their ten adult children and eighty-nine grandchildren. Prominent among the earliest pioneers who helped found the town of Bourke, they were honoured with a prominent memorial stone in the town cemetery and their memory is celebrated by thousands of descendants including the Anderson, Bannister, Barton,

Bradley, Brennan, Burnet, Dekker, Dickson, Farrell, Fleming, Flemming, Gibb, Harding, Helm, Honeyman, Hull, Jackson, Johnson, Kessey, Maxwell, Matthews, McCready, Moller, Murphy, Nicholls, Ralph, Reed, Tobin, Turner, Wall and Whye families.

May their souls rest in peace

The 89 grandchildren of James and Frances Reed

REED - John Benjamin Reed and Eliza Jane Green (2)
William John Reed (1858-7 Oct 1865)
Frances Eliza Reed (1860-8 Jul 1875)

REED - James "Jimmy" Reed and Eliza Bend (10)
John Reed (1859-31 Dec 1945)
Eliza Reed (1860-23 Dec 1942)
James Reed (1862-17 Dec 1906)
Charles Alexander Reed (ca Oct 1865-28 Mar 1919)
George Reed (1866-1887)
Henry Reed (16 Jan 1869-24 Nov 1951)
Frank Edward Reed (5 Jul 1871-1 Oct 1940)
Frances Reed (4 Feb 1874-20 Nov 1947)
Thomas Reed (21 May 1876-)
Mary Jane Reed (6 Jul 1878-26 Oct 1948)

REED - Alexander Reed and Mary Eckel (7)
Margaret "Maggie" Reed (8 Jul 1879-13 Mar 1959)
Eliza Jane Reed (28 Dec 1880-25 Dec 1964)
Christina Wingfield Reed (1 Feb 1883-18 Dec 1950)
Henry James Reed (5 Dec 1885-26 Apr 1953)
George Charles Alexander Reed (28 Nov 1887-1966)
William Edward "William Frederick" Reed (6.4.90-4.8.50)
Ernest John Reed (19 Jul 1891-19 May 1919)

JOHNSON - Eliza Emily Reed and Henry Johnson (10)
Frances Eliza Johnson (1866-bef 22 Aug 1925)
James Henry Johnson (9 Feb 1868-1938)
Alexander George Oxley Johnson (22 Dec 1869-1946)
Sarah Jane Heazle "Heazle" Johnson (29.11.71-28.7.60)
John Benjamin Linley "Benjamin" Johnson (11.73-1955)
George Johnson (20 Apr 1876-)
Henry Sampson "Sampson" Johnson (2 Mar 1878-1956)
Emily Jane Johnson (15 Oct 1879-1 Nov 1908)
Albert William Johnson (25 Sep 1881-)
Mary Ann Maud "Maud" Johnson (8 Mar 1884-)

BRENNAN - Sarah Ann Reed and Michael James "Mick" Brennan (11)
Sarah Ellen Brennan (24 Jul 1864-)
Frances Eliza Brennan (ca Oct 1865-29 Mar 1885)
Emeline Brennan (Jul 1867-)
Isabella Maude Mary "Maude" Brennan (15 Mar 1869-)
Victoria Prudence Brennan (7 Sep 1870-)
William J Brennan (Aug 1872-14 Aug 1876)
Mary Jane Heazle Brennan (23 Jul 1874-30 Nov 1944)
Josephine Whelan Brennan (28 May 1877-10 Jun 1956)
Annie Brennan (28 Dec 1878-4 Apr 1879)
Michael James Brennan (6 Oct 1881-)
Alfred John Brennan (28 Feb 1884-10 May 1947)

WHYE - Prudence Reed and Joseph Whye (9)
Frances Anna Whye (1864-1960)
William Whye (1865-9 Jul 1865)
Jane Elizabeth Whye (Jul 1866-12 Apr 1947)
Frederick Whye (1868-4 Jan 1868)
Emily Maude Mary Whye (1869-24 Aug 1940)
Albert George Henry Whye (26 Feb 1871-19 Jul 1927)
Kate Whye (28 Apr 1873-14 Jul 1878)
Josephine Heazle Whye (15 Mar 1875-)
Joseph Headland Whye (abt Jan 1877-21 Mar 1878)

MURPHY - Prudence Reed and James Murphy (5)
Daniel Reed Murphy (14 May 1879-24 Dec 1881)
George Charles Reed Murphy (24 Dec 1880-11 Dec 1949)
Nora Lilian Murphy (1882-)
Mary Ethel Murphy (4 Sep 1884-)
Lila Kate Murphy (13 Nov 1886-4 Nov 1941)

TOBIN - Frances Reed and James Tobin Junior (1)
Female Tobin (1864-1864)

REED - George Charles Reed and Mary Ann Peters (9)
Edward John Bloxham Reed (14 Dec 1878-4 Nov 1881)
Gilbert George Joseph Whye Reed (28.2.80-26.3.49)
Frances Heazle Reed (17 Feb 1882-)
Ethel Mary Ann Reed (28 Jul 1883-)
Emily Beatrice Reed (1 Jul 1885-3 Aug 1907)
Bertie Augustus Reed (17 Dec 1887-10 Jan 1952)
James Reed (13 Feb 1890-)
George Charles Reed (29 Jul 1892-22 Sep 1958)
William Reed (8 Aug 1895-9 May 1958)

GIBB - Mary Ann Reed and George Samson Gibb (2)
Jannet Frances Gibb (Oct 1873-)
Alexander James Boswell Gibb (3 Apr 1875-17 Oct 1947)

FARRELL - Mary Ann Reed and Timothy Farrell (1 + 7)
Hazle May Gibb Farrell
Thomas James Edmond Farrell (14 Sep 1882-6 Apr 1884)
Lila Rose Farrell (1884-)
Victoria K Farrell (1887-)
Timothy Oxley "Tim" Farrell (1889-23 May 1918)
Edwin Albert "Eddy" Farrell (1892-1958)
George Charles Reed Farrell (1896-15 Mar 1917)
Una Elsie Marie Farrell (1899-)

MAXWELL - Jane Elizabeth Reed and Joseph Maxwell Junior (15)
Alexander Maxwell (Aug 1871-Jul 1872)
Richard James Oxley "Oxley" Maxwell (Jul 1873-1950)
Kate Heazle Maxwell (26 Sep 1875-9 Nov 1936)
Frances Annie Maxwell (3 Dec 1877-May 1878)
Eliza Emily Tobin "Lila" Maxwell (11 Dec 1878-Dec 1973)
Augustus George Maxwell (23 Apr 1881-30 Apr 1881)
Albert Charles Maxwell (7 Feb 1883-1928)
Frances Prudence Maxwell (May 1885-4 Nov 1888)
Private Joseph Henry "Harry" Maxwell (9.87-3.5.17)
Edward H Maxwell (Feb 1890-)
Blanche Olive Maxwell (Mar 1892-)
Jane Elizabeth Maxwell (21 Sep 1894-aft 23 Sep 1894)
Norman Harold Maxwell (Aug 1895-)
William Walter Maxwell (Feb 1898-)
John S Maxwell (Oct 1903-)

Photographs 35 & 36 - Gravestone of James and Frances Reed in Bourke cemetery.
Author's photos

Photograph 37 - Eliza Emily Johnson in 1909.
Source: Kayleen Vallance.

Photograph 38 Murphy family of Bourke, ca 1910.

Source: Jennie Hull, Dubbo.

L to R: William Bede Bowen (Ellens brother), Ellen Ruby Murphy holding Ena Ruby Murphy (later Mrs Kessey), Lillian May Bowen (Ellens sister, later Mrs Sunderland), Jack Murphy, Alice Mary Bowen (Ellens sister, later Mrs Min Honeyman).

Photograph 39
Eliza Emily Johnson in her garden with daughter Maud and other family members in 1920.
Source: Kayleen Vallance.

**Photograph 40
Mary Ann Reed
nee Peters, ca
1920.**

**Photograph 41
Murphy family
Memorial,
Bathurst
cemetery.**
Author's photo.

CHAPTER TWENTY-ONE

Epilogue

Despite the death of the Reed matriarch and patriarch, the surviving members of the family in both Queensland and Bourke remained tightly knit. Relatives were also reliable close friends whose integrated lives helped to support each other into the unstoppable future.

The next family member to die was son-in-law Michael Brennan in 1908, aged 65.[822] After witnessing Frances' burial in 1895, he had continued working as a house painter right up until just before his death. An obituary in *The Worker* described him as *"a genial man who was widely respected[823]"*. His wife Sarah Ann would survive him by 24 years.

*

After providing the information for his father's death certificate, George Charles Reed continued working as a labourer. This was a significant come down for the adroit businessman who had successfully established both the *Bourke* and *Overland* hotels as profitable enterprises. The 1880 fire had, however, pushed him into bankruptcy and his finances had never recovered enough to support further business ventures.

In 1906 his 21-year-old daughter Emily Beatrice Reed contracted tuberculosis and she died after battling the disease for 18 months.[824] After his many trials it may have been this tragedy that finally triggered a breakdown in her father's mental health. Sadly, George Charles took his own life by phosphorous poisoning two years later.[825] His wife Mary Ann survived him by 35 years.

*

Unfortunately, Emily was not the only family member to die from tuberculosis around this time. Her first cousin, Emily Jane Johnson, also battled it for a long time before succumbing in November 1908. The *Western Herald* published a brief obituary.[826]

On Sunday night last, Miss Emily Johnson, daughter of Mr. and Mrs. H. Johnson of North Bourke, died in the Bourke District Hospital after a lingering illness, the cause being consumption. Miss Johnson was 29 years of age, and except for the past two years, was a splendid specimen of womanhood.

A year later her mother posed for a studio portrait (Photograph 37) that is now among a significant Johnson collection preserved by her descendant Kayleen Vallance. Two years after this picture was taken her 73-year-old husband Henry Johnson followed their daughter to the grave.[827] Eliza would survive him by 14 years.

*

Tuberculosis was not the only infectious disease endemic in Bourke during the early years of the twentieth century. The detritus that had settled in the soil after the 1890 flood continued to cause typhoid epidemics for more than two decades. In 1912, the wife of James and Frances' grandson, George Charles Reed Murphy, (Ellen Ruby Bowen) died of this disease leaving three young Murphy children to be raised by their maternal grandmother Alice Clarkson Bowen: Jack, Ena Ruby (Kessey) and Leila (Barton) - see Photograph 38.

*

Alexander Reed's marriage must have broken down around the turn of the century because, by 1903, his wife Mary was living apart from him in Emu Street Longreach with their daughters Christina and Eliza Jane.[828] Another daughter, Margaret, had married William John Swan in Longreach four years earlier while Christina would marry August Johann Gottleib Beutel three years later[829].

Alexander was still living at Springsure, 500 kilometres away, on the Sandy Creek Farm owned by his brother Jimmy.[830] This seems to have been a permanent arrangement, because it persisted in 1905[831] and 1906[832] before Jimmy unfortunately lost this farm.[833]

He was nevertheless still living at Springsure in 1913[834] but passed away in April 1916,[835] while his brother Alexander died eighteen months later.[836] Jimmy's widow Eliza survived him by 11 years while Alexander's widow Mary would remarry T O'Brien in 1921.[837]

***

At least nine of James' and Frances' grandsons
served in the First World War, six from Bourke and three
from Springsure. Three sons of Alexander Reed served
overseas throughout much of the war. Also joining up
were two sons of George Charles Reed, three sons of his
sister Mary Ann Farrell and one son of their sister Jane
Maxwell. Unfortunately, three of these grandsons would
pay the ultimate price and are now buried in France.

Two of Alexander's sons joined the Australian
Imperial Force (AIF) at Brisbane on 18 May 1915. **George
Charles Alexander Reed** was about 28 years old[838] while
William Edward Reed (who recorded his name as
William Frederick) was three years younger.[839] Their 30-
year-old brother **Henry James Reed** joined as James
Henry Reed at Darwin nine months later on 9 December
1915.[840]

George left Australia on 29 June 1915 and must
have served at Gallipoli because his wife's later
application for his Gallipoli medal was approved. From
there he disembarked from the *Mudros* at Alexandria in
Egypt in January 1916. Two months later he arrived at
Marseilles in France to join the British Expeditionary
Force which fought on the Western Front. A year later he
was admitted to hospital with influenza and was in and
out of hospital throughout 1917. When he wasn't sick he
rejoined his unit where he worked as a cook. After
promotion to acting Corporal and finally to Sergeant
(Cook) he attended the Australian Corps Cooking School
in between further bouts of hospitalisation for influenza.
In late 1918 he was treated for bronchial pneumonia.

Photograph 42 - Official enlistment portrait of George Charles Alexander Reed.
Pictorial supplement to The Queenslander, 15 August 1915.

His brother William had a similar war experience. He embarked from Australia on 8 November 1915 with the 31st Battalion. While he had signed up as a driver, the same job that his father Alexander had worked at for so many years, his role was soon changed at his own request to Stretcher Bearer. He too probably served at Gallipoli because he also arrived at Alexandria on the *Mudros* in January 1916. Six months later he embarked from there to join the British Expeditionary Force, disembarking from the *Hororata* at Marseilles, three months after his brother George. He was soon evacuated to hospital at Birmingham and Harefield in England for treatment of severe gunshot wounds to his eye, ear, neck and arm inflicted on 19 July. He had suffered a permanent injury that would afflict him for the remainder of his life. After several months of recovery, he was assigned light administrative duties but was readmitted several times with tonsilitis.

During this long period of convalescence, he met Hazel Cecilia White and they were married in the Parish

Church at Walthamstow on 2 January 1918. He was scheduled for a return to Australia aboard the *Demosthenes* in January 1919 but was delayed when it was discovered that he was suffering from trachoma. He eventually departed two months later aboard the *Euripedes*, arriving on 1 May. Presumably his wife travelled with him. He was discharged on 19 July 1919.

About a month after William boarded the *Euripedes*, his brother George was punished for providing a false reason in a leave application. It seems that he had not told his superiors that he had married Vera White in the Parish Church at Walthamstow in 15 January 1919, a year after his brother William had married her sister Hazel in the same church. He was soon granted leave and he and his new wife were transported to Australia aboard the *Borda*, disembarking on 2 February 1920 and discharged on 3 April 1920.

Their brother Henry James Reed was a Private in the Reserve Company from 17 February until 10 April 1916 before joining the 17/12th. He departed Australia on 20 April bound for Folkestone in England. In July he was hospitalised but a month later proceeded overseas to join his unit. Within a fortnight he was admitted to hospital in Etaples (France) suffering from trachoma and was soon returned to England by hospital ship from Calais. Following treatment in Leicester he was sent to work at the 2nd Australian Corn Depot at Weymouth. Four months later, persistent trachoma forced his evacuation to Australia aboard the *Ulysses* and he was discharged on 15 June 1917 with a pension of 3 pounds per fortnight.

Fortunately, all three brothers had made it home safely in time to reunite with their father during the last few months of his life. Their youngest brother, Ernest

John Reed, had not fought in the war but ironically, while his brothers returned home safely, he died in 1919 aged 27.[841]

*

George Charles Reed's son **Bertie Reed** joined the AIF at Dubbo on 18 October 1915, two months before his 28th birthday.[842] He was assigned to the 6th Australian Light Horse Regiment at Liverpool, near Sydney but, after just 3 months, was discharged at his own request.

A few days later his youngest brother, twenty-year-old **William Reed** (a stockman), joined at Charters Towers in Queensland. Within three months he boarded the *Hawkes Bay* at Sydney bound for Alexandria, arriving in early June. He remained aboard and finally disembarked at Portsmouth later that month.[843]

In late September William crossed to Etaples in France from where he was attached to the 47th Battalion on the battlefield. Two months later he was admitted to the Field Hospital suffering from bronchitis. His condition worsened and he was returned to Etaples where his condition developed into laryngitis after Christmas. This cleared up within a week and he was back in the combat zone from 5 January 1917.

In August he enjoyed two weeks leave in England but was then sent to Belgium. In January 1918 he was attached as a miner to a Canadian company of tunnellers for two months before rejoining his Battalion on 9 March.

He was listed as Missing in Action (MIA) on 5 April but two days later he was confirmed as a Prisoner of War (POW) in Germany.

It may have been the news of William's capture that prompted his older brother Bertie to rejoin, two years after his discharge. He re-enlisted at Brisbane on 27 May 1918 aged 30 years and 5 months. In July his portrait was published in The Queenslander newspaper[844] before he was posted to number 1 Depot Company for a few months before an assignment to the 3rd Reinforcements.

Photograph 43 - Official enlistment portrait of Bertie Reed.
Pictorial supplement to The Queenslander, July 1918.

Bertie embarked at Sydney aboard the HT *Wiltshire* in June and disembarked at Suez on 17 July 1918. After a period of training, he was allocated to the 2nd Light Horse Regiment. He spent time in hospital for an undisclosed illness between January and March 1919 before it was decided to repatriate him to Australia as medically unfit. He embarked aboard the HT *Dorset* at Port Said on 29 April, disembarked in Australia on 9 June and was discharged in September 1919.

Meanwhile his brother William spent about eight months in captivity before he was part of a prisoner exchange. It was a condition of such exchanges that the released soldiers would be repatriated to their home countries and take no further part in hostilities. After arriving in England on 1 December 1918 he was immediately hospitalised with skin infections including boils and impetigo that affected his upper body, arms and face. He recovered quickly and was discharged after four days. On 11 December his mother was informed that he would be returning home and he sailed aboard the *Plessy* in March 1919 arriving home on 30 April. He had beaten his brother Bertie home by about a month.

*

On Monday 10 April 1916 a large group of Bourke citizens gathered at the residence of Charles Campbell and his wife Mary Ann nee Farrell to give a hearty sendoff to three of her nephews. Tim, Eddie and George Farrell, who had all recently joined the armed forces, were the three surviving sons of Timothy Farrell and Mary Ann nee Reed. The Western Herald reported[845] that

> *Speeches ... were ... made by Messrs J Maxwell, Alexander Gibb and Watty Baker, all of whom expressed the hope that the three of them would return 'safe and sound'.*

Two days later the "Fighting Farrells" boarded the mail train for Sydney but unfortunately, those good wishes would not be realised.

Both **Timothy Oxley Farrell**[846] and **George Charles Reed Farrell** had joined the AIF at Dubbo on 22 January 1916[847]. George was just 19 years old and described as a fisherman while Tim was a 26-year-old shearer. Two weeks later their 23-year-old brother **Eddie Reed Farrell** (a labourer) also joined up at Dubbo[848] where the enlisting officer recorded that he already had a bullet wound on his upper left arm! Their 28-year-old cousin

Joseph Henry Maxwell, a labourer, also joined up as Henry Joseph Maxwell in Dubbo a few weeks later on 9 March.[849]

All three Farrell brothers embarked on the SS *Barambah* in June, arriving at Plymouth in late August. Three months later they proceeded from Folkestone aboard the SS *Onward* to Etaples in France. In late November and early December 1916, they marched out to join the 55th Battalion. In early January, George undertook two weeks training to use the new Lewis light machine gun, at the end of which he had to prove his proficiency by stripping the gun down completely and then reassembling its 104 parts within one minute - blindfolded.

Two months after his cousins' send-off, "Harry" Maxwell shared a grand Bourke send-off with fellow-Privates Archie and Bertie Thorne, sons of Mr and Mrs Willoughby Thorne. He soon followed his cousins to Plymouth aboard the *Wiltshire*, disembarking in mid-October. He arrived at Etaples on 14 December aboard the *Henrietta*, a few days after his cousins had been deployed to the 55th. He was attached to the 18th Battalion on 25 January 1917, but three months later was reported as Missing in Action during the first Battle at Bullecourt.

On 31 August the *Western Herald* published a report from a war correspondent.[850]

> *I rode a donk. over to an infantry battalion last week and saw a young Tim Farrell, from Bourke, and he gave me a little news concerning some of the lads from the Far West. I regretted to hear that he had lost a brother, and also a cousin, one of the Maxwells, was missing.*

Tim's 21 year old brother George Farrell had been killed in action on 6 March 1917 and was buried in the cemetery at Needle Dump between Les Boeufs and Flers, half a mile west of Les Boeufs. He was very unlucky, because the Germans withdrew from this area later that month. His remains were eventually removed to the Guards' Cemetery at Les Boeufs where he is interred in plot VII L 10.[851]

Following a Court of Enquiry in December 1917, his missing cousin Harry Maxwell was confirmed as killed in action on 3 May 1917, one of 7,400 Australian lives lost at Bullecourt. His sacrifice at age 29 is memorialised at MR 26 Part IV K-M on the Villers Bretonneux Memorial[852] and also on the gravestone of his aunt (Frances Tobin nee Reed) at Rookwood cemetery in Sydney.[853]

After serving in France for thirteen months, Tim Farrell was granted two weeks leave in the UK in early January 1918. Four months after his return to the field of battle he was admitted to the 14th Field Ambulance station on 19 May suffering from gunshot wounds to the chest and back that he had suffered the day before. Within a day he was removed to the 47th Casualty Clearing Station where he died of his wounds two days later, aged 29 years. Tim was buried in Crony British Cemetery ten miles northwest of Amiens on 26 July 1918. Six months later, his mother (Mary Ann Farrell nee Reed) received his effects, including a knife, fountain pen, handkerchief, two badges, a stamp, two shoulder titles, a wallet, photos and cards.

The late Harry Maxwell's father Joseph later served with Willoughby Thorne on the Bourke Soldiers Memorial Committee that raised funds and organised the construction of the Bourke War Memorial monument.[854]

It lists the names of 33 Bourke soldiers who had lost their lives in World War I, including his son Harry Maxwell and nephew George Farrell, but omits his other late nephew, Timothy "Oxley" Farrell. This is a major oversight that should be corrected.

Since the end of 1916, when Eddie Farrell arrived in France with his brothers, he had remained with his unit on active service for more than a year. He was finally rewarded with two weeks' leave in the field during March 1918. On the day of his return to duty he was wounded by gas and removed to the 15th Field Ambulance but was discharged back to duty five days later. He probably learned of the death of his brother Tim before he was sent to the Brigade School for three weeks in June.

Five months later the Armistice was signed and the hostilities ended; he had survived the war. After two years on active service in France, during which he had lost two brothers and a cousin, he was finally granted a month's leave in the UK during December 1918.

Promotion to Lance Corporal was confirmed a month after returning to his unit in Belgium during January 1919. He embarked for England on 30 April at Le Havre and was admitted to Bulford Hospital near Salisbury for two months from 27 May before returning to Australia aboard the *Ajana*, disembarking on 9 October. He arrived home in Bourke five days later to a huge welcome by all the dignitaries of the town and a long article headed "Welcome Home to Lance-Corp E Farrell" on the back page of the *Western Herald* a few days later.[855]

*After an enthusiastic reception at the train by the Mayor
and other members of the Reception League, (Lance-
Corporal E Farrell) was taken in Mr Green's specially
decorated motor car to Starr's Hotel, where the
"Welcome Home" was arranged. The banquet
commenced at 7.30 pm. His Worship, the Mayor (Ald. H
K Bloxham) occupied the chair and round the tables were
seated relatives, old Bourkeites, returned soldiers and
friends - all of whom joined together in welcoming "Ted"
home again. ... The chairman made a presentation to the
guest, consisting of a purse of notes, which had been
subscribed by his friends in the town. ... Ald. E B Mugg
said it was with great pleasure that he proposed the
health of "The Parents of our Guest" ... It was our duty
to do all we could for the bereaved parents, who had three
sons go to the front and had unfortunately lost two of
them.*

Five months after arriving home Eddie received a
letter, written in French, that had been forwarded via the
Military authorities. It had been written on 5 February
1920 by Monsieur L Draguet-Damat of Grand Rue in
Rance, Hainault, Belgium (35 kilometres south of
Charleroi and 100 kilometres south of Brussels). The
letter recalled that Eddie had arrived in Rance on
Christmas Eve 1918 and had left for the war zone near
Charleroi at the beginning of April and from there to
England. Clearly the two men had been acquainted for
about four months but then *"et puis je perdu sa trace"* (I
lost track of him). He wanted to know whether Eddie was
still living, married or single, his age and address. Eddie's
response is unknown, but he never married.

After living out most of his remaining years in
Bourke he died at Gilgandra in 1958 aged 66 years.

***

In 1898, James Tobin's *Union* hotel lost several bedrooms and stables to a fire that started in hessian window blinds attached to the house next door owned by Mrs RH Warmoll. A jury had returned an open verdict on the cause[856]. Nevertheless, nine months later the hotel hosted a reception for 50 people to celebrate the marriage of his adopted daughter Eliza Emily "Lila" Tobin (born Maxwell) to John McCready.[857]

In 1901 another fire caused the loss of the billiard room[858] but the main building survived to host a funeral and wake for Tobin's father in August.[859]

Seventy-year-old Tobin was still the hotel's licensee in 1913,[860] when he sold some of the family's land in River Street Gongolgon.[861] Soon afterwards the family moved to Sydney where he died at Petersham in 1918.[862] His wife Frances sold two of the family's blocks of land in Bourke during 1920 and 1921,[863] but she survived her husband by just four years, dying at Leichhardt in June 1922[864]. She is buried at Rookwood along with her granddaughter, Dorothy Frances McCready.[865] Frances Tobin's obituary was published in the *Western Herald* on 9 August.[866]

The death occurred on Saturday last at Leichhardt of Mrs Frances Tobin, relict of the late Mr. James Tobin. The deceased and her late husband were residents of Bourke for a great many years and kept the Union Hotel in the good old days. The deceased had been living in Sydney ever since she left Bourke and had been ailing for some considerable time. Mrs Brennan (of Bourke) is a sister of the deceased. To the relatives we extend our sincere sympathy. The deceased was 72 years of age; her husband died over three years ago.

*

During the 1890s, James Murphy held the license for his *Commercial* hotel at Gongolgon while also working the mail run between Byrock and Brewarrina via Gongolgon. At the same time, he leased the *Family* hotel in Bourke to a series of licensees, including his brother Daniel, but none of them lasted more than a year, signifying that the aging premises were struggling to attract clientele. In 1899 he leased the Gongolgon hotel to his wife's nephew (Alfred Haylock Whye) while returning himself to Bourke in an effort to revive the *Family* hotel. But his family was now struggling financially and in May 1900 he failed to pay council rates on four properties, including the hotel.[867] These financial woes clearly continued because, on 30 April 1903, the Supreme Court authorised a mortgagee sale of that hotel[868].

James and Prudence managed to avoid bankruptcy by liquidating all their interests in the Bourke District. They moved to Orange where he was soon owner and licensee of the *Green Gate* hotel that had previously been run by his brother Daniel.[869] Soon after, James' 83-year-old mother died and was buried alongside her husband in Bathurst, where they share a prominent grave monument[870] (see Photograph 41). James' own health was also deteriorating and he had to sell up three years later[871] and thereafter lived in retirement[872].

By 1909 Prudence had moved the family to Sydney[873] where she and her daughter Nora soon found that they could not care for him adequately. In the lead up to his death he was an inmate at the Lidcombe State Hospital. James Murphy was buried at Rookwood

Cemetery on 7 November 1919, survived by both his wives and seven of his ten children. Prudence erected the gravestone that still stands in weathered testament to the strong and successful partnership that they had forged[874].

*

After Jimmy Reed's death his widow Eliza lived at Thursby near Rolleston, 70 kilometres from her old home at Springsure in Queensland.[875] Sixty eight years earlier she had emerged from a similar background (as her father Charles Bend had also served as a Private in the 80th Regiment) to become the first Reed daughter-in-law. She died during the winter of 1924 aged 85 years.

*

Her much younger sister-in-law, Jane Maxwell, had died three months earlier, after a very arduous life based in Bourke and Gongolgon. Married at just 15 years, she had lost her first child within a year. Later, as the family grew and poverty made life extremely difficult, she had given up a baby to be raised by her sister, Frances Tobin. Her husband Joseph had tried his hand at many occupations but succumbed to bankruptcy twice after failing to succeed as a publican. Three more children had died before the family gained a surer financial footing as the older children married and left home. This afforded her the satisfaction of welcoming numerous grandchildren and watching her family grow even further. But then, just seven years earlier, she had suffered the sadness of losing her son Harry on a French battlefield, far away. Jane was survived by her husband

Joseph, nine of her fifteen children and twenty-four grandchildren. The Western Herald published a detailed obituary.[876]

On Monday morning last there passed away at Bourke, an old and respected resident, in the person of Mrs. Jane Elizabeth Maxwell, wife of Mr. Joseph Maxwell, of this town. The deceased had not enjoyed good health for some time past, and her death was not unexpected. The late Mrs Maxwell resided in Bourke practically all her life, and had reached the ripe old age of 67 years and 9 months. Mrs Maxwell, with her good old husband, reared a large family in Bourke, nine of whom are still alive to mourn the loss of a devoted mother. Mrs. McCready, who has been a resident of Sydney for some years made the journey to Bourke to cheer and assist her mother in her last days. The rest of the family are Oxley, Albert Norman, William, Edward and Sam, and Mrs W. Peter and Mrs A. Jenkins. They are all married with the exception of Albert and Sam. Deceased also has four sisters, Mrs A. Brennan, Mrs T Farrell, Mrs E. Johnson and Mrs P Murphy. One of her sons, Harry, paid the supreme sacrifice in the Great war. Deceased also leaves 24 grand children, and two great grand children. Mrs. Maxwell was the youngest daughter of the late Mr. and Mrs. James Reed, old pioneers of Bourke, who came to this district in the early sixties.

*

Four years after the return of her three sons from the war and the death of her estranged husband Alexander, Mary Reed nee Eckel remarried in August

1921 to T O'Brien.[877] Unfortunately she became ill about a year later and her health never recovered before her death in September 1925.[878] The *Longreach Leader* published a detailed obituary a few days after her burial.[879]

By the passing away of Mrs. M. E. O'Brien on Sept. 15th, at the General Hospital, another link with the West has been severed. Mrs. O'Brien, who was 65 years of age at the time of her death, came to Longreach from Barcaldine, when the Longreach Hotel was first built, and resided there for many years. For the last nine years she resided at West Longreach, to be near her daughter, Mrs. Swan. A few years ago deceased married Mr. O'Brien, and had been an invalid for the past three years. The deceased lady had four sons, all of whom enlisted for service overseas; one, however, Ernest, was rejected through ill-health, and he died at Toowoomba, during the war. Another son, William, received permanent injuries on the other side. Deceased had three daughters (Mrs. Swan of West Longreach, Mrs. Andrews, Longreach, and Mrs. Beutel, Mt. Mee); 33 grandchildren and 2 great grandchildren. Her only sister, Mrs. Dolgner, resides in Longreach. The Rev. J. H. Brown-Beresford officiated at the grave side.

*

Her widowed sister-in-law, Eliza Emily Johnson, had died a month earlier, a few years after being photographed relaxing in her garden in Mooculta Street Bourke along with her daughter Maud Jones and other family members (see Photograph 39).

Eighty-three-year-old Eliza died at her home in August 1925 from bronchopneumonia and chronic bronchitis and was buried in the local cemetery. After an ill-fated first marriage at age 18 to Anders Bufe, she had built a successful marriage with Henry Johnson over 46 years. They had run the *Mountain Home* hotel at Mount Oxley for a few years before settling to a life on small landholdings supplemented by Henry's work as a rural labourer. Together they raised ten children and later mourned their 29-year-old daughter Emily Jane, three years before Henry's death. Eliza had then enjoyed a further 14 years of widowhood. Her obituary was promptly published in the *Western Herald*.[880]

The 'Grim Reaper has taken away another of our old and respected residents in the person of Mrs Eliza Johnson, who passed away on Saturday last. Mrs Johnson was born in 1841 at Wollongong, and would have been 84 years of age next month. Deceased had been a resident of the Bourke District since early in the Sixties. Her husband predeceased her 14 years. She enjoyed the best of health up till about ten days ago; when all the family were summoned to her bedside, one daughter (Mrs Wall) coming the long distance of 800 miles by car, arriving just in time to see the last of her mother. The deceased had a family of four daughters (two of whom have died) and six sons. The surviving children are : — Mrs E. Jones, Mrs Steve Wall (Winton), and Messrs Albert, James, Samuel, Alexander, George and Benjamin. Deceased had 16 great grand children and 25 grand children.

*

In early 1926 came news of the death of another Reed son-in-law, Timothy Farrell, who had lived in the Bourke district for at least 62 of his 72 years, having arrived on the Culgoa River with his parents just ten years after his birth on the voyage to Australia. Tim had witnessed his father Edmund's drowning in the Culgoa in 1863 and (six years later) his brother Edmund's death by lightning.

On marriage to the widowed Mary Ann Reed at age 28, he had taken on immediate parental duties for her children Jannet, Alexander and Hazle Gibb. The family would eventually add a further seven children, but his eldest son had died in 1884 at two years old. Tim had run both the *Bourke* hotel (1882) and Gongolgon's *Lame Horse* hotel (1883) but surrendered to insolvency soon afterwards. He then returned to the rural work that had brought his family to the district in the first place. Later in life he became one of the few professional fisherman operating on the Darling. Three of his sons fought in World War I, but unfortunately two of them paid the ultimate sacrifice.

Tim Farrell was mourned by his wife Mary Ann, four children, three stepchildren, many grandchildren and his long-standing friend from Bourke's early days, Joseph Maxwell (his wife's brother-in-law). His status as one of the few remaining of Bourke's earliest residents was reflected in a lengthy obituary published in the *Western Herald*.[881]

Another old and respected resident of the West passed to "The Great Beyond" on January 7th, in the person of Mr. Timothy Farrell, at the ripe age of 73 years. The sad news was received with regret in town and district as the deceased was well and favorably known to all the residents of the western part of New South Wales, although his death was not unexpected. ... We learn that the deceased arrived in Bourke district about the 60's and that he was one of the early pioneers. Just a few years prior to his arrival here Mr. Willoughby Thorne came to Bourke and shortly after Mr. Joseph Maxwell and Mr. James Maxwell and we mention the names of these old townsmen as they were great associates of the deceased (Mr. Farrell) right from the time be came to Bourke. The deceased was in Bourke in 1863 and had the sad experience of losing his father by drowning in 1863 in the big flood in the Culgoa. He was proprietor of the 'Old Bourke Hotel' ... Some years later, the deceased kept 'The Lame Horse Hotel' at Gongolgon. After some years he was Overseer on the Winnalabrinna ... and followed in the occupations of drover, stock rider, shearing and fishing. He had for many years past been fishing at the river near Warraweena, and very few fisherman have not heard of the particular spot where deceased camped when fishing and which was known as 'Tim Farrell's Bend.' In our earlier remarks we omitted to mention that deceased was born at sea, on the voyage of his parents out from Ireland. He married a Mrs. Gibbs, and besides his wife leaves a grown-up family to mourn his loss, viz., Mrs. Henderson, Mrs. H. Honeyman, Mrs. Westbrook and one son Edward. Two of deceased's sons paid the supreme sacrifice at 'The Great War' which sad event caused the old couple many a sad hour.

*

Having survived his wife Jane by five years, Joseph Maxwell died at Bourke in February 1929, aged 83 years. He had been born at Montefiore near Wellington NSW and came to the Bourke district as an 18-year-old drover in about 1864. During the next few years, he worked as a stockman and drover on *Boonawanna* and *Warraweena* Stations before trying his hand in the butchery business in partnership with his brother-in-law WW Davis. At age 25 he married Jane Reed who was ten years younger and they produced a family of 15 children over the next 32 years. He worked for WW Davis as an innkeeper before later taking the license of the *Overland* hotel at North Bourke, but unfortunately he soon surrendered to insolvency. Later he worked as a pound keeper, drover, stockman, overseer, mail contractor and ranger for the Gongolgon Common.

His son Harry fought in World War I but paid the supreme sacrifice. Two other sons and three daughters also pre-deceased him. A few weeks after Joseph's burial, the Western herald published a lengthy obituary.[882]

An old and respected resident of the town in the person of Mr. Joseph Maxwell passed away on Wednesday night last, aged 82 years. The deceased leaves a family of five sons and three daughters, all of whom are married. His wife died some 4½ years ago; one son, Harry, was killed at the war and another son, Albert, died in Dubbo a few weeks ago. The surviving children are Mrs. McCreadie (Sydney), Mrs. A. Jenkins and Mrs. W. Peter (both of Bourke), Samuel (Bourke), William (Tarcoon), Norman (Byrock), Edward (Tarcoon) and Oxley (Sydney.) Deceased also leaves one brother, James Maxwell, of Bourke. ... In 1864 the late Mr. Joe Maxwell came from Butstone Station, off the Macquarie, and took a draft of bullocks from a Western Station back to that place. Whilst tracking some missing stock on Milroy, he accidentally discovered, a good distance off the river, a swamp, around which there was an abundance of feed, and for his fortunate discovery the owners of the Station made him a bonus of £25. He was a stockman on Boonawanna (about the year 1865) ... After two or three years ... he went to work for Warraweena and was droving their stock for some years. ... A few years later he joined the late W. W. Davis in a butchering business in Bourke about the year 1870. He was on and off butchering in partnership here with Alf Hickles ... It was shortly after this that he took on teamstering and made several trips to Cunnamulla. He also had an hotel at Mount Oxley for a short period, and it was there his first child was born. He married a daughter of Mrs. Read, and several sisters of his late wife now reside in town, viz., Mrs. Brennan, Mrs. Farrell and a sister-in-law, Mrs. Read. ... The call of the land again appealed to him and we find him in several land deals in conjunction with the late William Tobin, in Byrock and Nyngan districts His last business venture was the Gongolgon Hotel. He came back to Bourke in 1903 and has practically resided here ever since. Old age and delicate health prevented him doing hard work for a good many years past. At one time we hear that deceased was for 7 years a stockman on Charlton station, on the Bogan, where he had numerous adventure with wild pigs, and deceased could give some glowing accounts when the humor took him. Mr. Willoughby Thorne, is a 68 years old acquaintance of the deceased and we are indebted to him for most of the information above stated.

*

The health of Sarah Ann Brennan started to decline at the start of the 1930s and she died at Bourke in May 1932 aged 88. She had married Michael Brennan in Sydney at the start of 1863, a year before they came to Bourke on a bullock spring dray, arriving during the 1864 flood. Her first child had been born at Wellington as the family made its way westwards. Eventually her family comprised eight girls and three boys with two girls and a boy dying as children. The family lived frugally on her husband's income from the family timber business, his early work as a storeman/labourer and his lifetime work as a house painter. For a couple of years, they had tried unsuccessfully to make a good business running a hotel at Native Dog Springs, 44 kilometres north of Bourke on the Enngonia Road.

She lived as a widow for 24 years and was survived by two sons, four daughters, 62 grandchildren, 93 great-grandchildren and one great-great grandchild. The *Western Herald* published a long obituary.[883]

Death took from our midst on Monday last Mrs. Sarah Ann Brennan, one of the pioneers of Bourke, who had reached the age of 87 years. Deceased had not enjoyed the best of health for the past two years and her death was not unexpected. The deceased was born in Barrack Street and was married at an early age. She came westward at the age of 20 with her husband and brothers in a bullock waggon. From Wellington to Bourke the means of travel was in a bullock spring dray and from the time the party left Sydney until their arrival in Bourke was just on six months. It was a strenuous trek and before reaching town the whole of the country westward from Mount Oxley was a sea of water, indicating a big flood in the river at that period. For 67 years deceased resided in Bourke; her husband predeceased her 24 years ago. The husband was employed as back-storeman by the late Mr. August Becker 'King of Bourke' in those days. ... One notable item in connection with the deceased was that she has been a neighbour of Mr and Mrs W Bell for the past 60 years. Deceased leaves two sons, Alfred (Bourke) and Michael (Griffith) and four daughters, Mrs C Matthews, Mrs. J. Newman and Mrs. Bishop. There are 62 grand children, 93 great grand children, and one great great grand child.

*

Her 81 year old sister Mary Ann Farrell followed her to the grave two years later in the winter of 1934. At nineteen years old in 1872 she had married the Scottish mining entrepreneur George Samson Gibb soon after he and his partners made the discovery of copper at Cobar. He had died suddenly three years later leaving her with two young children and a hotel to run. She had another daughter out of wedlock before marrying Timothy Farrell in 1882 and completing the family with another seven children. She had lost a son in infancy and only one of three sons who fought in World War I had returned alive. She was survived by her older sister (Prudence Murphy), three daughters, two sons, 23 grandchildren and 25 great-grandchildren. Her obituary was soon after published in the *Western Herald*.[884]

With the passing away of Mrs. Mary Ann Farrell, on 21st June, another old and respected resident of the West has gone to rest. The deceased was born in Sydney in

*1852 and therefore 82 years of age. She came to Bourke
at the early age of 10 and has resided here practically all
her life, with the exception of a short stay in Brewarrina
and Byrock. Deceased was married twice, her first
husband being George Gibb, one of the discoverers of the
Cobar mining belt. Her second husband Timothy Farrell
died on 7th January, 1926. She leaves a grown up family
of three daughters and two sons, to mourn their loss, viz.,
Mrs. H. Honeyman, Mrs. L. Westbrook, and Mrs.
Anderson (Balladoran), and Messrs. Alec. Gibb,
(Brewarrina) and E. Farrell. Two sons paid the supreme
sacrifice in the Great War. One sister of deceased (Mrs.
Murphy) resides at Hurlstone Park and is 87 years of
age. Some 50 years ago Mrs. Farrell's husband kept the
'Bourke Hotel' which was on the site where now stands
a Chinese Garden, but the hotel was pulled down many
years ago. Deceased also leaves 23 grand children, and
25 great grand children.*

*

The sole survivor of James' and Frances' children,
Prudence Murphy, had been living in the household of
her daughter Nora Lilian (Murphy) and son-in-law
Edward Burnet at 19 Fernhill Street in the Sydney suburb
of Hurlstone Park at the time of her husband's death in
1919; and still lived there when she died, aged 94, in
October 1940.[885] She was buried in the Church of England
Cemetery at Randwick.

After a childhood spent mainly in the central
business district of Sydney, Prudence had travelled to
Bourke in 1862 with her parents as a fifteen-year-old. She
worked as a servant on *Gongolgon* Station 18 where she

met Joseph Whye. Within three years of their marriage the young couple had produced three children and built the *Lame Horse* hotel, first licensed in 1866. The business boomed and six more children followed before her husband's untimely death in 1877, aged 41 years.

With the help of her brother George Charles Reed, Prudence kept the hotel afloat for the next two years before marrying divorcee James Murphy in 1879. He proved to be a good publican who expanded their business interests over the next few years. Five Murphy children were added to her nine Whye children, but Prudence had to mourn the deaths of six of her offspring.

The coming of the railway dealt a blow to their Gongolgon business and a decline in her husband's health undermined the Bourke businesses to the extent that they lost the *Family* hotel to a mortgagee sale in 1903, just months before it burnt to the ground. By then they had moved to Orange where they ran the *Green Gate* hotel for a few years.

By 1912, Prudence had moved her family to Sydney where James, now suffering badly from senile decay, was admitted to Rookwood Asylum where he died in 1919. She then spent the remaining twenty one years of her life living with the Burnet family. She was survived by eight children, 73 grandchildren and 33 great-grandchildren, one of whom was my mother, Halvene Therese Kessey, then six years old.

While no obituary was published for Prudence, she had been the subject of a *Sydney Sun* article and photograph that celebrated her ninetieth birthday[886] four years earlier.

Mrs. Prudence Murphy, of Fernhill Street, Hurlstone Park, who is 90 years old to-day, claims to be the first white girl to travel by coach from Parramatta to Gongolgon, on the Bogan River. Mrs. Murphy made the journey to visit her brother. Mrs. Murphy was born in a house behind St. Andrew's Cathedral. Her maiden name was Reed. She married James Murphy, a well-known hotel proprietor, who was established for many years at the Family Hotel, Bourke, and the Greengate Hotel, Orange. He died 16 years ago. Eight of Mrs. Murphy's 14 children are still living, and she has 73 grandchildren and 33 great-grandchildren. Her father died at the age of 87 and her mother at 82.

*

Prudence's death marked the end of the second generation of the Reed family in Australia. Nevertheless, one member of her generation survived: the widow of her brother George Charles Reed, Mary Ann nee Peters. She would eventually survive her husband by nearly thirty-five years before dying from heart failure in Bourke, aged 87 years.[887]   Her obituary was published in the *Western Herald* in mid-February 1944.[888]

A very old identity of Bourke in the person of Mrs. Mary Ann Reed died on Monday morning last from heart failure, at the age of 84 years. The deceased, although she enjoyed good bodily health has for the past ten years not had good eye-sight. In fact for the past few years she has been practically blind and had to be led about. She was married in Bourke in 1887 and has resided ever since that year in Bourke. She leaves a grown-up family, viz.: —

William (Lane Cove), James (Bourke), George (Brisbane), Bert. (Brisbane), Mrs. E. Mayoh (Sydney) and Mrs C. Bye (Bourke).

She had been photographed about twenty years earlier with one of her grandchildren (see Photograph 40).

***

With the demise of its two elders and the beginning of a new century, the Reed family had moved imperceptibly into a new era. During the first few months and years, the lives of the next generations had gone on in much the same way as before but, gradually and inevitably, members of the extended family had started to grow apart. Siblings came to see less of each other and some moved away from Bourke. As the surviving members of the next generation died, some grandchildren learnt little or nothing about their second and third cousins, even those living in the same town. But, despite this process of fragmentation, the history of the Reed family endures, swaddling all members of the clan with a shared heritage.

APPENDIX ONE

Bourke hotels

In researching this book, I delved into the history of Bourke hotels because most of the senior members of the Reed family held a publican's license in the Bourke Licensing District at some time. Information sources included the official Licensing Notices published in the NSW Government Gazette; advertisements published in the *Western Herald* (from 1887); land records; and earlier research published in various volumes of the *History of Bourke* journal. Unfortunately, the hotel information in that journal (while largely correct) is scattered, confused and contains some mistakes. This Appendix is designed to succinctly present my research findings for the benefit of future local historians.

*

One erroneous statement made in the History of Bourke journal is the claim on page 121 of volume 8 that *"there were 21 hotels doing business in Bourke in 1882"*. In fact, there were nine - Tattersalls, Royal, Shakespeare, Bourke (later Family), Trafalgar (later Telegraph), Turf, Commercial, Carriers' Arms and Jolly Waggoner. When we add in two each at North Bourke (Bridge, Overland) and Gongolgon (Lame Horse, Royal) the grand total reaches just thirteen.

The year of peak hotels was 1892 when there were 20. The nine listed above were supplemented by another eleven comprising the Four Mile (Carrington), Union, Central Australian, Great Western (Empire), Club House, Oxford, Royal Exchange (Caledonian), Railway (Cambridge), Gladstone, Post Office and Federal. The two at North Bourke had been supplemented by the Occidental, the Halfway House and Murphy's Australian but the Royal hotel at Gongolgon had ceased operating, giving a grand total of twenty-six.

*

Another furphy relates to the apocryphal Bourke Club hotel. No such hotel ever held a license. This was, in fact, a gentleman's club that was operating by 1873 when it obtained a billiard table.[889] The club's premises were in the former Commercial Bank building on the corner of Mitchell and Richard Streets (see Photograph 13). When the club disbanded in 1888,[890] the building was converted into the Gladstone hotel by JS Donohoe.

Much of the confusion in the History of Bourke journal stems from the fact that the NSW Gazette never published the hotels' full addresses. With ten in Mitchell Street, for example, it is often difficult to work out which one the official notice refers to. This is exacerbated by the use, over time, of different names for a single premises. In the worst case, the hotel that was originally named the Exchange was later the Royal Exchange, then the Harp of Erin and finally the Caledonian, but was popularly known as the Golden Stairs! The original Carriers Arms changed its name to the Commercial after two years, but the Commercial name was also used at various times for both the Old Fort and the Union. In fact, during 1890 advertisements appeared for two different Commercial hotels in the same issue of the *Western Herald*[891], one licensed to E Dorrington (which had been formerly known as Deignan's and was later the Union) and the other licensed to Mrs E Peter. When you throw in the widespread practice of referring to hotels by nicknames (Bond's, Deignan's, Donohoe's, Dorrington's, Eccles' Fitz's, Gale's, Lennon's, Luscombe's, Murphy's, Sly's, Whittaker's) the task of a researcher becomes very complicated.

*

One of the most confusing episodes in the history of Bourke's hotels is the sequence of events relating to the Old Fort, Royal and Shakespeare hotels. Bourke historian Bill Cameron advanced an hypothesis that JE Kelly's original 1863 hotel (initially called the "Fort Bourke", then the "Old Fort") was finally known as the Old Royal and that the subsequent Royal hotel was eventually built in its place. While there is a grain of truth in this, it is not quite right because the old Royal and the subsequent Royal were on different sites.

The confusion is based partly on the use of the Royal name for two different premises and partly on an article about Bourke that was published in the Town and Country Journal on 28 October 1871.[892]

> *There are three hotels. Tattersall's, by Henry Colless, in the centre of the main street, is a handsome brick building with a verandah, supported with fluted Tuscan pillars; and for excellence of design exteriorly, and for comfort and convenience in the interior, is excelled by very few houses of the kind out of Sydney. The Commercial, by Mr Joseph*

Maxwell (brother-in-law of the owner, Mr W. W. Davis) is also an excellent brick and wood building; and doubtless, under the energetic management of its owner, who has but recently purchased it, this hotel will obtain a large share of public support. The Royal, by Mr George Harris, is the first house on entering Bourke from the Sydney road; there is a large brick-built assembly room attached, admirably adapted for dancing, music and theatricals.

The main street that he refers to was Mitchell Street, on either side of the junction with Sturt Street. WW Davis had recently purchased his premises from Henry Nancarrow. It was the site of the Old Fort hotel but Nancarrow had, apparently, demolished the old building and constructed a new hotel that Davis had renamed the Commercial (see photographs 8 and 9).

Cameron's hypothesis is conveyed in his entry for "The 'Old Fort' or 'Royal' hotel" on pages 67-68 of volume 4 of the History of Bourke journal.[893] He notes that the hotel was first licensed to John Edward Kelly in 1863; still licensed to Kelly in 1865; to Henry Nancarrow in 1870; before noting the reference to Mr G Harris' "Royal" hotel in the article reproduced above as if it is the same hotel. He then points to an 1872 report that Russell Barton had bought the "Old Royal" and intended to convert it into a soap and candle factory after offering it for use as a school. Cameron concludes:

There is confusion here, and obviously there were two "Royal" Hotels. In 1872 Harris had taken over the "Commercial Inn" and called it the "Royal".

This conclusion is correct, but unfortunately Cameron did not explain how he had reached it. On face value it doesn't stand scrutiny, because licenses existed for BOTH the Commercial and the Royal in both 1871 and 1872. Furthermore, George Harris had first been licensed for the Royal hotel in 1866 while the earlier license for the Old Fort hotel continued[894]. So, the two hotels had coexisted from 1866 until 1872.

The answer to this conundrum lies in the fact that the premises licensed to George Harris as the Royal from 1866 to 1872 are different from the premises licensed to him as the Royal from 1873 to 1883. He had moved his hotel business but retained the name. This is clear from an article published in the *Central Australian and Bourke Telegraph* on 30 November 1872.[895]

Mr WW Davis has disposed of his "Commercial Hotel" and is expected to move nearer the coast. ... George Harris has moved his Royal hotel to the more central and commodious premises in Mitchell Street, lately occupied by Mr WW Davis of the 'Commercial'. It still retains the title of 'Royal'.

In September 1872, WW Davis sold lots 2 and 3 in section 2 (the site of his Commercial hotel) to George Harris[896] who promptly renamed it as the Royal, a name that was long associated with the site thereafter. Davis had acquired the site from the Nancarrow family[897] who had bought it in 1869 from the first licensee, JE Kelly[898]. Henry Nancarrow had held the license for the Old Fort in 1870, which confirms that this hotel sat on the land he had just bought, lot 2.

So, while this confirms Bill Cameron's hypothesis, it begs the question: where was the <u>old</u> Royal situated? Reference to the deeds that these hotels stood on sorts out the confusion. This would have been difficult to achieve in the 1970s when Cameron advanced his hypothesis but is much simpler now because early land deeds are freely available online. Cameron rightly highlighted a clue in an 1872 report (quoted below) that Russell Barton intended to convert the "Old Royal" into a soap and candle factory. Another clue is the fact that a publican's license was granted in 1873 to Donald J McDonald for the Old Victoria, a name that appears only once in the records. This was George Harris's former Royal hotel, but where was it?

The 1871 article reports that Harris's hotel was "*the first house on entering Bourke from the Sydney road*", meaning that it must have been to the east of the Old Fort. In August 1866, Harris had obtained title to lot 2 in <u>section 10</u> - a block and a half east of the Old Fort hotel.[899] It seems likely that this was the site of the "*large brick-built assembly room attached*" to his first Royal hotel. The hotel itself was on lot 1 (the block next door on the north-east corner of Mitchell and Glen Streets) which was at that time owned by one Charles Cheshire. Harris may have been frustrated in his attempts to buy the land on which his hotel sat because the owner seems to have disappeared. He may be the Charles Rowe Cheshire who had died at Liverpool on 8 March 1864.[900]

That the old Royal hotel was on this corner block is clear from subsequent events. The *Empire* newspaper reported in September 1872 that a public meeting had considered an offer that the "Old Royal" hotel be used as a Public School, but the idea did not meet with approval.[901] This offer presumably came from Harris, who was keen to sell because he had just bought the Commercial hotel. But, since Harris did not own the old Royal hotel building, it seems more likely he was proposing his large brick-built assembly room, not the hotel itself.

The same article reported that Russell Barton *"has since purchased the Royal to be converted into a soap and candle factory"*. Six months later he reported that *"Messrs Barton and Topham have advertised for 40,000 bricks, and next August a soap and candle factory will be one of our institutions"*.[902] The transfer of the land from Harris to Barton was not confirmed legally until 1876.

The site of the old Royal was re-licensed to Donald J McDonald as the Old Victoria hotel in 1873; and subsequently to Ephraim Smith and his licensee successors as the Shakespeare hotel from 1875. Edward Dugan (licensee from 1886 to 1889) bought the land in 1882.[903] His son-in-law Donald Shaw then took over the license for several years.

Meanwhile, Harris retained his license for the new Royal hotel until 1883 before Thomas Huggins had it from 1884 to 1887; Richard Green in 1888 and 1889; and Samuel Davis in 1890 and 1891. By 1892 the hotel was in the hands of George Colless and the *Western Herald* newspaper reported[904] that he

> has almost completed a most substantial and imposing two-storey brick addition to his Royal Hotel. This new building contains at present seven large rooms, one of which, a dining room, will easily accommodate 60 persons at a sitting. A balcony will be erected in front and, altogether the hotel will be a credit to the town, besides showing the enterprise of its proprietor. Mr Colless has built having consideration for the future, and will easily be able to add to his premises.

It seems likely that Colless' extension was built on the other lot so that the whole building would have now straddled both lots 2 and 3. It was ultimately demolished in 1941 when a new building (which is still standing) was constructed on the site.[905]

*

The first member of the extended Reed family to be granted a publican's license by the Bourke District Licensing Court was Prudence's husband, **Joseph Whye**, for the Lame Horse hotel at Gongolgon in 1866. These premises would remain in family ownership into the twentieth century and, during those 35 years, its license was held by five other family members including **Prudence Whye** herself, her second husband **James Murphy**, her brother-in-law **Timothy Farrell**, her son-in-law **Thomas Ralph** and **Alfred Whye**, nephew of her first husband.

Next came **James Reed** himself, who was granted a license for the Mountain Home hotel at Mount Oxley in 1870. His son-in-law **Henry Johnson** took over the license in 1875 for four years.

George Charles Reed was the original licensee for both the Bourke (later Family) hotel in 1873 and the Overland hotel at North Bourke in 1876. The license for the Overland was held briefly by his brother-in-law **Joseph Maxwell** (who had also run the Old Fort hotel in 1872, but not as licensee). The license for the Bourke was later held by George's brother-in-law **George Samson Gibb**, sister **Mary Ann Gibb** and her third husband **Timothy Farrell** (whose brother-in-law Charles Campbell ran several different Bourke hotels from the late 1890s).

Daniel Murphy (Prudence's brother-in-law) held a license for the Carrington in 1891-2 and for the Family in

1893. Both James and Daniel Murphy were subsequently licensees of the Greengate hotel in Orange. **Michael Brennan** held the license of the Native Dog hotel at Native Dog Springs from 1879 to 1881. **James Tobin junior** took over the license of the Commercial hotel in Sturt Street in 1895 and changed its name to the Union hotel.

So, that is a total of fifteen members of the extended Reed family who were involved with seven Bourke hotels during the 19th century.

*

The list that follows includes all the hotels that were licensed in Bourke, North Bourke and Gongolgon during the nineteenth century, in chronological order of license issue. To avoid needless repetition, the relevant source citations for each annual Licensing Notice are as follows: 1866[906], 1867[907], 1868[908], 1869[909], 1870[910], 1871[911], 1872[912],1873[913], 1874[914], 1875[915], 1876[916], 1877[917], 1878[918], 1879[919], 1880[920], 1882[921], 1881[922], 1883[923], 1884[924], 1885[925], 1886[926], 1887[927], 1888[928], 1889[929], 1890[930], 1891[931], 1892[932], 1893[933], 1894[934], 1895[935], 1896[936], 1897[937], 1898[938], 1899[939], 1900[940], 1901[941].

1863 - Bourke Hotel
See Photograph 10 on page 232
Southwestern corner of Mitchell and Sturt Streets
Bourke's first completed building. Also known as Sly's hotel; briefly Bond's hotel; later Tattersall's hotel

1863[942]: William Sly (28 April) was an American who had shouted free drinks when the first paddle-steamer brought supplies in 1859. He had come to the district a few years earlier as a representative of Jeffrey Bros who owned *Toorale* Station and established a timber mill near the future Wortumertie Street, with much of the timber that it produced being used on *Toorale*. He later built the first building in the town (this hotel) and is often referred to as the Founder of Bourke[943]. His daughter Emily Celia Sly was the first colonial child born in the town on 20 August 1862 (although five other births were recorded in the district before that). Sly left Bourke in 1867-8 and settled at Gayndah in Queensland, although he retained an interest in the Bourke hotel until 1872.

1866[944]: Frederick Bond (when the hotel was temporarily referred to as **Bond's hotel**). 1867[945]: Joshua Free, then Alfred Merriel. 1868: Henry Colless who added a new wing and changed the name to **Tattersall's hotel**. He had started as a bullocky at 12 years old and was a pioneer grazier (along with his brother George) at Weilmoringle (170 kilometres northeast of Bourke) by 1857. He was a Bourke businessman, Alderman and prominent Anglican.

1875: Oliver Sproule. 1879: Joseph Mandelson. 1882: Edward Prevot. 1885: Arthur Charles Bilton. 1890: William Morgan. 1892: Francis Paget. 1893: Henry McCullagh. 1896: James McLennan. 1897: Charles Campbell (brother-in-law of Timothy Farrell). 1898: Donald Shaw until 1900.

*

Photograph 44 - The Royal hotel, ca 1895.

1863: Old Fort Hotel; 1873: Royal Hotel
Lots 2 and 3, Section 2, Mitchell Street (southern side)
Rebuilt in 1871 and renamed the Commercial; renamed the Royal 1873

1863[946]: John E Kelly (28 April) licensed for the *Fort Bourke* hotel that was soon known as the *Old Fort*. Kelly was head stockman for Vincent Dowling and came to the district in about 1860 with a herd of cattle for *Fort Bourke* Station.[947] He later owned *Pirillie* Station. He claimed to have erected the first building post in Bourke (for this hotel) and to have sunk the first well. Kelly played a leading part in the arrest of James Stewart who was committed for trial at Bathurst on 8 March 1864 on a charge of murder. After leaving the Bourke district in 1881, he was elected in 1887 as the MLA for Bogan and re-elected in 1888. He was the first mayor of Peak Hill where he died in 1896, aged 57. 1866[948]: Richard James Kelly (son of John E Kelly). 1867[949]: John E Kelly.

1870: Henry Nancarrow. He and his brothers James and Richard were prominent businessmen with interests in a large store and copper mining as well as the hotel. He moved to Wellington in 1873 but his son remained in Bourke to run a real estate and auction business. 1871: Henry Nancarrow, then William Batten. Nancarrow demolished the original Old Fort premises and constructed a new hotel building see *Photograph 8.*

1871: Renamed the **Commercial hotel** by the new owner, WW Davis,[950] who employed his brother-in-law (Timothy Farrell) to manage it. 1872: WW Davis.

1873[951]: The land and building was sold to George Harris, formerly licensee of the old Royal Hotel further east. Harris brought the name **Royal hotel** with him. 1884: Thomas Huggins. 1888: Richard Green. 1890: Samuel C Davis. 1892[952]: George Colless. Extended 1892[953] to occupy both lots 2 and 3; 1893: Simeon S Moses until after 1900. Rebuilt 1941; Renovated 1968 and still in use.

*

1863 - Lame Horse Hotel
See Photograph 12 on page 233
Gongolgon
Renamed the Commercial in 1885; renamed the Gongolgon hotel 1895

Note that Chapter 13 includes a detailed analysis of the photograph labelled "Bourke's First Hotel 1866" held in the National Archive, leading to the hypothesis that this photograph captures the Lame Horse hotel at Gongolgon, not William Sly's Bourke hotel of 1863.

7 Sep 1866: Joseph Whye. 1877: his widow Prudence Whye nee Reed. 1879: John Joseph Dempsey. 1880: James Murphy, Prudence Whye's second husband. 1883: Timothy Farrell, Prudence Murphy's brother-in-law. 1884: James Murphy. 1885: Renamed the **Commercial hotel**. 1886: Thomas Ralph, Prudence Murphy's son-in-law. 1888: Unlicensed. 1891: Thomas Ralph. 1893: James Murphy. 1895: Renamed the **Gongolgon hotel**. 1899: Alfred Whye (nephew of Prudence Murphy's first husband). 1901: not licensed after the railway reached Brewarrina in 1901.

*

1866: Royal Hotel; 1875: Shakespeare Hotel
Northeastern corner of Mitchell and Glen Streets
Briefly the Old Victoria 1873; renamed the Shakespeare 1875; briefly the Bushman's Arms 1882-1885

1866[954]: George Harris. In 1873 Harris moved his business to the former Commercial hotel (previously the Old Fort) and took the Royal name with him. 1873: Donald J McDonald, who re-named it the **Old Victoria**.

1875[955]: Ephraim Smith, who re-named it the **Shakespeare**. During 1877 Smith was twice refused a license due to police objections that "the applicant kept a disorderly house". In February 1878 George Charles Reed applied for the license but must have withdrawn. In December 1878 a license was granted to Ephraim Smith's son Charles William Smith. 1879: This may be the premises called "the Shades" where Edward Dugan was granted a wine license. Henry Waldron was refused a license in 1880; and Thomas Giddens was refused a wine license in 1881.

1882: James McCabe renamed it the **Bushman's Arms** and transferred it to Patrick Welden;[956] 1884: Thomas Reynolds; 1885: Frank Riley.

1886: Edward Dugan (the new owner) resurrected the **Shakespeare** name, which it retained thereafter. (See more details of the Dugan family in the section on the Commercial hotel below.) On 2 Oct 1886 the second branch of the Australian Shearers' Union was formed at a meeting held here. 1890: Donald Shaw (Dugan's son-in-law). 1895[957]: James Stibbard. 1900[958]: Charles Stagg. In 1901 Stibbard was the building's owner when it burnt to the ground.[959]

*

1869: West Bourke Hotel; later Bridge Hotel
Western side of the Enngonia Road at North Bourke

1869: Joseph Lunn, the Founder of North Bourke. He was also a storekeeper and butcher and owned a pontoon bridge nearby. He had built the old slab and shingle Police Station on the corner of Richard and Oxley Streets in Bourke which was later rebuilt at North Bourke. 1884[960]: JC Tighe, who renamed it the **Bridge hotel**. 1885: George Rolfe.

1886: James Maxwell (brother of Joseph Maxwell), Lunn's son-in-law, who had come to the district to work on *Toorale* and later worked as a teamster with both bullock and horse wagons. He had a 10,000 acre homestead lease a few miles from North Bourke. 1887: William Quinn. 1889: Walter Fry. 1890: William Murphy. 1892: James Maxwell until the turn of the century and beyond until the building was demolished.

*

1870: Mountain Home Hotel; later Mount Oxley Hotel
At the northernmost tip of Oxley's Tableland
1870: James Reed (see chapter 13). 1873: John Hancock. 1875: Henry Johnson (Reed's son-in-law). 1879: Patrick Welden. Welden's renewal application was refused in 1882 and the hotel was never again licensed.

*

1870: Royal Hotel at Gongolgon
Gongolgon
1870: John Hawthorne, an ex-policeman who had been part of a team that captured the bushranger John Dunn in 1866. 1875: William Hartnett. 1878: John Willcock. 1880: John Cowell. 1884: Alexander Shaw. 1885: John Willcock. 1886: Thomas L Morris.

Following the opening of the railway service to Bourke in 1885, the hotel appears to have been unlicensed from 1887 to 1889 before James A Robb obtained a license during 1890. 1895: John Willcock.[961] 1897: Richard James Oxley Maxwell. Maxwell retained the license in 1898 but the premises were never again licensed.

*

1873: Bourke Hotel; 1884: Family Hotel
Northwest corner of Darling and Wilson Streets
Previously a boarding house; renamed the Family hotel in 1884; colloquially "Lennon's hotel" in 1887-9.

The premises were most probably previously used by members of the Reed family as a boarding house. 1873[962] (Bourke hotel): George Charles Reed. 1875: George Samson

Gibb (Reed's brother-in-law). 1876: Mary Ann Gibb nee Reed (Gibb's widow). 1882: Transferred ownership to her brother-in-law, James Murphy.[963] He employed his wife's brother in law, Timothy Farrell[964], to manage it. Farrell was declared insolvent in 1884.[965] James Murphy then changed the name to the **Family hotel** and found a new licensee - Joseph Donohoe.[966] 1887: John Lennon. During his tenancy the hotel was sometimes referred to as *Lennon's hotel*. 1890: James Murphy. 1892[967]: James Murphy, then James Draper. 1893: Daniel Murphy (brother of James Murphy). 1894: Thomas Dillon. 1895: William O'Connor. 1896: John Hunter. 1897[968]: George Astill. 1899: James Murphy. 1903: James Murphy was forced into a mortgagee sale.[969] The land and premises were sold by the Sheriff of NSW to Alexander Valentine Gow on 12 June 1903. (Murphy moved to Orange where he was soon licensee of the Green Gate hotel.) Gow advertised as the new owner of the Family hotel on 29 July 1903.[970] The premises were burnt to the ground in 1904.[971]

*

1874: Trafalgar Hotel; 1882: Telegraph Hotel
Mitchell Street (northern side)
Previously a boarding house; renamed the Telegraph hotel in 1882.

1866[972]: Matthew Good ran a boarding house which was probably in this building. He was an Irishman who had reputedly made money on the Victorian goldfields and bought several town allotments in late 1867. Five years later he was involved in the mining boom at Cobar and, a year later, built "a fine stone and brick edifice in Mitchell Street" which was licensed as the Trafalgar hotel (later renamed the Telegraph hotel) in 1875. He owned houses in "rotten row" and was a member of the building committee for the Anglican church. After leasing his hotel to Arthur Meadows in 1886 he retired to focus his energies on running a successful horse stud. He died at Bourke on 9 August 1909 aged 77.

1875[973]: Matthew Good. 1882: Good changed the name to the **Telegraph hotel**. 1887: Arthur Meadows. 1892: Cornelius J Drew. 1895[974]: Francis Good. 1901: Charles Campbell (brother-in-law of Timothy Farrell). JS Donohoe transferred to the Telegraph from the Gladstone about 1902. This building is currently used as the Riverside Motel.

*

1876: Overland Hotel
Eastern side of the Enngonia Road at North Bourke

1876: George Charles Reed. The premises were owned by Joseph Lunn, licensee of the 8-year-old West Bourke hotel across the road. He clearly had so much business that he had opened a second premises - see chapter 16. 1877: Joseph Maxwell (Reed's brother-in-law) who was declared insolvent two years later. 1878: David Neale. 1870: George Charles Reed. The premises were **destroyed by fire** in September 1880 and Reed was declared insolvent two years later.

The hotel must have been **rebuilt** as Thomas A Willoughby held the license from 1882. 1886: John Willoughby. 1888: William Quinn. 1889: Thomas A Willoughby. 1892: Dick Barlow. 1895: William Worthington who held the license into the new century until the building was demolished in 1902.

*

1877: Turf Hotel

Northern side of Mitchell Street, lot 4 in section 10, next to the Carrier's Arms

1877[975]: Edward Warmoll, who acquired the land from Joseph Becker in 1880.[976] He was a prominent businessman from Enngonia, before becoming a Bourke hotelier and Alderman who died in 1892.[977] Warmoll held the license until 1885 except for 1878 (Alfred Eccles) and 1883 (Charles Warren). 1886/7 - Robert Warmoll.

It seems to have been unlicensed between 1888 and 1891. In 1892 both R Anderson and Robert S Martlew held licenses for premises in Mitchell Street, one of which may have been the old Turf hotel building. Both were re-licensed in 1893.

*

1877: Carrington Hotel

Four miles from Bourke on the Brewarrina Road
Colloquially known as the Four Mile

1876[978]: James Nathan Taylor. 1880/1: George Warren. 1882: James Maxwell was refused a license.[979] 1887[980]: Alfred Eccles. 1888[981]: Charlotte Larkins. 1889[982]: Robert Cross. 1890/1: James Edward Floyd (with James Mallon as owner). 1892: Daniel Murphy (brother of James Murphy). 1893: Alfred Eccles transferred to Julia Celia Holmes. 1894: Julia Celia Holmes. 1895/6: Stephen Wood.

*

1877: Commercial Hotel

*Southwest corner of Tudor and Wilson Streets, lot 7 in section
26; site of the cordial factory*

**Originally named the Carrier's Arms; colloquially
"Whittaker's" in the twentieth century**

(The Old Fort and Union were both briefly the Commercial.)

1877: Edward Dugan was the first licensee of these premises, then named the Carrier's Arms,[983] before the license was transferred to his son-in-law David Peter in the same year. Dugan was originally a bullock wagon driver who first came to Bourke in 1865 with his wife Clementina (nee Barry). Two years after opening the Carrier's Arms he was granted a license for a wine bar called "the Shades" on Mitchell Street (possibly in the premises that normally operated as the Shakespeare hotel). He was the first licensee of the Jolly Waggoner hotel in 1881 and was later owner and licensee of the Shakespeare (from 1886). He owned the Union hotel briefly in 1900-01. His daughter Elizabeth married David Peter (second licensee of this hotel) and secondly Donald Shaw (licensee from 1887; later licensee of the Shakespeare from 1890; licensee of the Caledonian in 1896-7; licensee of Tattersalls 1897-1900). Elizabeth was herself licensee of the Commercial in 1891 and, according to her obituary, later had a financial interest in both the Shakespeare and Tattersalls hotels.[984]

The name was changed to the Commercial hotel in 1878 when Henry Wilson was licensee. 1879: David Peter. 1884: Nicholas Dugan (Edward's brother; he was later owner and licensee of the Club House hotel). 1887: Donald Shaw (Edward Dugan's son-in-law); 1891: Mrs Elizabeth Peter (Dugan's daughter). 1893: Donald Mathison. 1894: Clementina Dugan (Dugan's wife).

1896: Percy Whittaker (husband of Dugan's granddaughter, Martha Peter). 1897: William Alexander Peter (Dugan's grandson and husband of Kate Hazle Maxwell). 1899: Charles Stagg, then Edward Dugan. 1902: Robert Peter (another grandson). 1907: Henry C Whittaker (husband of Dugan's granddaughter, Elizabeth Peter and brother of Percy Whittaker) who held the license until 1909.

The land that this hotel was built on was originally owned by David Peter from April 1874.[985] In May 1880 it was transferred to Edward and Nicholas Dugan who transferred it back to David Peter in August 1883. Peter promptly transferred it to Edward Dugan and William Alexander Peter. The latter became sole owner on the death of his grandfather, Edward Dugan, and promptly sold it to John Rice in September 1907. The Peter family had operated a cordial factory at the rear of the hotel, an enterprise that was continued by the Rice family thereafter. The hotel building was pulled down early in the Rice family's ownership.

*

1879: Carrier's Arms Hotel
Northwestern corner of Mitchell and Wilson Streets[986]
(The Commercial was initially called the Carrier's Arms.)

1879[987]: John Fletcher for 3 years. He was fined 40 shillings for "furious driving" in 1880.[988] 1882-84: no record. 1885: John Dowling. 1886: Edwin Field. 1888: Denis Houlahan. 1890[989]: Donald Mathison. 1892: Watson Braithwaite. 1893: Alexander Stevenson. 1896: Hugh Langwell. 1897: Watson Braithwaite. 1898: George Walsh. 1900: EJ Watkins. 1901[990]: lease advertised? 1902: George Walsh until at least 1906.

Photograph 45 - The Carriers' Arms hotel, ca 1898.

*

1881: Jolly Waggoner Hotel
Northwest corner of Mitchell and Glen Streets

1881: Edward Dugan was the first licensee, four years after he had opened the Commercial. 1884 - John Murray; 1886[991]: damaged by fire but saved from total destruction. 1886[992]: John McLaughlan, who seems to have retained the license until 1893. 1894: Donald Mathison seems to have retained the license until about 1902 when the hotel was again badly damaged by fire.[993] 1905: Charles Campbell (brother-in-law of Timothy Farrell). 1908: George Alfred Wall. Demolished in 1962.[994]

*

451

Photograph 51: The Union hotel, 1919
Source: Janet Rice

1884: Union Hotel
Southeast corner of Mertin and Sturt Streets
Originally Deignan's Commercial hotel; briefly Dorrington's

1884: Built by and licensed to Bernard Deignan, a prominent citizen and builder, who retained it until 1888. 1889: William Glover. 1890/1: Edward Dorrington. 1892: George E Drew. 1893: Thomas Ralph and Donald Mathison. 1894: Clementina Dugan. 1895-98: James Tobin junior (son-in-law of James and Frances Reed).

In March 1899 a fire started in hessian window blinds that were attached to the house next door owned by Mrs RH Warmoll. The hotel lost several bedrooms and stables. A jury could not determine the cause of the fire.[995] Three months later Tobin's hotel hosted a reception for the marriage of his adopted daughter Eliza Emily Tobin Maxwell to Jack McCready.[996]

1899: Arthur J Hobson. 1900/01: Edward Dugan. 1901: James Tobin junior. April 1901: The billiard room was lost to fire.[997] Four months later the hotel hosted a funeral ceremony for Tobin's late father, James Tobin senior.[998] Tobin, still licensee in 1913,[999] died in 1918.[1000]

In 1919 the hotel was licensed to my great-grandfather, James Kessey, a new arrival in the town who had moved his family from Orange to escape the Spanish Influenza epidemic.

*

1884: Club House Hotel
Northwestern corner of Hope and Wilson Streets
1884[1001]: Patrick Nash (the hotel's builder). 1885[1002]: Alexander Shaw, grandson of Donald Shaw[1003] who held the license of several Bourke hotels at various times. 1886: James McPherson. 1887/90[1004]: Nicholas Dugan[1005] (brother of Edward Dugan of the Commercial hotel). 1891: license transferred from Pearce to James Stibbard who retained it until 1893. 1894: George Rorke. 1895: Thomas Hand, who held the license until his death in 1901.[1006] 1903: TM Green. 1905[1007]: William Hatten.

Between 1908 and 1921 the license was held by William Pearce, who died in 1926 aged 75.[1008]

The hotel's license was transferred by its owner, Tooth's Brewery, to Leura in 1947.[1009]

*

1885: Central Australian Hotel
See Photograph 29 on page 349
Northwest corner of Anson and Richard Streets
1885: Built by and licensed to William Gale close to the new railway station. It was one of the largest hotels in

the west, comprising two stories with fifty bedrooms. Gale had been born in Penrith into a family with extensive farming interests and became a bullock wagon carrier who ran a service over the Blue Mountains to Bourke for many years. He bought riverside land at Bourke to spell his bullocks, leasing some land to Chinese men who created a successful market garden. Before moving to Bourke permanently he had run hotels in both Orange and Dubbo.[1010] He held the license uninterrupted into the twentieth century and had a variety of other business interests in the district, including breeding and dealing in draft horses and a steam saw and planing mill. He owned many Bourke properties and served the community on the Hospital Board, Pastoral Society and the Jockey Club.[1011]

The hotel hosted an 1890 reception for the Governor of NSW and his wife who had come to inspect the town's flood defences. A valuable set of photographs were taken from the hotel's roof observatory during the flood.[1012]

Gale's original premises burnt down in the 1930s and were replaced by an art deco building in 1937.

*

1885: Great Western Hotel
Western side of Richard Street on the Southern side of the corner with Mertin Lane
Renamed the Empire hotel in 1897.

1885: Built by and licensed to Edward Heseler in anticipation of increasing trade from the new railway station. (The railway line to Bourke was called the Great Western line.) He was a builder and businessman of German origin who had come from Brewarrina in 1872 for an 1874 contract to build Bourke's Anglican church.[1013] He

454

also built the Public School 1874,[1014] the Post Office 1878[1015], McKenzie's Store (corner of Mitchell and Richard Streets) 1882,[1016] and had a later contract to make bricks for the North Bourke Bridge which opened in 1883.

During 1892, the famous poet and short story writer, Henry Lawson, worked as a house painter in renovating the hotel premises.

1886[1017]: Austin O'Grady. 1887: Licensed transferred from David Peter to Daniel Dewhurst who held in in 1888. Heseler advertised the lease of the premises in 1889.[1018] 1890/01[1019]: John Lennon. 1892[1020]: Charles Septimus Smith. 1893: Michael Carroll. 1895/06: James Cornelius Drew. 1897: Samuel Davis who changed the name to the Empire hotel and held the license until at least 1902.

In 1904 the license was transferred from O Gibson to DJ Grogan. In 1914 the license was withdrawn and the building pressed into service as an internment camp. In later years it was a boarding house.

*

1885: Occidental Hotel
North Bourke, near the end of the bridge
Third hotel at North Bourke

1885[1021]: Thomas Manning, formerly proprietor of the local newspaper. There is no record of a license between 1886 and 1889. 1890[1022] until 1904: Isaac James. The positioning of this building created a need to alter the bridge approaches, completed in 1903.[1023] No sooner had this work been completed than James transferred the hotel's license to the newer Australian hotel nearby from 1905.[1024]

Photograph 46
The Occidental hotel and the North Bourke bridge, 1885

*

1886: Oxford Hotel

Eastern side of the corner of Anson and Glen Streets

1886: William Robinson. He seems to have held the license through until at least 1913 except for 1898-1900 when GPW Heathcote held it.[1025] Unspecified additions were added in 1890.[1026] 1906[1027]: T Green. Robinson had reportedly left Bourke in 1905 to take over the license of the Great Western hotel in Orange,[1028] but he again held the Oxford's license in 1908.[1029] At the time that my great-grandfather James Kessey took over the lease in 1923 the hotel had two storeys, but it was rebuilt as single storey soon after the photo was taken.[1030]

Photograph 47 - The Oxford hotel, ca 1930.

*

1886: Royal Exchange Hotel
Northern side of Mitchell Street between the Shakespeare and Turf hotels
Originally the Exchange; Harp of Erin 1894/5; Caledonian from 1896; popularly called the Golden Stairs

1886: **Exchange hotel** licensee Richard Green, a storekeeper (in partnership with Joseph Becker), butcher, cattle dealer, Alderman and Mayor on several occasions. His wife had formally opened the North Bourke Bridge in 1883. He was a former licensee of the Salmonford hotel at Fords Bridge and was later licensee of Bourke's Royal hotel. He died in 1900 and is buried on *Kerribree* Station.

1887[1031]: Walter Fry, who renovated the premises, changed the name to the **Royal Exchange** and retained the license until at least 1890. 1891: Euphemia Crane. 1893: Bennet Bentick.

1894: John McLaughlin, who changed the name to the **Harp of Erin**. 1895: John McLaughlin.

1896: Donald Shaw, who changed the name to the **Caledonian**. 1897: William Alexander Peter (Shaw's stepson and husband of Kate Hazel Maxwell). 1898: Richard Laffin. 1900: William Alexander Peter.

1900: RC Marsh (Peter's brother-in-law). In 1903[1032] the hotel was saved by a great effort from the fire brigade despite the loss of nine shops and a horse bazaar. 1905: RC Marsh. 1906 until at least 1909: Henry Moxham.

*

1887: Railway Hotel
Northern side of Hope Street near the Club House hotel
Renamed the Cambridge hotel in 1895

1887[1033]: James Lynch, until 1890 when the license was transferred to William Quinn. 1891[1034]: Alexander Barry. 1892[1035]: Thomas Hand. There is no record of the hotel in 1893. 1894[1036]: Percy Whittaker.

1895[1037]: SC Davis, who changed the name to the **Cambridge hotel**. Later that year Doctors Kane and Scott performed emergency surgery at the hotel to amputate the leg of Mr Edward Broderick, a railway shunter whose limb had been run over by a train carriage.[1038] 1896[1039]: Edward Charles Davis. 1897[1040]: Abraham Wade. 1898-1901: Thomas Green. 1902: Clementina Dugan. 1902: E C Davis. 1903/1905: William Heuston.

*

1888: Gladstone Hotel
See Photographs 13 (page 231) and 48 (below)
Northeastern corner of Mitchell and Richard Streets; a substantial brick building
Named after the Grand Old Man[1041]

1888: Joseph Donohoe, a stock dealer and Alderman

who had run Murphy's Family hotel for three years previously. In setting up his hotel, he had acquired and renovated the former premises of the Bourke Club[1042] (previously the Commercial Bank).[1043] He seems to have continued at the Gladstone until 1901[1044] when he transferred to the Telegraph.

1902: Charles Warmoll. 1904: James Warmoll, who died in September 1905.[1045] Then Charles Bernard James Warmoll until 1918.[1046] 1919: James Hackett

The building was later used as a store and, later still, as a boarding house until it was condemned in 1953.[1047]

Photograph 48 - The Gladstone hotel, 1890.

*

1889: Post Office Hotel

Southern side of Oxley Street, roughly opposite the Post Office

1889/90[1048]: Built in 1888 by its first licensee, Edward Luscombe, who claimed it as the premier hotel in the west. He was an Englishman who had previously run a hotel on the Culgoa River where he and his family had been forced to live on floating pontoons for six weeks during the 1890 flood.[1049] He switched to the Federal hotel from 1892 and died in 1915.

1891 until 1957[1050]: Patrick Fitzgerald, from whom it acquired its long-standing colloquial name *Fitz's*. Except that Edward Rich was licensee in 1904. When the above photo was taken the hotel was presenting the 1921 movie *The Wakefield Case* starring Herbert Rawlinson.

Photograph 49 - The Post Office hotel, ca 1922.

*

1892: Australian Hotel
Corner of the Wanaaring and Enngonia Roads at North Bourke
Later called the Riverview hotel; popularly known as Northy's hotel

1892: Built by William Murphy (previously licensee of the Bridge hotel and originally the Enngonia hotel), but the first licensee was Alfred Wall,[1051] previously (and later) licensee of the Gidgie Camp hotel on the Barringun Road. 1893: William Murphy until 1900. He was not related to James or Daniel Murphy. 1901: Alfred Lyon Hart. 1904:

George Wall.

1905: Isaac James transferred from the Occidental hotel nearby, which closed. He held the license until 1909 when it ceased operating. In 1925 it was revived by Mrs MA White of the Gumbalie hotel who ran it for some time. From 1938 it was run by Fred Warmoll who changed the name to the Riverview hotel after WW2.[1052] Warmoll's son-in-law Alan Groube ran it until 1984.

*

1892: Halfway House Hotel
Halfway between Bourke and North Bourke
1892[1053]: Edward Mathew Warmoll. He died soon after and his wife Louisa took over the license. 1893: William Quinn (previously licensee of the Bridge hotel). 1894: Alexander Barry who previously held the license of the Cambridge hotel and had worked as a policeman for many years before entering business as a baker, storekeeper and publican.[1054] 1895: Patrick Kennedy. 1896/99: Alexander Barry. 1900/01: James Dutton.

*

1892: Federal Hotel
Southwestern corner of Mitchell and Warraweena Streets
1892[1055]: Built by its first licensee Edward Luscombe, formerly of the Culgoa and Post Office hotels. He retained the license until his death in 1915 when it was taken over by his wife. After her death in 1922 the license was taken over by their son Richard Luscombe until it was sold in 1927.

Photograph 50 - The Federal hotel, built 1892.

APPENDIX TWO

Family Group Sheets

FATHER Private James Reed 80th Regiment of Foot		
BIRTH	14 Dec 1808	Ash Green, Trentham, Stone, Staffordshire, England
DEATH	30 Jan 1898	senile decay, North Bourke
BURIAL	31 Jan 1898	Bourke cemetery, central eastern side,
MARRIAGE	28 Jun 1830	St Peter's church, Monkwearmouth, Sunderland, England
FATHER	Thomas Reed 1765-1853	
MOTHER	Elizabeth Sutton 1767-1809	
MOTHER Frances Heazle		
BIRTH	1812	Canterbury, England
DEATH	5 Apr 1895	Apoplexy, Bourke
BURIAL	7 Apr 1895	Bourke Cemetery
FATHER	Sergeant Benjamin Heazle 1791-1850	
MOTHER	Elizabeth Wilson	
CHILDREN		
M	**William Reed**	
	BIRTH	ca Apr 1831	Southsea Castle, Portsmouth, England
	DEATH	bef 1836	
M	**John Benjamin Reed**	
	BIRTH	1832	Belfast, Northern Ireland
	DEATH	15 Sep 1881	Bourke
	BURIAL	16 Sep 1881	Bourke
	SPOUSE	Eliza Jane Green 1830-1879	
	MARRIAGE	Oct 1857	Sydney

M	James "Jimmy" Reed		
	BIRTH	ca Mar 1835	Manchester, England
	DEATH	19 Apr 1916	Queensland
	SPOUSE	Eliza Bend 1839-1924	
	MARRIAGE	5 Dec 1856	Anglican church of St John the Baptist, Wellington, New South Wales

M	Alexander Reed		
	BIRTH	10 Jul 1837	Linden, NSW
	DEATH	21 Nov 1917	Queensland
	SPOUSE	Mary Eckel 1860-1925	
	MARRIAGE	5 Dec 1877	Wesleyan Minister's Residence, Rockhampton, Qld, Australia

F	Sarah Reed		
	BIRTH	20 Nov 1839	Military Barracks, Sydney
	DEATH	11 May 1843	Military Barracks, Sydney
	BURIAL	14 May 1843	St Phillips church, Sydney

F	Eliza Emily Reed		
	BIRTH	22 Oct 1841	Wollongong Stockade
	DEATH	22 Aug 1925	bronchopneumonia and chronic bronchitis, Mooculta Street, Bourke
	SPOUSE	Henry Johnson 1838-1911	
	MARRIAGE	12 Sep 1865	Bourke
	SPOUSE	Anders Bufe 1834-1865	
	MARRIAGE	Aug 1860	Sydney

F	Sarah Ann Reed		
	BIRTH	21 Mar 1844	York Street, Sydney
	DEATH	May 1932	a long illness, Bourke
	BURIAL	May 1932	Bourke Church of England Cemetery
	SPOUSE	Michael James Brennan 1843-1908	
	MARRIAGE	6 Jan 1863	Sydney

F	Prudence Reed		
	BIRTH	3 Jul 1846	Kent Street, Sydney
	DEATH	29 Oct 1940	19 Fernhill Street, Hurlstone Park
	BURIAL	30 Oct 1940	C of E, Randwick
	SPOUSE	James Murphy 1843-1919	
	MARRIAGE	18 May 1879	Gongolgon
	SPOUSE	Joseph Whye 1836-1877	
	MARRIAGE	28 Apr 1863	Bourke

F	Frances Reed		
	BIRTH	16 Jun 1848	Clarence Street, Sydney
	DEATH	5 Jun 1922	Leichhardt
	BURIAL	6 Jun 1922	Rookwood Cemetery, Sydney
	SPOUSE	James Tobin Junior 1843-1918	
	MARRIAGE	25 Nov 1863	Bourke

M	George Charles Reed		
	BIRTH	23 Sep 1850	Clarence Street, Sydney
	DEATH	19 Sep 1909	phosphorous poisoning Bourke Hospital
	SPOUSE	Mary Ann Peters 1856-1944	
	MARRIAGE	1 Jan 1877	St Stephen's Church of England at Bourke

465

F	Mary Ann Reed		
BIRTH	23 Dec 1852	Clarence Street, Sydney	
DEATH	21 Jun 1934	Bourke	
BURIAL	23 Jun 1934	Bourke Church of England Cemetery	
SPOUSE	Timothy Farrell 1853-1926		
MARRIAGE	Jan 1882	Bourke	
SPOUSE	George Samson Gibb 1840-1875		
MARRIAGE	25 Apr 1872	Bourke	
F	**Jane Elizabeth Reed**		
BIRTH	16 Jun 1856	17 Clarence Street, Sydney	
DEATH	31 Mar 1924	her residence, Bourke	
BURIAL	31 Mar 1924	Bourke Church of England Cemetery	
DEATH			
SPOUSE	Joseph Maxwell Junior 1846-1929		
MARRIAGE	Jul 1871	Bourke	

FATHER	John Benjamin Reed	
BIRTH	1832	Belfast, Northern Ireland
DEATH	15 Sep 1881	Bourke
BURIAL	16 Sep 1881	Bourke
MARRIAGE	Oct 1857	Sydney
FATHER	Private James Reed 80th Regiment of Foot 1808-1898	
MOTHER	Frances Heazle 1812-1895	

MOTHER	Eliza Jane Green	
BIRTH	Jun 1830	Great Surry Street, Southwark now Blackfriars Road, London
DEATH	23 Nov 1879	Bourke
BURIAL	24 Nov 1879	Bourke
FATHER	John Green 1786-	
MOTHER	Jane Hutton 1801-1857	

CHILDREN

M	William John Reed	
BIRTH	1858	Sydney
DEATH	7 Oct 1865	drowned in the Darling River Bourke

F	Frances Eliza Reed	
BIRTH	1860	Sydney
DEATH	8 Jul 1875	when her clothes caught on fire Bourke hotel in Darling Street, Bourke

FATHER	James "Jimmy" Reed	
BIRTH	ca Mar 1835	Manchester, England
DEATH	19 Apr 1916	Queensland
MARRIAGE	5 Dec 1856	Anglican church of St John the Baptist, Wellington, New South Wales
FATHER	Private James Reed 80th Regiment of Foot 1808-1898	
MOTHER	Frances Heazle 1812-1895	

MOTHER	Eliza Bend	
BIRTH	1839	Norfolk Island
DEATH	11 Jun 1924	Queensland
FATHER	Private Charles Bend 80th Regiment of Foot 1806-1845	
FATHER	John Atkins 1815-1863	
MOTHER	Eliza Hood	

CHILDREN

M	John Reed	
BIRTH	1859	Wellington, NSW
DEATH	31 Dec 1945	Homehill, Queensland
SPOUSE	Elizabeth Mary Ahern 1868-1961	
MARRIAGE	30 Apr 1890	Hughenden, Queensland

F	Eliza Reed	
BIRTH	1860	Wellington, NSW
DEATH	23 Dec 1942	Rolleston, Queensland
SPOUSE	George Henry Horsfield 1842-1897	
MARRIAGE	8 Apr 1878	Rockhampton, Queensland
SPOUSE	Joseph Fisher 1843-1912	

M	James Reed		
	BIRTH	1862	Wellington, NSW
	DEATH	17 Dec 1906	Cowra, New South Wales
	SPOUSE	Alice Elizabeth Foote 1867-1948	
	MARRIAGE	12 Jun 1885	Queensland
M	Charles Alexander Reed		
	BIRTH	ca Oct 1865	Bourke
	DEATH	28 Mar 1919	Emmaville, New South Wales
	SPOUSE	Margaret Maguire 1864-1896	
	MARRIAGE	10 May 1886	Queensland
M	George Reed		
	BIRTH	1866	Bourke, New South Wales, Australia
	DEATH	1887	Queensland
M	Henry Reed		
	BIRTH	16 Jan 1869	Queensland
	DEATH	24 Nov 1951	Queensland
M	Frank Edward Reed		
	BIRTH	5 Jul 1871	Queensland
	DEATH	1 Oct 1940	Queensland
	SPOUSE	Agnes Grace Royalson 1911-2004	
	MARRIAGE	7 Feb 1935	Queensland
F	Frances Reed		
	BIRTH	4 Feb 1874	Queensland
	DEATH	20 Nov 1947	Springsure Hospital, Queensland
	SPOUSE	Michael Martin Kavanagh 1871-1953	
	MARRIAGE	18 Nov 1893	Springsure, Queensland

M	Thomas Reed		
	BIRTH	21 May 1876	Queensland
F	Mary Jane Reed		
	BIRTH	6 Jul 1878	Queensland
	DEATH	26 Oct 1948	Milton Street, Mackay, Queensland
	SPOUSE	James Lewis Doyle 1872-1941	
	MARRIAGE	25 Dec 1895	Springsure, Queensland

FATHER	Alexander Reed	
BIRTH	10 Jul 1837	Linden, NSW
DEATH	21 Nov 1917	Queensland
MARRIAGE	5 Dec 1877	Wesleyan Minister's Residence, Rockhampton, Qld
FATHER	Private James Reed 80th Regiment of Foot 1808-1898	
MOTHER	Frances Heazle 1812-1895	

MOTHER	Mary Eckel	
BIRTH	25 Apr 1860	Dalby, Queensland, Australian Colonies
DEATH	15 Sep 1925	invalidity of three years duration General Hospital, Longreach, Queensland
FATHER	Henry Eckel 1825-1899	
MOTHER	Christina Erskine 1825-1916	
OTHER SPOUSE	T O'Brien 1855-	
MARRIAGE	25 Aug 1921	

CHILDREN

F	Margaret "Maggie" Reed	
BIRTH	8 Jul 1879	Queensland
DEATH	13 Mar 1959	Longreach, Queensland, Australia
SPOUSE	William John Swan 1869-1939	
MARRIAGE	2 Sep 1899	Longreach, Queensland

F	Eliza Jane Reed	
BIRTH	28 Dec 1880	Queensland
DEATH	25 Dec 1964	Longreach, Queensland, Australia
SPOUSE	Robert George Andrews- 876-1950	

F	Christina Wingfield Reed		
	BIRTH	1 Feb 1883	Queensland
	DEATH	18 Dec 1950	Woody Point, Queensland
	SPOUSE	August Johann Gottleib Beutel	
	MARRIAGE	22 Feb 1906	Queensland
M	Henry James Reed-6630		
	BIRTH	5 Dec 1885	Queensland
	DEATH	26 Apr 1953	Queensland
M	George Charles Alexander Reed		
	BIRTH	28 Nov 1887	Queensland
	DEATH	1966	Greenslopes Hospital, Brisbane
	SPOUSE	Lavinia Alice White 1894-1978	
	MARRIAGE	15 Jan 1919	Walthamstow, Essex
M	William Edward "William Frederick" Reed		
	BIRTH	6 Apr 1890	Queensland
	DEATH	4 Aug 1950	Queensland
	SPOUSE	Hazel Cecilia White 1891-	
	MARRIAGE	2 Jan 1918	St Michael and All Angels church, Walthamstow, Essex
M	Ernest John Reed		
	BIRTH	19 Jul 1891	Queensland
	DEATH	19 May 1919	Queensland

FATHER	Anders "Andrew" Bufe	
BIRTH	1834	USA
DEATH	bef 1865	
MARRIAGE	Aug 1860	Sydney
FATHER		
MOTHER		

MOTHER	Eliza Emily Reed	
BIRTH	22 Oct 1841	Wollongong Stockade, Wollongong
DEATH	22 Aug 1925	bronchopneumonia and chronic bronchitis, Mooculta Street, Bourke
FATHER	Private James Reed 80th Regiment of Foot 1808-1898	
MOTHER	Frances Heazle 1812-1895	
OTHER SPOUSE	Henry Johnson 1838-1911	
MARRIAGE	12 Sep 1865	Bourke

NO CHILDREN

FATHER	Henry Johnson		
	BIRTH	ca 1838	Richmond, New South Wales, Australian Colonies
	DEATH	3 Apr 1911	North Bourke, Bourke, New South Wales, Australia
	MARRIAGE	12 Sep 1865	Bourke, New South Wales, Australian Colonies
	FATHER	William Johnson 1796-1854	
	MOTHER	Bridget Caton (or Keating) 1797-1846	
MOTHER	**Eliza Emily Reed**		
	BIRTH	22 Oct 1841	Wollongong Stockade, Wollongong, NSW, Australia
	DEATH	22 Aug 1925	bronchopneumonia and chronic bronchitis, Mooculta Street, Bourke
	FATHER	Private James Reed 80th Regiment of Foot 1808-1898	
	MOTHER	Frances Heazle 1812-1895	
	OTHER SPOUSE	Anders Bufe 1834-1865	
	MARRIAGE	Aug 1860	Sydney
CHILDREN			
F	**Frances Eliza Johnson**		
	BIRTH	1866	Bourke, New South Wales, Australia
	DEATH	bef 22 Aug 1925	
M	**James Henry Johnson**		
	BIRTH	9 Feb 1868	Bourke, New South Wales, Australia
	DEATH	1938	Bourke, New South Wales, Australia

M	**Alexander George Oxley Johnson**		
	BIRTH	22 Dec 1869	Bourke
	DEATH	1946	
	SPOUSE	Maria Mary Mapstone 1870-	
	MARRIAGE	20 Sep 1897	Queensland
F	**Sarah Jane Heazle "Heazle" Johnson**		
	BIRTH	29 Nov 1871	Bourke
	DEATH	28 Jul 1960	Winton, Queensland
	SPOUSE	Stephen Wall 1870-	
	MARRIAGE	28 Dec 1892	Bourke
M	**John Benjamin Linley "Benjamin" Johnson**		
	BIRTH	Nov 1873	Bourke
	DEATH	1955	
M	**George Johnson-6644**		
	BIRTH	20 Apr 1876	Bourke
M	**Henry Sampson "Sampson" Johnson**		
	BIRTH	2 Mar 1878	Mount Oxley, Bourke
	DEATH	1956	Wellington, New South Wales
F	**Emily Jane Johnson**		
	BIRTH	15 Oct 1879	Mount Oxley, Bourke
	DEATH	1 Nov 1908	Consumption, Bourke
	BURIAL	2 Nov 1908	Bourke Cemetery
M	**Albert William Johnson**		
	BIRTH	25 Sep 1881	Bogan
F	**Mary Ann Maud "Maud" Johnson**		
	BIRTH	8 Mar 1884	Mooculta, Bourke
	SPOUSE	Jones	

FATHER	Michael James "Mick" Brennan		
	BIRTH	3 Mar 1843	Prince's Street, The Rocks, Sydney
	DEATH	9 Dec 1908	Sydney, New South Wales
	BURIAL	10 Dec 1908	Rookwood Cemetery, Sydney
	MARRIAGE	6 Jan 1863	Sydney
	FATHER	William Brennan 1810-1872	
	MOTHER	Ellen Whelan 1813-1888	
MOTHER	Sarah Ann Reed		
	BIRTH	21 Mar 1844	York Street, Sydney
	DEATH	May 1932	a long illness, Bourke
	BURIAL	May 1932	Bourke Church of England Cemetery
	FATHER	Private James Reed 80th Regiment of Foot 1808-1898	
	MOTHER	Frances Heazle 1812-1895	
CHILDREN			
F	Sarah Ellen Brennan		
	BIRTH	24 Jul 1864	Ponto, Wellington
	SPOUSE	Unknown	
	SPOUSE	Edward James Freeman 1860-	
	MARRIAGE	1882	Bourke
F	Frances Eliza Brennan		
	BIRTH	ca Oct 1865	Bourke
	DEATH	29 Mar 1885	Bourke
	SPOUSE	Frederick Jackson 1860-	
	MARRIAGE	5 Mar 1883	Bourke

F	**Emeline Brennan**	
BIRTH	Jul 1867	Bourke
SPOUSE	John S Harding 1865-1888	
MARRIAGE	1887	Bourke

F	**Isabella Maude Mary "Maude" Brennan**	
BIRTH	15 Mar 1869	North Bourke
SPOUSE	Charles Devine Mathews son of the founder of Louth 1866-1950	
MARRIAGE	1891	Bourke

F	**Victoria Prudence Brennan**	
BIRTH	7 Sep 1870	Bourke
SPOUSE	James C Hudson 1780-	
MARRIAGE	1893	Bourke

M	**William J Brennan**	
BIRTH	Aug 1872	Bourke
DEATH	14 Aug 1876	Bourke

F	**Mary Jane Heazle Brennan**	
BIRTH	23 Jul 1874	Bourke
DEATH	30 Nov 1944	
SPOUSE	Albert J Huckle 1870-1930	
MARRIAGE	1894	Bourke
SPOUSE	Frederick C Bishop 1871-	
MARRIAGE	1933	Canterbury, New South Wales

F	Josephine Whelan Brennan		
	BIRTH	28 May 1877	Bourke
	DEATH	10 Jun 1956	
	SPOUSE	James P Costello 1875-1905	
	MARRIAGE	1895	Bourke
	SPOUSE	Malcolm I Newman 1875-	
	MARRIAGE	1917	Bourke
F	Annie Brennan		
	BIRTH	28 Dec 1878	Native Springs, Bourke
	DEATH	4 Apr 1879	Bourke
M	Michael James Brennan		
	BIRTH	6 Oct 1881	Bourke
	SPOUSE	Mabel Dyball 1884-	
	MARRIAGE	1904	Bourke
M	Alfred John Brennan		
	BIRTH	28 Feb 1884	Bourke
	DEATH	10 May 1947	Bourke
	SPOUSE	Bertha Jane Frances Wood 1885-1929	
	MARRIAGE	1914	Bourke

FATHER	Joseph Whye		
BIRTH	1836	Waterbeach, Cambridgeshire	
DEATH	6 May 1877	inflammation of the lungs over 5 days Gongolgon, New South Wales	
BURIAL	8 May 1877	Gongolgon Cemetery	
MARRIAGE	28 Apr 1863	Bourke	
FATHER	William Whye 1801-		
MOTHER	Hannah Headland 1804-		

MOTHER	Prudence Reed		
BIRTH	3 Jul 1846	Kent Street, Sydney	
DEATH	29 Oct 1940	19 Fernhill Street, Hurlstone Park	
BURIAL	30 Oct 1940	C of E, Randwick	
FATHER	Private James Reed 80th Regiment of Foot 1808-1898		
MOTHER	Frances Heazle 1812-1895		
OTHER SPOUSE	James Murphy 1843-1919		
MARRIAGE	18 May 1879	Gongolgon	

CHILDREN

F	Frances Anna Whye		
BIRTH	1864		
DEATH	1960		
SPOUSE	Augustus Sullivan 1855-1937		
MARRIAGE	31 May 1881	Bourke	

M	William Whye		
BIRTH	1865	Gongolgon	
DEATH	9 Jul 1865	*Nidgerie* Station, Gongolgon	

F	Jane Elizabeth Whye		
	BIRTH	Jul 1866	
	DEATH	12 Apr 1947	Bathurst, New South Wales, Australia
	SPOUSE	Thomas Ralph 1856-1900	
	MARRIAGE	1886	Brewarrina
	SPOUSE	William Henry Fuller 1878-1954	
	MARRIAGE	18 Feb 1901	Bourke
M	**Frederick Whye**		
	BIRTH	1868	Bourke
	DEATH	4 Jan 1868	Bourke
F	**Emily Maude Mary Whye**		
	BIRTH	1869	
	DEATH	24 Aug 1940	Goondiwindi, Queensland
	SPOUSE	William Joseph Clendinen 1865-1906	
M	**Albert George Henry Whye**		
	BIRTH	26 Feb 1871	Gongolgon
	DEATH	19 Jul 1927	73 Great Buckingham Street, Redfern
	SPOUSE	Annie M Roberts 1872-	
	MARRIAGE	1892	Brewarrina
	SPOUSE	Rose A J Walls 1873-	
	MARRIAGE	1897	Brewarrina
F	**Kate Whye**		
	BIRTH	28 Apr 1873	Gongolgon
	DEATH	14 Jul 1878	whooping cough, Gongolgon
	BURIAL	15 Jul 1878	Gongolgon Cemetery

F	Josephine Heazle Whye		
	BIRTH	15 Mar 1875	
	DEATH		
	SPOUSE	John Joseph Francisco 1866-1937	
M	Joseph Headland Whye		
	BIRTH	abt Jan 1877	
	DEATH	21 Mar 1878	continued illness of 4 months duration
	BURIAL	28 Mar 1878	Gongolgon Cemetery

FATHER	James Murphy		
	BIRTH	Nov 1843	Keelnabrack, Kerry, Ireland
	DEATH	5 Nov 1919	senile decay, Rookwood Asylum, Granville, New South Wales
	BURIAL	7 Nov 1919	Catholic Cemetery, Rookwood, New South Wales
	MARRIAGE	18 May 1879	Gongolgon
	FATHER	John Murphy 1819-1894	
	MOTHER	Mary Shea 1821-1904	
	OTHER SPOUSE	Ann Malcolm 1847-1922	
	MARRIAGE	28 Dec 1864	Church of Saints Michael and John, Bathurst
MOTHER	Prudence Reed		
	BIRTH	3 Jul 1846	Kent Street, Sydney
	DEATH	29 Oct 1940	19 Fernhill Street, Hurlstone Park
	BURIAL	30 Oct 1940	C of E, Randwick
	FATHER	Private James Reed 80th Regiment of Foot 1808-1898	
	MOTHER	Frances Heazle 1812-1895	
	OTHER SPOUSE	Joseph Whye 1836-1877	
	MARRIAGE	28 Apr 1863	Bourke
CHILDREN			
M	**Daniel Reed Murphy**		
	BIRTH	14 May 1879	
	DEATH	24 Dec 1881	diphtheria for 4 days, Gongolgon
	BURIAL	28 Dec 1881	Gongolgon Cemetery

M	George Charles Reed Murphy		
	BIRTH	24 Dec 1880	Gongolgon
	DEATH	11 Dec 1949	Donald Street, Goondiwindi
	BURIAL	12 Dec 1949	Goondiwindi Cemetery
	SPOUSE	Ellen Ruby Bowen 1882-1912	
	MARRIAGE	18 Oct 1905	St Ignatius Catholic Church, Bourke
	SPOUSE	Grace Isabel Cox 1888-1924	
	MARRIAGE	2 Jul 1918	Court House, Winton, Queensland
	SPOUSE	Kathleen Teresa White 1885-1949	
	MARRIAGE	12 Feb 1934	St Patricks Catholic Church, Brewarrina
F	Nora Lilian Murphy		
	BIRTH	1882	
	DEATH		
	SPOUSE	Edward Burnet 1882-	
	MARRIAGE	abt 1913	Sydney
F	Mary Ethel Murphy		
	BIRTH	4 Sep 1884	
	DEATH		
	SPOUSE	Francis P Bradley 1884-	
	MARRIAGE	abt 1912	Sydney
F	Lila Kate Murphy		
	BIRTH	13 Nov 1886	Darling Street, Bourke
	DEATH	4 Nov 1941	
	SPOUSE	Neills Moller 1886-	
	MARRIAGE	16 Nov 1904	Orange, New South Wales

FATHER	James Tobin Junior		
	BIRTH	abt 1843	Hunter's River, NSW
	DEATH	1918	Petersham, NSW
	MARRIAGE	25 Nov 1863	Bourke, New South Wales, Australia
	FATHER	James Tobin senior 1813-1901	
	MOTHER	Catherine Maloney 1817-1869	
MOTHER	Frances Reed		
	BIRTH	16 Jun 1848	Clarence Street, Sydney
	DEATH	5 Jun 1922	Leichhardt
	BURIAL	6 Jun 1922	Rookwood Cemetery, Sydney
	FATHER	Private James Reed 80th Regiment of Foot 1808-1898	
	MOTHER	Frances Heazle 1812-1895	
CHILDREN			
F	Female Tobin-3884		
	BIRTH	1864	Dubbo
	DEATH	1864	Dubbo
F	Eliza Emily Tobin "Lila" Maxwell		
	BIRTH	11 Dec 1878	Gongolgon
	DEATH	Dec 1973	
	SPOUSE	John S McCready 1875-1932	
	MARRIAGE	12 Jun 1899	Presbyterian Church Bourke, Bourke

FATHER George Charles Reed		
BIRTH	23 Sep 1850	Clarence Street, Sydney
DEATH	19 Sep 1909	phosphorous poisoning, Bourke Hospital
MARRIAGE	1 Jan 1877	St Stephen's Church of England, Bourke
FATHER	Private James Reed 80th Regiment of Foot 1808-1898	
MOTHER	Frances Heazle 1812-1895	

MOTHER Mary Ann Peters		
BIRTH	9 Nov 1856	Windsor Road, Windsor
DEATH	7 Feb 1944	heart failure, Bourke
FATHER	William Peters 1832-	
MOTHER	Mary Ann Smith 1835-	

CHILDREN

M	Edward John Bloxham Reed		
	BIRTH	14 Dec 1878	Bourke
	DEATH	4 Nov 1881	Bourke

M	Gilbert George Joseph Whye Reed		
	BIRTH	28 Feb 1880	Bourke
	DEATH	26 Mar 1949	

F	Frances Heazle Reed		
	BIRTH	17 Feb 1882	North Bourke

F	Ethel Mary Ann Reed		
	BIRTH	28 Jul 1883	East Bourke, Bourke

F	Emily Beatrice Reed		
	BIRTH	1 Jul 1885	Charlton, Bourke
	DEATH	3 Aug 1907	Consumption, Bourke

M	Bertie Augustus Reed		
	BIRTH	17 Dec 1887	Bourke
	DEATH	10 Jan 1952	Bourke
M	James Reed		
	BIRTH	13 Feb 1890	Bourke
M	George Charles Reed		
	BIRTH	29 Jul 1892	Bourke
	DEATH	22 Sep 1958	road accident, Bourke
M	William Reed		
	BIRTH	8 Aug 1895	Bourke
	DEATH	9 May 1958	Bourke

FATHER	George Samson Gibb	
BIRTH	8 Apr 1840	Blackston, Auchinleck, Scotland
DEATH	9 Dec 1875	Intemperance, Bourke
BURIAL	10 Dec 1875	Bourke Cemetery
MARRIAGE	25 Apr 1872	Bourke
FATHER	Alexander Boswell Gibb 1804-	
MOTHER	Janet Samson 1810-	

MOTHER	Mary Ann Reed	
BIRTH	23 Dec 1852	Clarence Street, Sydney
DEATH	21 Jun 1934	Bourke
BURIAL	23 Jun 1934	Church of England Cemetery, Bourke
FATHER	Private James Reed 80th Regiment of Foot 1808-1898	
MOTHER	Frances Heazle 1812-1895	
OTHER SPOUSE	Timothy Farrell 1853-1926	
MARRIAGE	Jan 1882	Bourke

CHILDREN

F	Jannet Frances Gibb	
BIRTH	Oct 1873	Bourke
SPOUSE	William Power 1870-	
MARRIAGE	1893	

M	Alexander James Boswell Gibb of "Collerina"	
BIRTH	3 Apr 1875	Bourke
DEATH	17 Oct 1947	Brewarrina
SPOUSE	Mercy Archer1880-1934	
MARRIAGE	1902	Bourke, New South Wales, Australia

FATHER (adoptive) Timothy Farrell		
BIRTH	10 May 1853	at sea
DEATH	7 Jan 1926	Bourke
BURIAL	7 Jan 1926	Bourke Roman Catholic Cemetery
FATHER	Edmund Farrell 1828-1863	
MOTHER	Eleanor Ryan 1830-	
MARRIAGE	Jan 1882	Bourke
MOTHER Mary Ann Reed		
BIRTH	23 Dec 1852	Clarence Street, Sydney
DEATH	21 Jun 1934	Bourke
BURIAL	23 Jun 1934	Church of England Cemetery, Bourke
FATHER	Private James Reed 80th Regiment of Foot 1808-1898	
MOTHER	Frances Heazle 1812-1895	
OTHER SPOUSE	George Samson Gibb 1840-1875	
MARRIAGE	25 Apr 1872	Bourke
CHILDREN		
F **Hazle May Gibb Farrell-6748**		
BIRTH	6 Aug 1879	Bourke
DEATH	24 Jun 1909	
SPOUSE	Daniel Power-6806 1875-	
MARRIAGE	18 Aug 1897	Bourke
SPOUSE	Henry Shallvy 1870-1940	
MARRIAGE	17 Nov 1903	Nyngan, New South Wales

FATHER (natural) Timothy Farrell		
BIRTH	10 May 1853	at sea
DEATH	7 Jan 1926	Bourke
BURIAL	7 Jan 1926	Roman Catholic Cemetery, Bourke
MARRIAGE	Jan 1882	Bourke
FATHER	Edmund Farrell 1828-1863	
MOTHER	Eleanor Ryan 1830-	

MOTHER Mary Ann Reed		
BIRTH	23 Dec 1852	Clarence Street, Sydney
DEATH	21 Jun 1934	Bourke
BURIAL	23 Jun 1934	Church of England Cemetery, Bourke
FATHER	Private James Reed 80th Regiment of Foot 1808-1898	
MOTHER	Frances Heazle 1812-1895	
OTHER SPOUSE	George Samson Gibb 1840-1875	
MARRIAGE	25 Apr 1872	Bourke, New South Wales, Australia

CHILDREN

M	Thomas James Edmond Farrell	
BIRTH	14 Sep 1882	Bourke
DEATH	6 Apr 1884	Bourke

F	Lila Rose Farrell	
BIRTH	1884	Bourke
SPOUSE	Charles Westbrook -1934	

F	Victoria K Farrell	
BIRTH	1887	Brewarrina, NSW, Australia
SPOUSE	Walter Anderson	

M	Timothy Oxley "Tim" Farrell		
	BIRTH	1889	Brewarrina, NSW, Australia
	DEATH	23 May 1918	of wounds received in action, France
M	**Edwin Albert "Eddy" Farrell**		
	BIRTH	1892	Brewarrina
	DEATH	1958	Gilgandra
M	**George Charles Reed Farrell**		
	BIRTH	1896	Brewarrina
	DEATH	15 Mar 1917	killed in action, France
	BURIAL	1921	Guards Cemetery plot 7 row L grave 10, Les Boeufs, France
F	**Una Elsie Marie Farrell**		
	BIRTH	1899	Cobar
	SPOUSE	H G Honeyman	

FATHER Joseph Maxwell Junior		
BIRTH	1846	Montefiore, Wellington, NSW
DEATH	6 Feb 1929	Bourke
BURIAL	7 Feb 1929	Church of England Cemetery, Bourke
BURIAL		
MARRIAGE	Jul 1871	Bourke
FATHER	Richard James Maxwell 1810-1898	
MOTHER	Ann Cross 1819-1878	

MOTHER Jane Elizabeth Reed		
BIRTH	16 Jun 1856	17 Clarence Street, Sydney
DEATH	31 Mar 1924	her residence, Bourke
BURIAL	31 Mar 1924	Church of England Cemetery, Bourke
FATHER	Private James Reed 80th Regiment of Foot 1808-1898	
MOTHER	Frances Heazle 1812-1895	

CHILDREN

M	Alexander Maxwell	
BIRTH	Aug 1871	Bourke
DEATH	Jul 1872	Bourke

M	Richard James Oxley "Oxley" Maxwell	
BIRTH	Jul 1873	Bourke
DEATH	1950	Parramatta

F	Kate Heazle Maxwell		
	BIRTH	26 Sep 1875	Bourke
	DEATH	9 Nov 1936	
	SPOUSE	William Alexander Peter 1874-1962	
	MARRIAGE	2 Feb 1897	Brewarrina

F	Frances Annie Maxwell		
	BIRTH	3 Dec 1877	North Bourke
	DEATH	May 1878	Bourke

F	Eliza Emily Tobin "Lila" Maxwell		
	BIRTH	11 Dec 1878	Gongolgon
	DEATH	Dec 1973	
	SPOUSE	John S McCready 1875-1932	
	MARRIAGE	12 Jun 1899	Presbyterian Church, Bourke

M	Augustus George Maxwell		
	BIRTH	23 Apr 1881	Bourke
	DEATH	30 Apr 1881	bronchitis of 2 days duration, Bourke
	BURIAL	30 Apr 1881	Cemetery, Bourke

M	Albert Charles Maxwell		
	BIRTH	7 Feb 1883	Gongolgon
	DEATH	1928	Bourke

F	Frances Prudence Maxwell		
	BIRTH	May 1885	Nyngan
	DEATH	4 Nov 1888	Gongolgon

M	Private Joseph Henry "Harry" Maxwell		
	BIRTH	Sep 1887	Brewarrina
	DEATH	3 May 1917	killed in action, France
M	Edward H Maxwell		
	BIRTH	Feb 1890	Brewarrina
F	Blanche Olive Maxwell		
	BIRTH	Mar 1892	Brewarrina
	SPOUSE	Angus Jenkins -1925	
	MARRIAGE	Aug 1911	St Stephen's Church of England, Bourke
F	Jane Elizabeth Maxwell-6654		
	BIRTH	21 Sep 1894	Gongolgon
	DEATH	aft 23 Sep 1894	Bourke
M	Norman Harold Maxwell-6662		
	BIRTH	Aug 1895	Bourke
M	William Walter Maxwell-6663		
	BIRTH	Feb 1898	Bourke
M	John S Maxwell-6658		
	BIRTH	Oct 1903	Bourke

Bibliography

Bibliography

Abbott, G. J. 'Kemp, Charles (1813–1864)'. *Australian Dictionary of Biography*. Canberra: National Centre of Biography, Australian National University, 1967. Trove at https://adb.anu.edu.au/biography/kemp-charles-2295.

Abbott, J. H. M. *The Newcastle Packets and the Hunter Valley.* Currawong Publishing Co, Sydney 1942.

Backhouse, Tim. *St. Paul's Church, Southsea.* History in Portsmouth at http://historyinportsmouth.co.uk/places/st-pauls.htm.

Bamford, Andrew. 'Dastardly and Atrocious': Lieutenant Blake, Captain Clune and the Recall of the 55th Foot from the Netherlands, 1814'. *Journal of the Society for Army Historical Research* 92, no. 371 (Autumn 2014): 210–22.

Bamford, Andrew. 'The British Army in the Low Countries 1813-14'. *The Waterloo Association*, Napoleon Series, 2013 at https://www.napoleon-series/military-info/battles/1814/c_lowcountries1814.pdf.

Barnett, Harvey. 'Memoirs of Harvey Barnett'. In *History of Bourke Journal*, volume 4:8–46. Bourke and District Historical Society, 1972.

G C Baugh, W L Cowie, J C Dickinson, Duggan A P, A K B Evans, R H Evans, Una C Hannam, P Heath, D A Johnson, Hilda Johnstone, Ann J Kettle, J L Kirby, R Mansfield and A Saltman, 'Houses of Augustinian canons: The priory of Trentham', in *A History of the County of Stafford: Volume 3*, ed. M W Greenslade and R B Pugh (London, 1970), pp. 255-260. British History Online at http://www.british-history.ac.uk/vch/staffs/vol3/pp255-260.

Cable, K. J. 'Fulton, Henry (1761–1840)'. *Australian Dictionary of Biography*. Canberra: National Centre of Biography, Australian National University, 1966 at https://adb.anu.edu.au/biography/fulton-henry-2074/text2593.

Cable, K. J. 'Macarthur, George Fairfowl (1825–1890)'. *Australian Dictionary of Biography:* National Centre of Biography, Australian National University, 1974 at https://adb.anu.edu.au/biography/macarthur-george-fairfowl-4060/text6467.

Cameron, Bill. *Bourke, a Pictorial History.* 2 vols. Bourke Wool Press, 1982.

Cameron, William et al. *History of Bourke Journal.* 13 vols. Bourke: Bourke and District Historical Society, 1966-1992.

Cooper, Paul F. 'Penny Banks in Colonial NSW: banking that sought to serve'. *Philanthropy and Philanthropists in Australian Colonial History,* June 25, 2018 at https://colonialgivers.com/2018/06/23/penny-banks-in-colonial-nsw-banking-that-sought-to-serve/

Davis, Joseph L. *The Spotless Reputation of the Reverend Matthew Devenish Meares (1800-1878) at Wollongong.* Academia.edu at https://www.academia.edu/39765539/

Delbridge, Kristina. *Saxby/Delbridge Family Tree.* Online family tree, Ancestry.com at https://www.ancestry.com.au/family-tree/tree/76413441?dtid=100.

Evans, William. *Journal of His Majesty's Convict Ship Earl Grey 1836.* Royal Navy Medical Journals 1817-1857. The British Admiralty, 1837.

Foott, Bethia. 'Of Henrietta, Marooned'. *History of Bourke Journal,* 1:27–33. Bourke and District Historical Society, n.d.

Gapps, Dr Stephen. *The Sydney Wars.* New South Books, 2018. https://thesydneywars.com/.

Gould, John, and Henry Constantine Richter. *The Mammals of Australia.* 3 vols. London: The Author, 1863. https://nla.gov.au/nla.obj-55392912.

Greaves, Bernard. 'Blackman, James (1792–1868)'. *Australian Dictionary of Biography.* Canberra: National Centre of Biography, Australian National University at https://adb.anu.edu.au/biography/blackman-james-1790.

Jenkins J G (ed.), 'Stoke-upon-Trent: Local government, economic history and social life'. *A History of the County of Stafford: Volume 8,* (London, 1963), pp. 194-205. British History Online at http://www.british-history.ac.uk/vch/staffs/vol8/

Jervis, James. 'The Exploration and Settlement of the Western Plains'. *Royal Australian Historical Society* 42, no. Part 1 (1956).

Jewitt, Llewellyn Frederick William. *The Wedgwoods: Being a Life of Josiah Wedgwood; with Notices of His Works and Their Productions, Memoirs of the Wedgewood and Other Families, and a History of the Early Potteries of Staffordshire.* Virtue Brothers and Company, 1865.

King, Hazel. 'Sir Richard Bourke'. *Australian Dictionary of Biography.* National Centre of Biography, Australian National University, 1966 at https://adb.anu.edu.au/biography/bourke-sir-richard-1806.

Krefft, Gerard. *Transactions of the Philosophical Society of New South Wales.* Sydney: Printed by Reading and Wellbank, 1862. https://www.biodiversitylibrary.org/item/73082.

McCance, H M. 'How the Colours of the 55th Foot Were Saved at Bergen-Op-Zoom, in March, 1814.' *Journal of the Society for Army Historical Research* 7, no. 30 (October 1928): 201–4.

McCulloch, Samuel Clyde. 'Gipps, Sir George (1791–1847)'. *Australian Dictionary of Biography.* Canberra: National Centre of Biography, Australian National University at https://adb.anu.edu.au/biography/gipps-sir-george-2098.

McDonald, Peter F. *Age at First Marriage and Proportions Marrying in Australia 1860-1971.* Doctoral thesis, Department of Demography, Australian National University, 1972 at http://hdl.handle.net/1885/117075

McIntyre, Alastair. *Boswell.* History website. Electric Scotland at https://electricscotland.com/history/nation/boswell.htm.

McKenzie, Joan. *The Vision Splendid: The History of Coonamble Town and District.* Coonamble: J McKenzie, 1988.

McKillop, Bob. 'Saint Mary MacKillop: a brief overview'. *Willoughby History Chatters*, volume 44, number 1, pages 4-5, February 2018, Willoughby District Historical Society Inc., Chatswood.

McQueen, Ken. 'Hidden Copper: The Early History of the Cornish, Scottish and Australian (C.S.A.) Mine, Cobar, NSW'. *Journal of Australasian Mining History* volume 4, no. September 2006 (2006): pages 20-46.

Nicholson, Ian. *Log of Logs*. 3 vols. Nambour, Queensland: The Australian Association for Maritime History, n.d.

Organ, Michael K, and Robert Hardy. 'Pioneers of the Illawarra - a History of the Family of Elias Organ in Wollongong, 1839-1869'. *Research Online*, 1984, 131 at https://ro.uow.edu.au/asdpapers/128/

Piggin, Stuart. *Faith of Steel, a History of the Christian Churches in Illawarra, Australia*. The University of Wollongong, 1984 at https://issuu.com/libuow/docs/faith_of_steel

Pollard, N. S. 'Cowper, William (1778–1858)'. *Australian Dictionary of Biography*. National Centre of Biography, Australian National University, 1966 at https://adb.anu.edu.au/biography/cowper-william-1929/text2301

Randell, William. 'Voyage up the Darling and Barwon'. *Journal of the Royal Geographical Society* 31 (1861): 145–48. Reprinted in the History of Bourke Journal, 2:82-85.

Readford, Edward. 'Reminiscences of Early Days'. *History of Bourke Journal*, 6:71–73. Bourke and District Historical Society.

Ryan, Lyndal et al. *Colonial Frontier Massacres in Eastern Australia 1788 to 1930*. Centre for 21st Century Humanities, University of Newcastle, 2018 at http://hdl.handle.net/1959.13/1340762

Sargent, Clem. *The British Garrison in Australia 1788-1841: The Mutiny of the 80th Regiment at Norfolk Island*. The Free Library at https://www.thefreelibrary.com/The+British+Garrison+in+A ustralia+1788-1841%3a+the+mutiny+of+the+80th...-a0137872263

Smith, Rev Herbert. *Correspondence, Containing Some ... Particulars Concerning the Lord's Day, Published for the Purpose of Promoting Well Organized Sabbath Societies throughout England*. Piccadilly, London: J Hatchard & Son, 1830 at https://www.google.com.au/books/edition/Correspondence_ containing_some_particula/_TwozpyVNsgC?hl=en&gbpv=0.

Surtees, Robert. 'Parish of Monk-Wearmouth'. *The History and Antiquities of the County Palatine of Durham*, Volume 2, Chester ward. London: Nichols and Son, 1820 at https://www.british-history.ac.uk/antiquities-durham/vol2/pp1-39

Teale, Ruth. 'Marsden, Samuel Edward (1832–1912)'. *Australian Dictionary of Biography*. Canberra: National Centre of Biography, Australian National University at https://adb.anu.edu.au/biography/marsden-samuel-edward-4155.

Thomasson, Rose Maree. *Thomasson Family Tree*. Online family tree, Ancestry.com at https://www.ancestry.com.au/family-tree/tree/22762359.

Turnbull, Lucy. 'The End of Transportation'. *Dictionary of Sydney*, NSW State Library, 2008 at https://dictionaryofsydney.org/entry/the_end_of_transportat ion.

Unknown. *Camp Followers and Family Members*. Internet Archive Wayback Machine at http://users.hunterlink.net.au.

Unknown. *Photograph Captioned 'Bourke's First Hotel 1866'*. 1866. Image. Tooth and company photographs of country hotels. Noel Butlin Archive, Australian National University at https://openresearch-repository.anu.edu.au/handle/1885/254838?mode=full.

Unknown. *Regimental History, 80th Regiment of Foot, Staffordshire Volunteers*. Internet Archive, Wayback Machine at https://web.archive.org/web/20080116203826/http://users.hu nterlink.net.au/~ddchr/Regimental%20History.htm.

Unstated. *80th Regiment Record of Stations 1793-1905*. Australian Joint Copy Project. Trove at https://nla.gov.au/nla.obj-1379847382.

Ibid. *Digest, Vol. 1, 1793-1897; Vol. 2, 1793-1899*. https://nla.gov.au/nla.obj-2387560815.

Unstated. 'Archibald Bell - Settler'. *Hunter Valley History*. Free Settler or Felon at https://www.freesettlerorfelon.com/archibald_bell.htm.

Unstated. *Charles Kemp Monument, St James Church, Sydney*. Memorial. Monument Australia at https://monumentaustralia.org.au/themes/people/religion/di splay/23151-charles-kemp.

Unstated. *Convict Records: Bridget Keating*. Convict Records, State Library of Queensland at https://convictrecords.com.au/convicts/keating/bridget/14473 3.

Ibid. *Convict Records: William Johnson*. https://convictrecords.com.au/convicts/johnson/william/9108 3.

Unstated. *Senior Constable John McCabe Monument, Bourke Cemetery*. Memorial. Monument Australia at https://monumentaustralia.org.au/themes/people/crime/disp lay/114191-senior-constable-john-mccabe.

Van Heyden, Peter 'The Pottery Industry in Staffordshire', *The Industrial Revolution in England was not All Bad*, at https://history.pictures/2020/03/18/14-11-the-pottery-industry-in-staffordshire/

Various. *Medical Records Malta Garrison 1799-1979, 80th Regiment 1821-1830*. Royal Army Medical Corps, London at https://www.maltaramc.com/regmltgar/80th.html.

Walsh, G. P. 'Davis, William Walter (1840–1923)'. *Australian Dictionary of Biography*. Canberra: National Centre of Biography, Australian National University at https://adb.anu.edu.au/biography/davis-william-walter-5917/text10079.

White, William. *History, Gazetteer and Directory of Staffordshire*. Sheffield, 1851.

Willetts, Jen. *Convict Ship Canada 1817*. Free Settler or Felon at https://www.freesettlerorfelon.com/convict_ship_canada_18 17.htm.

Ibid. *Convict Ship Earl Grey 1836*. https://www.freesettlerorfelon.com/convict_ship_earl_grey_ 1836.htm.

Ibid. *William Evans Surgeon*. https://www.freesettlerorfelon.com/william_evans_surgeon. html.

End Notes

Chapter 1: James Reed's origins

[1] Baptism entry for James Rhead, born December 1808, baptised 22 Jan 1809. Father: Thos; Mother: Elizh. Anglican Parish of St Mary and All Saints, Trentham, Staffordshire. Staffordshire Baptisms, D4480/1/5, page 130. Digital image. 'Staffordshire Baptisms'. www.findmypast.com.

[2] White, William. *History, Gazetteer and Directory of Staffordshire*. 1834. Google Books at https://www.google.com.au/books/edition/History_Gazetteer_and_Directory_of_Staff/mw9Mgl6AHr8C

[3] G C Baugh, W L Cowie, J C Dickinson, Duggan A P, A K B Evans, R H Evans, Una C Hannam, P Heath, D A Johnson, Hilda Johnstone, Ann J Kettle, J L Kirby, R Mansfield and A Saltman, 'Houses of Augustinian canons: The priory of Trentham', in *A History of the County of Stafford: Volume 3*, ed. M W Greenslade and R B Pugh (London, 1970), 255-260. British History Online at http://www.british-history.ac.uk/vch/staffs/vol3/pp255-260.

[4] Wikipedia, s.v. "John Sutton II," https://en.wikipedia.org/w/index.php?title=John_Sutton_II

[5] Fernyhough, William. *Poems*. James Smith, 1786.

[6] Jewitt, Llewellyn Frederick William. The Wedgwoods: Being a Life of Josiah Wedgwood; with Notices of His Works and Their Productions, Memoirs of the Wedgewood and Other Families, and a History of the Early Potteries of Staffordshire. Virtue Brothers and Company, 1865. Page 357.

[7] Census record for Thomas Rhead, aged 86, 32 Ash Green, Trentham, Staffordshire, England. 1851 England and Wales Census. The National Archives, HO107, enumeration district 7 & 4, schedule 39, folio 631, page 12, line 3. 'UK Census Collection'. *www.ancestry.com.au*.

[8] Baptism entry for Thomas Reade, 27 September 1767. Anglican Parish of St Mary & All Saints, Trentham, Staffordshire. Staffordshire Baptisms, D4480/1/4, page 121. Digital image. 'Staffordshire Baptisms'. *www.findmypast.com*.

⁹ Baptism entry for Thomas Read, baptised 30 August 1765. Father: William, mother: Sarah. Anglican parish of St Mary and All Saints, Whitmore, Staffordshire, England. Christenings and Burials from 1765, p1. Staffordshire Archives, D3332/1/2. Digital image. 'Staffordshire Baptisms'. *www.findmypast.com*.

¹⁰ Marriage entry for William Read and Sarah Martin, married 26 December 1764. Anglican parish of St Peter Ad Vincula, Stoke upon Trent, Staffordshire, England. Marriage Banns Register, number 496, page 103. Staffordshire Archives, D1188/9. Digital image. 'Staffordshire Banns'. *www.findmypast.com*.

¹¹ Baptism entry for Ann Read, baptised 19 July 1767. Anglican parish of St Mary and All Saints, Whitmore, Staffordshire, England. Christenings and Burials from 1765, p2. Staffordshire Archives, D3332/1/2. Digital image. 'Staffordshire Baptisms'. www.findmypast.com.

¹² *Ibid*, baptism, William Reade, 5 May 1771, page 5.

¹³ *Ibid*, burial, William Reade, 7 Apr 1772,   page 7.

¹⁴ *Ibid*, baptism, William Reade, 29 Jun 1773, page 8.

¹⁵ Burial entry for William Read, buried 8 January 1786. Anglican parish of St Lawrence, Chapel Chorlton, Staffordshire, England. Register of Baptisms, Marriages and Burials, 21 May 1715 to 9 May 1813, 1st entry on p39. Staffordshire Archives, D3636/1/2. Digital image. 'Staffordshire Burials'. www.findmypast.com.

¹⁶ Burial entry for Sarah Rhead, buried 17 August 1802. Anglican parish of St Mary & All Saints, Whitmore, Staffordshire, England. Online Transcript. 'National Burial Index For England & Wales'. www.findmypast.com.

¹⁷ Baptism entry for Mary Reed, born 2 May 1790, baptised 15 August 1790. Father: Thomas, Mother: Elizabeth. Anglican parish of Trentham, Staffordshire, England. Parish Register of Baptisms, 1790-1812, p4. Staffordshire Record Office, D4480/1/5. Digital image. 'England Births & Baptisms 1538-1975'. www.findmypast.com.

¹⁸ *Ibid*, Ann Reed, page 12, 25 Dec 1791.

¹⁹ *Ibid*, Elizabeth Reed, page 25, 13 Apr 1794.

²⁰ *Ibid*, William Reed, page 39, 11 Dec 1796.

²¹ *Ibid*, Thomas Reed, page 47, 3 Feb 1799.

²² *Ibid*, John Reed, page 67, 14 Jun 1801.

²³ *Ibid*, Prudence Reed, page 81, 4 Sep 1803.

[24] *Ibid*, Edward Reed, page 100, 7 Feb 1806.

[25] *Ibid*, James Rhead, page 130, 22 Jan 1809.

[26] Burial entry for Elizabeth Read, buried 2 April 1809. Anglican parish of St Lawrence, Chapel Chorlton, Staffordshire, England. Staffordshire Archives, D3636/1/2. Digital image. 'Staffordshire Burials'. www.findmypast.com.

[27] Burial entry for Anne Rhead, buried 7 March 1810. Father: Thos; Mother: Elizh. Anglican parish of St Mary and All Saints, Trentham, Staffordshire, England. Burial register, p80. Staffordshire Archives, D4480/1/6. Digital image. 'Staffordshire Burials'. www.findmypast.com.

[28] Marriage entry for John Grindley and Mary Rhead, married 3 Feb 1823. Bachelor and spinster, both aged "21 years & upwards" and from Keele. Performed by George Styche, curate of Newcastle. Anglican parish of St John the Baptist, Keele, Staffordshire, England. Marriage register, number 58, p20. Staffordshire Archives, D3514/1/7. Digital image. 'Staffordshire Marriages'. www.findmypast.com.

[29] 'Stoke-upon-Trent: Local government, economic history and social life.' Jenkins, JG, ed. *A History of the County of Stafford: Volume 8*. London: Victoria County History, 1963. 194-205. *British History Online*. Web. 29 July 2022. http://www.british-history.ac.uk/vch/staffs/vol8/pp194-205.

[30] Van Heyden, Peter, 'The Pottery Industry in Staffordshire', in *The Industrial Revolution in England was not All Bad*. Web. 29 July 2020. https://history.pictures/2020/03/18/14-11-the-pottery-industry-in-staffordshire/

[31] Plot, Robert, *The natural history of Staffordshire*. Oxford: printed at the theatre, 1686. Web. 29 Jul 2020. http://name.umdl.umich.edu/A55155.0001.001

[32] Digital image of Regimental Register of Service for James Reed, 13 June 1827. 35th Foot Soldiers Depot, Durham, England. UK National Archives, WO 25/373, 61a and 61b. 'UK, Regimental Registers of Service, 1756-1900'. www.ancestry.com.au.

[33] Digital image of Record of Stations for 80th Regiment, 15 January 1821. Staffordshire, England. File 4, image 5. Australian Joint Copy Project. National Library of Australia, [M815]. 'Australia, Records of the 80th Regiment relating to Australia, 1793-1905'. *Trove (www.nla.gov.au)*.

34 Marriage entry for James Reed, bachelor of Monk Wr Mouth and Frances Hazle, spinster of Monk Wr Mouth, married 28 June 1830. Witnesses Margt Ann Wilson and A Robson. Anglican parish of Monkwearmouth, Durham, England. 1824-1837, number 587, page 194. Durham University Library, DDR/EA/PBT/2/182. Digital image. 'Durham Marriages'. *https://www.findmypast.com/*.

Chapter 2: Frances Heazle's origins

35 Baptism entry for Benjamin Heazle, 30 Jun 1791. Benjamin Heazle, of George. St Peter's Church, Ballymodan, Parish Baptisms, 1723-1812. Digital image. National Archives of Ireland, Irish Parish Register Baptisms & Confirmations, Ffolliott Collection. www.findmypast.com.

36 Burial entry for John Heazle, buried 6 Jul 1796. John Heazle of George. St Peter's Church, Ballymodan, Ballymodan Burials 1733-1832. Digital image. National Archives of Ireland, Irish Parish Register Burials & Marriages, Ffolliott Collection. www.findmypast.com.

37 Baptism entry for Frances Heazle, 16 Apr 1796. Father George, Mother Frances. Christchurch, Kilbrogan, Baptisms, 1707-1902. Digital image. National Archives of Ireland, Dublin, Irish Parish Register Baptisms & Confirmations, Ffolliott Collection. www.findmypast.com.

38 *Ballymodan Burials 1733-1832*, Ellen Heazle, 26 Aug 1799. Ellen Heazle of George.

39 *Ballymodan Burials 1733-1832*, George Heazle, 17 Dec 1803. George Heazle of George.

40 *Kilbrogan Baptisms 1707-1902*, Catherine Heazle, 19 Apr 1802. Catherine Heazle, of George and Frances, born Apl 14.

41 *Ballymodan Baptisms 1723-1812*, Mary Heazle, 23 Mar 1807. Mary Heazle, of George.

42 *Ballymodan Baptisms 1723-1812*, Jane Heazle, 3 Feb 1809. Jane Heazle, of George.

43 *Kilbrogan Baptisms, 1707-1902*, twins Rachel and Ellen Heazle, 29 Apr 1811. Twins Rachel and Ellen Heazle, of George and Frances, born Apl 28.

44 Digital image of Regimental Register of Service for Benjamin Heazle. 55th Foot Soldiers Depot, Durham, England. UK National Archives, WO 25/421. 'UK, Regimental Registers of Service, 1756-1900'. *www.ancestry.com.au*.

45 Digital image of Length of Service Pensions, Admission Books for Benjamin Heazle. UK National Archives, WO 117/03, 1832-1839; WO 97/901, 1809-1832. *www.fold3.com*.

46 Death Certificate, Frances Reed, 1895. Registry of Births Deaths and Marriages, NSW, Australia, 1895/4274.

47 Unknown author, *Camp Followers and Family Members*, captured from *www.users.hunterlink.net.au*. on Nov 28 2017 by the Internet Archive Wayback Machine, *www.web.archive.org*.

48 Andrew Bamford, 'Dastardly and Atrocious: Lieutenant Blake, Captain Clune and the recall of the 55th from the Netherlands, 1814', *Journal of the Society for Army Historical Research*, 92 (371), 210-222. *www.jstor.org*

49 Bamford, Andrew. 'The British Army in the Low Countries 1813-14'. *The Waterloo Association*, Napoleon Series, 2013. *www.napoleon-series.org*

50 McCance, H M. 'How the Colours of the 55th Foot Were Saved at Bergen-Op-Zoom, in March, 1814.' *Journal of the Society for Army Historical Research* 7, no. 30 (October 1928): 201–4.

51 Unknown author, *55th Foot Regiment*. Cumbria's Museum of Military Life. *www.cumbriasmuseumofmilitarylife.org*

52 Baptism transcription entry for Eliza Heazle, 1814. Eliza Heazle, 1814, 55th Regiment of Foot. GRO Regimental Birth Indices, 1761-1924, British Armed Forces, REG1, Volume 1088, page 5, line 56. *www.findmypast.com*.

53 Record of Stations 1793-1815, 55th Regiment. Transcribed by The Waterloo Association. *www.napoleon-series.org*.

54 Muster Rolls and Pay Lists, 55th Regiment of Foot 1815-1816. British Army Muster Books and Pay Lists, 1812-1817. UK National Archives, WO 12/06485.

55 Length of Service Pensions, Admission Books for Benjamin Heazle. UK National Archives, WO 117/03, 1832-1839; WO 97/901, 1809-1832. *www.fold3.com*.

56 Digital image of Record of Stations for 80th Regiment, 15 January 1821. Staffordshire, England. File 4, image 5. Australian Joint Copy Project. National Library of Australia, [M815]. 'Australia, Records of the 80th Regiment relating to Australia, 1793-1905'. *Trove (www.nla.gov.au)*

57 Burial entry for Benjamin Heazle, buried 26 Jan 1819. Aged 1, resident of Citadel. Anglican parish of St Andrew, Drypool, Hull, Yorkshire, England. Burial register, p75. East Riding Archives & Local Studies Centre, PE109/67. Digital image. 'Yorkshire Burials'. *www.findmypast.com*.

58 Baptism transcription for Benjamin Heazle, 25 January 1818. Father: Sizer Hazel, mother: Maria. Flowton, Suffolk. FHL Film number 952327. 'England, Select Births and Christenings, 1538-1975'. *www.ancestry.com.au*.

59 Memorial for Benjamin Heazle, died 27 Jun 1875. Appleton City, Missouri, USA. Plot 20, Ward 3, memorial ID 42307959. Digital image. 'Appleton City Cemetery'. *www.findagrave.com*.

60 Digital image of Regimental Diary for 80th Regiment, September 1821. Staffordshire, England. Digest, Volume 2, 1793-1899, File 2. Australian Joint Copy Project. National Library of Australia, [M815]. 'Australia, Records of the 80th Regiment relating to Australia, 1793-1905'. *Trove (www.nla.gov.au)*.

61 Royal Army Medical Corps. *Medical Records Malta Garrison 1799-1979, 80th Regiment 1821-1830*. Royal Army Medical Corps, London. *www.maltaramc.com*.

62 *Ibid*, 20 Oct James Heagle son of Sgt Benjamin Heagle and Elizabeth, born on 24 September 1822.

63 Digital image of Burial Register for James Heazle, 21 June 1824. Military and Civilian Burials, Malta. 1823-1829, p7. Aged 2 y 1m, father a Sergeant, 80th Regiment. UK National Archives, WO 156/111. 'United Kingdom, Military Records of Baptisms, Confirmations, Marriages and Burials, 1813-1957'. www.ancestry.com.

64 *80th Regiment Digest 1793-1899*, citing image 16, the Depot arrived from Sunderland on 22 March 1831.

65 *80th Regiment Digest 1793-1899*, citing image 16, on 30 May 1831 orders were received to march to Stafford.

66 Length of Service Pensions, Admission Books, Benjamin Heazle, discharge 23 Jan 1832.

[67] Digital image of census schedule for Benjamin Heazle, smith, aged 20, born Ireland, March 1841. Liverpool Registration District, Lancashire, England. St Thomas Sub-District, piece 566, book 22, folio 37, page 18. Household of John and Eliza Walsh within a boarding house run by Frances and Margaret Mead in Park Lane. UK National Archives, HO 107/566/22. 'England, Census, 1841'. *www.ancestry.com.*

[68] Thorne, Jill. 'Thorne Family Tree' pedigree chart, citing Benjamin Heazle 1820-1875, https://www.ancestry.com.au/family-tree/person/tree/18383754/person/652454789. *www.ancestry.com.au.*

[69] Digital image of residential valuation for No 2, Boyle Street, Bandon. 22 Nov 1848, George Heazle, lessee, George Bennett lessor, 24' x 186' x 15'6", quality 1B, 44 measures, 2 pounds, 13 shillings, 2 pence. Cork Sheriff's Office, Houses in the Town of Bandon, pages xii, 158, Cloghmacsimon, Carberry East ED, Parish of Ballymodan, Cork, Ireland. National Archives of Ireland, Cork, House Book, OL/5/2458, microfilm MFGS/46/79. *www.findmypast.com.*

[70] Digital image of residential valuation for No 2, Boyle Street, Bandon. 24 Jul 1851, George Heazle, lessee, George Bennett lessor, house and yard, 2 pounds, 15 shillings. Cork Sheriff's Office, Houses in the Town of Bandon, pages xii, 158, Cloghmacsimon, Carberry East ED, Parish of Ballymodan, Cork, Ireland. National Archives of Ireland, Griffiths Valuation 1847-1864, Act 1846 (9 & 10) Victoria. *www.findmypast.com.*

[71] Typescript of burial entry for Fanny Heazle, buried 21 Sep 1865, aged 99. Ballymodan Parish, Cork, Ireland, 1812-1878, p 628. National Archives of Ireland. 'Irish Parish Register Burials, ffolliott Collection'. *www.findmypast.com.*

[72] Township of Ballynadeige, Parish of Lismore & Mocollop, Barony of Coshmore & Coshbride, County of Waterford, *Township of Ballynadeige*, (Ireland: The National Archives), 1848, page 23. Number 3b.

[73] Wikipedia, s.v. "William Cavendish, 6th Duke of Devonshire." https://en.wikipedia.org/wiki/William_Cavendish,_6th_Duke_of_Devonshire

Chapter 3: Married life

74 Marriage entry for James Reed, bachelor of Monk Wr Mouth and Frances Hazle, spinster of Monk Wr Mouth, married 28 June 1830. Witnesses Margt Ann Wilson and A Robson. Anglican parish of Monkwearmouth, Durham, England. 1824-1837, number 587, page 194. Durham University Library, DDR/EA/PBT/2/182. Digital image. 'Durham Marriages'. https://www.findmypast.com/.

75 Surtees, Robert. 'Parish of Monk-Wearmouth'. *The History and Antiquities of the County Palatine of Durham*, Vol. Volume 2, Chester ward. London: Nichols and Son, 1820 at https://www.british-history.ac.uk/antiquities-durham/vol2/pp1-39.

76 Wikipedia, s.v. "Benjamin Kennicott", https://en.wikipedia.org/w/index.php?title=Benjamin_Kennicott

77 Death Certificate, Frances Reed, Registry of Births Deaths and Marriages, NSW, Vol 1895 No 4274.

78 Digital image of 80th Regiment Digest, Vol 1, 1793-1897; Vol 2, 1793-1899. Australian Joint Copy Project, *www.trove.nla.gov.au.*

79 Wikipedia, s.v. "Southsea Castle https://en.wikipedia.org/w/index.php?title=Southsea_Castle

80 Baptism entry for William Reed, baptised 24 April 1831. Parents James and Frances Reed, Southsea Castle, Private. Anglican parish of St Pauls Chapel, St Mary, Portsea, Hampshire, England. 1831, number 320, page 40. Hampshire Archives and Local Studies, Winchester, Bishops' Transcripts, 21M65/F8/211/21. Digital image. 'Hampshire, England, Church of England Baptisms, 1813-1921'. *www.ancestry.com.au.*

81 Smith, Rev Herbert. Correspondence, Containing Some ... Particulars Concerning the Lord's Day, Published for the Purpose of Promoting Well Organized Sabbath Societies throughout England, 1830. https://www.google.com.au/books/edition/Correspondence_containing_some_particula/_TwozpyVNsgC?hl=en&gbpv=0.

82 Backhouse, Tim. 'St. Paul's Church, Southsea'. *History in Portsmouth at* http://historyinportsmouth.co.uk/places/st-pauls.htm.

83 Digital image of 80th Regiment Record of Stations 1793-1905. Australian Joint Copy Project, *www.trove.nla.gov.au.*

84 Marriage entry for John Grindley and Mary Rhead, 3 Feb 1823. England & Wales Marriages, 1538-1988. Keele, Staffordshire, England; Date Range: 1734 - 1852; Film Number: 1040762. *www.ancestry.com.au.*

85 Lola Cormie. Back to Bourke: Court House Death and Marriage Records 1862-1974. John Benjamin Reed, aged 49, 15 Sep 1881.

86 Wikipedia, s.v. "Peterloo Massacre", https://en.wikipedia.org/w/index.php?title=Peterloo_Massacre

87 Baptism entry for James Reed, baptised 5 April 1835. Parents James and Frances Reed, Infantry Barracks, Private in 80th Regt, minister J Robley. Anglican parish of St Philips Church, Salford, Manchester, Lancaster, England. 1835, number 329, page 42. Manchester Libraries, Information and Archives, Archive Roll 955. Digital image. 'Manchester, England, Church of England Births and Baptisms, 1813-1915'. *www.ancestry.com.au.*

88 Wikipedia, s.v. "Earl Grey (1835 ship)," https://en.wikipedia.org/w/index.php?title=Earl_Grey_(1835_ship)

89 Wikipedia, s.v. "Earl Grey tea," https://en.wikipedia.org/w/index.php?title=Earl_Grey_tea

90 Willetts, Jen. 'William Evans Surgeon'. *Free Settler or Felon* at https://www.freesettlerorfelon.com/william_evans_surgeon.html.

91 Ibid. 'Convict Ship Earl Grey 1836'. https://www.freesettlerorfelon.com/convict_ship_earl_grey_1836

92 Evans, William. *Journal of His Majesty's Convict Ship Earl Grey 1836.* Royal Navy Medical Journals 1817-1857. The British Admiralty, 1837.

Chapter 4: Emigration

93 Ship News. (1837, January 3). The Sydney Gazette and New South Wales Advertiser, p. 3.

94 Wikipedia, s.v. "Edmund Burke," https://en.wikipedia.org/w/index.php?title=Edmund_Burke

95 King, Hazel. 'Sir Richard Bourke'. *Australian Dictionary of Biography, 1966.* https://adb.anu.edu.au/biography/bourke-sir-richard-1806.

96 Advertising (1837, February 14). The Australian (Sydney, NSW), p. 2. Retrieved August 9, 2022, from http://nla.gov.au/nla.news-article36853211

97 Gapps, Dr Stephen. *The Sydney Wars.* New South Books, 2018 at https://thesydneywars.com/.

98 Views of Sydney, ca. 1843-1865, watercolours by George Roberts, number 5. Barracks, George Street, Barracks Street Gate, 1845. State Library of NSW at https://collection.sl.nsw.gov.au/record/9AL4avJY/JByB0AQplAvmq

Chapter 5: Duty and discharge

[99] K. J. Cable, 'Fulton, Henry (1761–1840)', *Australian Dictionary of Biography*, National Centre of Biography, Australian National University,1966 at https://adb.anu.edu.au/biography/fulton-henry-2074/text2593

[100] St James church (Sydney, NSW), FHL film number 993952, Sarah Reed, 1 Dec 1839; digital index, *Ancestry* (www.ancestry.com.au : online index 31 January 2022).

[101] *A Venerable Clergyman, The Late Reverend GN Woodd, Half a century of work,* Australian Town and Country Journal (Sydney, NSW) Sat 16 Sep 1893, Page 10 at http://trove.nla.gov.au/newspaper/article/71189218

[102] Turnbull, Lucy. 'The End of Transportation'. NSW State Library, Dictionary of Sydney, 2008 at https://dictionaryofsydney.org/entry/the_end_of_transportation

[103] 1841 census of England, Staffordshire, Trentham, folio 9, page 9, line 14, Thomas Rhead; HO107, Stone district, Trentham sub-District, enumeration district 7 & 4, schedule 39; The National Archives, Kew; FHL microfilm.

[104] 1841 census of England, Staffordshire, Keele, John Grindley household, Class: HO107; Piece: 988; Book: 23; Civil Parish: Keele; County: Staffordshire; Enumeration District: 12; Folio: 5; Page: 3; Line: 23; GSU roll: 474620

[105] 1841 census of England, Staffordshire, Trentham, Edward Rhead household, Class: HO107; Piece: 993; Book: 7; Civil Parish: Trentham; County: Staffordshire; Enumeration District: 2; Folio: 8; Page: 8; Line: 1; GSU roll: 474622

[106] 1841, NSW, Australia: "NSW Census of the year 1841, Alexandria, Sydney," Surry Hills, page 15 line 288, James Reed household; Records NSW, Kingswood.

[107] 1842-3, NSW, Country: "Citizen Roll," City of Sydney, Cook's Ward, number 184. Records NSW, Kingswood.

[108] Anglican churches (Sydney), page 8, St Michael's church, Wollongong, number 113, Eliza Reed, 7 Nov 1841; Sydney Anglican Church Diocesan Archives, Sydney.

[109] Davis, Joseph L. *The Spotless Reputation of the Reverend Matthew Devenish Meares (1800-1878) at Wollongong*. Academia.edu. https://www.academia.edu/39765539/

[110] Advertising (1841, October 14). *The Sydney Herald (NSW: 1831 - 1842)*, p. 1.

[111] Various. 'Sophia Jane'. *Flotilla Australia*. https://www.flotilla-australia.com/iscsnco.htm.

[112] Wikipedia, s.v. "Sophia Jane," https://en.wikipedia.org/w/index.php?title=Sophia_Jane

[113] Organ, Michael K, and Robert Hardy. 'Pioneers of the Illawarra - a History of the Family of Elias Organ in Wollongong, 1839-1869'. *Research Online*, 1984, 131. Pages 22-23.

[114] Reminiscences of Illawarra. (1924, May 9). *Illawarra Mercury (Wollongong, NSW : 1856 - 1950)*, p. 1.

[115] Watercolour, *Wollongong, from the stockade, April 20th, 1840*. National Library of Australia, PIC Drawer 2655 #R4105-Wollongong at http://nla.gov.au/nla.obj-135201895

[116] Piggin, Stuart. *Faith of Steel, a History of the Christian Churches in Illawarra, Australia*. The University of Wollongong, 1984 at https://issuu.com/libuow/docs/faith_of_steel.

[117] Burial Register of St Phillips Church, Sydney, NSW for Sarah Reed, Reel 91, Society of Australian Genealogists, Kent St, Sydney, 14 May 1843.

[118] Normal Institution. (1837, December 15). *The Australian (Sydney, NSW : 1824 - 1848)*, p. 2.

[119] Bathurst. (1838, April 10). The Australian (Sydney, NSW : 1824 - 1848), p. 2.

[120] Advertising (1838, July 31). The Australian (Sydney, NSW : 1824 - 1848), p. 5.

[121] General Order.—No. 211. (1838, September 14). *The Australian (Sydney, NSW: 1824 - 1848)*, p. 2.

[122] Law. (1838, August 3). *The Australian (Sydney, NSW : 1824 - 1848)*, p. 2.

[123] Missions. (1838, October 13). *The Australian (Sydney, NSW : 1824 - 1848)*, p. 2.

[124] Supreme Court—Criminal Side. (1842, January 18). *The Australian (Sydney, NSW : 1824 - 1848)*, p. 2.

[125] Unknown. *Regimental History, 80th Regiment of Foot*. Internet Archive, Wayback Machine. 80th Regiment of Foot, Staffordshire Volunteers, at https://web.archive.org/web/20080116203826/http://users.hunterlink.net.au/~ddchr/Regimental%20History.htm.

[126] Roberts, George, *Views of Sydney, ca. 1843-1865*, watercolours, number 5. Barracks, George Street, Barracks Street Gate, 1845. State Library of NSW at https://collection.sl.nsw.gov.au/record/9AL4avJY/JByB0AQplAvmq

Chapter 6: Turbulent years

[127] Lew, *Lew's Directory for the City of Sydney* (Sydney: Lew, 1844), page 92.

[128] St James church (Sydney, NSW), Baptism, Sarah Ann Reed baptised 26 May 1844, FHL film number 993955, SAG Reel 61; digital index, *Ancestry* (www.ancestry.com.au, 1 February 2022).

[129] Abbott, G. J. 'Kemp, Charles (1813–1864)'. *Australian Dictionary of Biography*. National Centre of Biography, Australian National University, 1967. https://adb.anu.edu.au/biography/kemp-charles-2295.

[130] 'Charles Kemp Monument, St James Church, Sydney'. Archive. *Monument Australia at* https://monumentaustralia.org.au/themes/people/religion/display/23151-charles-kemp.

[131] City of Sydney, *Assessment Book*. City of Sydney Archives. Brisbane Ward, 1845, https://archives.cityofsydney.nsw.gov.au/nodes/view/1842293#idx2575038, page 11, assessment number 283, Jas Reid, Clarence Street, a house of stone and shingles valued at 15 pounds and owned by Thomas Leary, rented weekly.

[132] Police Reports. (1845, November 8). Bell's Life in Sydney and Sporting Reviewer (NSW : 1845 - 1860), p. 2.

[133] 'Cataraqui Shipwreck'. National Museum of Australia at https://www.nma.gov.au/defining-moments/resources/cataraqui-shipwreck.

[134] NSW Police Salary Register, 1846. Ancestry.com. *Records NSW, Australia, Miscellaneous Records, 1787-1976*, page 107 of 669.

[135] Ibid. 1847, page 117 of 669.

[136] St James church (Sydney, NSW), Baptisms, FHL film number 993935, Frances Reid, 2 Jul 1848. Digital index, www.ancestry.com.au.

[137] K. J. Cable. 'Macarthur, George Fairfowl (1825–1890)', *Australian Dictionary of Biography*, National Centre of Biography, Australian National University, 1974 at https://adb.anu.edu.au/biography/macarthur-george-fairfowl-4060/text6467

[138] City of Sydney, *Assessment Book*. City of Sydney Archives, Sydney, Brisbane Ward, 1848, page 4, assessment number 77, James Reed, 68 Clarence Street, a house of brick and shingles valued at 13 pounds and owned by Thomas Whitney.

[139] St James church (Sydney, NSW), Baptisms, George Charles Reed, 13 Oct 1850. Digital index, www.ancestry.com.au.

[140] Paul F Cooper, 'Penny Banks in Colonial NSW: banking that sought to serve'. *Philanthropy and Philanthropists in Australian Colonial History*, June 25, 2018 at https:/colonialgivers.com/2018/06/25/penny- banks- in- colonial-nsw-banking- that- sought- to- serve

[141] War Office, "Length of Service Pensions, Admission Books," Benjn Heazle, 8 Jan 1832, Regimental Register of Pensioners, digital images, Fold3, *Ancestry* (www.fold3.com), WO117, piece 03: 1832-1839; WO97, 1809-1832, piece 901.

[142] 1851 census of England, Staffordshire, Trentham, folio 631, page 12, line 3, Thomas Rhead. HO107, Stone district, Trentham sub-District, enumeration district 7 & 4, schedule 39. The National Archives, Kew. FHL microfilm .

[143] City of Sydney, *Assessment Book*. City of Sydney Archives, Sydney, Assessment Books, Brisbane Ward, 1851, page 31, assessment number 647, James Reeds, Clarence Street, a house of brick and shingles owned by the Trustees of R Wilson.

[144] St Philip's church (Sydney), "Baptism Register," number 3750, page 254, Baptism of Mary Ann Reed, 27 Feb 1853. SAG film 91, Society of Australian Genealogists, SAG library, Sydney.

[145] N. S. Pollard, 'Cowper, William (1778–1858)', Australian Dictionary of Biography, National Centre of Biography, Australian National University, 1966 at https://adb.anu.edu.au/biography/cowper-william-1929/text2301

[146] Death Certificate, Thomas Reed, General Register Office, London, March Quarter, vol 6B, page 30.

[147] St Mary and All Saints (Trentham), Burial Register, Thomas Rhead, 20 Feb 1853. Digital image, www.findmypast.com.

[148] Wikipedia, s.v. "Australian gold rushes." https://en.wikipedia.org/wiki/Australian_gold_rushes

[149] Council Paper. (1854, March 28). *The Sydney Morning Herald (NSW: 1842 - 1954)*, p. 2.

Chapter 7: Inexorable expansion

[150] City of Sydney, *Assessment Book,* City of Sydney Archives at - https://archives.cityofsydney.nsw.gov.au/nodes/view/1842286?key words=&type=all#idx2575383. Brisbane Ward, 1854, page 24, assessment number 491, James Reid, 1 Back of 122 Clarence Street, a house of stone and shingle valued at 22 pounds and owned by Stubbs.

[151] Baptismal Record: Reed, Jane Elizabeth, Vol 1856 Baptism Register of St Philip's church, Sydney, No 409 on page 28, SAG Reel 91, (24 August 1856), Sydney Anglican Parishes, Sydney

[152] Greaves, 'Blackman, James (1792–1868)'.

[153] Wikipedia, s.v. "Windradyne". https://en.wikipedia.org/w/index.php?title=Windradyne

[154] Jervis, 'The Exploration and Settlement of the Western Plains', *Occupation of the Bogan Country.*

[155] McKenzie, *The Vision Splendid,* p.17.

[156] Ibid, p.18.

[157] *England, Births and Christenings, 1538-1975.* Salt Lake City, Utah: FamilySearch, 2013. Baptism of Charles Bend, 12 Sep 1806, Tamworth, Stafford, parents Joseph and Margaret Bend. Ancestry.com.

[158] Bishop's Transcripts, St Oswald Shincliffe, Durham, Durham Baptisms 1773-1869, Durham University Library, DDR/EA/PBT/2/87, Charles Bend, 28 Sep 1806, father John, Private in the Durham Militia, mother Isabella Carr.

[159] Qld Registry of Births Deaths and Marriages, *Index to Qld Deaths,* (Registry of BDM), Eliza Reed, 1924/C/3168.

[160] NSW Registry of Births Deaths and Marriages, *Index to NSW Births and Baptisms,* (Registry of BDM), John Bend, 46/1836 CAG (St Philip's church, Sydney).

[161] NSW Registry of Births Deaths and Marriages, *Index to NSW Births and Baptisms,* (Registry of BDM), Eliza Bend, parents Charles and Eliza, 1459/1839 V1839145944A CG (Norfolk Island); and 1546/1839 V1839145923A CG (Norfolk Island).

[162] Sargent, Clem. 'The British Garrison in Australia 1788-1841: The Mutiny of the 80th Regiment at Norfolk Island'. The Free Library. https://www.thefreelibrary.com/The+British+Garrison+in+Australia +1788-1841%3a+the+mutiny+of+the+80th...-a0137872263.

163 NSW Registry of Births Deaths and Marriages, *Index to NSW Births and Baptisms*, (Registry of BDM), Baptism of George Bend, 1755/1841 V18411755 25 CH (Christ church, Hexham, Newcastle), father Charles, mother Eliza.

164 Deed: Land Grant Register, 25 ac Maroota, Gov Gipps - Charles Bend, 9 Jan 1843, number 76 folio 143, Archives Office of NSW, Land Grant Register.

165 Pasturage Licenses. (1845, November 18). New South Wales Government Gazette (Sydney, NSW : 1832 - 1900), p. 1296.

166 NSW Registry of Births Deaths and Marriages, *Index to NSW Births and Baptisms*, (Registry of BDM), Baptism of Charles Atkins, 1939/1846 V18461939 32A MM (Montefiore, Wellington), father John, mother Elizabeth.

167 NSW Registry of Births Deaths and Marriages, *Index to NSW Deaths and Burials*, (Registry of BDM), Burial of Charles Atkins, infant,758/1848 V1848758 33B MM (Montefiore, Wellington).

168 NSW Registry of Births Deaths and Marriages, *Index to NSW Births and Baptisms*, (Registry of BDM), Baptism of Mary Atkins, 1711/1848 V18481711 33A MM (Montefiore, Wellington), father John, mother Elizabeth.

169 Ibid, Baptism of John Atkins, 2464/1851 V18512464 37A MM (Montefiore, Wellington), father John, mother Elizabeth.

170 Ibid, Baptism of William Atkins, 1203/1853 V18531203 40 MM (Montefiore, Wellington), father John, mother Elizabeth.

171 NSW Registry of Births Deaths and Marriages, *Index to NSW Marriages*, (Registry of BDM), Marriage of James Ried and Eliza Bend, 2075/1856 at Wellington.

172 St John the Baptist church (Wellington), "Marriage Register," page 44, James Ried and Eliza Bend, 5 December 1856; SAG film 342, Society of Australian Genealogists, SAG library, Sydney.

173 "Advertising" *The Sydney Herald (NSW : 1831 - 1842)* 11 December 1839: 4.

174 Advertising (1854, November 25). Bathurst Free Press and Mining Journal (NSW : 1851 - 1904), p. 4. Advertising (1856, August 20). Bathurst Free Press and Mining Journal (NSW : 1851 - 1904), p. 4.

175 McKillop, Bob. Saint Mary MacKillop: a brief overview, Willoughby History Chatters, volume 44, number 1, pages 4-5, February 2018, Willoughby District Historical Society Inc., Chatswood.

[176] NSW Registry of Births Deaths and Marriages, *Index to NSW Marriages*, (Registry of BDM), John Benjamin Reed and Eliza Jane Green, 796/1857, Sydney.

[177] Lola Cormie, *Back to Bourke: Court House Death and Marriage Records 1862-1974*, Eliza Jane Reed, death aged 47, 24 Nov 1879, parents John Green and Jane Hutton, born in London England, 35 years in the colonies.

[178] Marriage entry for John Green and Jane Hutton, married 21 October 1828. Bachelor and spinster, both of this Parish, married by licence by Frederick Hamilton, witnessed by Charles Evans and John Geo Leigh. Church of England parish of St George, Hanover Square, London, England. Marriage Register for 1828, number 819, folio 241. City of Westminster Archives, ATG/PR/7/15. Online image. 'Westminster, London, England, Church of England Marriages and Banns, 1754-1935'. *www.ancestry.com.au.*

[179] Baptism entry for Eliza Jane Green, baptised 14 July 1830. Daughter of John and Jane Green, Great Surry Street, Oilman, baptised by W Blunt. Church of England parish of Christ Church, Southwark, Surrey, England. Baptism Register, number 36, page 5. London Metropolitan Archives, P92/Ctc/010. Online image. 'London, England, Church of England Births and Baptisms, 1813-1923'. *www.ancestry.com.au.*

[180] Census entry for the household of John Green, merchant, aged 55, born in another county, recorded at Bedford Row, St Mary Islington, Finsbury, London, Middlesex. Listed household members: Jane Green, 40, another county; John Green, 15, same county; Samuel Green, 10, same county; Elizabeth Green, 8, same county; Jane Green, 6, same county; Elizabeth Sparrow, 25, female servant, another county; Jane Ayers, 23, female servant, another county. The National Archives, England, HO107, registration district Islington, subdistrict Islington West, piece 665, book 2, folio 12, page 18, schedule 401. Online image. '1841 England, Wales & Scotland Census'. *www.findmypast.com.*

[181] Baptism entry for John Green, born 19 August 1825, baptised 21 September 1825. Father John, Mother Jane. Anglican parish of Old Church, St Pancras, London, England. Family History Library, films numbered 597808, 598162, 598163, 598164. Online transcript. 'Select Births and Christenings, 1538-1975'. *www.ancestry.com.au.*

[182] Baptism entry for Samuel Green, born 17 January 1830, baptised 31 March 1830. Parents John and Jane Green, gentleman of Guildford Street, born 17 Jan 1830, minister Rev Hannan. Anglican parish of Old St Pancras, Camden, London, England. Parish Baptisms 1830, number 469, page 427. London Metropolitan Archives, Church of England Parish Registers, P90/Pan1/016. Online image. 'London, England, Church of England Births and Baptisms, 1813-1923'. *www.ancestry.com.au.*

[183] Baptism entry for Anna Maria Green, born 4 January 1829, baptised 4 February 1829. Father John Green, gentleman, mother Jane, abode Northampton Place, minister Rev J Carver. Anglican parish of St Mary, Islington, London, England. Parish Baptisms 1829, number 450, page 57. London Metropolitan Archives, Church of England Parish Registers, P83/Mry1/1174. Online image. 'London, England, Church of England Births and Baptisms, 1813-1923'. *www.ancestry.com.au.*

[184] Burial entry for Ann Lucy Green, buried 10 May 1831. Aged 3 years, abode Bedford Row, minister Rev. TM Fallow. Anglican parish of St Mary, Islington, London, England. London Metropolitan Archives, Church of England Parish Registers, P83/Mry1/1272. Online image. 'London, England, Church of England Deaths and Burials, 1813-2003'. *www.ancestry.com.au.*

[185] Baptism entry for Elizabeth Hannah Green, born 23 May 1832, baptised 10 August 1832. Father John, gentleman, mother Jane, abode Bedford Row, minister Mark Cooper. Anglican parish of The Holy Trinity, Islington, London. England, Baptism Register, number 225, page 29. London Metropolitan Archives, Church of England Parish Registers, P83/Tri/001. Online image. 'Church of England Births and Baptisms, 1813-1923'. *www.ancestry.com.au.*

[186] Burial entry for Anna Maria Green, buried 27 December 1832. Aged 4, abode Princes Street. Anglican parish of St John the Evangelist, Lambeth, London, England. Burials 1825-1875, number 1129, page 142. London Metropolitan Archives, Church of England Parish Registers, P85/Jna3/089. Online image. 'London, England, Church of England Deaths and Burials, 1813-2003'. *www.ancestry.com.au.*

[187] Burial entry for Elizabeth Green, died 1833, buried 1833. Harriet Street. Anglican parish of St John the Evangelist, Lambeth, Surrey, England. Online transcript. 'www.findmypast.com'. *Greater London Burial Index, South London Burials Index 1545-1905.*

[188] Baptism entry for Jane Green, baptised 14 February 1836. Father John, mother Jane. Anglican parish of St Mary, Lambeth, London, England. London Metropolitan Archives, Church of England Parish Registers, P85/Mry1/359. Online image. 'Church of England Baptisms, 1813-1923'. *www.ancestry.com.au*.

[189] "Family Notices," Death Notice for Jane Green aged 54 years, *Sydney Morning Herald, Sydney*, 5 June 1857, p 1, col 1 and p 4; online image, *www.trove.nla.gov.au*. On the 2nd instant, at 82 Prince St Sydney, Jane, the beloved wife of John Green, daughter of the late Mr John Hutton of Ashford, Kent.

[190] John Sands Ltd, *Sands Directories: Sydney and New South Wales*, www.ancestry.com.au. Original record: W. & F. Pascoe Pty Ltd, Balgowlah, Sands Directories: Sydney and New South Wales, Australia, 1858-1933, 1858-59, Commercial Directory page 132.

[191] City of Sydney, *Assessment Book*, City of Sydney Archives, Gipps Ward, 1861, page 36, assessment number 711, John Reed, 105 Princes Street, a house of stone and slates owned by Robert Watson. *www.archives.cityofsydney.nsw.gov.au*.

[192] NSW Registry of Births Deaths and Marriages, *Index to NSW Births and Baptisms*, (Registry of BDM), William John Reid, 1422/1858 Sydney, father John, mother Eliza J.

[193] Ibid, Frances Eliza Reed, 765/1860, Sydney, father John B, mother Eliza J.

[194] NSW Registry of Births Deaths and Marriages, *Index to NSW Births and Baptisms*, (Registry of BDM), John Reed, 13479/1859, Wellington, father James, mother Eliza.

[195] Ibid, Eliza Reed, 13234/1860, Wellington, father James, mother Eliza.

[196] Ibid, James Reed, 14581/1862 Wellington, father James, mother Eliza.

Chapter 8: Impetus for change

[197] McKenzie, page 18.

[198] Ryan, *Colonial Frontier Massacres in Eastern Australia 1788 to 1930*, Bogan River beyond Mt Harris, Oct 1841. https://c21ch.newcastle.edu.au/colonialmassacres/detail.php?r=587

[199] McCulloch, 'Gipps, Sir George (1791–1847)'.

[200] Jervis, 'The Exploration and Settlement of the Western Plains', *Occupation of the Bogan Country*.

[201] A Brief Aboriginal History, Aboriginal Heritage Office website, https://www.aboriginalheritage.org/history/history/

202 Poulton family entry, *Fitzjames*, Passenger List, 20 Feb 1860; in (Kingswood: Archives Office of NSW), microfilm roll 2480.

203 John Sands Ltd, *Sands Directory*. City of Sydney Archives, Sydney, Sands Suburban and Country Commercial Directory, 1858, page 61, Kent Street, 78 James Reid.

204 City of Sydney, *Assessment Book* at - https://archives.cityofsydney.nsw.gov.au/nodes/view/1842090?key words=&type=all#idx2531271. City of Sydney Archives, Sydney, Gipps Ward, 1861, page 45, assessment number 871, James Reed, 80 Kent, a large house of stone and shingles owned by John Glovett.

205 City of Sydney, *Assessment Book* at - https://archives.cityofsydney.nsw.gov.au/nodes/view/1842221?key words=&type=all#idx2577216. City of Sydney Archives, Sydney, Brisbane Ward, 1858, page 17, assessment number 292, rate book number 11779, James Reid, 165 Clarence Street, a dwelling house of brick and shingle valued at 34 pounds and owned by Joseph Spinks.

206 "Advertisement," Classified Advertisement, *Sydney Morning Herald, Sydney*, 24 November 1858, Notice re board.

207 City of Sydney, *Assessment Book* at - https://archives.cityofsydney.nsw.gov.au/nodes/view/1842090?key words=&type=all#idx2531271. City of Sydney Archives, Sydney, Gipps Ward, 1861, page 45, assessment number 871, James Reed, 80 Kent, a large house of stone and shingles owned by John Glovett.

208 City of Sydney, *Assessment Book* at - https://archives.cityofsydney.nsw.gov.au/nodes/view/1842090?key words=&type=all#idx2531271. City of Sydney Archives, Sydney, Brisbane Ward, 1861, page 16, assessment number 291, rate book number 11990, James Reid, 171 Clarence Street, a house of wood and shingle valued at 45 pounds owned by Mrs Jones.

209 NSW Registry of Births Deaths and Marriages, *Index to NSW Marriages*, (Registry of BDM), 788/1860, Andrew Bufe and Eliza Reed, Sydney.

210 Shipping Intelligence. (1849, September 15). *Adelaide Observer (SA: 1843 - 1904)*, p. 1.

211 Danksagung. (1849, September 13). Die Deutsche Post für die Australischen Colonien = The German Australian Post (Adelaide, SA: 1848 - 1851), p. 59.

212 Manifest, Minnie Ha Ha, 22 May 1860, Andrew Buff, carpenter on arrival at Sydney, crew list, *Ancestry.com*

213 Manifest, Matilda, 18 October 1859, Anders Buff, carpenter on arrival at Sydney, crew list, *Ancestry.com*

214 Advertising, *Sydney Morning Herald*, 26 Aug 1863, page 1.

215 Marriage Certificate, Henry Johnson and Eliza Bufe nee Reed, 12 Sep 1865, Registry of Births Deaths and Marriages, NSW. 18/1865.

Chapter 9: Bourke

216 Cameron, *History of Bourke Journal*, volume 9, page 309.

217 NSW land deed volume 72 folio 206, section 21, lot 5, 1 acre in Anson Street Bourke purchased by Alexander Reed, bullock driver, 25 Nov 1867.

218 Wikipedia, s.v. "Thomas Mitchell (explorer)." https://en.wikipedia.org/wiki/Thomas_Mitchell_(explorer)

219 Cameron, *History of Bourke*, volume 2, page 61.

220 Ibid, page 60.

221 Ibid, page 62.

222 Ibid, page 67.

223 Glover, W. K., *Some early settlers*, History of Bourke Journal, volume 1, page 27.

224 Cameron, *History of Bourke*, volume 2, page 67.

225 Ibid, page 46.

226 Ibid, page 8.

227 Cameron, History of Bourke Journal, volume 6, page 71.

228 Ibid, page 19.

229 1859 'Yesterday's Sydney News.', The Maitland Mercury and Hunter River General Advertiser (NSW: 1843 - 1893), 22 March, p. 2.

230 1859 'South Australia.', *The Sydney Morning Herald (NSW: 1842 - 1954)*, 22 April, p. 5.

231 1859 'Local Intelligence.', The Goulburn Herald and County of Argyle Advertiser (NSW: 1848 - 1859), 30 April, p. 2.

232 The Empire. (1859, December 1). *Empire (Sydney, NSW: 1850-1875)*, p. 4.

233 Inland Mails. (1859, December 22). *The Sydney Morning Herald (NSW: 1842 - 1954)*, p. 6.

234 Pioneers of the West (1928, September 12). *Sydney Mail (NSW: 1912 - 1938)*, p. 53.

[235] Cameron, *History of Bourke Journal,* volume 1, page 28.

[236] Last of the Culgoa Blacks (1911, October 24). *The Farmer and Settler (Sydney, NSW: 1906 - 1955),* p. 5.

[237] Heritage Office (HO) and Department of Urban Affairs and Planning (DUAP). *Regional Histories of New South Wales.* Sydney. Page 193.

[238] Kamien, M. *The Dark People of Bourke: A study of planned social change.* Australian Institute of Aboriginal Studies, Canberra, and Humanities Press Inc, New Jersey. Page 15.

[239] Gould and Richter, *The Mammals of Australia.*

[240] Krefft, Transactions of the Philosophical Society of New South Wales.

[241] Hapalotis Apicalis (White-tipped Hapalotis) Tillikin. (1862, October 24). *The Sydney Morning Herald (NSW: 1842 - 1954),* p. 2.

[242] Various. 'Species: Leporillus Apicalis (Lesser Stick-Nest Rat)'. https://bie.ala.org.au/species/https://biodiversity.org.au/afd/taxa/5a c0db97-0266-442f-86b3-f21c3f98f58a.

Chapter 10: Life on the frontier

[243] Sands Street Index Sydney 1861, 37 Cambridge Steet, The Rocks, James Reed household, 39 Cambridge Street, household of John Reed, waterman, Ancestry.com, https://www.ancestry.com.au/imageviewer/collections/1907/images /rdaus1863_078553__0000_02_g-0016

[244] John Sands Limited, *Sands Street Index, Sydney* at - https://www.ancestry.com.au/discoveryui-content/view/30345:1907. Original record: Sands Directories: Sydney and New South Wales, Australia, 1858–1933. W. & F. Pascoe Pty, Ltd., Balgowlah, Sands Directory, 1861, page 84, William Brennan, 110 Prince's Street, The Rocks.

[245] 1863 'Advertising', *The Sydney Morning Herald (NSW: 1842 - 1954),* 11 February, p. 1.

[246] Cameron, *History of Bourke Journal,* Volume 7, page 30, baptism of William Wright on 27 Nov 1862.

[247] Willrene1086, "Bourke Family Tree," online pedigree chart, (https://www.ancestry.com.au/family-tree/tree/23954802/: online 5 May 2023), Peter Sloey - https://www.ancestry.com.au/family-tree/person/tree/23954802/person/100068670402; citing Aileen Roberson, Families of Molong and District, 1993, page 18.

248 NSW Registry of Births Deaths and Marriages, *Index to NSW Births and Baptisms*, (Registry of BDM), Sarah A Sloey, 9294/1858, mother Mary, Molong.

249 William Wright (bachelor and storekeeper of Kangaroo Bay) and Mary Sloey (spinster resident at Brookeville), Marriage Certificate number 2577/1859 (6 September 1859), Orange, NSW Registry of Births, Deaths and Marriages, Sydney. Peter Sloey gave his consent to the marriage as Mary Sloey was under 21 years.

250 NSW Registry of Births Deaths and Marriages, *Index to NSW Births and Baptisms*, (Registry of BDM), John T Wright, 10151/1860 at Orange, parents William and Mary.

251 "Miscellaneous Information," news article, *NSW Police Gazette, Sydney*, 6 March 1878, Mr Wright was the station manager of Nidgerie who identified the body of a shepherd; page 89.

252 "Legal Notices," notice, *The Daily Telegraph, Sydney*, 31 May 1893, Estate of William Wright, intestate; page 2.

253 "Some small cemeteries", Bill Cameron, *History of Bourke Journal*, Volume 12 (Bourke NSW: Bourke and District Historical Society, 1966-1992), page 51, William Wright, Byrock, 6 Apr 1893 aged 56.

254 Mary Wright nee Sloey, Death Certificate number 12633/1910 (7 November 1910), Brewarrina, NSW Registry of Births, Deaths and Marriages, Sydney. Informant: BJ Rogan, son-in-law. Maiden name Sloey, parent details unknown, married at Wellington to William Wright at age 18, buried at Brewarrina Cemetery 7 Nov 1910.

255 Biographies, Bill Cameron, *History of Bourke Journal*, Volume 10 (Bourke NSW: Bourke and District Historical Society, 1966-1992), page 120, Bob Wright.

256 Coroner, *Register of Coroners' Inquests* at - https://www.ancestry.com.au/discoveryui-content/view/7646:1785. Original record: State Records Authority of New South Wales, Kingswood, Registers of Coroners' Inquests and Magisterial Inquiries, 1834-1942, 1908-1913, series 2764, item X2089, roll 343, page 141, number 1045, William Wright, 28 August 1912.

257 Fort Bourke. (1863, March 31). *Empire (Sydney, NSW: 1850 - 1875)*, p. 8.

258 Ibid.

259 Readford, 'Reminiscences of Early Days'.

260 Foott, 'Of Henrietta, Marooned'.

261 Ibid.

[262] The Modern Crusoe. (1862, March 3). *Empire (Sydney, NSW: 1850 - 1875)*, p. 8.

[263] Fort Bourke. (1862, October 15). Bathurst Free Press and Mining Journal (NSW: 1851 - 1904), p. 3.

[264] Fort Bourke. (1862, December 10). Bathurst Free Press and Mining Journal (NSW: 1851 - 1904), p. 2.

[265] NSW Registry of Births Deaths and Marriages, *Index to NSW Deaths*, (Registry of BDM), 12370/1908 Sydney, aged 66, parents William and Ellen.

[266] NSW Registry of Births Deaths and Marriages, *Index to NSW Births and Baptisms*, (Registry of BDM), 2837/1843 V18432837 133, Catholic, parents William and Ellen.

[267] NSW Registry of Births Deaths and Marriages, *Index to NSW Marriages*, (Registry of BDM), 18/1863 Sydney.

[268] Ibid. 1368/1863 Bourke.

[269] Ibid. 1371/1863 Bourke.

[270] McDonald, 'Age at First Marriage and Proportions Marrying in Australia 1860-1971'. Figure 3.2, p. 40.

[271] Ibid. Table 4.1. p. 62.

[272] Ibid. Table 4.3, p. 73.

[273] Ibid. p. 79.

[274] Randell, 'Voyage up the Darling and Barwon'.

[275] Friday, March 14th (1862, March 19). Bathurst Free Press and Mining Journal (NSW: 1851 - 1904), p. 2.

Chapter 11: Reunited

[276] Cameron, *History of Bourke Journal*, volume 3 page 127.

[277] NSW Registry of Births Deaths and Marriages, *Index to NSW Marriages*, (Registry of BDM), 1368/1863 Bourke.

[278] Cameron, *History of Bourke Journal*. First Marriage registered at Bourke, page 1. Joseph Whye and Prudence Reed, 28 Apr 1863.

[279] Bishop's Transcript, Waterbeach Marriages, William Wey and Hannah Headley, 2 Oct 1821, https://familysearch.org/ark:/61903/3:1:3Q9M-C9TN-T3NJ-5?cc=1465708&c=2KFFW4V%3A1590153757

[280] 1841 census of England, Cambridgeshire, Waterbeach, piece 69, book 14, ED 18, folio 4, page 2, line 24, household of William Whye; HO107; The National Archives of the UK, Kew; FHL microfilm GSU roll 241224.

[281] 1851 census of England, Cambridgeshire, Trumpington, Enumeration district 19, book 14, piece 74, folio 4, page 2, line 13, household of Joseph Headland; HO107; The National Archives of the UK, Kew; FHL microfilm GSU roll 241225.

[282] 1851 census of England, Cambridgeshire, Waterbeach, Enumeration district 14a, piece 1759, folio 315, page 27, household of John Stacey Youngman; HO107; The National Archives of the UK, Kew; FHL microfilm GSU roll 193649-193650.

[283] Manifest, Gilmore, 18 October 1855, Joseph Wye aged 19, passengers, www.ancestry.com.

[284] Nicholson, Log of Logs Volume 1, Gilmore, page 204

[285] "The English Mail per the Champion of the Sea," shipping news article, *Sydney Morning Herald, Sydney*, 19 October 1855, page 4.

[286] Cameron, *History of Bourke Journal*, volume 12, page 88.

[287] Ibid. Volume 8, page 188.

[288] NSW Registry of Births Deaths and Marriages, *Index to NSW Births and Baptisms*, (Registry of BDM), 4985/1864, Bourke, Anna Whye.

[289] Ibid. 5208/1865, Bourke, William Whye.

[290] NSW Registry of Births Deaths and Marriages, *Index to NSW Deaths*, (Registry of BDM), 2449/1865, Bourke, William Whye. Also, the Burial Register for Brewarrina dated 12 Jan 2012, William Whye, infant, 9 July 1865, Nidgerie, https://www.brewarrina.nsw.gov.au/f.ashx/death-register-2011.pdf, page 67.

[291] James Tobin and Frances Reed, 25 Nov 1863, unstated author, *History of Bourke Journal* (Bourke NSW: Bourke and District Historical Society, 1966-1992), First Marriages at Bourke.

[292] Delbridge, 'Saxby/Delbridge Family Tree'.

[293] "Insolvency" Freeman's Journal (Sydney, NSW: 1850 - 1932) 10 October 1863: 5.

[294] NSW Registry of Births Deaths and Marriages, *Index to NSW Marriages*, (Registry of BDM), 590/1840 V1840590 123, Tobin-Maloney.

[295] Convict Permission to Marry, *James Tobin senior to Catherine Maloney*, (Kingswood: NSW Archives), 9 June 1840.

296 James Tobin, *Convict Indent 1830 NSW Dunvegan Castle: James Tobin*, (Kingswood NSW: NSW State Archives), 30 Mar 1830, Dunvegan Castle. State Archives NSW; Series: NRS 12188; Item: [4/4015]; Microfiche: 675.

297 Court Report, Old Bailey, London, case 890 on the second day of the fourth session, 1827, James Tobin, aged 12, guilty, transported for life.

298 "Workhouse Admission and Discharge Records, 1659-1930," admission and discharge register, www.ancestry.com, Castle Street Workhouse Register: Tobin family, 10 Feb 1827, reference number: WEBG/SM/038/001.

299 NSW Registry of Births Deaths and Marriages, *Index to NSW Deaths*, (Registry of BDM), 8665/1901, James Tobin of Bourke, father William.

300 Unstated, 'Archibald Bell'.

301 NSW Registry of Births Deaths and Marriages, *Index to NSW Births and Baptisms*, (Registry of BDM), 2326/1841 V18412623 121A, Amelia Tobin, Maitland, parents James and Catherine.

302 James Tobin junior and Frances Reed, 25 Nov 1863, unstated author, *History of Bourke Journal*, First Marriages at Bourke (Bourke NSW: Bourke and District Historical Society, 1966-1992), page 1.

303 James Tobin and Frances Reed, 25 Nov 1863, unstated author, *History of Bourke Journal* (Bourke NSW: Bourke and District Historical Society, 1966-1992), First Marriages at Bourke. Margaret Tobin was a witness.

304 "Death of Mr Tobin," obituary, *The Cumberland Argus and Fruitgrowers Advocate, Parramatta*, 14 February 1917, page 2. Late of Baulkham Hills and Bourke.

305 NSW Registry of Births Deaths and Marriages, *Index to NSW Births and Baptisms*, (Registry of BDM), 204/1848 V1848204 66, Ambrose Tobin, Maitland, parents James and Catherine.

306 Ibid. 2102/1852 V18522102 69, Edward Tobin, Whittingham, parents James and Catherine.

307 Ibid. 2103/1852 V18522102 69, Henry Tobin, Whittingham, parents James and Catherine.

308 Second Class Conditional Pardon, pages 277-8, 2 March 1846, James Tobin, per Dunvegan Castle 1830.

309 1901 'Local and General.', *Western Herald (Bourke, NSW: 1887 - 1970)*, 31 August, p. 2.

[310] NSW Registry of Births Deaths and Marriages, *Index to NSW Deaths*, (Registry of BDM), 2722/1869, Catherine Tobin, Bourke.

[311] NSW Hospital and Asylum Records, 1840-1913, James Tobin, 15 Aug 1895, Bourke, Ancestry.com.

[312] "Local and General," obituary, *The Western Herald, Bourke*, 31 August 1901, page 2.

[313] Ibid.

[314] NSW Registry of Births Deaths and Marriages, *Index to NSW Births and Baptisms*, (Registry of BDM), 7980/1864 Dubbo, parents James and Frances.

[315] Email from Charles Price to James Michael Fleming, June 2 2020. Copy held by the author.

[316] Bourke. (1863, June 30). *Empire (Sydney, NSW: 1850 - 1875)*, p. 2.

[317] NSW land deeds for section 11, lot 1, 2 roods, Darling Street, Town of Bourke, volume 10 folio 147; volume 612 folio 133; volume 636 folio 59.

[318] First Marriages, Bourke Registry Office, *History of Bourke Journal*, First Marriages (Bourke NSW: Bourke and District Historical Society, 1966-1992), page 2, Charles May and Mahalath Witmarsh, married 6 Jan 1864, witnesses Frances Reed and William Sly.

[319] Telegraphic Intelligence. (1862, October 23). *Empire (Sydney, NSW: 1850 - 1875)*, p. 5.

[320] Floods on the Lower Bogan. (1864, April 19). *The Sydney Morning Herald (NSW: 1842 - 1954)*, p. 8.

[321] Bourke. (1864, April 20). *Empire (Sydney, NSW: 1850 - 1875)*, p. 8.

[322] Death of a Pioneer. (1932, May 20). *Western Herald (Bourke, NSW: 1887 - 1970)*, p. 3.

[323] NSW Registry of Births Deaths and Marriages, *Index to NSW Births and Baptisms*, (Registry of BDM), Sarah E Brennan, parents Michael and Sarah A, 7949/1864, Dubbo.

[324] No. 10. List of Letters Returned from the Country, and now lying at this office unclaimed. (1863, June 5). *New South Wales Government Gazette (Sydney, NSW: 1832 - 1900)*, p. 1291.

[325] Bourke. (1865, October 24). *Empire (Sydney, NSW : 1850 - 1875)*, p. 5.

[326] The Climate on the Darling. (1885, December 31). The Maitland Mercury and Hunter River General Advertiser (NSW: 1843 - 1893), p. 2.

[327] General News. (1864, August 13). The Maitland Mercury and Hunter River General Advertiser (NSW: 1843 - 1893), p. 5.

[328] Unstated, "Convicts," database, Coding Labs, Convict Records (https://convictrecords.com.au: online 7 March 2023), William Johnson arrived 1819, Lord Sidmouth; citing various.

[329] List of convicts disembarked from the "Lord Sidmouth" and forwarded to Parramatta for distribution, 18 March 1819, [4/3500], page 40, reel 6006, index number 99, INX-99-69106, William Johnson. Records NSW.

[330] List of convicts employed by William Lawson from August 1817 to 1820, Colonial Secretary's Papers, 1788-1825, [4/1771], page 313, reel 6058, index number 99, INX-99-71779, Bridget Caton and William Johnson. Records NSW.

[331] Unstated, "Convicts," database, Coding Labs, Convict Records (https://convictrecords.com.au: online 7 March 2023), Bridget Keating arrived 1817, Canada; citing various.

[332] Willetts, Jen. 'Convict Ship Canada 1817'. https://www.freesettlerorfelon.com/convict_ship_canada_1817.htm.

[333] William Johnson and Bridget Caton, Convict PM: 1820 Johnson Caton granted, (Kingswood: NSW Archives), 7 Feb 1820, Rev. Samuel Marsden. Granted.

[334] Marriage Register, St James church, Parramatta, 1790-1966, William Johnson and Bridget Caton on 28 Feb 1820. Ancestry.com.

[335] Re permission to marry at Parramatta, Colonial Secretary's Papers, 1788-1825, James Stinson per Archduke Charles of 1813, 1 February 1819, [4/3499], page 302, reel 6006, index number 99, INX-99-12446. Records NSW.

[336] Registers of Certificate of Freedom, number 151/3379, 17 March 1825, William Johnson, Lord Sidmouth of 1819, Ancestry.com. Butts of Certificates of Freedom, NRS 1165, 1166, 1167, 12208, 12210, reels 601, 602, 604, 982-1027. State Records Authority of New South Wales, Kingswood, New South Wales.

[337] 1828 NSW census, household of William Johnstone, Cambridge Street, Sydney, HO 10/24, Ancestry.com.

[338] 1841 census, NSW, statistical return for Ham Common parish, Windsor district, Cumberland county, household of William Johnson of Richmond. Ancestry.com

[339] NSW Registry of Births Deaths and Marriages, Index to NSW Deaths, (Registry of BDM), 4845/1911, Henry Johnson aged 78 years.

[340] NSW burial record, V18541453 41A, William Johnson aged 56, shoemaker, Parish of Richmond, County of Cumberland.

[341] Early baptisms at St Stephen's Anglican church Bourke, Sarah Jane Hazel Johnson, parents Henry and Eliza, 26 May 1872.

[342] Tuesday, Jan 7,1858. Before Dr. Palmer P.M. (1858, January 9). *Bathurst Free Press and Mining Journal (NSW: 1851 - 1904)*, p. 2.

[343] Wednesday, June 23. (1858, June 26). Bathurst Free Press and Mining Journal (NSW: 1851 - 1904), p. 2.

[344] NSW Registry of Births Deaths and Marriages, *Index to NSW Marriages*, (Registry of BDM), Henry Johnson and Eliza Bufe, 1466/1865.

[345] NSW Registry of Births Deaths and Marriages, *Index to NSW Births*, (Registry of BDM), Frances E Johnson, parents Henry and Eliza, 5179/1866, Bourke.

[346] Ibid. James H Johnson, parents Henry and Eliza,5643/1868, Bourke.

[347] Ibid. Alexander G O Johnson, parents Henry and Eliza,7359/1870, Bourke.

[348] Ibid. Sarah J H Johnson, parents Henry and Eliza, 7867/1871, Bourke. Also, Early baptisms at St Stephen's Anglican church Bourke: 1870-1900 extracted from Reel 335, Society of Australian Genealogists. Sarah Jane Hazel Johnson, 26 May 1872, page 2.

[349] Brewarrina. (1871, October 21). *Empire (Sydney, NSW: 1850 - 1875)*, p. 3.

[350] Criminal Depositions (Deposition Books) Index 1849-1949, series NRS 849, item number 4, page 9, reel 2760, entry numbers 3224 and 3225, Henry Johnson, Brewarrina, 30 Sep 1871. Records NSW https://search.records.nsw.gov.au/permalink/f/1ebnd1l/INDEX1593 124 and https://search.records.nsw.gov.au/permalink/f/1ebnd1l/INDEX1593 123

[351] Bourke. (1871, November 27). *Evening News (Sydney, NSW: 1869 - 1931)*, p. 4.

[352] Return of Prisoners Discharged Free since last publication. (1874, May 20). *New South Wales Police Gazette and Weekly Record of Crime (Sydney :1860 - 1930)*, Henry Johnson, Darlinghurst, p. 145.

[353] NSW Registry of Births Deaths and Marriages, *Index to NSW Births and Baptisms*, (Registry of BDM), John Benjamin Linley Johnson, 7903/1873, parents Henry and Eliza, Bourke.

[354] Bourke. (1865, October 24). *Empire (Sydney, NSW: 1850 - 1875)*, p. 5.

[355] NSW Registry of Births Deaths and Marriages, *Index to NSW Births and Baptisms*, (Registry of BDM), Frances E Brennan, 5217/1865, Bourke, parents Michael and Sarah A.

[356] Ibid. Emeline Brenan, parents Michael and Sarah A, 5670/1867, Bourke.

Chapter 12: Work, save, invest

[357] Death of a Pioneer. (1932, May 20). *Western Herald (Bourke, NSW: 1887 - 1970)*, p. 3.

[358] NSW land deeds for section 11, lots 3,4 and 5 of 2 roods each, Darling Street, Town of Bourke, volume 38 folios 27, 28 and 29;   volume 260 folios 197 and 245;   volume 342 folio 211.

[359] Bourke. (1865, February 16). The Maitland Mercury and Hunter River General Advertiser (NSW: 1843 - 1893), p. 3.

[360] "Timber Licenses," public notice, *NSW Government Gazette, Sydney*, 14 August 1865, page 1772.

[361] "Timber Licenses," notice, *NSW Government Gazette, Sydney*, 8 February 1866, James Reed, Warrego, hardwood; page 418.

[362] "Timber Licenses," notice, *NSW Government Gazette, Sydney*, 23 July 1867, James Reed, Bourke, hardwood, one pound.

[363] "Timber Licenses," notice, *NSW Government Gazette, Sydney*, 3 July 1868.

[364] "Timber Licenses," notice, *NSW Government Gazette, Sydney*, 30 September 1869, Jas Reid, Hardwood, Warrego, 5 shillings.

[365] "Timber Licenses," notice, *NSW Government Gazette, Sydney*, 22 December 1871, J Ried, hardwood, Warrego, 5 shillings.

[366] "Timber Licenses," notice, *NSW Government Gazette, Sydney*, 23 December 1874, J Reed, hardwood, Warrego, 5 shillings.

[367] "Timber Licenses," notice, *NSW Government Gazette, Sydney*, 3 July 1868.

[368] Timber Licenses, &c. (1866, October 1). New South Wales Government Gazette (Sydney, NSW: 1832 - 1900), p. 2329.

[369] "Timber Licenses," public notice, *NSW Government Gazette, Sydney*, 14 August 1865, page 1772.

370 "Timber Licenses," public notice, *NSW Government Gazette, Sydney,* 14 August 1865, page 1772 - Michael Brennan 1865. Timber Licenses, &c. (1866, October 1). *New South Wales Government Gazette (Sydney, NSW: 1832 - 1900),* p. 2323 - Alexander Reed. "Timber Licenses," notice, *NSW Government Gazette, Sydney,* 3 July 1868 - James Reed junior.

371 District News. (1865, November 11). The Maitland Mercury and Hunter River General Advertiser (NSW: 1843 - 1893), p. 3.

372 Bourke. (1866, October 10). *Empire (Sydney, NSW: 1850 - 1875),* p. 2.

373 Cameron, *History of Bourke Journal.* Volume 9, page 79.

374 Bourke. (1869, April 22). The Maitland Mercury and Hunter River General Advertiser (NSW: 1843 - 1893), p. 1.

375 The Climate on the Darling. (1885, December 31). The Maitland Mercury and Hunter River General Advertiser (NSW: 1843 - 1893), p. 2.

376 "Bourke," news article, *Maitland Mercury, Maitland,* 16 January 1868.

377 The Diseases, Medicine in Bourke 1900 compared to 1963, Dr RE Coolican, History of Bourke journal volume 1, page 128.

378 Bourke. (1867, November 26). The Maitland Mercury and Hunter River General Advertiser (NSW: 1843 - 1893), p. 3.

379 Land deeds, Bourke NSW. Section 18, lot 5, 1 acre, Anson Street, volume 72 folio 204. Section 18, lot 6, 1 acre, corner of Anson Street and the billabong, volume 72 folio 205. Section 21, lot 5, 1 acre, Anson Street, volume 72 folio 206. Section 21, lot 6, 1 acre, corner Anson and Richard Streets,   volume 72 folio 207.

380 "Horses and Cattle," public notice, *NSW Police Gazette, Sydney,* 20 May 1868, page 157.

381 Land purchase 29 Jun 1868, section 4, lot 5, 2 roods, North Bourke, Vol 82 Fol 20.

382 Baptism Register, St Stephen's Anglican church Bourke, Society of Australian Genealogists Reel 335: 1870-1900, Victoria Prudence Brennan, parents Michael and Sarah Ann, painter, 6 Feb 1871.

383 Bourke. (1867, November 14). The Maitland Mercury and Hunter River General Advertiser (NSW : 1843 - 1893), p. 4.

384 Bourke. (1868, October 20). The Maitland Mercury and Hunter River General Advertiser (NSW: 1843 - 1893), p. 3.

385 NSW Registry of Births Deaths and Marriages, *Index to NSW Births and Baptisms,* (Registry of BDM), Isabella MM Brennan, parents Michael and Sarah A, 6186/1869, Bourke.

386 *Women of the West - Maude Brennan*, Bill Cameron, biography, History of Bourke journal, volume 13, page 47.

387 Ibid.

388 Baptism Register, St Stephen's Anglican church Bourke, Society of Australian Genealogists Reel 335: 1870-1900, Victoria Prudence Brennan, parents Michael and Sarah Ann, painter, 6 Feb 1871.

389 NSW Registry of Births Deaths and Marriages, *Index to NSW Births and Baptisms*, (Registry of BDM), William J Brennan, parents Michael and Sarah A, 7580/1872 Bourke.

390 NSW Land Deeds, Vol 82 Fol 20, section 4, lot 5, 2 roods, North Bourke.

391 NSW land deed number 776 in book 106, lots 5 and 6 in section 1, Town of Bourke, 2 January 1868.

392 NSW land deed volume 64 folio 144, lots 5 and 6 in section 1, Town of Bourke, 27 April 1868.

393 1868 'Bourke.', The Maitland Mercury and Hunter River General Advertiser (NSW: 1843 - 1893), 30 July, p. 4.

Chapter 13: The Lame Horse and the Mountain Home

394 NSW Registry of Births Deaths and Marriages, *Index to NSW Deaths*, (Registry of BDM), 2449/1865 Bourke, William Whye.

395 NSW Registry of Births Deaths and Marriages, *Index to NSW Births and Baptisms*, (Registry of BDM), 5185/1866 Bourke, Female Whye. Death Certificate, Prudence Murphy, Registry of Births Deaths and Marriages, NSW, Vol 1940 No 526.

396 Joseph Whye, 17 Sep 1866 Publican's License, NSW, Gongolgon, State Records of NSW, Lame Horse hotel at Gongolgon.

397 Cameron, Bourke Pictorial History Volume 1, page 8.

398 Bourke. (1867, August 8). The Maitland Mercury and Hunter River General Advertiser (NSW: 1843 - 1893), p. 4.

399 A Tour to the North-Western Interior. (1874, October 17). *Australian Town and Country Journal (Sydney, NSW: 1870 - 1919)*, p. 22.

400 "Notes of a journey from Sydney to Bourke." *Empire (Sydney, NSW: 1850 - 1875)* 3 October 1866: 8.

401 Cameron, *History of Bourke Journal*. Volume 3, page 122.

402 No. XVII. An Act to authorize the Sale of certain Improved Lands. [Assented to, 23rd December, 1867.] (1867, December 27). *New South Wales Government Gazette (Sydney, NSW: 1832 - 1900)*, p. 3634.

403 Land Deeds, NSW Land Titles Office, vol 92 fol 215-217, lot 4 in section 33 and lots 4 & 5 section 3, Gongolgon.

404 NSW Registry of Births Deaths and Marriages, *Index to NSW Births and Baptisms*, (Registry of BDM), 5637/1868 Bourke, Frederick Whye. NSW Registry of Births Deaths and Marriages, *Index to NSW Deaths*, (Registry of BDM), 2802/1868 Bourke, Frederick Whye.

405 NSW Registry of Births Deaths and Marriages, *Index to NSW Births and Baptisms*, (Registry of BDM), 6170/1869 Bourke, Emily M M Whye, parents Prudence and Joseph

406 Ibid. 7824/1871 Bourke, Albert G H, parents Prudence and Joseph. Baptism Register, St Stephen's Anglican church Bourke, Society of Australian Genealogists Reel 335: 1870-1900, Albert George Henry Whye, 23 April 1871.

407 Early baptisms at St Stephen's Anglican church Bourke: 1870-1900, Albert George Henry Whye, 23 April 1871.

408 Land Deeds, NSW Land Titles Office, vol 85 fol 170-174, lots 4, 5 & 6 section 2 and lots 1 and 2 in section 10, Gongolgon.

409 Gongolgon Lot 1 sec 33, vol 85 fol 155, 10 November 1868; Purchase, Land Deeds; NSW Land Titles Office, Sydney.

410 Section 2, lots 1 and 3, Gongolgon, volume 85, folios 167 and 168, 10 November 1868; Purchase, Land Deeds; NSW Land Titles Office, Sydney.

411 "Bourke", Maitland Mercury, 16 December 1868, quoted in the History of Bourke journal, volume 9, page 193.

412 Unstated. 'Senior Constable John McCabe'. Memorial. Monument Australia. https://monumentaustralia.org.au/themes/people/crime/display/114191-senior-constable-john-mccabe.

413 Smith, Jane. 'Captain Starlight'. Captain Starlight website. https://www.starlightjanesmith.com/.

414 Smith, Jane. 'Charley Rutherford'. Captain Starlight website. https://www.starlightjanesmith.com/.

415 Bourke. (1869, February 11). The Maitland Mercury and Hunter River General Advertiser (NSW: 1843 - 1893), p. 1.

416 Cameron, *History of Bourke Journal*. Volume 4, page 62.

417 Government Gazette Notices (1870, March 15). New South Wales Government Gazette (Sydney, NSW: 1832 - 1900), p. 624.

418 Government Gazette Notices (1871, March 3). *New South Wales Government Gazette (Sydney, NSW: 1832 - 1900)*, p. 496.

[419] Timber Licenses. (1870, January 11). *New South Wales Government Gazette (Sydney, NSW: 1832 - 1900)*, p. 36.

[420] Timber Licenses. (1871, October 20). *New South Wales Government Gazette (Sydney, NSW: 1832 - 1900)*, p. 2398.

[421] Land Deeds, NSW Land Titles Office, vol 92 fol 215-217, lot 4 in section 33 and lots 4 & 5 section 3, Gongolgon.

[422] Ibid. Volume 135, folio 78, portion 2, Gongolgon.

[423] Wikipedia, s.v. "Fred Lowry". https://en.wikipedia.org/w/index.php?title=Fred_Lowry

[424] Exciting chase after and capture of bushrangers. (1871, June 29). *The Maitland Mercury and Hunter River General Advertiser (NSW: 1843 - 1893)*, p. 4.

[425] Land deeds, Cowper County NSW, unnamed Parish (later named Booda). Portions 8/1 and 8/2, 40 acres each, volume 103 folio 240.

[426] Pise or Clay Buildings. (1871, November 11). Australian Town and Country Journal (Sydney, NSW: 1870 - 1919), p. 13.

[427] Government Gazette Notices (1873, February 26). *New South Wales Police Gazette and Weekly Record of Crime (Sydney: 1860 - 1930)*, p. 64.

[428] Miscellaneous Information. (1873, January 8). New South Wales Police Gazette and Weekly Record of Crime (Sydney: 1860 - 1930), p.15.

[429] Miscellaneous Information. (1878, June 26). *New South Wales Police Gazette and Weekly Record of Crime (Sydney: 1860 - 1930)*, p. 235.

Chapter 14: Jimmy, Alexander and Jane

[430] NSW Registry of Births Deaths and Marriages, *Index to NSW Births and Baptisms*, (Registry of BDM), Charles A Reid, Bourke, 1865/5197, parents James and Eliza.

[431] Ibid. George Reed, parents James and Eliza, 5195/1866, Bourke.

[432] Wikipedia, s.v. "Springsure", https://en.wikipedia.org/w/index.php?title=Springsure

[433] The Wills' Tragedy. (1861, November 16). *The Sydney Morning Herald (NSW: 1842 - 1954)*, p. 7.

[434] Wikipedia, s.v. "Cullin-la-ringo massacre", https://en.wikipedia.org/w/index.php?title=Cullin-la-ringo_massacre

435 The Sydney Morning Herald. (1861, December 11). *The Sydney Morning Herald (NSW: 1842 - 1954)*, p. 5.

436 Wikipedia, s.v. "Tom Wills", https://en.wikipedia.org/w/index.php?title=Tom_Wills

437 Wikipedia, s.v. "Australian Aboriginal cricket team in England in 1868", https://en.wikipedia.org/w/index.php?title=Australian_Aboriginal_cricket_team_in_England_in_1868

438 Qld Registry of Births Deaths and Marriages, *Index to Qld Births*, (Registry of BDM), Henry Reed, born 16/1/1869, mother Eliza Bend, 2766/1869, page 12376.

439 Ibid. Frank Edward Reed born 5 Jul 1871, parents James Reed and Eliza bend, 2917/1871, page 12375.

440 Ibid. Frances Reed born 4 Feb 1874, parents James Reed and Eliza Bend, 2600/1874, page 12375.

441 Ibid. Thomas Reed born 21 May 1876, parents James Reed and Eliza Bend, 59/1876, page 12380.

442 Ibid. Mary Jane Reed born 6 Jul 1878, parents James Reed and Eliza Bend, 90/1878, page 12379.

443 Qld Registry of Births Deaths and Marriages, *Index to Qld Marriages*, (Registry of BDM), George Horsfield and Eliza Reed, 1878/C/756, 8 April 1878.

444 Rose Maree Thomasson, "Thomasson Family Tree," online pedigree chart, *Ancestry* (https://www.ancestry.com.au/family-tree/tree/22762359:), https://www.ancestry.com.au/family-tree/person/tree/22762359/person/29340548340

445 Ibid.

446 Alexander Reed and Mary Eckel, (5 December 1877), Certificate of Marriage: 1877/C/848; Queensland BDM, Brisbane.

447 Qld Registry of Births Deaths and Marriages, *Index to Qld Births*, (Registry of BDM), Mary Ann Eckel, parents Christina Tomb and Henry Eckel, 25 Apr 1860, 1860/C/76.

448 Qld Registry of Births Deaths and Marriages, *Index to Qld Marriages*, (Registry of BDM), Henry Eckel and Christina Erskine, 4 Jun 1859, 1859/C/26.

449 Qld Registry of Births Deaths and Marriages, *Index to Qld Births*, (Registry of BDM), 5266/1879, page 12378.

450 Ibid. 125/1881.

451 NSW Land Deed, Volume 72, folio 206, Section 21, Lot 5, 1 acre, Anson St Bourke.

452 Qld Registry of Births Deaths and Marriages, *Index to Qld Births*, (Registry of BDM), 138/1883.

453 Ibid. 1524/1886, page 12377.

454 Government of Queensland, "Selections," register of selection under the Queensland crown lands act 1884, 1 August 1887, ITM24016, Land records; Queensland Archives Repository, Brisbane. Selection 23, Springsure, Alexander Reed, 1887, microfilm number Z5422, page 41, 30 Sep 1889.

455 Qld Registry of Births Deaths and Marriages, *Index to Qld Births*, (Registry of BDM), 10446/1887, page 12376.

456 Ibid. 208/1890, page 21748.

457 Ibid. 258/1891, page 21740.

458 NSW Registry of Births Deaths and Marriages, *Index to NSW Marriages*, (Registry of BDM), Joseph Maxwell and Jane Elizabeth Reed, Bourke, 1806/1871.

459 NSW Registry of Births Deaths and Marriages, *Index to NSW Births and Baptisms*, (Registry of BDM), Alexander Maxwell, parents Joseph and Jane Elizabeth, Bourke, 7581/1872.

460 NSW land deed volume 137 folio 23, 2 roods, section 8 lot 3, Oxley Street, Bourke

461 NSW land deed Vol 6629 Fol 54, 22.75 perches, part of lot 3, section 8, Oxley Street, Bourke

462 NSW Registry of Births Deaths and Marriages, *Index to NSW Births and Baptisms*, (Registry of BDM), Joseph Maxwell, parents Richard and Ann, church code MM, CofE Montefiores, Wellington, 2941/1846 V18462941 31A.

463 Barnett, 'Harvey Barnett Memoirs'. Pages 8-12.

464 NSW Registry of Births Deaths and Marriages, *Index to NSW Births and Baptisms*, (Registry of BDM), Catherine Maxwell, parents Richard and Ann, church code MI, CofE Gundaroo, Gunning, Yass, 2183/1844 V18442183 28.

465 Ibid, Joseph Maxwell, parents Richard and Ann, church code MM, C of E Montefiores, Wellington, 2941/1846 V18462941 31A.

466 Ibid. Jane Maxwell, parents Richard and Ann, church code MM, C of E Montefiores, Wellington, 1702/1848 V18481702 33A.

467 Ibid. James Maxwell, parents Richard and Ann, church code MM, CofE Montefiore near Wellington, 2431/1850 V18502431 37A.

468 Ibid. Margaret H Maxwell, parents Richard and Ann, church code PU, Presbyterian, Carcoar, 1108/1852 V18521108 52.

[469] Bourke. (1863, June 11). The Maitland Mercury and Hunter River General Advertiser (NSW : 1843 - 1893), p. 3.

[470] Barnett, 'Harvey Barnett Memoirs'.

[471] Obituary. (1929, February 13). *Western Herald (Bourke, NSW: 1887 - 1970)*, p. 3.

[472] *Baldy Thompson*, Henry Lawson, Complete Works, A Camp-fire Yarn, compiled and edited by Leonard Cronin, Lansdowne Press, Sydney, 1984. Page 400.

[473] Barnett, 'Harvey Barnett Memoirs'. *History of Bourke Journal*. Volume 5, page 23.

[474] Walsh, 'Davis, William Walter (1840–1923)'.

[475] Bourke. (1871, October 28). *Australian Town and Country Journal (Sydney, NSW: 1870 - 1919)*, p. 16.

[476] Census figures for Bourke, 1871, History of Bourke journal, volume 7, page 61.

[477] NSW Registry of Births Deaths and Marriages, *Index to NSW Deaths*, (Registry of BDM), Alexander Maxwell, parents Joseph and Jane E, Bourke, 3393/1872.

[478] NSW Registry of Births Deaths and Marriages, *Index to NSW Births and Baptisms*, (Registry of BDM), Richard James O Maxwell, parents Joseph and Jane Elizabeth, Bourke, 7880/1873.

[479] Obituary. (1929, February 13). *Western Herald (Bourke, NSW: 1887 - 1970)*, p. 3.

[480] New Journal. (1872, January 10). Bathurst Free Press and Mining Journal (NSW : 1851 - 1904), p. 2.

[481] "History", The Western Herald, online, https://www.thewesternherald.com.au/history

[482] A Tour to the North-West. (1872, June 8). Australian Town and Country Journal (Sydney, NSW: 1870 - 1919), p. 24.

Chapter 15: The mining boom

[483] Baptism of George Samson Gibb on 8 Apr 1840 at Auchinleck, Ayrshire, Scotland. Parents Alexander Boswell Gibb and Janet Samson of Blackston. Page 140, OPR 577/2, 1820-1854, item 4, Scotland, Parish Births and Baptisms 1564-1929, www.findmypast.com. Also, NSW Registry of Births Deaths and Marriages, *Index to NSW Deaths*, (Registry of BDM), George S Gibb, parents Alexander B and Janet, 5200/1875 Bourke. Also, Cameron, *History of Bourke Journal*. Volume 11, page 117.

[484] 1851, Scotland, Country: "Scotland Census of the year 1851," Auchinleck, Ayrshire, 577/4/11, Household of Gibb, Alexander, aged 47; National Records of Scotland, Edinburgh.

[485] McIntyre, 'Boswell'.

[486] Boswell Collection. General Collection, Beinecke Rare Book and Manuscript Library. https://archives.yale.edu/repositories/11/archival_objects/291592.

[487] 1861, Scotland, Country: "Scotland Census of the year 1861," Galston, 593/5/3, household of William Lennox, a farmer of 62 acres; National Records of Scotland, Edinburgh.

[488] Wikipedia, s.v. "Auchinleck House", https://en.wikipedia.org/w/index.php?title=Auchinleck_House

[489] Death Certificate, Alexander Boswell Gibb, Victoria, 8527/1872. Father Andrew, mother Agnes.

[490] 1862 'Eastern Police Court.', *The Star (Ballarat, Vic. : 1855 - 1864)*, 7 October, p. 1. (Supplement to the Star). Also, General Sessions. (1862, December 18). *The Star (Ballarat, Vic. : 1855 - 1864)*, p. 4.

[491] Public Record Office of Victoria, Inward Overseas Passenger Lists, Olympia, 1859, https://prov.vic.gov.au/archive/3B109F91-F96C-11E9-AE98-93E32FF6E163?image=70

[492] Wikipedia, s.v. "Cobar", https://en.wikipedia.org/w/index.php?title=Cobar

[493] McQueen, 'Hidden Copper'. Page 21

[494] Ransley, Robyn. 'Cobar Copper and Mining Heritage'. Tourism website. Geological sites of NSW. http://www.geomaps.com.au/scripts/cobarcopper.php.

[495] Stele Monument, Cobar. Monument Australia. https://monumentaustralia.org.au/themes/technology/industry/display/20806-stele-monument

[496] Notes from Fort Bourke. (1871, November 30). *The Herald (Melbourne, Vic.: 1861 - 1954)*, p. 3.

[497] Advertising (1872, July 22). The Sydney Morning Herald (NSW: 1842 - 1954), p. 7.

[498] Mining Intelligence. (1872, January 19). *Empire (Sydney, NSW: 1850 - 1875)*, p. 4.

[499] McQueen, 'Hidden Copper'. Page 22

[500] Cameron, *History of Bourke Journal*. Volume 4, page 146.

501 Bourke. (1872, May 4). Australian Town and Country Journal (Sydney, NSW: 1870 - 1919), p. 7.

502 No title (1872, June 26). *Empire (Sydney, NSW: 1850 - 1875)*, p. 2.

503 A Visit to the Cobar Copper Mine. (1872, July 6). *Australian Town and Country Journal (Sydney, NSW: 1870 - 1919)*, p. 15.

504 Pastoral Notes. (1873, August 23). Wagga Wagga Express and Murrumbidgee District Advertiser (NSW: 1858 - 1859; 1866; 1872 - 1875), p. 2.

505 Barnett, 'Harvey Barnett Memoirs'. *History of Bourke Journal*. Volume 5, page 23.

506 Advertising (1875, January 5). *Empire (Sydney, NSW: 1850 - 1875)*, p. 1.

507 McQueen, 'Hidden Copper'. Page 25

508 "The Bourke Hotel," advertisement, *The Central Australian and Bourke Telegraph, Bourke*, 2 August 1875; print, *National Library of Australia* (transcribed by JM Fleming in 1991).

509 Government Gazette Notices (1875, September 9). *New South Wales Government Gazette (Sydney, NSW: 1832 - 1900)*, p. 2763.

510 Baptism Register, St Stephen's Anglican church Bourke, SAG Reel 335: 1870-1900, Alexander James Boswell Gibb and Mary Jane Hazel Brennan, 1 Jun 1875.

511 Bourke. (1875, July 22). The Maitland Mercury and Hunter River General Advertiser (NSW: 1843 - 1893), p. 3.

512 NSW Registry of Births Deaths and Marriages, *Index to NSW Deaths*, (Registry of BDM), George S Gibb, parents Alexander B and Janet, 5200/1875 Bourke.

513 Bourke. December 12. (1876, January 3). *Evening News (Sydney, NSW: 1869 - 1931)*, p. 3.

514 Government Gazette Notices (1885, June 12). *New South Wales Government Gazette (Sydney, NSW: 1832 - 1900)*, p. 3707.

515 Supreme Court of NSW, "Probate," file, 13 February 1877, [17/1812], series 3, 1031, NRS 13660-3; State Records of NSW, Kingswood. George Samson Gibb, died intestate 12 Dec 1875, granted to Mary Ann Gibb, widow.

516 Government Gazette Notices (1876, September 13). *New South Wales Government Gazette (Sydney, NSW: 1832 - 1900)*, p. 3645.

517 Baptism Register, St Stephen's Anglican church Bourke, SAG Reel 335: 1870-1900, Hazel May Gibb, 5 Oct 1879.

518 Government Gazette Notices (1882, September 13). *New South Wales Government Gazette (Sydney, NSW: 1832 - 1900)*, p. 4735.

Chapter 16: The Bourke and the Overland

519 Sale of lots 5 and 6 in section 18, 2 acres in Anson Street Bourke, 10 Sep 1873, George Reed to James Moloney (Customs Officer), NSW land deed volume 72 folios 204 and 205.

520 "Bourke," news, *Australian Town and Country Journal, Sydney*, 27 September 1873, Mr G Reed opened the Bourke Hotel, page 7.

521 The Treasury, *Lists of Licenses Issued*, www.ancestry.com.au. Original record: State Records Authority of New South Wales, Kingswood, Certificates for Publicans' Licenses, 1830-1849, 1853-1899, 1873, Printed lists of licenses issued, 1866-82, 1895-1900, 1907-10, NRS 14411, reel 1243, page 2245, Treasury Notice, 14 Oct 1873.

522 Bill Cameron, "Jolly Waggoners Hotel", History of Bourke Journal, volume 4, page 60.

523 Government Gazette Notices (1881, September 13). *New South Wales Government Gazette (Sydney, NSW: 1832 - 1900)*, p. 4697.

524 Government Gazette Notices (1875, September 9). *New South Wales Government Gazette (Sydney, NSW: 1832 - 1900)*, p. 2763.

525 Government Gazette Notices (1869, August 24). *New South Wales Government Gazette (Sydney, NSW: 1832 - 1900)*, p. 2133.

526 Bourke. (1875, March 13). The Maitland Mercury and Hunter River General Advertiser (NSW: 1843 - 1893), p. 8.

527 NSW land deed, lot 2, section 11, Darling Street, Town of Bourke, volume 223, folio 81, transfer from JE Kelly to GC Reed on 19 June 1875.

528 "Apprehensions," public notice, *NSW Police Gazette, Sydney*, 10 March 1875, page 72.

529 "Return of Prisoners tried at different Circuit Courts and Courts of Quarter Sessions," notice, *NSW Police Gazette, Sydney*, 27 May 1875, Henry Hackley, 4 months for stealing George Reed's horse; Thomas Collins 12 months for larceny from Joseph Lunn; page 156.

530 The Treasury, *Return of Publican's Licenses* www.ancestry.com.au. Original record: State Records Authority of New South Wales, Kingswood, Printed lists of licenses issued, 1866-82, NRS 14411, reel 1243, page 174, 21 Jan 1876, George C Reed, West Bourke, the Overland hotel.

531 Timber Licenses. (1871, October 20). New South Wales Government Gazette (Sydney, NSW: 1832 - 1900), p. 2398.

532 NSW Land Deed volume 85 folios 170-174, lot 6, sec 2, Gongolgon, 1 rood and 6 perches, transferred from Joseph Whye to Thomas Davis of *Milroy* Station, Dubbo on 20 Nov 1871.

533 Ibid. Transferred from Joseph Whye to William Cleaver, carrier of Dubbo on 20 Jan 1873.

534 Baptism register, St Stephen's church, Bourke. Kate Whye on 10 May 1873; Josephine Hazel Whye on 7 Oct 1875.

535 Teale, 'Marsden, Samuel Edward (1832–1912)'.

536 1851 census of England, Cambridgeshire, Waterbeach, Enumeration district 14a, piece 1759, folio 315, page 27, household of John Stacey Youngman; HO107; The National Archives of the UK, Kew; FHL microfilm GSU roll 193649-193650.

537 Chesterton District, *marriage index*, www.ancestry.com.au. Original record: General Register Office, London, England & Wales, Civil Registration Marriage Index, 1837-1915, Oct-Dec quarter 1864, page 1118, volume 3b, Cambridgeshire, Jane Why.

538 Captain Wakeham, *Passenger List, Zoroaster, arrival at Brisbane, 25 Sept 1874,* Queensland State Archives at - https://www.archivessearch.qld.gov.au/api/download_file/DR39711 . Original record: Queensland State Archives, Brisbane, Register of passengers on immigrant ships arriving in Queensland, No. 2, IMM/115; PRV8879/1/4; A1 Item ID 18477, Alfred Whye, age 21, Free passengers, number 386, page 766.

539 C Knight Captain of steamship "City of Brisbane", arrival at Sydney, *4 January 1875,* www.ancestry.com.au. Original record: State Records Authority of New South Wales, Kingswood, Unassisted Immigrant Passenger Lists, 1826-1922, Series 13278, Reels 399-560, 2001-2122, 2751, INX-49-50676, page 94, Alfred Whye.

540 NSW Registry of Births Deaths and Marriages, *Index to NSW Births and Baptisms,* (Registry of BDM), Joseph E Whye, 8877/1877 at Bourke, parents Joseph and Prudence.

541 Joseph Whye, Death Certificate number 4163/1877 (6 May 1877),
     Bourke, NSW Registry of Births, Deaths and Marriages, Sydney.
     Informant: Prudence Whye, wife. Publican aged 42 of Gongolgon,
     inflammation of the lungs, 5 days (James M McPherson); born
     Cambridgeshire, parents William Whye and Hannah Headland;
     spouse Prudence Whye; children Frances Anna 13, Jane Elizabeth
     11, Emily Maude May 8, Albert George Henry 6, Kate 4, Josephine
     Hazel 2, Joseph Headland 4 months; buried at Gongolgon on 8 May
     1877 by Rev McCoy, Wesleyan, witnesses George Reed and
     Dominick Fowey; William Wright undertaker. Transcribed by NSW
     Family History Transcriptions Pty Ltd for James Fleming on 3 May
     2023 (reference number 10408906).

542 Supreme Court of NSW, "Joseph Whye Probate," file, 2 August 1877,
     [17/1824] Series 3-1515, NRS 13660-3; NSW State Archives,
     Kingswood. Joseph Whye, died 6 May 1877.

543 Government Gazette Notices (1877, August 31). *New South Wales
     Police Gazette and Weekly Record of Crime (Sydney: 1860 - 1930)*, p.
     3369 (Supplement to the NSW Government Gazette).

544 NSW Registry of Births Deaths and Marriages, *Index to NSW
     Marriages*, (Registry of BDM), 2323/1877, George Charles Reed and
     Mary Ann Peters, Bourke.

545 Lola Cormie, *Back to Bourke: Court House Death and Marriage Records
     1862-1974* (N.p.: n.p., n.d.), Mary Ann Reed nee Peters, burial, 7 Feb
     1944, aged 84, born Windsor, parents William Peters and Sophie
     Smith.

546 NSW Registry of Births Deaths and Marriages, *Index to NSW Births
     and Baptisms*, (Registry of BDM), Mary A Peters, 8237/1856,
     Windsor, parents William and Mary A.

547 Joseph Headland Whye, Death Certificate number 04742/1878 (21
     March 1878), Bourke, NSW Registry of Births, Deaths and
     Marriages, Sydney. Informant: Prudence Whye, mother. Aged 14
     months, continued illness of 4 months; parents Joseph (deceased
     publican) and Prudence Whye; buried 28 Mar 1878 at Gongolgon
     by Jacob Jonson, witnessed by Thos. Hatton and James Tobin, no
     Minister. Transcribed by Joy Murrin for James Fleming on 24 May
     2023 (reference number 327902).

[548] Kate Whye, Death Certificate number 04784/1878 (14 July 1878), Bourke, NSW Registry of Births, Deaths and Marriages, Sydney. Informant: Alfred P Gunning, no relation. Aged 5 years, whooping cough; parents Joseph (innkeeper) and Prudence Whye (nee Reed); buried 15 Jul 1878 at Gongolgon by Henry Graham, witnessed by John Ward and Frank Wright, AP Gunning Minister. Transcribed by Joy Murrin for James Fleming on 24 May 2023 (reference number 327901).

[549] Baptismal Record: James Murphy 1843, Vol Glenbeigh baptisms, No KY-RC-BA-245651, entry number 21 on page 14 of book 1, (12 Nov 1843), Kilnabrack, near Glenbeigh, General Register Office, Ireland

[550] Shea family entry, *Panama*, Passenger list, 14 Sep 1849; in (Kingswood: Archives Office of NSW).

[551] Denis Shea entry, *SS Blenheim*, Convict Arrival Indent, 14 Nov 1834; in *Convict Records* (Kingswood: NSW Archives).

[552] Denis Shea, *Convict Assignment 1834 NSW: Shea Denis*, (Kingswood NSW: NSW State Archives), November 1834, HO 10/30. Goulburn Plains.

[553] Denis Shea, *Convict Ticket of Leave Butt: Shea Denis 1842*, (Kingswood: NSW State Archives), 12 Dec 1842. Bathurst District.

[554] Denis Shea, *Conditional Pardon*, (NSW: Colonial Secretary), 1847, 1310

[555] Denis Shea, *Convict family 1847 NSW: Shea Denis*, (Kingswood NSW: NSW State Archives).

[556] Shea family entry, *Panama*, Passenger list, 14 Sep 1849; in (Kingswood: Archives Office of NSW).

[557] Marriage Certificate, John Murphy and Mary Shea, 1 Feb 1836, General Register Office, Ireland. Glenbeigh marriages.

[558] Murphy family entry, *Talavera*, Passenger list, 6 Sep 1853; in 4/4935 (Kingswood: Archives Office of NSW), 2465.

[559] Marriage Certificate, James Murphy and Ann Malcolm, 28 Dec 1864, Registry of Births Deaths and Marriages, NSW. 1864/1546, Bathurst.

[560] NSW Registrar of Births, Deaths and Marriages. Birth Certificate 1865/5526, James Murphy, 3 Jun 1865, Campbell's River, parents James Murphy (farmer) and Ann Malcolm, no previous issue, witness Mrs Murphy. Transcribed on 11 Jun 1998 by Joy Murrin Transcription Agent for Edward Malcolm.

[561] NSW Registry of Births Deaths and Marriages, *Index to NSW Deaths*, Bernard Murphy, parents James and Ann, 2726/1863 Bathurst.

[562] Apprehensions. (1866, February 28). New South Wales Police Gazette and Weekly Record of Crime (Sydney: 1860 - 1930), p. 77.

[563] October 16th. (1866, October 19). *Empire (Sydney, NSW: 1850 - 1875)*, p. 5.

[564] Government Gazette Notices (1866, May 9). New South Wales Police Gazette and Weekly Record of Crime (Sydney: 1860 - 1930), p. 170.

[565] Divorce file, 83/1878. State Archives, Kingswood, NSW, Australia. NRS 13495, 1873-1967, 1969-1976, James Murphy v Ann Murphy and Henry Herring, Affidavit of Petitioner, James Murphy, dated 29 July 1878, filed 9 Aug 1878, clause 5.

[566] NSW Registry of Births Deaths and Marriages, *Index to NSW Births and Baptisms*, Abbey E Murphy, parents James and Ann, 6343/1867 Bathurst. Also, Mary Murphy, parents James and Ann, 6342/1867 Bathurst.

[567] NSW Registrar of Births, Deaths and Marriages, Death Certificate 1867/4129, Mary Murphy, 12 Dec 1867, Campbell's River, 3 days old, elder of twins; parents James Murphy (labourer) and Ann Malcolm. Also, Death Certificate 1867/4130, Abbey Elizabeth Murphy, 19 Dec 1867, Campbell's River, 10 days old, younger of twins; parents James Murphy (labourer) and Ann Malcolm. Both transcribed on 11 Jun 1998 by Joy Murrin Transcription Agent for Edward Malcolm.

[568] NSW Registrar of Births, Deaths and Marriages, Birth Certificate 1868/06313, Mary Murphy, 30 Nov 1868, Campbell's River, parents James Murphy (farmer) and Ann Malcolm. Transcribed on 22 Oct 1999 by Joy Murrin Transcription Agent for E&T Malcolm. Also, NSW Registry of Births Deaths and Marriages, *Index to NSW Births and Baptisms*, (Registry of BDM), Catherine Murphy, parents James and Ann, 6653/1870 Bathurst. And John Murphy, parents James and Ann, 6722/1873 Bathurst.

[569] NSW Registry of Births Deaths and Marriages, *Index to NSW Deaths*, Bernard Murphy, parents James and Ann, 2726/1863 Bathurst.

[570] Edited, "James Murphy, Esquire," in *Australian Men of Mark, Vol. 2, Series 2*. (Sydney: Charles F Maxwell, 1889), p 321.

[571] Edited. 'Divorce Records Guide'. NSW State Archives. https://mhnsw.au/guides/divorce-records-guide/.

[572] NSW Registrar of Births, Deaths and Marriages, Marriage Certificate 1879/2580, James Murphy (butcher; bachelor - sic - aged 33) and Prudence Whye (widow aged 33), both of Gongolgon, 18 May 1879, Gongolgon. Transcribed on 1 Jul 1998 by Joy Murrin Transcription Agent for Edward Malcolm.

[573] Divorce file, 83/1878. State Archives, Kingswood, NSW, Australia. NRS 13495, 1873-1967, 1969-1976, James Murphy v Ann Murphy and Henry Herring, Decree Nisi, granted 4 Nov 1878.

[574] NSW Registry of Births Deaths and Marriages, *Index to NSW Marriages*, 6761/1884 at Orange, Henry Heron and Ann Malcolm.

[575] NSW Registry of Births Deaths and Marriages, *Index to NSW Births and Baptisms*, (Registry of BDM), Daniel Reed Murphy, 10313/1879 Bourke, parents James and Prudence.

[576] NSW land deeds volume 342, folios 209 and 210. Portion 2 of 48 acres; lot 4 in section 33; lots 4 & 5 in section 3; and lots 1 & 2 in section 10; all at Gongolgon.

[577] NSW land deed volume 223, folio 181. Lot 2 in section 11, Darling Street, Bourke. Transferred on 4 Sep 1878 from George Charles Reed to Edward Warmoll, publican.

[578] Government Gazette Notices (1875, September 9). *New South Wales Government Gazette (Sydney, NSW: 1832 - 1900)*, p. 2763.

[579] Government Gazette Notices (1882, September 13). *New South Wales Government Gazette (Sydney, NSW: 1832 - 1900)*, p. 4760.

[580] Government Gazette Notices (1876, September 13). *New South Wales Government Gazette (Sydney, NSW: 1832 - 1900)*, p. 3645.

[581] Government Gazette Notices (1877, August 31). *New South Wales Police Gazette and Weekly Record of Crime (Sydney: 1860 - 1930)*, p. 3369 (Supplement to the NSW Government Gazette).

[582] *History of Bourke* journal, volume 4 page 56.

[583] The Treasury, NSW, 9 Oct 1874, page 2118, Ebenezer Timothy Smith, Criterion Hotel, Bourke District. Printed lists of licenses issued, 1866-82, 1895-1900, 1907-10. NRS 14411, reel 1243. State Records Authority of New South Wales, Kingswood at https://www.ancestry.com.au/imageviewer/collections/1792/images/41718_329539-00224

[584] Baptism of Edward John Bloxham Reed, St Stephen's Anglican church, Bourke, SAG Reel 335: 1870-1900, 10 March 1879.

[585] Petition for a Municipality - Bourke," public notice, *NSW Government Gazette, Sydney*, 11 January 1878, page 175.

586 Baptism of Gilbert George Joseph Whye Reed, St Stephen's Anglican church, Bourke, SAG Reel 335: 1870-1900, 16 May 1880.

587 District News. (1880, September 18). The Maitland Mercury and Hunter River General Advertiser (NSW: 1843 - 1893), p. 6.

588 NSW land deed volume 72, folio 206. Lot 5 in section 21, one acre in Anson Street, Bourke. Transferred on 11 Oct 1881 from Alexander Reed to Cavendish Lister Neville, solicitor.

589 NSW land deed volume 82, folio 18. Lot 10 in section 4, 2 roods on the corner of Darling and Narran streets, North Bourke. Transferred on 30 Jun 1881 from Joseph Becker to George Charles Reed. Mortgaged on 14 Apr 1881 to Thomas Campbell Ranken, stock and station agent. Transferred on 11 Jul 1881 from George Charles Reed to Alfred Kirkpatrick.

590 Government Gazette Notices (1882, September 13). *New South Wales Government Gazette (Sydney, NSW: 1832 - 1900)*, p. 4735.

591 Baptism of Frances Hazel Reed, St Stephen's Anglican church, Bourke, SAG Reel 335: 1870-1900, 1 May 1882.

592 NSW Registry of Births Deaths and Marriages, *Index to NSW Deaths*, (Registry of BDM), 5529/1881 Bourke.

593 Baptism of Frances Hazel Reed, St Stephen's Anglican church, Bourke, SAG Reel 335: 1870-1900, 1 May 1882.

594 "New Insolvents," public notice, *The Daily Telegraph, Sydney*, 29 September 1882, page 3.

595 Marriage Certificate, James Murphy and Prudence Whye nee Reed, 18 May 1879, Registry of Births Deaths and Marriages, NSW. 1879/2580.

596 NSW Registry of Births Deaths and Marriages, *Index to NSW Births and Baptisms*, (Registry of BDM), Daniel Reed Murphy, 10313/1879 Bourke, parents James and Prudence.

597 NSW Registrar of Births, Deaths and Marriages, Deaths 1855-1922. Death Certificate 1879/04301, Mary Murphy, 12 Aug 1879, Bathurst, 10 Years and 9 months old, pericarditis, buried 14 Aug 1879; parents James Murphy (carrier) and Ann Malcolm; informant Andrew Cavanagh, uncle, Campbell's River; undertaker Thomas M Wellington, minister P Riordan, witnesses James Morris, Henry Weeks. Transcribed on 22 Oct 1999 by Joy Murrin Transcription Agent for E&T Malcolm.

598 Government Gazette Notices (1880, September 17). *New South Wales Government Gazette (Sydney, NSW: 1832 - 1900)*, p. 4831.

[599] Birth Certificate Vol 1880 No 11867, George Charles Reed Murphy, (11 February 1881), NSW Registry of Births Deaths and Marriages.

[600] NSW Registry of Births Deaths and Marriages, *Index to NSW Marriages*, (Registry of BDM), Augustus Sullivan and Frances Whye, 3276/1881, 31 May 1881, Bourke.

[601] Daniel Reed Murphy, Death Certificate number 06313/1881 (28 December 1881), Gongolgon, NSW Registry of Births, Deaths and Marriages, Sydney. Informant: James Murphy, father. Aged 2 years and 7 months, diphtheria for 4 days; parents James Murphy (publican) and Prudence Reed; buried 28 Dec Apr 1881 at Gongolgon by Jacob Johnson, witnessed by Henry Starr and HM Graham; Augustus Sullivan read prayers. Transcribed by Joy Murrin for James Fleming on 24 May 2023 (reference number 327904).

Chapter 17: The worst of times

[602] Baptism of Kate Hazle Maxwell, St Stephen's Anglican church, Bourke, SAG Reel 335: 1870-1900, 2 Nov 1875.

[603] Bourke. (1876, October 7). The Maitland Mercury and Hunter River General Advertiser (NSW: 1843 - 1893), p. 7.

[604] "Bourke," news article, *Maitland Mercury, Maitland*, 7 October 1876, page 7.

[605] Baptism of Frances Annie Maxwell, St Stephen's Anglican church, Bourke, SAG Reel 335: 1870-1900, 3 Jan 1878.

[606] NSW Registry of Births Deaths and Marriages, *Index to NSW Deaths*, (Registry of BDM), Frances A Maxwell, parents Joseph and Jane E, Bourke, 4765/1878.

[607] Insolvency Court. (1879, February 4). *Evening News (Sydney, NSW: 1869 - 1931)*, p. 3.

[608] Government Gazette Notices (1878, August 27). New South Wales Police Gazette and Weekly Record of Crime (Sydney: 1860 - 1930), p. 3425.

[609] NSW Registry of Births Deaths and Marriages, *Index to NSW Births and Baptisms*, (Registry of BDM), 9685/1878 Bourke.

[610] In Insolvency. (1879, February 11). New South Wales Government Gazette (Sydney, NSW: 1832 - 1900), p. 652.

[611] "In Insolvency," public notice, *NSW Government Gazette, Sydney*, 27 February 1880, page 1016.

612 NSW Registry of Births Deaths and Marriages, *Index to NSW Births and Baptisms*, (Registry of BDM), Augustus George Maxwell, parents Joseph and Elizabeth J, 11896/1881 Bourke.

613 NSW Registry of Births Deaths and Marriages, *Index to NSW Deaths*, (Registry of BDM), Augustus G Maxwell, parents Joseph and Elizabeth J, 5485/1881 Bourke.

614 Section 2, lots 1 and 3, Gongolgon, volume 85, folios 167 and 168, 10 November 1868; Purchase, Land Deeds; NSW Land Titles Office, Sydney.

615 Land District of Brewarrina. (1880, January 30). *New South Wales Government Gazette (Sydney, NSW: 1832 - 1900)*, p. 514.

616 Approved Claims for defined pre-emptive leases. (1875, March 23). *New South Wales Government Gazette (Sydney, NSW: 1832 - 1900)*, p. 882.

617 Timber Licenses. (1870, January 11). New South Wales Government Gazette (Sydney, NSW: 1832 - 1900), p. 36.

618 Horses and Cattle. (1870, December 14). New South Wales Police Gazette and Weekly Record of Crime (Sydney: 1860 - 1930), p. 335.

619 Apprehensions. (1871, May 24). New South Wales Police Gazette and Weekly Record of Crime (Sydney: 1860 - 1930), p. 142.

620 Approved Claims for defined pre-emptive leases. (1871, June 16). *New South Wales Government Gazette (Sydney, NSW: 1832 - 1900)*, p. 1284.

621 New South Wales. (1888, May 12). *The Australasian (Melbourne, Vic.: 1864 - 1946)*, p. 22.

622 Dubbo. (1875, February 4). The Sydney Morning Herald (NSW: 1842 - 1954), p. 6.

623 Reed family baptisms, 27 Oct 1879, Henry Sampson Johnson, Emily Jane Johnson and Eliza Emily Tobin Maxwell, St Stephen's Anglican church Bourke, Society of Australian Genealogists Reel 335.

624 Lola Cormie, *Back to Bourke: Court House Death and Marriage Records 1862-1974* (N.p.: n.p., n.d.), Eliza Jane Reed, aged 47, 24 Nov 1879

625 Ibid. John Benjamin Reed, aged 49, 15 Sep 1881.

626 Government Gazette Notices (1873, March 26). *New South Wales Police Gazette and Weekly Record of Crime (Sydney: 1860 - 1930)*, p. 96.

627 Cameron, *History of Bourke Journal*. Volume 4, page 62.

628 The Anglican Church in Bourke and District, compiled by Brother Richard Stamp, *History of Bourke Journal*, volume 1 (Bourke NSW: Bourke and District Historical Society, 1966-1992), page 156.

629 Transfer from James Reed to Joseph Whye of lot 3 in section 11, Darling Street, Bourke on 13 August 1875. NSW land deed volume 38 folio 27.

630 Transfer from James Reed to Michael Brennan of lot 4 in section 11, Darling Street, Bourke on 13 August 1875. NSW land deed volume 38 folio 28.

631 Transfer from Frances Reed to James Tobin junior of lot 1 in section 11, corner of Darling and Glen Streets, Bourke on 2 August 1876. NSW land deed volume 10 folio 147.

632 Baptism of Sarah Jane Heazle Johnson, St Stephen's Anglican church, Bourke, SAG Reel 335: 1870-1900, 26 May 1872.

633 "Timber Licenses," notice, *NSW Government Gazette, Sydney*, 11 June 1872, H Johnson, general, Brewarrina, 15 shillings. Also "Timber Licenses," notice, *NSW Government Gazette, Sydney*, 20 August 1872, H Johnson, general, Brewarrina, 15 shillings.

634 "Timber Licenses," notice, *NSW Government Gazette, Sydney*, 13 December 1872, H Johnson, hardwood, Bourke, 5 shillings.

635 "Timber Licenses," notice, *NSW Government Gazette, Sydney*, 18 June 1875, H Johnson, hardwood, Warrego, 5 shillings.

636 Government Gazette Notices (1874, June 5). *New South Wales Government Gazette (Sydney, NSW: 1832 - 1900)*, p. 1712. And Government Gazette Notices (1874, September 2). *New South Wales Government Gazette (Sydney, NSW: 1832 - 1900)*, p. 2639.

637 Government Gazette Notices (1875, September 9). *New South Wales Government Gazette (Sydney, NSW: 1832 - 1900)*, p. 2763.

638 "The Mount Oxley Hotel," advertisement, *The Central Australian and Bourke Telegraph, Bourke*, 2 August 1875; print, *National Library of Australia* (transcribed by JM Fleming 1991).

639 Government Gazette Notices (1876, September 13). New South Wales Government Gazette (Sydney, NSW: 1832 - 1900), p. 3645. Also, 1877, August 31, NSW Gazette and Weekly Record of Crime (Sydney: 1860 - 1930), p. 3369 (Supplement to the New South Wales Government Gazette). Government Gazette Notices (1878, August 27). New South Wales Police Gazette and Weekly Record of Crime (Sydney: 1860 - 1930), p. 3425.

640 Land deeds, Cowper County NSW, unnamed Parish (later named Booda). Portions 8/1 and 8/2, 40 acres each, volume 103 folio 240.

641 Baptism of George Johnson, St Stephen's Anglican church, Bourke, SAG Reel 335: 1870-1900, 28 September 1876.

[642] "Bourke," news item, *Maitland Mercury, Maitland*, 13 December 1877, page 7.

[643] Baptisms of Henry Sampson Johnson, Emily Jane Johnson and Eliza Emily Tobin Maxwell, St Stephen's Anglican church, Bourke, SAG Reel 335: 1870-1900, 27 October 1879.

[644] Government Gazette Notices (1879, September 12). New South Wales Government Gazette (Sydney, NSW: 1832 - 1900), p. 4075. Also, 1880, September 17, p. 4831. Also, 1881, September 13, p. 4697.

[645] History of Bourke Journal, Volume 4, p 62.

[646] Baptism of Albert William Johnson, St Stephen's Anglican church, Bourke, SAG Reel 335: 1870-1900, 25 September 1881.

[647] *History of Bourke Journal*, volume 4 (Bourke NSW: Bourke and District Historical Society, 1966-1992), Wine licenses, page 79, Henry Johnson 1 Aug 1882.

[648] Baptism of Mary Ann Maud Johnson, St Stephen's Anglican church, Bourke, SAG Reel 335: 1870-1900, 25 May 1885.

[649] Land Deeds, NSW Land Titles Office, Sydney, Book 378 No 473, 40 ac, Parish of Booda portion 9, 4 August 1887.

[650] Ibid. Book 378 No 474, 40 ac, Parish of Booda portion 8, 4 August 1887.

[651] Baptisms of Alexander James Boswell Gibb and Mary Jane Hazle Brennan, St Stephen's Anglican church, Bourke, SAG Reel 335: 1870-1900, 1 June 1875.

[652] NSW Registry of Births Deaths and Marriages, *Index to NSW Deaths*, (Registry of BDM), William J Brennan, 5134/1876 at Bourke, parents Michael and Sarah A.

[653] Cameron, Bill. History of Bourke journal, volume 4, page 63.

[654] Baptism of Annie Brennan, St Stephen's Anglican church, Bourke, SAG Reel 335: 1870-1900, 29 March 1879.

[655] NSW Registry of Births Deaths and Marriages, *Index to NSW Deaths*, (Registry of BDM), 6111/1879 Bourke.

[656] The Great Tragedy at Bourke. (1877, September 20). The Maitland Mercury and Hunter River General Advertiser (NSW: 1843 - 1893), p. 3.

[657] Murder of Senior-Sergeant Wallings. (1878, September 27). *The Burrowa News (NSW: 1874 - 1951)*, p. 2.

[658] Murderer of Sergeant Wallings Arrested: (1878, October 12). *Evening News (Sydney, NSW: 1869 - 1931)*, p. 5.

Chapter 18: Life goes on

[659] Baptism of Josephine Whelan Brennan, St Stephen's Anglican church, Bourke, SAG Reel 335: 1870-1900, September 1877.

[660] Apprehensions. (1877, October 24). *New South Wales Police Gazette and Weekly Record of Crime (Sydney: 1860 - 1930)*, p. 353.

[661] Government Gazette Notices (1877, November 21). New South Wales Police Gazette and Weekly Record of Crime (Sydney: 1860 - 1930), p. 382.

[662] Petition for a Municipality.—Bourke. (1878, January 11). *New South Wales Government Gazette (Sydney, NSW: 1832 - 1900)*, p. 175.

[663] Government Gazette Notices (1879, September 12). *New South Wales Government Gazette (Sydney, NSW: 1832 - 1900)*, p. 4053.

[664] Government Gazette Notices (1880, September 17). *New South Wales Government Gazette (Sydney, NSW: 1832 - 1900)*, p. 4829.

[665] Government Gazette Notices (1881, September 13). *New South Wales Government Gazette (Sydney, NSW: 1832 - 1900)*, p. 4697.

[666] Transfer from Michael Brennan to Edward Warmoll of lot 4 in section 11, Darling Street, Bourke on 20 Apr 1880. NSW land deed volume 260 folio 245.

[667] Baptism of Michael James Brennan, St Stephen's Anglican church, Bourke, SAG Reel 335: 1870-1900, 20 February 1882.

[668] NSW Registry of Births Deaths and Marriages, *Index to NSW Marriages*, (Registry of BDM), Edward James Freeman and Sarah Ellen Brennan, 3735/1882, Bourke.

[669] Ibid. Frederick Jackson and Frances E Brennan, 3967/1883, Bourke.

[670] "Timber and Other Licenses," public notice, *NSW Government Gazette, Sydney*, 1 June 1883, page 3049.

[671] NSW Registry of Births Deaths and Marriages, *Index to NSW Births and Baptisms*, (Registry of BDM), 14902/1884 Bourke

[672] Baptism of Mary Ann Maud Johnson, Frederick George Brennan and Alfred John Brennan, St Stephen's Anglican church, Bourke, SAG Reel 335: 1870-1900, 8 Mar 1885.

[673] NSW Registry of Births Deaths and Marriages, *Index to NSW Deaths*, (Registry of BDM), Frances E Jackson, 7727/1885 at Bourke, parents Michael and Sarah A.

[674] NSW Registry of Births Deaths and Marriages, *Index to NSW Births and Baptisms*, (Registry of BDM), Emeline Brenan, parents Michael and Sarah A, 5670/1867, Bourke.

675 Census figures for the Bourke District in 1881, History of Bourke journal, volume 7, page 61.

676 History of Bourke, volume 7, page 71.

677 NSW Land Deeds, volume 544, folio 108 (Sarah Ann Brennan) 4 Feb 1881. Volume 544, folio 134, James Tobin junior 4 Feb 1881 and Frances Tobin 19 Jun 1888.

678 M Brennan household, Oxley Street, 5 Apr 1891 Census, NSW, Bourke, NSW Records Authority.

679 NSW Land Deed, volume 636, folio 59, 19 Jun 1888.

680 NSW Registry of Births Deaths and Marriages, Index to NSW Marriages, (Registry of BDM), 3729/1882 Bourke, Timothy Farrell and Mary Ann Gibb.

681 Farrell family information, History of Bourke journal, volume 12, page 71.

682 Government Gazette Notices (1882, September 13). *New South Wales Government Gazette (Sydney, NSW: 1832 - 1900)*, p. 4735.

683 "Apprehensions," public notice, NSW Government Gazette, Sydney, 10 May 1882, page 185.

684 NSW Registry of Births Deaths and Marriages, Index to NSW Births and Baptisms, (Registry of BDM), 12543/1882 Bourke, Thomas James Farrell.

685 St Stephen's Anglican church Bourke, 1870-1900, Thomas James Edmond Farrell, 22 Oct 1882, Extracted from Reel 335, Society of Australian Genealogists.

686 NSW land deed volume 38, folio 29, section 11, lot 5, 2 roods, corner of Darling and Wilson Streets, Bourke, transfer dated 25 April 1882 from Mary Ann Farrell to James Murphy.

687 Cameron, Family Hotel Bourke, History of Bourke journal, volume 6, page 35.

688 Government Gazette Notices (1883, August 31). New South Wales Government Gazette (Sydney, NSW: 1832 - 1900), p. 4737.

689 NSW Registry of Births Deaths and Marriages, *Index to NSW Births and Baptisms*, (Registry of BDM), 14988/1884 Bourke, Lila Rose Farrell

690 In Insolvency. (1884, March 28). New South Wales Government Gazette (Sydney, NSW: 1832 - 1900), p. 2125.

691 Government Gazette Notices (1884, August 29). *New South Wales Government Gazette (Sydney, NSW: 1832 - 1900)*, p. 5880-1.

692 NSW Registry of Births Deaths and Marriages, *Index to NSW Deaths*, (Registry of BDM), 7059/1884 Bourke, Thomas J E Farrell.

693 "Death of an Old Resident," obituary, The Western Herald, Bourke, 13 January 1926, page 2.

694 NSW Registry of Births Deaths and Marriages, *Index to NSW Births and Baptisms*, 16694/1887 Brewarrina, Victoria K Farrell.

695 Ibid. 16320/1889 Brewarrina, Timothy O Farrell.

696 Botfields.—Impounded at Botfields, Gongolgon, on the (1884, September 5). *New South Wales Government Gazette (Sydney, NSW: 1832 - 1900)*, p. 6037.

697 Botfields.—Impounded at Botfields, Gongolgon, on the 7th day of April, 1879, from Cultivation Paddock, by Mr. (1879, April 16). *New South Wales Government Gazette (Sydney, NSW: 1832 - 1900)*, p. 1735.

698 NSW Registry of Births Deaths and Marriages, *Index to NSW Births and Baptisms*, 12559/1882 Bourke, Nora Lilian Murphy.

699 Ibid. 15004/1884 Bourke, Mary Ethel Murphy.

700 Ibid. 16331/1886 Bourke, Lila K Murphy.

701 NSW Registry of Births Deaths and Marriages, *Index to NSW Marriages*, (Registry of BDM), 4378/1886, Thomas Ralph and Jane Elizabeth Whye, Brewarrina.

702 A Short History of Bourke, History of Bourke journal, volume 11, p 282-287.

703 Wikipedia, s.v. "Bourke railway station", https://en.wikipedia.org/w/index.php?title=Bourke_railway_station

704 Government Gazette Tenders and Contracts (1896, February 19). *New South Wales Government Gazette (Sydney, NSW: 1832 - 1900)*, p. 1250.

705 Government Gazette Notices (1884, September 19). *New South Wales Government Gazette (Sydney, NSW: 1832 - 1900)*, p. 6307.

706 Government Gazette Appointments and Employment (1895, April 2). *New South Wales Government Gazette (Sydney, NSW: 1832 - 1900)*, p. 2219.

707 The Commons Acts, 1873-86. (1894, October 26). *New South Wales Government Gazette (Sydney, NSW: 1832 - 1900)*, p. 6788.

708 NSW Land Deed, volume 846, folio 160, December 1886.

709 NSW Land Deeds, volume 342, folios 209 and 210, December 1886.

710 Government Land Business. (1887, July 26). *Evening News (Sydney, NSW: 1869 - 1931)*, p. 7.

711 Reserves from sale for Special Lease. (1888, August 11). *New South Wales Government Gazette (Sydney, NSW: 1832 - 1900)*, p. 5667.

712 Pastoral Memoranda. (1890, September 27). *Western Herald (Bourke, NSW: 1887 - 1970)*, p. 3.

713 Government Gazette Notices (1888, February 10). *New South Wales Government Gazette (Sydney, NSW: 1832 - 1900)*, p. 1203. Also, 1889, February 22, p. 1476.

714 'Ninety to-day', Sydney Sun. 3 Jul 1936, p.19.

715 Mr. Waddell at Byrock (1891, May 9). *Western Herald (Bourke, NSW: 1887 - 1970)*, p. 2.

716 Government Gazette Notices (1891, May 15). New South Wales Government Gazette (Sydney, NSW: 1832 - 1900), p. 3609.

717 Advertising (1887, December 17). *Western Herald (Bourke, NSW: 1887 - 1970)*, p. 5.

718 Sporting News. (1905, November 3). *The West Australian (Perth, WA: 1879 - 1954)*, p. 7; and many other newspapers around this date.

719 NSW Land Deed, volume 10, folio 147. Mortgage 15 Dec 1879; Discharge 22 Oct 1881; Transfer of 35 perches to Mary Ann Farrell 25 Aug 1882.

720 Government Gazette Notices (1886, December 8). *New South Wales Government Gazette (Sydney, NSW: 1832 - 1900)*, p. 8390.

721 "Albury," news article, *The Australasian, Melbourne*, 12 May 1888, page 22.

722 Baptism Register, St Stephen's Anglican church Bourke, SAG Reel 335: 1870-1900, Albert Charles Maxwell, 27 May 1883.

723 NSW Registry of Births Deaths and Marriages, *Index to NSW Births and Baptisms*, Frances P Maxwell, parents Joseph and Jane E, 15192/1885 Nyngan.

724 Ibid. Joseph H Maxwell, parents Joseph and Jane E, 16716/1887 Brewarrina.

725 Baptism Register, St Stephen's Anglican church Bourke, SAG Reel 335: 1870-1900, Ethel Mary Ann Reed, 6 Sep 1883.

726 Ibid. Emily Beatrice Reed, 27 Oct 1886.

727 Ibid. Bertie Augustus Reed, 10 Jun 1888.

[728] Brewarrina Historians, *Index to Burials at Brewarrina NSW,* (Brewarrina Shire Council), Frances Prudence Maxwell, aged 3, No 2349, page 38, 4 Nov 1888, Gongolgon. Also, NSW Registry of Births Deaths and Marriages, *Index to NSW Deaths,* 7497/1888 Brewarrina.

[729] "Weather, Wool, Movements of Stock," news article, *Australian Town and Country Journal, Sydney,* 1 August 1885, page 23.

[730] Crown Lands Commissioner, *Government Gazette* at - https://www.ancestry.com.au/discoveryui-content/view/3252454:2172. Original record: State Records Authority of New South Wales, Kingswood, Timber Licenses, April-June 1884, New South Wales Government Gazette. Assorted volumes, 1853–1899, page 3805.

[731] Baptism Register, St Stephen's Anglican church Bourke, SAG Reel 335: 1870-1900," Bertie Augustus Reed, 10 Jun 1888, number 1146, page 83, born 17 Dec 1887 at Bourke.

[732] Trade Union and Political History in Bourke, History of Bourke journal, volume 2, pp 205-216.

Chapter 19: Flood and strife

[733] River and Floods, Alan R Barton, History of Bourke journal, volume 1, page 81.

[734] Public Meeting in Bourke. (1890, March 17). *Evening News (Sydney, NSW: 1869 - 1931),* p. 6.

[735] Edited, "James Murphy, Esquire," in *Australian Men of Mark, Vol. 2, Series 2.* (Sydney: Charles F Maxwell, 1889), p 321.

[736] Flood of 1890, extracts from The Central Australian and Bourke Telegraph, 18 April 1890 edition, History of Bourke journal, volume 8, page 318.

[737] Diary of Lady Carrington, Thursday April 17 1890, Bourke, Papers of Charles Robert Wynn-Carrington, 1st Earl of Carrington, Australian Joint Copy Project, National Library of Australia, Reel M930,_ http://nla.gov.au/nla.obj-952930984

[738] History of Bourke journal, volume 8, page 315.

[739] Mrs Glover, Bourke 1890, including extracts from the Central Australian and Bourke Telegraph, History of Bourke journal, volume 1, pages 111 - 124.

740 NSW Census, 1891, County Cowper, District 69, Sub-District D, East Ward, Darling Street, North Bourke, page 23, https://www.ancestry.com.au/discoveryui-content/view/169671:1733 (J Reid, Darling St, number 547; H Johnson, Culgoa Street, number 546) and https://www.ancestry.com.au/discoveryui-content/view/185699:1733 (James Reed, Culgoa St).

741 History of Bourke journal, volume 4, page 46; also, volume 5 page 27.

742 Baptism Register, Stephen's Anglican church Bourke, 1870-1900, Reel 335, Society of Australian Genealogists, James Reed, 6 Aug 1890, number 1245, page 90, born 13 Feb 1890 at Bourke.

743 NSW Registry of Births Deaths and Marriages, *Index to NSW Births and Baptisms*, (Registry of BDM), Edward H Maxwell, parents Joseph and Jane E, 7972/1890 Brewarrina.

744 NSW Census, 1891, County Cowper, District 69, Sub-District D, Middle Ward, James Murphy, numbers 323, 324 and 692(?), Darling Street, page 18, https://www.ancestry.com.au/discoveryui-content/view/169551:1733 and https://www.ancestry.com.au/discoveryui-content/view/185755:1733

745 NSW Census, 1891, County Cowper, District 69, Sub-District D, East Ward, James Murphy, number 628, Wilson Street, page 21, https://www.ancestry.com.au/discoveryui-content/view/185647:1733 and https://www.ancestry.com.au/discoveryui-content/view/185714:1733 and https://www.ancestry.com.au/discoveryui-content/view/185790:1733

746 NSW Census, 1891, County Barrona, District 69, Sub-District 4, J Murphy, number 15, Wanaaring Road, page 1,_ https://www.ancestry.com.au/discoveryui-content/view/169877:1733

747 NSW Census, 1891, County Clyde and Gregory, District 68, Sub-District L, J Murphy, number 1, Clyde, page 1, https://www.ancestry.com.au/discoveryui-content/view/168787:1733

748 History of Bourke journal, volume 3, page 127.

749 Ibid. Volume 4, pages 51 and 56.

750 Government Gazette Notices (1893, August 18). *New South Wales Government Gazette (Sydney, NSW: 1832 - 1900)*, p. 6430.

751 1894 'Government Gazette Notices', New South Wales Government Gazette (Sydney, NSW: 1832 - 1900), 24 August, p. 5351.

752 NSW Census, 1891, County Cowper, District 69, Sub-District D, East Ward, E Brennan, number 326, Darling Street, page 19, https://www.ancestry.com.au/discoveryui-content/view/169557:1733

753 NSW Registry of Births Deaths and Marriages, *Index to NSW Marriages*, John S Harding and Emaline Brennan, 4138/1887, Bourke.

754 NSW Registry of Births Deaths and Marriages, *Index to NSW Births and Baptisms*, 16990/1880 at Bourke, Arthur W Harding, son of John and Emmaline.

755 Ibid. 16217/1889 at Bourke, Alfred I Harding son of John and Emmaline.

756 NSW Registry of Births Deaths and Marriages, *Index to NSW Deaths*, 7341/1888, Bourke, John W Harding, son of John and Annie.

757 NSW Census, 1891, County Cowper, District 69, Sub-District D, Middle and East Ward, M Brennan, number 125, Oxley Street, page 4; GC Reid, number 376, Darling Street, page 5,_ https://www.ancestry.com.au/discoveryui-content/view/185462:1733

758 NSW land deed, volume 960, folio 158, transfer dated 23 Jan 1890 (Kay).

759 "The Municipal District of Bourke," notice, *The Western Herald, Bourke*, 24 February 1900, Mary Ann Reed, lot 5, sec 10, East Bourke, 2 pounds 1 shilling and three pence.

760 NSW land deed, volume 960, folio 173, transfer dated 2 Dec 1927 (Rogers).

761 NSW Census, 1891, County Cowper, District 69, Sub-District C, Jos Maxwell, number 25, *Tarcoon* Station, Commercial Hotel,_ https://www.ancestry.com.au/discoveryui-content/view/169130:1733

762 Local and General. (1891, March 28). *Western Herald (Bourke, NSW: 1887 - 1970)*, p. 2.

763 "Bourke Licensing District," public notice, *NSW Government Gazette, Sydney*, 17 May 1892, page 4153.

764 "Sequestration Orders," public notice, *Sydney Morning Herald, Sydney*, 8 November 1893, page 3.

[765] NSW Census, 1891, County Cowper, District 69, Sub-District C, Gongolgon. Households of Thos Ralph of Bogan Street (number 31), Jas Tobin of Bridge Street (number 32) and MA Farrell of Bridge Street (number 33), https://www.ancestry.com.au/discoveryui-content/view/169044:1733

[766] "Notice," public notice, *The Western Herald, Bourke*, 27 June 1891, page 5.

[767] "Homestead Leases Refused," public notice, *NSW Government Gazette, Sydney*, 24 December 1891, page 10065.

[768] History of Bourke journal, volume 1, page 335.

[769] NSW Census, 1891, County Cowper, District 69, Sub-District D, Aboriginal Camp, number 816, Middle Ward, Municipality of Bourke, https://www.ancestry.com.au/imageviewer/collections/1733/images/32094_223354-00606

[770] History of Bourke journal, volume 12, page 14.

[771] Ibid. Volume 7, page 7.

[772] Telegraphic Intelligence (1880, December 16). The Maitland Mercury and Hunter River General Advertiser (NSW: 1843 - 1893), p. 3.

[773] Telegrams. (1889, June 1). The Sydney Mail and New South Wales Advertiser (NSW: 1871 - 1912), p. 1165.

[774] Camel transport, History of Bourke journal, volume 2, page 269.

[775] NSW Census, 1891, County Cowper, District 69, Sub-District D, West Ward, Gunny Khan, number 261, Billabong, page 22, https://www.ancestry.com.au/discoveryui-content/view/169645:1733

[776] Some swearing. (1916, January 22). *Western Herald (Bourke, NSW: 1887 - 1970)*, p. 4.

[777] At Gongolgon. (1893, October 25). *Western Herald (Bourke, NSW: 1887 - 1970)*, p. 2.

[778] NSW Registry of Births Deaths and Marriages, *Index to NSW Births and Baptisms*, 7555/1892.

[779] Ibid. Blanche O Maxwell, parents Joseph and Jane E, Brewarrina, 7970/1892.

[780] Ibid. 7978/1892 Brewarrina.

[781] Coolican, RE, Medicine in Bourke 1900 compared to 1963, History of Bourke journal, volume 1, page 128.

[782] NSW Registry of Births Deaths and Marriages, *Index to NSW Births and Baptisms*, 7251/1894 Bourke.

[783] NSW Registry of Births Deaths and Marriages, *Index to NSW Deaths*, (Registry of BDM), 3180/1894 Bourke.

[784] NSW Registry of Births Deaths and Marriages, *Index to NSW Births and Baptisms*, Norman H Maxwell, parents Joseph and Jane E, 20903/1895 Bourke.

[785] The Commons Acts, 1873-86. (1894, October 26). *New South Wales Government Gazette (Sydney, NSW: 1832 - 1900)*, p. 6788.

[786] Government Gazette Appointments and Employment (1895, April 2). *New South Wales Government Gazette (Sydney, NSW: 1832 - 1900)*, p. 2219.

[787] Official Correspondence. (1895, June 19). *Western Herald (Bourke, NSW: 1887 - 1970)*, p. 2.

[788] Local and General. (1895, April 10). *Western Herald (Bourke, NSW: 1887 - 1970)*, p. 2.

Chapter 20: Brassy skies and bare plains

[789] St Stephen's Anglican church Bourke, *Baptism of William Reed, 8 Mar 1896*, born 8 Aug 1895 at Bourke, Society of Australian Genealogists Reel 335: 1870-1900, number 1663, page 118.

[790] NSW Registry of Births Deaths and Marriages, *Index to NSW Births and Baptisms*, 2090/1896 Brewarrina.

[791] "Bourke Races 1896," Advertisement, *The Western Herald, Bourke*, 29 April 1896, page 3.

[792] WA Baker, Pastoral Inspector 1963, *Closer Settlement in the Western Division*, History of Bourke Journal, volume 2, page 124.

[793] Unknown author, *The Heatwave of 1896*, History of Bourke Journal, volume 1, pages 150-153

[794] Terrible Heat at Bourke. (1896, January 17). *The Sydney Morning Herald (NSW: 1842 - 1954)*, p. 5.

[795] Terrible Heat at Bourke. (1896, January 18). *The Sydney Morning Herald (NSW: 1842 - 1954)*, p. 9.

[796] The Excessive Heat at Bourke. (1896, January 22). *The Sydney Morning Herald (NSW: 1842 - 1954)*, p. 5.

[797] Ten More Deaths at Bourke. (1896, January 23). *The Sydney Morning Herald (NSW: 1842 - 1954)*, p. 5.

[798] Weather in Australia. (1896, January 24). *Launceston Examiner (Tas: 1842 - 1899)*, p. 6.

[799] Circuit Courts. (1896, February 4). *The Sydney Morning Herald (NSW: 1842 - 1954)*, p. 5.

[800] What Bourke Says. (1896, January 25). *The Sydney Morning Herald (NSW: 1842 - 1954)*, p. 9.

[801] NSW Registry of Births Deaths and Marriages, *Index to NSW Marriages*, James P Costello and Josephine W Brennan, 771/1895, Bourke.

[802] Ibid.   5103/1897, Bourke, Daniel Power, Hazel Farrell.

[803] Ibid.   794/1896, Bourke, John Murphy and Honorah Rawson.

[804] Government of Queensland, "Registers Of Selection," land record, 25 May 1897, ITM24016, Land selections; Queensland State Archives, Brisbane. James Reed, selection 227, Springsure, microfilm number Z5422, series S13955.

[805] Government of Queensland, "Dead Farm Files," land record, 19 March 1906, ITM3674747, Land selection; Queensland State Archives, Brisbane. James Reed, Springsure, selection 227.

[806] WA Crothers, Bourke Commercial and Industrial History, Climax and Decline 1892-1931, History of Bourke Journal, volume 1, page 39.

[807] "Notice," advertisement, *The Western Herald, Bourke*, 31 July 1897, Notice published by Henry Johnson of North Bourke warning to people against cutting timber on Hazelwood selection.

[808] Qld Registry of Births Deaths and Marriages, *Index to Qld Marriages*, Alexander George Oxley Johnson and Maria Mary Mapstone, 20 Sep 1897, No 418, page 13095.

[809] "Conveyance of Mails," public notice, *NSW Government Gazette, Sydney*, 22 October 1897, page 7681.

[810] NSW Registry of Births Deaths and Marriages, *Index to NSW Marriages*, William Peter and Kate Hazel Maxwell, 752/1897, Brewarrina.

[811] *David Peter biography*, History of Bourke Journal, volume 8, page 69.

[812] "Forfeiture of Special Lease," notice, *NSW Government Gazette, Sydney*, 1 December 1893, page 9102 . Lease 215 of 93-3900 for 320 acres in the parish of East Bourke in the County of Cowper was cancelled for non-payment of 45 pounds in rent.

[813] Government Gazette Tenders and Contracts (1896, February 19). *New South Wales Government Gazette (Sydney, NSW: 1832 - 1900)*, p. 1250.

[814] Government Gazette Tenders and Contracts (1897, February 16). *New South Wales Government Gazette (Sydney, NSW: 1832 - 1900)*, p. 1134.

[815] "Conveyance of Mails," public notice, *NSW Government Gazette, Sydney*, 22 October 1897, page 7681.

[816] Government Gazette Notices (1899, February 24). *New South Wales Government Gazette (Sydney, NSW: 1832 - 1900)*, p. 1615.

[817] Death Certificate, James Reed, Registry of Births Deaths and Marriages, NSW, Vol 1898 No 5.

[818] Local and General. (1898, February 2). *Western Herald (Bourke, NSW: 1887 - 1970)*, p. 2.

[819] NSW Registry of Births Deaths and Marriages, *Index to NSW Births and Baptisms*, 11208/1899 Cobar.

[820] Ibid. William W Maxwell, parents Joseph and Jane E, 1667/1898 Bourke.

[821] Ibid.   John S Maxwell, parents Joseph and Jane E, 28550/1903 Bourke.

Chapter 21: Epilogue

[822] NSW Registry of Births Deaths and Marriages, *Index to NSW Deaths* 12370/1908 Sydney, aged 66, parents William and Ellen.

[823] "Bourke Branch," obituary, *The Worker, Wagga*, 16 December 1908, page 3.

[824] At the Council Chambers," news article, *The Western Herald, Bourke*, 7 August 1907, page 2.

[825] "Verdict of Suicide," news article, *The Daily Telegraph, Sydney*, 13 October 1909, page 10.

[826] Local and General. (1908, November 4). *Western Herald (Bourke, NSW: 1887 - 1970)*, p. 2.

[827] NSW Registry of Births Deaths and Marriages, *Index to NSW Deaths*, 4845/1911, Henry Johnson aged 78 years.

[828] Electoral Roll, Queensland, Australia. Longreach, Emu Street, Mary Reed, domestic servant; Christina Reed, domestic servant; Eliza Jane Reed, domestic servant; Queensland Government, Brisbane; FHL microfilm.

[829] Rose Maree Thomasson, "Thomasson Family Tree," online pedigree chart, https://www.ancestry.com.au/family-tree/tree/22762359, https://www.ancestry.com.au/family-tree/person/tree/22762359/person/29340548340.

830 Electoral Roll, Queensland, Australia. 1903, Springsure, Sandy Creek Farm, James Reed, selector; Eliza Reed, domestic duties; Thomas Reed, labourer; Alexander Reed, labourer; Queensland Government, Brisbane.

831 Ibid. 1905, Springsure, Sandy Creek Farm, James Reed, selector; Eliza Reed, domestic duties; Thomas Reed, labourer; Alexander Reed, labourer; Queensland Government, Brisbane.

832 Ibid. 1906, Springsure, Sandy Creek Farm, Alexander Reed, labourer, electoral register number 207; Queensland Government, Brisbane.

833 Government of Queensland, "Dead Farm Files," land record, 19 March 1906, ITM3674747, Land selection; Queensland State Archives, Brisbane. James Reed, Springsure, selection 227.

834 Antony James Cumming, Government Printer, *Queensland Brands Directory* (Brisbane: Queensland Government Printing Office, 1913), James Reed, Springsure, cattle brand, Ancestry.com, Australia, City Directories, 1845-1948, Original data: Various publishers. Australian City Directories. Gould Genealogy & History, South Australia, Australia.

835 Qld Registry of Births Deaths and Marriages, *Index to Qld Deaths*, James Reed died 19 Apr 1916, parents James Reed and Frances Hazel, 1916/C/2718.

836 Ibid. Alexander Reid, parents James Reid and Frances Hazel, 21 Nov 1917, 4554/1917, page 1679.

837 Qld Registry of Births Deaths and Marriages, *Index to Qld Marriages*, T O'Brien and Mary Reed ne Eckel, 1921/C/2078.

838 National Archives of Australia; Canberra, Australian Capital Territory, Australia; B2455, First Australian Imperial Force Personnel Dossiers, 1914-1920, George Charles Alexander Reed, service number 1686,_ https://www.ancestry.com.au/imageviewer/collections/60864/images/8027558_0001

839 Ibid. William Frederick Reed, service number 83, https://www.ancestry.com.au/discoveryui-content/view/290376:60864

840 Ibid. James Henry Reed, service number 5640, https://www.ancestry.com.au/imageviewer/collections/60864/images/8025728_0001

841 Qld Registry of Births Deaths and Marriages, *Index to Qld Deaths*, 3029/1919, page 1675.

842 National Archives of Australia; Canberra, Australian Capital Territory, Australia; B2455, First Australian Imperial Force Personnel Dossiers, 1914-1920, Bertie Reed, service number 56923, https://www.ancestry.com.au/discoveryui-content/view/289417:60864

843 Ibid.   William Reed, service number 1729, https://www.ancestry.com.au/discoveryui-content/view/290368:60864

844 Portrait of B Reed, The Queenslander Pictorial supplement to The Queenslander, July 1918, https://www.ancestry.com.au/discoveryui-content/view/2986:61489

845 Send-Off To Soldiers. (1916, April 15). *Western Herald (Bourke, NSW: 1887 - 1970)*, p. 4.

846 National Archives of Australia; Canberra, Australian Capital Territory, Australia; B2455, First Australian Imperial Force Personnel Dossiers, 1914-1920, Timothy Oxley, service number 1920, https://www.ancestry.com.au/discoveryui-content/view/163731:60864

847 Ibid. George Charles Farrell, service number 1921, https://www.ancestry.com.au/discoveryui-content/view/163561:60864

848 Ibid. Edward Albert Farrell, service number 1919, https://www.ancestry.com.au/imageviewer/collections/60864/images/3548806_0001

849 Ibid. Henry Joseph Maxwell, service number 5364, https://www.ancestry.com.au/discoveryui-content/view/347828:60864

850 From the war zone. (1917, August 31). *Western Herald (Bourke, NSW : 1887 - 1970)*, p. 2.

851 Commonwealth War Graves Commission website, George Charles Farrell, service number 1921, https://www.cwgc.org/find-records/find-war-dead/casualty-details/542826/george-charles-farrell/

852 Commonwealth War Graves Commission website, Henry Joseph Maxwell, service number 1921, Private Henry Joseph Maxwell, War Casualty Details 1456625, CWGC

853 *Find a Grave,* database and images
(https://www.findagrave.com/memorial/197325900/henry_joseph-
maxwell, memorial page for PVT Henry Joseph Maxwell
(unknown–3 May 1916), Find a Grave Memorial ID 197325900,
citing Rookwood General Cemetery, Rookwood, Cumberland
Council, New South Wales, Australia; Maintained by alisonc1109
contributor 48349597).

854 Bourke Memorial Fund. (1923, June 20). *Western Herald (Bourke, NSW:
1887 - 1970),* p. 2.

855 Welcome Home (1919, October 18). *Western Herald (Bourke, NSW:
1887 - 1970),* p. 2.

856 "The conflagration in Mertin Street," coroner's court report, *The
Western Herald, Bourke,* 4 March 1899, page 2.

857 "Marriage," public notice, *Illawarra Mercury, Wollongong,* 17 June 1899,
page 2.

858 "Fire at the Union," coroner's court report, *The Western Herald, Bourke,*
24 April 1901, page 2.

859 "Local and General," obituary, *The Western Herald, Bourke,* 31 August
1901, page 2.

860 "Licensing Court," Article, *The Western Herald, Bourke,* 18 June 1913,
page 2.

861 Section 2, lots 1 and 3, Gongolgon, volume 85, folios 167 and 168, 10
November 1868; Purchase, Land Deeds; NSW Land Titles Office,
Sydney.

862 NSW Registry of Births Deaths and Marriages, *Index to NSW Deaths,*
9858/1918 Petersham.

863 NSW land deeds, volume 544 folio 134 and volume 636 volume 59,
NSW Land Titles Office.

864 NSW Registry of Births Deaths and Marriages, *Index to NSW Deaths,*
10407/1922 Petersham.

865 *Find A Grave Index, 1800s-Current,*
https://www.findagrave.com/memorial/189208368/dorothy-frances-
mccready.

866 Death of Mrs Tobin. (1922, August 9). *Western Herald (Bourke, NSW :
1887 - 1970),* p. 2.

867 Advertising (1900, March 7). Western Herald (Bourke, NSW: 1887 -
1970), p. 3.

868 NSW Land Registry Services, Sydney. 4 roods sold after fieri facias, lots 4 and 5 in section 11, corner Darling and Wilson Streets, Bourke. Land deeds volume 38 folio 29 and volume 260 folio 245.

869 Government Gazette Notices (1904, August 23). *Government Gazette of the State of New South Wales* (Sydney, NSW: 1901 - 2001), p. 6417.

870 Obituary: Mary Murphy (nee Shea) 1821-1904, *The Orange Leader*, 24 Jun 1904, p2.

871 Commercial News (1907, May 11). *Leader (Orange, NSW: 1899 - 1945)*, p. 4.

872 Marriage Certificate, George Charles Reed Murphy and Isobel Cox, 2 Jul 1918, Registry of Births Deaths and Marriages, Queensland. 1918/2177 677.

873 Watches and Jewellery Reported Stolen, Missing, Etc. (1909, June 2). *New South Wales Police Gazette and Weekly Record of Crime (Sydney: 1860 - 1930)*, p. 194.

874 Gravestone of James Murphy, 1843-1919, Rookwood Catholic Cemetery, Sydney, NSW. (Mortuary 2, 5, grave 539).

875 Electoral Roll, Queensland, Australia. 1919, Springsure, page 13, Eliza Reed, home duties, Thursby, Rolleston; 1921, Capricornia, Springsure, page 12, Eliza Reed, home duties, Thursby, Rolleston; 1922, Capricornia, Springsure, page 12, Eliza Reed, home duties, Thursby, Rolleston; Queensland Government, Brisbane.

876 Death of A Well Known Resident (1924, April 2). *Western Herald (Bourke, NSW: 1887 - 1970)*, p. 2.

877 Qld Registry of Births Deaths and Marriages, *Index to Qld Marriages* T O'Brien and Mary Reed nee Eckel, 1921/C/2078.

878 Qld Registry of Births Deaths and Marriages, *Index to Qld Deaths*, Mary O'Brien formerly Reed nee Eckel, 15 Sep 1925, 2809/1925, page 1326.

879 Obituary. (1925, September 25). *The Longreach Leader (Qld.: 1923 - 1954)*, p. 5.

880 Mrs. Eliza Johnson (1925, August 26). *Western Herald (Bourke, NSW: 1887 - 1970)*, p. 2.

881 Death of an old Resident. (1926, January 13). *Western Herald (Bourke, NSW: 1887 - 1970)*, p. 2.

882 Obituary. (1929, February 13). *Western Herald (Bourke, NSW: 1887 - 1970)*, p. 3.

[883] Death of a Pioneer. (1932, May 20). *Western Herald (Bourke, NSW: 1887 - 1970)*, p. 3.

[884] Death of Mrs. M. A. Farrell. (1934, July 6). *Western Herald (Bourke, NSW: 1887 - 1970)*, p. 4.

[885] Death Certificate, Prudence Murphy, Registry of Births Deaths and Marriages, NSW, Vol 1940 No 526.

[886] Ninety To-day (1936, July 3). *The Sun (Sydney, NSW: 1910 - 1954)*, p. 19 (Country Edition).

[887] NSW Registry of Births Deaths and Marriages, *Index to NSW Deaths*, 1095/1944 Bourke, parents William and Sophia.

[888] Deaths. (1944, February 11). Western Herald (Bourke, NSW: 1887 - 1970), p. 3.

Appendix 1: Bourke hotels

[889] Datelining Bourke from the Town and Country Journal files, History of Bourke journal, volume 5 page 94.

[890] Advertising (1888, January 7). *Western Herald (Bourke, NSW: 1887 - 1970)*, p. 4.

[891] (1890, June 4). Western Herald (Bourke, NSW : 1887 - 1970), p. 1.

[892] Bourke. (1871, October 28). Australian Town and Country Journal (Sydney, NSW: 1870 - 1919), p. 16.

[893] Cameron, *History of Bourke Journal*. Volume 4, pages 67-68.

[894] License year 1866, Ancestry.com. *New South Wales, Australia, Certificates for Publicans' Licenses, 1830-1849, 1853-1899*. Original data: Butts of publicans' licences, 1830-1849. NRS 14401, reels 5049-5062, 1236. Certificates for publicans' licences, 1853-1861. NRS 14403, reels 5063-5066, 1236-1242. Index to certificates of publicans' licences. NRS 14402, reel 5063. Printed lists of licenses issued, 1866-82, 1895-1900, 1907-10. NRS 14411, reel 1243. State Records Authority of New South Wales, Kingswood, New South Wales, Australia. https://www.ancestry.com.au/imageviewer/collections/1792/images/41718_329539-00010?usePUB=true&_phsrc=pvd990&_phstart=successSource&usePUBJs=true&pId=900142903

[895] Central Australian and Bourke Telegraph, 30 November 1872, republished in the Western Herald on January 24 1975 and quoted in the History of Bourke journal, volume 7, pages 53-55.

[896] NSW land deed volume 140, folio 42, 2 roods, lot 2, section 2, Bourke. NSW land deed volume 130, folio 19, 2 roods, lot 3, section 2, Bourke.

[897] Ibid.   Volume 137, folio 245, 2 roods, lot 2, section 2, Bourke.

[898] Ibid. Volume 38, folio 22, 2 roods, lot 2, section 2, Bourke. NSW land deed volume 92, folios 121 and 122, 2 roods, lot 2, section 2, Bourke.

[899] Ibid. Volume 31 folio 47, section 10 lot 2, Bourke. Bought by George Harris on 2 August 1866, transferred to Russell Barton on 30 May 1876, transferred to Charles Warren 1882.

[900] Family Notices (1864, May 17). The Sydney Morning Herald (NSW: 1842 - 1954), p. 1.

[901] Bourke. (1872, September 28). *Empire (Sydney, NSW: 1850 - 1875)*, p. 4.

[902] Bourke. (1873, March 28). Evening News (Sydney, NSW: 1869 - 1931), p. 3.

[903] NSW Land Deeds, volume 596 folios 135 and 136. Primary Application Packet number 5435.

[904] Local and General. (1892, May 21). *Western Herald (Bourke, NSW: 1887 - 1970)*, p. 2.

[905] New Royal Hotel. (1941, March 14). *Western Herald (Bourke, NSW: 1887 - 1970)*, p. 4.

[906] Government Gazette Notices (1866, September 18). *New South Wales Government Gazette (Sydney, NSW: 1832 - 1900)*, p. 2171.

[907] NSW Certificates for Publicans' Licenses, 1830-1849 and 1853-1899, 13 August 1867, https://www.ancestry.com.au/discoveryuicontent/view/900140551:1792?tid=&pid=&queryId=2a9d7592caf6147c2fbea484fd7a7c3c&_phsrc=NJn1520&_phstart=successSource

[908] Government Gazette Notices (1869, August 24). New South Wales Government Gazette (Sydney, NSW : 1832 - 1900), p. 2133.

[909] Ibid. (1869, August 24)   p. 2133.

[910] Ibid. (1870, September 9) p. 1925.

[911] Ibid. (1871, September 1) p. 1953.

[912] Ibid. (1872, September 20) p. 2409.

[913] NSW Certificates for Publicans' Licenses, 1830-1849 and 1853-1899, 1873, https://www.ancestry.com.au/discoveryuicontent/view/197345:1942?tid=&pid=&queryId=2a9d7592caf6147c2fbea484fd7a7c3c&_phsrc=NJn1520&_phstart=successSource

914 Government Gazette Notices (1874, September 2). *New South Wales Government Gazette (Sydney, NSW: 1832 - 1900)*, p. 2639.

915 Ibid. (1875, September 9) p. 2763.

916 Ibid. (1876, September 13) p. 3645.

917 Government Gazette Notices (1877, August 31). *New South Wales Police Gazette and Weekly Record of Crime (Sydney: 1860 - 1930)*, p. 3369 (Supplement to the NSW Government Gazette.)

918 Government Gazette Notices (1878, August 27). New South Wales Police Gazette and Weekly Record of Crime (Sydney: 1860 - 1930), p. 3425.

919 Ibid. (1879, September 12) p. 4053.

920 Ibid. (1880, September 17) p. 4829.

921 Ibid. (1882, September 13) p. 4760.

922 Ibid. (1881, September 13) p. 4697.

923 Ibid. (1883, March 16) p. 1458.

924 Ibid. (1884, August 29) p. 5879.

925 Ibid. (1885, August 19) p. 5399.

926 Ibid. (1886, August 10) p. 5365.

927 Ibid. (1887, August 3) p. 5066.

928 Ibid. (1888, February 10) p. 1203.

929 Ibid. (1889, February 22) p. 1476.

930 Ibid. (1890, February 13) p. 1287.

931 Ibid. (1891, August 21) p. 6526.

932 Ibid. (1892, February 26) p. 1621.

933 Ibid. (1893, August 18) p. 6430.

934 Ibid. (1894, August 24) p. 5339.

935 Ibid. (1895, August 27) p. 5502.

936 Ibid. (1896, February 18) p. 1225.

937 Ibid. (1897, February 20) p. 1334.

938 Ibid. (1898, August 26) p. 6861.

939 Ibid. (1899, August 22) p. 6333.

940 Ibid. (1900, August 21) p. 6515.

941 Ibid. (1901, August 23) p. 6482.

942 HOB v3 p127, p129; HOB v6 p31 June 1863 Squatters Party

943 Readford, Edward. 'Reminiscenses of Early Days'. In History of Bourke Journal, 6:71–73. Bourke and District Historical Society, 1903.

944 Ancestry.com. *New South Wales, Australia, Certificates for Publicans' Licenses, 1830-1849, 1853-1899.* Original data: Butts of publicans' licences, 1830-1849. NRS 14401, reels 5049-5062, 1236. State Records Authority of New South Wales, Kingswood, New South Wales, Australia. Also, Certificates for publicans' licences, 1853-1861. NRS 14403, reels 5063-5066, 1236-1242. Also, Index to certificates of publicans' licences. NRS 14402, reel 5063. Also, Printed lists of licenses issued, 1866-82, 1895-1900, 1907-10. NRS 14411, reel 1243. License Year: *1866.*
https://www.ancestry.com.au/imageviewer/collections/1792/images/41718_329539-00010?usePUB=true&_phsrc=pvd990&_phstart=successSource&usePUBJs=true&pId=900142903

945 Ancestry.com. *New South Wales, Australia, Certificates for Publicans' Licenses, 1830-1849, 1853-1899.*
https://www.ancestry.com.au/discoveryui-content/view/900140551:1792?tid=&pid=&queryId=2a9d7592caf6147c2fbea484fd7a7c3c&_phsrc=NJn1520&_phstart=successSource

946 HOB v3 p127, p129; HOB v6 p31 June 1863 Squatters Party

947 History of Bourke volume 1, page 27.

948 Readford, Edward. 'Reminiscences of Early Days'. In History of Bourke Journal, 6:71–73. Bourke and District Historical Society, 1903.

949 Ancestry.com. New South Wales, Australia, Certificates for Publicans' Licenses, 1830-1849, 1853-1899.
https://www.ancestry.com.au/discoveryui-content/view/900140551:1792?tid=&pid=&queryId=2a9d7592caf6147c2fbea484fd7a7c3c&_phsrc=NJn1520&_phstart=successSource

950 Bourke. (1871, October 28). *Australian Town and Country Journal (Sydney, NSW: 1870 - 1919)*, p. 16.

951 NSW land deed volume 140, folio 42, 2 roods, lot 2, section 2, Bourke. Also, volume 130, folio 19, 2 roods, lot 3, section 2, Bourke.

952 Local and General. (1892, May 21). *Western Herald (Bourke, NSW: 1887 - 1970)*, p. 2.

953 Government Gazette Notices (1879, September 12). New South Wales Government Gazette (Sydney, NSW : 1832 - 1900), p. 4053.

954 Readford, Edward. 'Reminiscences of Early Days'. In History of Bourke Journal, 6:71–73. Bourke and District Historical Society, 1903.

955 History of Bourke journal, vol 4, p 72.

956 Government Gazette Notices (1882, November 7). New South Wales Government Gazette (Sydney, NSW: 1832 - 1900), p. 5909. Also, 1883, March 16, p. 1458.

957 Special Licensing Court (1895, June 22). *Western Herald (Bourke, NSW: 1887 - 1970)*, p. 2.

958 Government Gazette Notices (1900, August 21). New South Wales Government Gazette (Sydney, NSW: 1832 - 1900), p. 6500.

959 Large fire at Bourke. (1901, August 21). *The Sydney Morning Herald (NSW: 1842 - 1954)*, p. 10.

960 Bridge Hotel, North Bourke, History of Bourke journal, volume 6 page 31.

961 Royal Hotel, Gongolgon, History of Bourke journal, volume 4 page 69.

962 Ancestry.com. New South Wales, Australia, Certificates for Publicans' Licenses, 1830-1849, 1853-1899. https://www.ancestry.com.au/imageviewer/collections/1792/images/41718_329539-00196?usePUB=true&_phsrc=pvd139&_phstart=successSource&usePUBJs=true&pId=900156600

963 NSW Land deed volume 38 folio 29. Transfer dated 25 April 1882 to James Murphy.

964 History of Bourke journal, vol 6, p 31. Also "Apprehensions," public notice, *NSW Government Gazette, Sydney*, 10 May 1882, page 185.

965 "In Insolvency," public notice, NSW Government Gazette, Sydney, 28 March 1884, page 2125.

966 Government Gazette Notices (1884, August 29). New South Wales Government Gazette (Sydney, NSW: 1832 - 1900), p. 5879.

967 Sundry Notes. (1893, May 27). Western Herald (Bourke, NSW: 1887 - 1970), p. 2.

968 Government Gazette Notices (1897, August 24). New South Wales Government Gazette (Sydney, NSW: 1832 - 1900), p. 6077.

969 Advertising (1903, April 29). Western Herald (Bourke, NSW: 1887 - 1970), p. 2.

970 Ibid.

971 Fire at the Family Hotel 1904, Editor, History of Bourke Journal, vol VI (Bourke NSW: Bourke and District Historical Society, 1966-1992), page 26.

972 Bourke. (1866, October 10). Empire (Sydney, NSW: 1850 - 1875), p. 2.

973 Ancestry.com. New South Wales, Australia, Certificates for Publicans' Licenses, 1830-1849, 1853-1899. https://www.ancestry.com.au/imageviewer/collections/1792/images/41718_329539-00234

974 Special Licensing Court (1895, June 22). Western Herald (Bourke, NSW : 1887 - 1970), p. 2.

975 Government Gazette Notices (1877, June 8). New South Wales Government Gazette (Sydney, NSW: 1832 - 1900), p. 2237.

976 NSW Land Deed, Book 207 Number 31, section 10 lot 4, Bourke.

977 EM Warmoll Snr, History of Bourke journal, volume 11 page 265.

978 Four Mile, History of Bourke journal, volume 4 page 56.

979 Wine Licenses, History of Bourke journal, volume 4 page 79.

980 (1887, October 26). Western Herald (Bourke, NSW: 1887 - 1970), p. 6.

981 (1888, June 2). Western Herald (Bourke, NSW: 1887 - 1970), p. 8.

982 The Four Mile, History of Bourke journal, volume 3 page 126.

983 Government Gazette Notices (1877, January 23). New South Wales Government Gazette (Sydney, NSW: 1832 - 1900), p. 331.

984 Family Notices (1907, June 26). *Western Herald (Bourke, NSW: 1887 - 1970)*, p. 2.

985 NSW Land Deed, volume 238 folio 81, lot 7 in section 26, Bourke.

986 Bourke Town Map, History of Bourke journal, volume 5 page 90.

987 Government Gazette Notices (1879, December 5). *New South Wales Government Gazette (Sydney, NSW: 1832 - 1900)*, p. 5375.

988 John Fletcher, History of Bourke journal, volume 11 page 109.

989 (1890, December 3). Western Herald (Bourke, NSW: 1887 - 1970), p. 3.

990 Advertising (1901, December 4). *Western Herald (Bourke, NSW: 1887 - 1970)*, p. 2.

991 Patrick Murray, History of Bourke journal, volume 10 page 77.

992 (1887, October 26). Western Herald (Bourke, NSW: 1887 - 1970), p. 1.

993 The Bourke Fire Brigade, History of Bourke journal, volume 7 page 34.

994 JP O'Mara, History of Bourke journal, volume 10 page 90.

995 "The conflagration in Mertin Street," coroner's court report, *The Western Herald, Bourke,* 4 March 1899, page 2.

996 "Wedding Bells," news article, *The Western Herald, Bourke,* 14 June 1899, page 2.

997 "Fire at the Union," coroner's court report, *The Western Herald, Bourke,* 24 April 1901, page 2.

998 "Local and General," obituary, *The Western Herald, Bourke,* 31 August 1901, page 2.

999 "Licensing Court," Article, *The Western Herald, Bourke,* 18 June 1913, page 2.

1000 NSW Registry of Births Deaths and Marriages, *Index to NSW Deaths,* (Registry of BDM), 9858/1918 Petersham.

1001 Club House Hotel, History of Bourke journal, volume 6 page 32.

1002 Government Gazette Notices (1885, October 13). *New South Wales Government Gazette (Sydney, NSW: 1832 - 1900),* p. 6725.

1003 Alexander Shaw (2), History of Bourke journal, volume 11 page 240.

1004 (1887, October 26). Western Herald (Bourke, NSW: 1887 - 1970), p. 4.

1005 (1890, July 23). Western Herald (Bourke, NSW: 1887 - 1970), p. 2.

1006 Thomas Hand, History of Bourke journal, volume 11 page 133.

1007 Club House Hotel, History of Bourke journal, volume 8 page 130.

1008 William Pearce, History of Bourke journal, volume 11 page 218.

1009 Frederick John Gaiter, History of Bourke journal, volume 11 page 116.

1010 William Gale (1848-1917), Early Bullock Teamster, History of Bourke journal, volume 10 page 62.

1011 William Gale, History of Bourke journal, volume 3 page 47.

1012 Central Australian, History of Bourke journal, volume 4 page 52.

1013 Brother Richard Stamp, *The Anglican Church in Bourke and District,* History of Bourke journal, volume 1, pages 153-170.

1014 Bourke Public School, History of Bourke journal, volume 1 pages 207-217.

1015 Post Office Building, History of Bourke journal, volume 1 page 200.

1016 Robinson and Sons, History of Bourke journal, volume 10 page 94.

1017 Great Eastern (sic) Hotel, History of Bourke journal, volume 6 page 36.

1018 (1889, February 27). Western Herald (Bourke, NSW: 1887 - 1970), p. 3.

[1019] 1891, June 6). Western Herald (Bourke, NSW: 1887 - 1970), p. 1.

[1020] Empire Hotel, History of Bourke journal, volume 4 page 55.

[1021] Government Gazette Notices (1885, June 12). New South Wales Government Gazette (Sydney, NSW: 1832 - 1900), p. 3707.

[1022] Ibid. (1890, August 22) p. 6645.

[1023] The North Bourke Bridge over the Darling River, History of Bourke journal, volume 9 page 292-293.

[1024] The North Bourke Hotel, History of Bourke journal, volume 13 page 340.

[1025] Oxford Hotel, Bourke History journal, volume 4 page 64.

[1026] Bourke Municipal Council. (1890, February 19). *Western Herald (Bourke, NSW: 1887 - 1970)*, p. 2.

[1027] North Bourke Amateur Race Club. (1907, May 22). *Western Herald (Bourke, NSW: 1887 - 1970)*, p. 2.

[1028] Hotels, Bourke History journal, volume 6 page 28.

[1029] Oxford Hotel, Bourke History journal, volume 8 page 136

[1030] Oxford Hotel. (1923, February 21). *Western Herald (Bourke, NSW : 1887 - 1970)*, p. 2.

[1031] Advertising (1887, December 14). *Western Herald (Bourke, NSW: 1887 - 1970)*, p. 5.

[1032] A Great Fire. (1903, March 11). *Western Herald (Bourke, NSW: 1887 - 1970)*, p. 2.

[1033] (1887, October 26). Western Herald (Bourke, NSW: 1887 - 1970), p. 5.

[1034] (1891, January 24). Western Herald (Bourke, NSW: 1887 - 1970), p. 1.

[1035] (1892, September 9). New South Wales Government Gazette (Sydney, NSW: 1832 - 1900), p. 7315.

[1036] Athletics. (1895, January 23). *Western Herald (Bourke, NSW: 1887 - 1970)*, p. 2.

[1037] Local and General. (1895, May 11). *Western Herald (Bourke, NSW: 1887 - 1970)*, p. 2.

[1038] A Serious Accident. (1895, November 23). *Western Herald (Bourke, NSW: 1887 - 1970)*, p. 2.

[1039] Government Gazette Notices (1896, September 18). *New South Wales Government Gazette (Sydney, NSW: 1832 - 1900)*, p. 6557.

[1040] (1897, January 13). Western Herald (Bourke, NSW: 1887 - 1970), p. 3.

[1041] (1888, June 2). Western Herald (Bourke, NSW: 1887 - 1970), p. 5.

[1042] Advertising (1888, January 7). *Western Herald (Bourke, NSW: 1887 - 1970)*, p. 4.

[1043] AK McKenzie, History of Bourke journal, volume 11 page 201.

[1044] Gladstone Hotel, History of Bourke journal, volume 4 page 58.

[1045] James Warmoll, History of Bourke journal, volume 11 page 265.

[1046] CBJ Warmoll, History of Bourke journal, volume 11 page 265.

[1047] History of Bourke journal, volume 13 page 184.

[1048] (1889, November 13). Western Herald (Bourke, NSW: 1887 - 1970), p. 2.

[1049] Account of a relief trip, History of Bourke journal, volume 1 page 120.

[1050] Updated Red Arrow Tour Guide, number 18 Post Office Hotel, History of Bourke journal, volume 12 page 135.

[1051] Gidgie Camp Hotel, History of Bourke journal, volume 8 page 133.

[1052] The North Bourke Hotel, History of Bourke journal, volume 13 page 340.

[1053] Halfway House, History of Bourke journal, volume 4 page 59.

[1054] Obituary of Mr A Barry, History of Bourke journal, volume 4 page 83.

[1055] Edward Mann Luscombe, Bourke History journal, volume 11 page 174.

Index

B

C

D

E

F

G

H

J

R

S